Promoting Democracy in Postconflict Societies

D1522597

A project of Clingendael,
the Netherlands Institute of International Relations

Promoting Democracy IN Postconflict Societies

edited by
Jeroen de Zeeuw
Krishna Kumar

LYNNE
RIENNER
PUBLISHERS

BOULDER
LONDON

Published in the United States of America in 2006 by
Lynne Rienner Publishers, Inc.
1800 30th Street, Boulder, Colorado 80301
www.rienner.com

and in the United Kingdom by
Lynne Rienner Publishers, Inc.
3 Henrietta Street, Covent Garden, London WC2E 8LU

Library of Congress Cataloging-in-Publication Data
Promoting democracy in postconflict societies / Jeroen de Zeeuw
    and Krishna Kumar, editors.
    p. cm.
    Includes bibliographical references and index.
    ISBN-13: 978-1-58826-446-6 (hardcover : alk. paper)
    ISBN-10: 1-58826-446-7 (hardcover : alk. paper)
    ISBN-13: 978-1-58826-422-0 (pbk. : alk. paper)
    ISBN-10: 1-58826-422-X (pbk. : alk. paper)
        1. Democracy. 2. Democratization—Case studies. 3. Human rights.
I. Zeeuw, Jeroen de. II. Kumar, Krishna, 1940–
JC423.P877 2006
321.8—dc22

                                                    2006011921

British Cataloguing in Publication Data
A Cataloguing in Publication record for this book
is available from the British Library.

Printed and bound in the United States of America

        The paper used in this publication meets the requirements
   ∞   of the American National Standard for Permanence of
        Paper for Printed Library Materials Z39.48-1992.

    5 4 3 2 1

Contents

Foreword

Since the fall of the Berlin Wall and the worldwide rejection of single-party and military rule, democracy promotion has become a major component of bilateral and multilateral assistance. Consequently, democracy assistance by development/cooperation agencies and international nongovernmental organizations is one of the largest growth industries in the world today. While it best manifests itself through the large number of organizations taking part in electoral observation in troubled areas, democracy assistance involves a wide range of activities designed to nurture fragile democratic institutions in such diverse places as Afghanistan, East Timor, Liberia, Sudan, and Iraq.

This book deals with three key areas of democracy development: postconflict elections and political party development, human rights assistance, and media assistance. These areas are critical not only for postconflict reconciliation in the short term, but also for sustainable peace and for capacity development of democratic institutions in the long term.

The book provides a timely account of both progress and shortcomings in all three areas. With respect to electoral assistance and political party development, there is the risk of focusing too much on electoral organization and mechanisms, to the detriment of addressing the fundamental issue of democracy as a system of rule that maximizes popular consent and participation, the legitimacy and accountability of rulers, and the responsiveness of the latter to the expressed interests and needs of the public. In this regard, the violence that took place in the wake of the general elections of 2005 in Ethiopia supports a contention made in the book that international assistance programs have failed to address the fundamental problems plaguing the Ethiopian political system. Likewise, international support for the "movement regime" or the "no-party" system in Uganda is said, correctly, to have impeded the development of multiparty democracy.

In the areas of human rights and media assistance, progress is being made in addressing the consequences of heinous crimes in postgenocide Rwanda and in postwar Cambodia and Sierra Leone. War crime tribunals, truth commissions, and the promotion of responsible journalism through competent and human rights–based media development are among the best results of international assistance in democracy promotion. On the other hand, shortcomings do exist, and these are most manifest in Guatemala, where political impunity and criminal violence are on the rise despite enormous international assistance for human rights promotion and protection.

Despite these shortcomings—for which the editors make excellent recommendations with respect to security sector reform, grassroots participation, donor coherence and coordination, sustainability and long-term capacity development, and utilization of regional experience and expertise in democracy assistance, among other aspects—the general conclusion of the book is that international assistance has made a positive impact in nurturing fragile democratic institutions in Africa, Asia, and Central America. The book is strongly supportive of a comprehensive approach to reconstruction and development, with a focus on democracy as legitimate rule; the building of effective state institutions, with a fundamental change in the security sector; the promotion of peace, reconciliation, and human rights, including minority rights; and the satisfaction of basic needs of the population through long-term capacity building for sustainable development.

Both scholars and development practitioners will find this book rich in ideas and suggestions for further research. Its comparative perspective provides fertile ground for testing theories of democracy and development as well as those of social change. Its empirical groundings will be useful to policymakers as they weigh choices with respect to democracy assistance. I highly recommend it to all readers.

—Georges Nzongola-Ntalaja
Africa Governance Institute/
United Nations Development Programme
New York

Acknowledgments

This volume is the result of an international research project coordinated by the Conflict Research Unit at Clingendael, the Netherlands Institute of International Relations. However, it would not have been possible without generous support from the Netherlands Ministry of Foreign Affairs. Apart from being thankful for the financial support that was extended to the Clingendael Institute, I greatly appreciate the personal support received from Fon van Oosterhout, Piet den Heijer, and Johanna Spreeuwenberg, all based at the ministry's Division for Research and Communication. In addition, the project benefited from regular feedback from several people at the Peacebuilding and Good Governance Division.

At the Clingendael Institute, I am grateful to Georg Frerks, head of the Conflict Research Unit during my work on this project, who generously allowed me the necessary time, as well as to my other colleagues in the unit who provided me with many useful suggestions. Pyt Douma's valuable assistance with two of the nine country case studies enabled me to concentrate on other necessary aspects of the project. Moreover, I particularly benefited from the advice and high-quality support of Luc van de Goor, who despite his many other tasks in the unit always found the time to provide extremely useful suggestions for dealing with the many substantive and managerial complexities of this project.

The chapters in this volume have gone through several rounds of commenting. For their useful reviews, I thank the following: Chris van der Borgh, David Holiday, Cynthia Arnson, Guillermo Fernández-Maldonado, Peter Uvin, Michael Twaddle, Timothy Shaw, Marie Hulsman-Vejsova, Siegfried Pausewang, Jon Abbink, John Harbeson, James Polhemus, Joseph Hanlon, Louise Ludlam-Taylor, John Vijghen, and two anonymous reviewers. In addition, I would like to thank Benjamin Reilly, William O'Neill, and Ross Howard, whose excellent thematic review papers on electoral, human rights, and media assistance gave us a headstart with the actual country studies. Moreover, Jane Carroll, Kathy Ogle, Susan Greenblatt, Ricardo Roque Baldovinos, David Hedges, and Peter Schregardus proved indispensable with their substantial editorial and translation skills. Also, Anna Little, Steven Schoofs, and Carola van der Heiden kindly assisted me with the seemingly trivial but indispensable tasks of collecting facts, figures, references, and other logistic support—tasks not to be underestimated in a project covering multiple postconflict countries with a poor record of data availability. In addition, Krishna Kumar and I would particularly like to thank two gifted editors: Dan de Luce who helped us revise many of the original documents into more focused book chapters; and Marilyn Grobschmidt of Lynne Rienner Publishers, whose thoughtful and efficient comments helped us to finalize this volume in a timely manner.

Most important, I am grateful for having had the opportunity to work with a remarkable group of researchers in Cambodia, Ethiopia, Rwanda, Uganda, Mozambique, Sierra Leone, El Salvador, and Guatemala, who all did an amazing job under sometimes extremely difficult circumstances: Samnang Ham, Sisowath Chanto, Bophany Un, Kum Kim, Sovirak Seng, Fassil Yenealem, Noël Twagiramungu, Samson Opolot, Peter Otim, Carlos Serra, Teles Huo, Hélder Ossemane, João Carlos Colaço, Roberto Rubio-Fabián, José Antonio Morales Tomás, Florentín Meléndez, Carlos Mendoza, Evelyn Blanck, and Ligia Blanco.

Moreover, Krishna Kumar and I are particularly indebted to the authors of this volume: Dinorah Azpuru, John-Jean Barya, Marc de Tollenaere, Dessalegn Rahmato, Charlie Hughes, Christopher Kayumba, Jean-Paul Kimonyo, Anne Germain Lefèvre, Meheret Ayenew, Sorpong Peou, Mohamed Gibril Sesay, Luc van de Goor, and Marieke Wierda. Without their stamina, the book would not have been possible.

Finally, Krishna Kumar and I would like to thank Ananda van Wessel and Parizad Tahbazzadeh for their love, patience, and support.

— *Jeroen de Zeeuw*

1

Democracy Assistance to Postconflict Societies

Krishna Kumar and Jeroen de Zeeuw

Since the early 1990s, autocratic regimes appear to have been on a steady decline, collapsing under their own weight.[1] Popular rejection of authoritarian rule in Georgia and Ukraine provide the latest examples. This decline has been combined with a trend toward elected governments. Although many of the elections held in transitional countries may fail to conform to the standards of Western democracies, these ballots represent a major step forward for democratic reform. Despite setbacks, democratic consolidation continues to progress in a majority of the countries that have discarded authoritarian governments over the past two decades. In Africa, Asia, and Latin America, political and civil rights are expanding, civil society is developing, media free from state control is emerging, and democratic norms are taking root on an unprecedented scale.

Multilateral and bilateral donor agencies and their partners have responded to this trend by providing assistance in countries that have initiated democratic reforms or have shown an inclination toward reform. Donors have devoted hundreds of millions of dollars each year to support and strengthen nascent democratic institutions in these countries. Much of the international assistance has been channeled through nongovernmental organizations (NGOs). Although questions have been raised about the effectiveness of some democracy programs, a consensus has emerged among donors that international assistance has had a positive effect in nurturing fragile democratic institutions. For example, a recent quantitative study conducted by Vanderbilt University and the University of Pittsburgh has found a positive relationship between democracy assistance and the consolidation of democracy in developing and transition countries.[2]

This book focuses on democracy assistance to societies that are recovering from prolonged violent conflicts.[3] In such countries, referred to as "postconflict societies," war ended through a peace process brokered by outside powers, international military interventions, or the outright victory of one faction over another, as was the case in Rwanda. Postconflict societies vary considerably, depending on criteria such as the length of conflict and the devastation brought about by it, the way the war ended, and the way relative peace was restored,[4] all of which have implications for economic and political development in these societies. However, as used here, the term "postconflict societies" simply refers to the societies in which intrastate conflict has ended and the international community has recognized the government as legitimate.

This book has three distinctive features. First, it discusses the role of democracy assistance to postconflict societies in a comparative perspective. While the literature on the reconstruction of postconflict societies has grown rapidly in recent years, enriching our understanding of their nature, problems, and challenges, the field of democracy assistance has not received the attention that it deserves. Much of the literature on democracy assistance is country-specific or deals with a specific topic such as human rights or civil society. In many cases, it deals with the assistance provided by a single bilateral or multilateral donor. This book makes a radical departure from that tradition. Instead of concentrating on a single country or topic, it covers postconflict elections and political party development, human rights, and independent media development, and presents case studies from nine countries in Africa, Asia, and Latin America.

Second, the contributors are mostly researchers from postconflict countries or have spent considerable time in them. Most of the authors are native scholars who possess intimate knowledge of the political developments in their countries. Unlike development "tourists," they were in a unique position to bring an insider's perspective, which is conspicuously missing in most of the literature on postconflict societies. And yet they have developed their concepts and approaches in close cooperation with Western scholars. Consequently, the book represents a unique blend of scholarship from the West and the developing world.

Third, all the contributors have used multiple data collection strategies. In practically all cases, they analyzed available documents, interviewed officials of donor agencies and their local partners, and conducted interviews with other key informants. In many cases, they organized focus-group discussions and meetings both to generate information and to discuss their findings. They were also able to discuss their data, findings, and conclusions with a wide range of scholars both within and outside the country. This gives the book a solid empirical grounding.

▓ International Assistance for Rebuilding War-Torn Societies

The international community started focusing on postconflict societies during the early 1990s.[5] During this period, international intervention helped to resolve a number of violent conflicts that had caused untold suffering, uprooted civilian populations, and destroyed both the physical and institutional infrastructure of the affected societies. Peace was restored in countries as diverse as Cambodia, Mozambique, Ethiopia, El Salvador, Guatemala, and Nicaragua. Unfortunately, as the old conflicts subsided, new ones arose in Bosnia-Herzegovina, Serbia, Kosovo, Congo, East Timor, Sudan, Sierra Leone, and Liberia. Some of these wars have since been resolved. While the future for some of these states remains uncertain, there are indications that the number of armed conflicts has been steadily declining since the late 1990s.[6]

International assistance to postconflict societies has been based on three general premises, which were articulated in the early 1990s and continue to provide a loose framework for humanitarian and development programs. First, the purpose of postconflict assistance is not merely to rehabilitate the shattered system and restore the status quo ante that existed before the conflict. The assistance should also help to build new institutions and promote changes in national policies to prevent the reoccurrence of violent conflict and to promote development. Such thinking represented a significant departure from the earlier practice of focusing on relief and rehabilitation in the case of physical or human-made disasters. It was in this context that many international experts proposed the paradigm of relief to development.[7] This paradigm proposed that during conflict, international assistance should focus on relief operations and, when possible, on the rehabilitation of shattered physical infrastructure. Once this was accomplished, assistance should seek to change national policies, restructuring existing institutions and establishing new ones to pave the way for sustainable development. The new approach did not suggest that the international community follow this sequence. However, it highlighted the importance of focusing on reconstruction and development.

The second premise, which follows from the first, is that international assistance should be comprehensive, covering social, political, and economic sectors. Reconstruction of postconflict societies requires redefining and reorienting the relationship between the citizenry and political authority, revisiting relationships between different ethnic and social groups, creating a "civil society" in the broadest sense of the term, and promoting the healing of social divisions. It also requires reforming economic institutions and changing macroeconomic policies to promote local entrepreneurship and initiative. Above all, such assistance requires a fundamental change in the security sector. Therefore, any isolated or piecemeal efforts by the international community are insufficient.

Since the 1990s, the donor community has concluded that postconflict societies must undergo a threefold transition; war to peace, command economy to free market enterprise, and authoritarian system to open political order.[8] The war-to-peace transition generally requires disarmament, demobilization, and reintegration of former combatants, the installation of democratic civilian control over the military, and other related security sector reforms. The economic transition involves macroeconomic reforms, promotion of property rights, and policies that stimulate the private sector. The political transition to a democratic model requires a conscious attempt to promote democratization. The international community has developed and implemented assistance programs in all these areas. Although the enthusiasm that international policymakers demonstrated during the 1990s to reconstruct postconflict societies has given way to a degree of fatigue and frustration, the same underlying philosophy continues to guide it.

The third premise underpinning assistance is the principle of "do no harm."[9] Simply stated, it implies that humanitarian and development assistance should not, intentionally or otherwise, promote attitudes, patterns of behavior, or institutions that obstruct sustainable development. For example, assistance should not create a subculture of dependency among the recipients. In prolonged emergencies, recipients can become accustomed to aid, and individual initiative will be stifled as a result. Moreover, many intermediary organizations emerge that have a stake in perpetuating donor assistance. In these circumstances, the result is that instead of promoting peace and development, international assistance helps to maintain the status quo. Through the implementation of various tools and techniques, such as the use of peace and conflict impact assessments, international agencies are gradually trying to minimize such negative effects.

■ Rationale for Promoting Democracy in Postconflict Societies

Although there are exceptions, the international community has generally emphasized the need for democracy in postconflict societies. For example, in Rwanda, the international donor community recognized that in the aftermath of genocide, it was almost impossible to have free and fair elections, as elections might bring back to power the political elites who had plunged the country into a bloodbath. Even then, international donors sought concrete assurances from the Rwandan government about its long-term commitment to democracy and took steps to promote civil society, independent media, and human rights in the country. In Uganda, the international community did pressure the government to hold elections, though not necessarily multiparty elections. Considerations of political stability and economic development were weighed by the international community in both the cases. Why does the international community support democracy in these difficult circumstances? There are both pragmatic and normative reasons.

At the end of a civil war, there is almost a universal demand in a postconflict country for establishing democracy. Citizens are disillusioned with the authoritarian regimes that existed previously and want greater civil liberties. Intellectuals, educators, and social and religious leaders tend to demand democracy and political participation. Major political parties are also inclined to experiment with democratic reform. Even political parties that previously established authoritarian regimes display a willingness to support democratic change, though out of political expediency if not genuine conviction. It is interesting to note that not a single major political party in all of the nine countries covered in this book publicly demanded an authoritarian government in the aftermath of violent conflict. Even the government of Paul Kagame in Rwanda, which assumed office in 1994, made a public pledge to bring back democracy in the future.

Moreover, there is an urgent need to form a government that enjoys national and international legitimacy. The incumbent rulers often lack legitimacy due to their role in the war and are unacceptable to a large section of the population. On the other hand, opposition parties have yet to demonstrate that they enjoy majority support. For example, in Cambodia the incumbent Cambodian People's Party (CPP), the main opposition party, the National United Front for an Independent, Neutral, Peaceful, and Cooperative Cambodia (FUNCINPEC), and the discredited Khmer Rouge all claimed to enjoy popular support. Similarly in Mozambique, both the Mozambican Liberation Front (FRELIMO) and the Mozambican National Resistance (RENAMO) insisted that the majority of citizens backed them. Such claims could only be settled through free and fair elections. Past experience has shown that despite problems plaguing postconflict voting, elections have been generally successful in forming legitimate, representative governments.[10] Although defeated parties have often alleged fraud and abuses, they have reluctantly accepted the outcome, barring a few exceptions such as in Angola. It is another matter that once in power, many of the elected leaders have failed to adhere to democratic norms, leading to what Marina Ottaway has called "semi-authoritarian" states.[11]

International donors believe—with considerable justification—that democracy offers the best chance to promote peace and heal the wounds of war in postconflict societies. This belief is partly based on the much debated "democratic peace thesis," which holds that democracies do not go to war with one another, thereby presenting an argument in favor of having a

democratic state in order to prevent future conflict.[12] More important, however, is that a democratic political order provides mechanisms to resolve
political conflicts in a peaceful manner. Elected authorities are less likely to
be challenged as "illegitimate" than are dictatorships. As the incumbents
must face elections, they are less apt to resort to violence to put down dissent.[13] A democratic order is founded on individual rights and the rule of
law, and provides citizens and groups unfettered opportunities to articulate
their interests and mobilize public opinion for them. A liberal democracy
protects minority rights, at least in theory if not always in practice. While
one should not idealize the role of democracy—and there are abundant
examples where political parties have shamelessly used the fear of a minority to capture power through elections—one cannot deny that democracies
fare better than authoritarian regimes in protecting ethnic and religious
minorities. Finally, it is important to note that many international policymakers view democracy promotion in war-torn societies as an important
element in combating international terrorism. Many experts believe that
autocratic regimes that prohibit political participation and freedom of
speech can serve as breeding grounds for international terrorists.

Some scholars have questioned the relationship between democratization and peacebuilding. For example, Edward Mansfield and Jack Synder
have argued that while mature democracies with well-established institutional structures are not prone to conflict, the case with transition democracies is different. According to them, "incomplete democratizing states"
are more likely to be bellicose, because—in the absence of strong institutions such as an effective state, political opposition parties, news media,
and the rule of law—politicians can easily mobilize nationalist support for
violent conflict in electoral competition.[14] Instead, as Morton Halperin,
Michael Weinstein, and Joe Siegle claim, "the rate of conflict in a democratizing society was no higher than the global norm in the 1980–2002
period."[15] In addition, they argue that low-income democracies tend to have
lower levels of conflict than do low-income autocracies.[16] That none of the
countries covered in this volume had a democratic system prior to peace
accords (with the possible exceptions of El Salvador and Guatemala) supports the hypothesis that authoritarian systems are not conducive to building peaceful coexistence.

It is beyond the scope of this chapter to settle this controversy. Perhaps
future research will generate greater insights and understanding. However,
the essential point is that policy communities in donor nations strongly
assume that democratic governments, even the weaker ones, manage political conflicts by channeling them into conventional politics. When divisive
ethnic or racial issues surface in democratic societies, they are expressed in
protests rather than rebellion, without undermining the legitimacy of the
state. More often than not, democratic protests result in genuine reforms or

the co-optation of leaders of the protesting group into government. In either case, the conflict is contained. This underlying reasoning, rather than a careful analysis of existing research findings, has provided a powerful rationale for democracy promotion.

Finally, all major donor countries, which themselves are established liberal democracies, subscribe to the view that a democratic system offers maximum opportunities for economic growth and social development. With the fall of the Soviet Union, socialism has lost its appeal to most of the third world, and to intellectuals in developing countries as well. Increasingly, leaders and experts recognize that many features of democracy, such as shared power, vertical and horizontal accountability, a free flow of information, and transparency of governance, usually provide an enabling environment for individual entrepreneurship and economic growth. On the other hand, autocratic regimes, with their concentration of power and control over the flow of information, stifle creativity and entrepreneurship. While the relationship between democracy and development is more complex than is generally assumed by the exponents of democracy, there is little doubt that a democratic society is more responsive to the material needs of its people than are authoritarian political regimes.

For all these reasons, the international community has promoted democratization in postconflict societies. However, it has no illusions about its role in crafting democracy. International policymakers recognize that they can only help and prod—and nothing more. It is up to the political and intellectual leadership of postconflict societies themselves to take the necessary initiative and push for democratization of their polity. Absent such visionary leadership, no amount of international assistance or diplomatic pressure can foster democracy. Fortunately, such leadership often emerges after war and bloodshed, contributing to the growth of democratic institutions and culture. For example, an overwhelming majority of the countries covered in this volume have progressed toward democracy, although the progress has been marked by sometimes serious setbacks.

◼ Obstacles to Democracy Promotion

Postconflict societies confront unique challenges on the path to democratization. The most critical barrier is the highly volatile security environment. Despite the meaning of "postconflict," most societies after prolonged and devastating conflicts suffer from continuing organized violence, rampant crime, and widespread lawlessness. Often the extreme elements of former warring parties are not reconciled to peace and continue their struggle in parts of the country (as in Uganda). As a result, the disarmament, demobilization, and reintegration of former combatants is not always completed before elections. The situation is worse in countries where one party gains a military victory over its opponents, as was the case in Rwanda, Uganda, and Ethiopia. In such countries, rebel forces often do not concede defeat and resort to insurgency. Moreover, in many postconflict societies, gangs of unemployed and marginalized youth, former militia, and antisocial elements emerge and terrorize the populace. In extreme cases, like the Democratic Republic of Congo (DRC), the government has no presence in remote parts of the country.

The problem is compounded by deep social divisions that exist in the aftermath of violent conflicts. War tends to exacerbate regional, ethnic, and religious cleavages and tensions. Most intrastate conflicts have their roots in socioeconomic grievances and mobilization. Even when they do not start as ethnic conflicts, they develop into ethnic conflicts, as their leaders use ethnicity to gain public support. This has been especially true in African countries such as Burundi, Rwanda, and the DRC. In the absence of integrative political and economic institutions, deep social divisions and hostilities can jeopardize the prospects for peaceful political change.

Moreover, war-torn societies tend to have little or no democratic experience. For example, none of the countries covered in this volume had historical experience with free and fair elections. Even when elections were held, the vote either was manipulated by the ruling regime or excluded significant segments of the population. Practically, none of these states had a free press that was independent of the state. Nor did they have civil societies that could effectively influence public policies. Their judiciaries were extremely weak and politically compromised. Conditions were not different in postconflict countries not covered in this volume. In many postconflict societies, government leaders are directly implicated in violations of human rights during the conflict and large parts of the population have serious grievances about discriminatory government policies, corruption, and nepotism.

Still another obstacle to democratic rule is the destruction of institutional infrastructure for governance. Not only are government buildings, roads, and bridges heavily damaged during wartime, but most government institutions cease to operate as personnel are forced to flee. At the end of the Pol Pot regime in Cambodia, for example, the corps of judicial professionals was decimated except for a handful of judges and lawyers. In Sierra Leone, the judiciary, police, and prison system almost ground to a halt during the conflict because of a total lack of resources. The truth is that many postconflict societies, especially former protracted authoritarian regimes, lack the elementary institutional infrastructure for crafting a democratic system.

These daunting conditions naturally reduce the effectiveness of international democracy assistance. Due to security risks, staff members with international agencies often cannot gain access to certain regions. The questionable background of some political actors also creates problems for international agencies. In the absence of alternatives, international staff members sometimes have to work with political leaders and government officials who were involved in large-scale killings and abuses. Moreover, the limited availability of qualified professionals creates obstacles to both the delivery of social services and the rebuilding of public institutions. International agencies have to bring in outside consultants, requiring considerable resources. Often these consultants are not familiar with local languages and cultures. Given these obstacles, it is clear that these countries are not ideal candidates for democratic development. Yet the international community sees no alternative but to keep pushing for reform.

■ Internationally Supported Democracy Programming

When democracy assistance to postconflict societies was launched in the early 1990s, the international donor community lacked a coherent strategy. Indeed, democracy programming evolved in response to the challenges faced in individual countries. While policymakers at international donor agencies constructed loose justifications for overarching interventions, the traditional development experts, usually with little background in political science, designed and implemented democracy projects. Under these circumstances, the influence of academic scholars who specialize in democracy was limited and at best indirect. Program and project documents from the early 1990s are conspicuous for their absence of references to the vast academic literature on democracy. Conditions have improved in recent years. Democracy specialists are increasingly consulted and sought out to identify new priorities and help design programming.

One of the most prevalent democracy assistance programs has been the organization of competitive elections. In practically all postconflict societies, initial democracy programs focused on holding competitive elections to elect new governments, to form a constitutional assembly, or both. Rwanda is the only country in our sample where the international community chose not to support elections for several years, because of the country's particular circumstances. The nature of electoral assistance has differed from country to country. For example, while the United Nations managed the entire election in Cambodia, from the establishment of the electoral administration to election monitoring, the international community sought to bolster existing electoral systems in El Salvador and Guatemala, which saved time and resources.

At a minimum, the international donor community has provided financial and technical assistance for reconstituting or improving the electoral administration, undertaking voter education programs and conducting election monitoring. In most cases, however, assistance programs were more ambitious. International agencies provided technical assistance to electoral boards, trained and funded electoral staff, helped in developing codes of conduct for political parties, provided funds for the printing of election ballots, fielded teams to monitor elections, and helped domestic NGOs to undertake voter education programs. Finally, in many contentious elections, in places like Cambodia, Mozambique, and Sierra Leone, the international community brokered agreements to coax the losing political parties into accepting the outcome of elections. As postconflict societies have acquired experience and have developed appropriate electoral institutions, the need for electoral assistance has declined, and the international community has increasingly started to focus on strengthening legislative practices.

While supporting postconflict elections, the international community became aware of the need to assist political parties—particularly opposition parties—to create a more level playing field. In most countries, incumbent political parties enjoy a dominant, powerful position. With access to state resources and patronage, these ruling parties are well organized and often discourage open debate. The opposition parties, by contrast, are often loose coalitions or quasi-military movements that hastily transformed themselves into political parties to contest elections. To address such imbalances, Western countries openly gave financial support to FUNCINPEC in Cambodia and RENAMO in Mozambique for postconflict elections. In addition, many international organizations held meetings and seminars to expose major political parties to the requirements of competitive elections. The international community has continued to provide such assistance after elections. However, resources devoted to political party assistance have been limited.[17]

Practically all postconflict societies witness systematic and severe violations of human rights. Genocide occurred in Cambodia and Rwanda. Massacres were common in Guatemala, Sierra Leone, and Uganda. Both ruling and opposition parties and their allied militias engaged in mass murder and terror. Consequently, the international community has also tried to improve the human rights situation in these countries. It has funded war crime tribunals and truth commissions to undermine the culture of impunity that has prevailed, and to plant the seeds for tolerance and peaceful coexistence. Although many high-profile, internationally funded tribunals and commissions have been beset with implementation problems, few people would deny that these bodies have made an important contribution to justice and postwar reconciliation.

The United Nations has supported human rights monitoring missions in the aftermath of peace accords. By monitoring human rights, such missions exert pressure on incumbent governments to improve their human rights records. More important, donors have supported an array of human rights training and education programs. The training usually is directed to senior- and middle-level functionaries in law enforcement agencies and the military. The international community also has supported the establishment of NGOs that monitor human rights and try to influence governmental policies. The overall objective of such efforts is to change the prevailing culture of impunity and to provide the basis for peaceful coexistence and eventual reconciliation. The international community has also assisted with constitutional and legal reforms. It has given financial and technical support for the drafting of constitutions based on democratic precepts and practices, and provided assistance to improve the functioning of the judiciary and law enforcement agencies.

In addition, the international community has provided assistance for the growth of independent media. The rationale for such assistance is that an independent and diverse media is essential for democracy, promoting transparency and accountability in public affairs, providing a voice for the people, and encouraging free and unfettered political debate. In the aftermath of conflict, the state and its cronies usually retain control and ownership of media. Only Latin American countries, such as El Salvador, Guatemala, and Nicaragua, permitted churches and civil society organizations to run community radio stations, which have limited reach. Independent print media tended to be nonexistent or extremely weak, with censorship or self-censorship prevailing. Under these conditions, the international community has exerted pressure on incumbent governments to open the media space. International media NGOs, with the generous assistance of bilateral and multilateral donor agencies, have also tried to promote independent media. They have trained local journalists, provided financial assistance to struggling independent media outlets, and helped to create a legal environment in which commercial media can flourish.

In retrospect, the international community failed to devote adequate attention to the media in the early 1990s. It gave only limited media assistance to countries such as El Salvador, Cambodia, Ethiopia, Mozambique, and Nicaragua. International attitudes evolved, however, as donors recognized the critical importance of media during peacebuilding efforts in the Balkans in the 1990s. In Bosnia-Herzegovina and Serbia (which was, strictly speaking, not a postconflict society), international donors designed innovative media programs that involved assistance to nonstate media entities, training of journalists, legal and regulatory reforms, and technical assistance to make the independent media economically viable and sustainable. Since then, international assistance to promote independent and responsible media has significantly increased. International media NGOs have carried out media interventions in Burundi, East Timor, Sierra Leone, and even Afghanistan with considerable success. There now exists a broad consensus among international policymakers that independent and responsible media should be supported in postconflict societies to promote democracy and pluralism while defusing political tensions.

Finally, the international community provided aid to civil society organizations at both local and national levels. Civil society assistance usually takes the form of training, technical advice, and financial support. The assistance is predicated on the premise that a dense network of civil society organizations and NGOs engaged in articulating different interests and mobilizing public opinion is essential for the consolidation of democracy. In the absence of strong political parties—as is generally the case in recovering fragile societies—many international policymakers see NGOs, in particular, as playing the role of de facto opposition parties. Donors have significantly increased their support of NGOs as a way of delivering social services and reducing the role of state authority. Unfortunately, these NGOs are often largely, if not totally, dependent on external assistance. Only a small minority is able to marshal local resources for their activities.

The nature and volume of democracy assistance has varied widely among recovering fragile states. For example, while the international community spent vast resources on holding elections in Cambodia, it allotted meager funds for the first postconflict election in Ethiopia. While donors initiated and implemented a range of democracy initiatives in Guatemala, relatively little democracy assistance was delivered to Rwanda. The nature and duration of the war, the terms of the peace agreements, the state of existing political institutions, and the strategic importance of the country all help explain the disparities in democracy assistance. Table 1.1 provides an outline of the various international democracy assistance efforts in the three areas highlighted in this volume.

■ Policy and Programmatic Choices

While providing democracy assistance, the international community is faced with difficult policy and programmatic choices. First, democracy promotion can collide with the equally important objective of ensuring political stability and peace in fragile, war-ravaged societies. Although the process of democratization tends to contribute to political stability over the long term, the institutional requirements of democracy can temporarily introduce instability and volatility. Two examples can be cited from the country cases discussed in this volume.

Rwanda was in total disarray after its 1994 genocide, in which the Tutsi minority as well as moderate Hutus suffered at the hands of extremist Hutus. In the aftermath of the conflict, the Tutsi-dominated government that came to power employed authoritarian methods, but was committed to

Table 1.1 Main Areas of Democracy Assistance

Election Assistance	Human Rights Assistance	Media Assistance
Constitutional and legal reforms	Human rights monitoring	Media and elections
Establishment of election administration (including national election commission)	Support for war crime tribunals and truth commissions	Legal and regulatory reforms
Training of election staff	Legal reforms and human rights commissions	Creation of "alternative" media
Political party assistance	Strengthening law enforcement agencies	Conflict resolution programming
International election monitoring	Assistance for nongovernmental human rights organizations	Training of media professionals
Civil society aid (e.g., voter education)		Support to media nongovernmental and other relevant organizations

Source: Previously published in *Democratization.* See de Zeeuw, "Projects Do Not Create Institutions," p. 484.

restoring peace and reducing ethnic tensions. The international community was faced with a dilemma. Should it support an incumbent government that seized power through military force and was in no way prepared to face the electorate? Or should it risk political instability and perhaps even a violent uprising by demanding competitive elections in which the sympathizers of the earlier regime might return to power? The international community followed the safe course and agreed with a postponement of the first post-conflict elections.

Cambodia provides another example. In the 1993 elections, the opposition party, FUNCINPEC, captured a majority of the seats in parliament. However, the incumbent party, the CPP, controlled all layers of state authority and was reluctant to surrender power to its rivals. An explosive situation arose, but the international community averted the crisis by brokering a compromise under which Cambodia had two prime ministers. However, as a result, the CPP was able to consolidate its power, and continued to perpetuate its authoritarian rule. In retrospect, many have questioned the wisdom of the international actors in choosing not to take a stronger stand in support of democracy in Cambodia and Rwanda. There is no need to revisit these disputes at this stage. However, these two examples show that the promotion of democracy is not necessarily the only goal, and that there are circumstances under which the international community has to make compromises in pursuit of competing objectives, such as avoiding a resumption of war.

Second, the international community is often forced to choose between attending to urgent needs on the one hand, and long-term institution building on the other. Postconflict societies require a slow nurturing of democratic structures that are sustainable over time. For example, these societies need a well-functioning electoral administration that can plan and implement free and fair elections. Organizations that can provide human rights training and monitor human rights violations are required. Independent regulatory agencies that can assign frequencies to broadcast media and prevent political interference are necessary. International policymakers are generally aware of such needs, and would like to assist in the development of all these democratic institutions.

The problem arises when international actors take actions, intentionally or not, that damage long-term institution building. For example, the UN Transitional Authority in Cambodia (UNTAC) was totally preoccupied with the organization of elections in 1993 and took no steps to sustain a rudimentary electoral administration. Even voter registration records, the list of trained polling-booth workers, and relevant protocols were not retained for future use. In the run-up to the 1993 elections, UNTAC contracted many functions, even the printing of ballots, to foreign firms. While it succeeded in holding elections, it failed to contribute to the building of institutions. Worse, it set a bad precedent by incurring huge expenditures on elections. Similarly, after the 1995 Dayton peace accord for the former Yugoslavia, many international agencies organized numerous training programs for journalists in Bosnia-Herzegovina. Outside consultants were brought in, who had little or no knowledge of the national language or the harsh realities that the reporters faced. Such training had little perceptible effect on improving professional standards. Progress came only after international media NGOs invested in expanding training capacities within local institutions and pushed for other reforms.

These shortcomings and mistakes arise from the rigid timetables that international donors adhere to. Often, international managers are under severe pressure to meet the stringent or unrealistic deadlines that are dictated by peace accords, funding requirements by donor countries, and pressing political problems in postconflict societies. In response, international managers follow an expedient course that involves minimal risks. They prefer to work with familiar foreign firms instead of contracting out to struggling local firms. They recruit experienced expatriate staff instead of training local talent. They directly manage training instead of helping local universities and organizations to manage the projects. The result is that their efforts fail to contribute to long-term capacity building, and even undermine it. There are also other reasons for the neglect of institution building, such as the limited time horizon of international donor agencies, a lack of donor coordination, an underestimation of local capabilities, and an unwillingness to make long-term commitments.

The third type of dilemma that the international community often faces is choosing between granting assistance and exerting political pressure. Depending on the donor's interest and resources, international agencies enthusiastically provide technical assistance, financial support, and other help to promote democracy in postconflict states. But internal and external political pressure on ruling governments, opposition parties, and other interest groups is also required to ensure that democratic norms are followed. There is a constant need for the international community to monitor the situation and use diplomatic influence as necessary. However, the international community is not always willing to spend its political capital on pressuring reluctant governments. Strategic and economic interests prevent it from following such a course. For example, many international powers overlooked restrictions on political rights by Yoweri Museveni's government in Uganda and continued to provide economic assistance. Such support strengthened the hands of the National Resistance Movement (NRM) and perhaps undermined the evolution of democracy in Uganda, as one of the authors in this volume argues.

■ Origin and Focus of the Book

This book has its origin in the Democratic Transition Project, a major col-
laborative project focusing on democracy assistance to postconflict societies, launched by the Conflict Research Unit of the Netherlands Institute of
International Relations 'Clingendael' in April 2002. This project analyzed
the nature, focus, effectiveness, and impact of democracy assistance in
eight countries—Cambodia in Asia, El Salvador and Guatemala in Central
America, and Ethiopia, Mozambique, Rwanda, Sierra Leone, and Uganda
in Africa.[18] Thus the project covered three continents and included some of
the most prominent civil wars in the post–Cold War era. The project excluded case studies on the Balkans, partly because much has already been
written on that region.

Completed in the summer of 2005, the project resulted in a dozen thematic and country publications and a large number of workshops in the
postconflict countries as well as donor capitals in Europe and North America.[19] This book heavily draws from the findings and country studies of the
project. Most of the contributors were involved in the multicountry research
endeavor, and the majority of the chapters are based on the extensive research done under its auspices. One additional chapter on a nonproject
country, Afghanistan, has been included to complement the findings.

Like the larger project, this book focuses on three important areas of
international assistance—postconflict elections, human rights, and independent media.[20] Each chapter presents a country case study focusing on
one of the above areas and seeks to answer the following questions:

- What was the overall political context in which the international
  community initiated and implemented its democracy promotion efforts
  in a country?
- What type of assistance did it provide in support of postconflict elections, human rights, or independent media?
- What was the overall impact of international assistance?
- Which factors affected (contributed to or limited) the overall impact
  of international assistance?
- What are the main lessons for improving future international assistance to support democratization in postconflict countries?

The cases indicate that international assistance has helped establish new
governmental and nongovernmental organizations working to strengthen
human rights protection, the electoral process, and media freedom. In addition, assistance has strengthened the capacities of existing institutions. Moreover, technical, logistical, and financial assistance have enabled free elections, promoted more open debate, raised public awareness about political

rights and civil liberties, eliminated or reduced gross human rights violations, opened up the media sector, and laid the foundation for reconciliation. International assistance has clearly served as a contributing factor in the democratization process in societies traumatized by conflict.

At the same time, however, our findings show that democracy assistance is plagued by several problems. First, many donor organizations do not have a coherent strategy for building democratic institutions and fostering a democratic political culture. Second, the time horizon for assistance programs often is far too short, especially considering the difficult conditions faced by these countries. Third, prospects for the sustainability of certain organizations and activities are often overlooked. Fourth, building the capacity of new domestic institutions receives too low of a priority. Fifth, the various case studies corroborate findings in other areas of assistance that coordination among donors remains problematic. Finally, the international community is often unwilling to apply strong political pressure, even when such pressure is pivotal in fostering long-term democratic development.

■ Organization of the Book

This book is organized into three central parts, each focusing on one thematic area of assistance—support for elections and political party development, human rights assistance, and support to independent media development.

Part 1 presents case studies of elections and electoral assistance to Uganda, Ethiopia, and Mozambique. In Chapter 2, John-Jean Barya focuses on international electoral assistance to Uganda following the dictatorial regime of Idi Amin and the bloody civil war that was won by the National Resistance Army (NRA) in 1986. It critically examines the nature and effects of international support for the national electoral commission, election observation missions, the 2000 referendum, and civil society organizations. The author concludes that international assistance helped sustain the peace and foster economic development in most parts of Uganda, but also legitimized Uganda's "no-party" system, delaying the development of a more pluralistic multiparty democracy in the country. The author raises important questions about electoral assistance in Uganda and a chronic lack of pluralism.

In Chapter 3, Dessalegn Rahmato and Meheret Ayenew examine the conduct of elections in Ethiopia after the Derg regime was overthrown in 1991. The case of Ethiopia is important because of the country's unique federal system based on relatively autonomous ethnic regions. Within this framework, donors provided technical and economic assistance to help with the design of a new electoral and governance system and to establish a national electoral commission that would organize four rounds of elections. The authors describe the difficult political conditions and the various forms of international aid delivered to the National Election Board of Ethiopia (NEBE), the body in charge of organizing fair elections. They suggest that international assistance programs failed to address fundamental problems plaguing the Ethiopian political system, which has undermined the long-term impact of international aid on consolidating democracy in the country.

In Chapter 4, Marc de Tollenaere takes a closer look at international aid to Mozambique in the aftermath of the 1992 peace agreement. Mozambique represents one of the few major attempts by the international community to develop a multiparty political system through direct support for political parties. The author discusses the nature, achievements, and shortcomings of international political party assistance. He not only focuses on the internationally assisted transformation of RENAMO into a political party, but also discusses various capacity-building activities for political parties. Taking into account the 2004 landslide victory of Mozambique's dominant political party, FRELIMO, and the structural problems of other, opposition parties, de Tollenaere wonders what the future role of international political party aid to Mozambique should be. He suggests that the brunt of international support was focused on the country's peace process, while only limited attention was devoted to consolidating a more pluralistic and democratic political system.

Part 2 deals with international human rights assistance to Guatemala, Cambodia, and Sierra Leone. In Chapter 5, Dinorah Azpuru looks at international efforts to promote human rights in Guatemala after the signing of the landmark peace accords in 1996. She examines the effects of international support to the Commission for Historical Clarification (CEH), the Office of the Human Rights Ombudsman (PDH), and numerous nongovernmental human rights organizations in the country. Azpuru concludes that while the overall human rights situation has greatly improved as compared to the late 1970s and 1980s, political impunity persists and criminal violence is on the rise. She argues that both the Guatemalan state and its international assistance partners seem ill equipped to deal with these problems.

In Chapter 6, Sorpong Peou examines international support for Cambodia's human rights institutions. He describes how, after the Paris peace agreement was signed in 1991, the international community donated considerable resources to promote free and fair elections and democracy. At the same time, the donors virtually ignored building capacity in key governmental and nongovernmental human rights institutions. As a result, the country's judiciary and other major human rights defenders are still deprived of basic equipment and resources, and lack independence. The author argues that domestic power struggles and regional political influences have impacted negatively on the fragile democratization process in Cambodia. The chapter shows how the good intentions of international democracy assistance can be hampered by other domestic and regional factors.

The next two chapters are devoted to Sierra Leone. In Chapter 7, Mohamed Gibril Sesay and Charlie Hughes provide a general overview and impact assessment of international assistance to institutions like the police, judiciary, prison system, national human rights commission, and human rights NGOs. According to the authors, the international community has paid too little attention to capacity building of domestic governmental and nongovernmental human rights institutions, which has hindered the process of democratization in the country. In Chapter 8, Marieke Wierda focuses exclusively on international support to the Special Court for Sierra Leone (SCSL) and the Truth and Reconciliation Commission (TRC). She argues that the simultaneous functioning of the SCSL and TRC was an appropriate strategy for transitional justice, addressing the complex legacy of human rights abuses in Sierra Leone. Although the international approach had some serious shortcomings, technical and financial assistance to the TRC and SCSL enabled each institution to have a major impact on the process of national reconciliation and justice. The author concludes that international support to these institutions has had a major impact on the fight against impunity of war crimes in Sierra Leone. However, international support is insufficient and focused too much on the short term, while widespread corruption and unaccountable governance continue to pose major threats to long-term stability.

Part 3 focuses on international efforts to develop and strengthen independent media in Rwanda, El Salvador, and Afghanistan. In Chapter 9, Christopher Kayumba and Jean-Paul Kimonyo give a comprehensive analysis of international aid to Rwanda's media sector. They assess the media scene before, during, and after the 1994 genocide and analyze the various media programs that the international community supported. These assistance programs included radio broadcasts to refugees and internally displaced citizens, training of journalists, and the establishment of a new journalism and communication school. Kayumba and Kimonyo outline the main obstacles to media development in Rwanda and provide a few lessons that will improve future international engagement in this field. They suggest that generous international assistance had a major impact, but was not sufficient to consolidate an independent and sustainable media sector in the country.

In Chapter 10, Anne Germain Lefèvre analyzes international assistance to strengthen the independent media sector after the 1992 peace accord in El Salvador, where there was no shortage of media outlets, but serious problems existed with ownership, (self-)censorship, and professionalism. Support to the Salvadoran media sector focused on developing new programming for broadcast media, training journalists, sustaining fledging media outlets that promoted peace and democracy, reforming media laws, and strengthening nongovernmental media organizations. The author concludes that the international community played a vital role in professionalizing and modernizing the Salvadoran media, but needs to reorient its media assistance programming to address the structural problems of the media landscape.

The last chapter in Part 3 focuses on media assistance to Afghanistan following the fall of the Taliban regime in 2001. In Chapter 11, Krishna Kumar highlights the main elements of a project, undertaken by Internews, an NGO, and funded by the US Agency for International Development (USAID), that set up a groundbreaking community radio network in Afghanistan. The author demonstrates that a project consisting of relatively small-scale radio initiatives can have a major impact on local news provision, grassroots democracy, and the creation of social networks, although financial sustainability remains a problem.

Finally, Part 4 presents some of the main lessons learned in democracy assistance. In Chapter 12, based on the findings of the various country case studies, Jeroen de Zeeuw and Luc van de Goor review some of the main strengths and weaknesses of democracy assistance and provide several concrete suggestions for improving future democracy assistance to postconflict states.

▨ Notes

1. See Marshall and Gurr, *Peace and Conflict 2005.* This report by the Center for International Development and Conflict Management notes that the number of democracies nearly doubled in the late 1980s and early 1990s, and continued to increase gradually in the first years of the twenty-first century (p. 16).

2. Finkel et al., *Effects of U.S. Foreign Assistance on Democracy Building.*

3. "Democracy assistance" refers to the nonprofit transfer of funds, expertise, and material to foster domestic groups, initiatives, and institutions that are working for a more democratic society. Democracy assistance is only a small part of the broader democracy promotion agenda. The latter may also include policy instruments like political dialogue and diplomacy, the use of sanctions and embargoes, the installation of international interim administrations, and, in exceptional cases, even military intervention. See also Burnell, *Democracy Assistance,* p. 5; and Carothers, *Aiding Democracy Abroad,* p. 6.

4. See also Stedman, Rothchild, and Cousens, *Ending Civil Wars.*

5. "International community" here refers to all bilateral and multilateral donor agencies, international organizations and associations, international nongovernmental organizations, political and private foundations, consultancy firms, and other organized groups engaged in international democracy assistance.

6. Marshall and Gurr, *Peace and Conflict 2005,* p. 1.

7. Kumar, *Rebuilding Societies After Civil War.*

8. Ibid., pp. 1–35.

9. Anderson, *Do No Harm.*

10. Kumar, *Postconflict Elections;* López-Pintor, "Postconflict Elections and Democratization."

11. Ottaway, *Democracy Challenged.*

12. One of the alleged problems with the democratic peace theory is that it applies mainly to liberal democracies and interstate wars and is of limited relevance to nonliberal democracies in the developing world and intrastate, civil wars. See Brown, Lynn-Jones, and Miller, *Debating the Democratic Peace.*

13. See Halperin, Weinstein, and Siegle, *The Democracy Advantage,* p. 96.

14. Mansfield and Snyder, *Electing to Fight,* p. 2.

15. Halperin, Weinstein, and Siegle, *The Democracy Advantage,* p. 100.

16. The analysis notes: "of the 49 low-income countries that faced civil conflicts from 1990 to 2000, only eight were democracies. By contrast, the 25 low-income autocracies were engaged in civil conflict nearly one-fourth of the time." Halperin, Weinstein, and Siegle, *The Democracy Advantage,* p. 96.

17. Kumar, *International Political Party Assistance.*

18. The three main criteria for case selection at the start of the project in 2002 were: (1) postconflict countries where there is clear end of the conflict (either by peace agreement or military victory) and where a first, and preferably second round of national elections has been held; (2) postconflict countries that have received substantial international (democracy) assistance; and (3) postconflict countries located in the developing world, with a strong emphasis on Africa.

19. The thematic publications include Reilly, *International Electoral Assistance;* O'Neill, *International Human Rights Assistance;* and Howard, *International Media Assistance.* The country publications include Azpuru et al., *Democracy Assistance to Postconflict Guatemala;* Rubio-Fabián et al., *Democratic Transition in Postconflict El Salvador;* Sesay and Hughes, *Go Beyond First Aid;* Barya, Opolot, and Otim, *The Limits of "No-Party" Politics;* Peou et al., *International Assistance for Institution-Building in Postconflict Cambodia;* Kimonyo, Twagiramungu, and Kayumba, *Supporting the Post-Genocide Transition in Rwanda;* and Dessalegn and Meheret, *Democracy Assistance to Postconflict Ethiopia.*

20. The focus on elections, human rights, and media assistance in this book is directly linked to the focus of Clingendael's Democratic Transition Project. The main reasons for focusing on these three areas of assistance are twofold. First, free and fair elections, respect for human rights, and the rule of law, as well as free and independent media, are widely considered key pillars of the process of democratization. Second, they have been major areas of democracy assistance.

PART 1

Elections and Political Parties

2

International Support to "No-Party" Democracy in Uganda

John-Jean Barya

International donors tend to view elections as catalysts for democratic development, and often offer substantial assistance to help organize, monitor, or otherwise support the electoral process. However, elections supported by international assistance do not necessarily produce the usually stated effect of strengthening the quality and breadth of democracy. This chapter examines the nature of international electoral assistance to Uganda since 1993, beginning with a description of the character and disputed legitimacy of the 1980 general elections. It then looks at elections held after 1986, when the National Resistance Movement (NRM) came to power. A review of the role of international assistance in those elections and general democratic development in Uganda indicates that international donations had little impact and at times aggravated national political disputes.[1]

■ Background

Uganda became a British protectorate in 1894 and secured independence in 1962. A ruling coalition of two parties collapsed and in 1967, the Ugandan People's Congress (UPC) operated as a one-party state, imprisoning its opponents. From 1971 to 1979, the notorious regime of Idi Amin instituted a reign of terror, suppressing virtually all forms of human expression and endeavor. An estimated 100,000 to 300,000 Ugandans lost their lives. In 1979, the Tanzania People's Defense Forces and a group of exiles in Tanzania known as the Uganda National Liberation Army ousted Amin's military dictatorship. A front of more than twenty Ugandan political parties formed a government and organized elections in 1980. The UPC abused state authority to manipulate the electoral process and subjected political opponents to intimidation and violence. The disputed elections led to civil war.

The National Resistance Movement, led by Yoweri Museveni and ignoring peace talks under way in Nairobi, overthrew the regime of Tito Okello in January 1986. Some elements of the former regime reorganized themselves into armed rebel groups in the north and northeast.

Continuous armed conflict in northern Uganda has complicated prospects for democratic development. The war has raged for two decades, since the NRM assumed power in 1986. The conflict pits the northern Lord's Resistance Army (LRA) against the government's Ugandan People's Defense Forces (UPDF). Children remain the main victims of the war, with the LRA having abducted an estimated 20,000 children, who are used as soldiers and sexual partners. The need to end the war has played a prominent role in national elections. The question of whether the conflict can be solved through military or political means lies at the heart of differences between the government on the one hand, and opposition parties and religious organizations on the other.

Compared to the systematic abuses of the past, there has been relative progress in human rights and economic development under Museveni's rule. A minimum respect for the rule of law has been established, non-governmental organizations (NGOs) have emerged, a degree of media freedom has evolved, and government policies have helped bolster economic growth. However, political opponents, journalists, and others with dissenting voices are still arbitrarily detained and sometimes tortured, according to Human Rights Watch and other international monitors.

Perhaps the most serious obstacle to building democracy has been Museveni's prohibition of political parties from electoral politics. Since 1986, Uganda has required prospective candidates to run only on an all-inclusive "movement" platform instead of with competing political parties. The movement system is based on the premise of one supposedly unified movement in which individual candidates run for elections based on their personal merit. This "no-party" system, which only came to an end in mid-2005, has served to stifle political debate and violate the civil rights of those in political opposition.

The first postindependence elections in Uganda were held in 1980 after the fall of dictator Idi Amin in 1979. The vote was organized under the 1967 constitution and the 1964 National Assembly (Elections) Act. The elections held under the ruling National Resistance Movement (1986–1995) and the Movement (1996–2001) were governed by the provisions of the 1967 constitution, several electoral laws passed before 1995, the 1995 constitution, and other new electoral laws passed after 1995. Between 1986 and 1996, elections were held for parliament under an indirect college system rather than by adult universal suffrage.

▉ International Electoral Assistance

Since the end of the Cold War, electoral assistance has been one of the major forms of support for democratic development in Africa. Given the political conditions required by Western states for continued economic assistance and loans, such assistance has taken on special importance. Donors hoped that election assistance and monitoring would help improve political conditions in states plagued by conflict or ruled by leaders of dubious legitimacy.[2]

It is worth noting that international donors did not provide funding for Uganda's 1980 general elections, the first since independence. Civil society groups, which were only beginning to emerge, played no important role. The elections were marred by violence and vote rigging, with state authorities and the state election commission supporting the UPC party at the expense of the other three parties competing in the election.

International monitors in the Commonwealth Observer Group (COG) issued a report concluding that the elections were generally free despite some "deficiencies." This conclusion sharply contrasted with widespread public perceptions of abuse and fraud, subsequently confirmed by scholars and human rights experts. This experience with international observers influenced public attitudes toward subsequent monitoring efforts.

In African states, donor governments, multilateral agencies, and nongovernmental organizations have delivered assistance through specific support for government initiatives and programs as well as assistance to "civil society," which in effect has mainly meant NGOs.[3] In the case of Uganda, however, this support has not been provided for political pluralism or multiparty democracy. Instead, the funding has been delivered within the rules of the so-called no-party political system set out by President Museveni.

Since the advent of the NRM and the Movement, the major donors in democracy and electoral assistance have included the UN Development Programme (UNDP), the Swedish International Development Agency (SIDA), Norway, Austria, Belgium, Ireland, Denmark, the European Union (EU), the United States, the US Agency for International Development (USAID), the World Bank, the Netherlands, and Canada. In addition to these major donors, assistance has also come from foundations, especially the Friedrich Ebert Stiftung and the Konrad Adenauer Stiftung of Germany, as well as the US-based Ford Foundation.

International support since 1986 has concentrated on the following elections: the 1993–1994 Constituent Assembly elections, the 1996 presidential and parliamentary elections, the 1997–1998 local council elections, the 2000 referendum on political systems, the 2001 presidential, parliamentary, and local elections, and the 2005 referendum on change of the political system. In addition, in October 2005 the country was preparing for a new round of presidential and parliamentary elections in February 2006. The latter elections fall outside the scope of this chapter, however.

◼ The 1993–1994 Constituent Assembly Elections

Constituent Assembly Commission and Donors

Under the Constituent Assembly Statute of 1993, the Commission for the Constituent Assembly was established with the task of organizing and supervising assembly elections. Appointed in July 1993, the commission was to operate until the promulgation of the 1995 constitution.

The Commission for the Constituent Assembly and subsequent election commissions have been presented by the state as impartial, but in practice the members are appointed by the president and approved by a parliament dominated by his supporters. As a result, since 1993 the election commission has been clearly biased in favor of the president's allies and failed to fulfill its role as independent arbiter.

Electoral assistance to the commission from international donors was overwhelming. While initially donors and the Ugandan government were each supposed to contribute 50 percent of the budget, donors ended up providing 71 percent, or US$10 million (10.8 billion Ugandan shillings). Donors included the European Commission (EC), USAID, Japan, Denmark (through the Danish International Development Agency [DANIDA]), Austria, Canada, Germany, and the United Kingdom (through the Overseas Development Agency [ODA]). Others contributed funds through the UNDP, including Austria, the Netherlands, Norway (through the Norwegian Agency for Development Cooperation [NORAD]), Sweden (SIDA), and USAID.

There were three forms of funding: government funds, donor funds through the UNDP, and bilateral donor funds. Each of these was managed and disbursed differently. The government and bilateral donor funds were directly controlled by the Commission for the Constituent Assembly under its finance and accounting unit. The UNDP managed a pool of donor funds on behalf of donor governments, employing the services of the financial management firm Price Waterhouse Coopers.

With the exception of money from USAID, the donor funds were all disbursed late. For example, the EC funds designated for election expenses arrived after the election and more than four months after being pledged. The Austrian donation promised for the printing of materials for the registration of voters arrived nearly three months after the printing had been completed.[4] The funds made available through the UNDP were governed by agreements signed between the donors and the UNDP and were difficult to obtain. The transfer of funds sometimes took a whole month between the advice of transfer and the actual receipt of funds. The cost of transfer increased, since funds had to be directed through New York rather than directly to a commercial bank in Uganda.[5]

The Commission for the Constituent Assembly had substantial support from a number of international consultants. There was a chief technical adviser, who assisted in setting up the commission and also managed the finances. In addition to the adviser, there were four national consultants and three main international consultants handling logistics, training, and civic education. Additional international consultants were also involved in the process. The international consultants served in various operational bodies, known as task forces, of the commission.

Civic Education and Election Monitoring During the 1993–1994 Elections

The Commission for the Constituent Assembly conceived and implemented a program of civic education and training. This included training civic education supervisors and instructors, presiding officers and tallying clerks, and returning officers and their assistants. The commission also sought to coordinate with NGOs that were responsible for training. Apart from the general objectives of civic education, the program was designed to enable citizens to see voting as a civic responsibility and as a fundamental right. It sought to clarify the differences between the assembly elections and general elections, assist voters to register and check for any anomalies on the voter register, help remind citizens of the date, time, and venue for voting, and explain correct voting procedures and the need to select whom they considered the best candidate.

Under the "no-party" system already mentioned, the Constituent Assembly elections were organized on the basis of individual merit rather than political and socioeconomic interests. As a result, civic education that was funded by the government and by donors over a series of elections failed to address the fundamental issues confronting the country. Voter education was carried out with this narrow, technical focus. NGO alliances or umbrella groups funded by donors formed haphazardly at election time to conduct education efforts and then would later fade away and dissolve, as they lacked an underlying civic goal or vision. In this context and within the confines of the commission's objectives, civic education had some successes. According to the commission, the efficacy of the training was illustrated by the high percentage of voter registration (83.5 percent), the high percentage of registered voters who voted (87.3 percent), the extensive use of civic education manuals and posters in all parts of the country, the cooperation of other organizations, especially the National Organization for Civic Education and Election Monitoring (NOCEM), the Ugandan Joint Christian Council (UJCC), the Muslim Supreme Council, the resistance councils, and others.

However, while the UJCC and NOCEM both carried out election monitoring, NOCEM was excluded from voter education because the commission alleged that some politicians used it for partisan purposes. The commission withdrew NOCEM's accreditation for civic education. Yet NOCEM appeared to be a credible organization, as it had among its members the most significant and widely representative NGOs, including the Ugandan Law Society, major women's groups, journalists, human rights NGOs, and Muslim representatives.[6] NOCEM had been set up with the assistance of USAID to carry out civic education and election monitoring. The other accredited organization, the UJCC, had a long history and comprised the three main Christian churches in Uganda: the Catholic Church, the Church of Uganda (Anglican), and the Orthodox churches.

Despite its positive impact, civic education had a number of limitations, according to the commission. Many citizens were unfamiliar with civic education and questioned its usefulness, especially given the novelty of a constituent assembly and the constitution-making process.[7] Time constraints meant that the training of trainers and civic educators was rushed. Many politicians, aspiring candidates, and organizations took it upon themselves to carry out civic education in a manner that was at times inaccurate or confusing. Civic education manuals were not translated into vernacular languages due to time and financial constraints. Some of the civic educators at the parish level failed to carry out their functions, and the commission "received numerous complaints in this regard."[8]

National monitors played a more important role than did the international observers. They observed procedures at every registration and polling station, while the smaller contingent of international observers reinforced the activities of the national monitors. The international observers were "a link between national monitors and the international community."[9]

The observers and monitors generally reported positively on the electoral process. The report of the joint international observers (including the UN Independent Secretariat, Australia, Denmark, Germany, the Netherlands, Norway, Sweden, the UK, the Organization of African Unity, and the African American Institute)[10] noted administrative failings but said that the elections were "well conducted and there was no evidence of systematic attempts to influence the outcome or alter the results."[11] NOCEM criticized the electoral law, which excluded opposition political parties, but stated: "Despite shortcomings, the electoral process was a positive step in the democratization process."[12]

■ The 1996 Presidential and Parliamentary Elections

Under the Parliamentary Elections Statute of 1996 and Article 64 of the constitution, the national electoral commission was charged with ensuring the vote was free and fair, supervising the election in line with the constitution and relevant legislation, declaring the results of the vote, updating the registration list of voters, hearing election complaints before and during polling, and preparing civic education programs.

International donors provided financial support for the whole electoral process. While the Ugandan government provided US$12.9 million (18.1 billion shillings), the donors provided US$8.9 million (12.5 billion shillings).[13] The contributions are outlined in Table 2.1.

In support of the government's pledge to hold free and fair elections, the donor community established the "Support to the Electoral Process" project. The government of Uganda and the UNDP, representing other donors, signed an agreement in July 1995 to provide assistance to the electoral commission and other aid for the electoral process.

All the donor contributions, other than those from Japan and Belgium, were channeled through the UNDP. The electoral commission again complained of delays in the transfer of money and of the costs associated with the transfer of funds from New York, saying: "While the donors pledged to support the elections, they pegged their funds on particular programs which might not have been the commission's priority."[14] The delay in disbursements arose because the financial management firm chosen by the donors, Price Waterhouse Coopers, did not perform as expected and had a high turnover of foreign experts, who were recommended by the donors. As a result, there were gaps in the service provided, and even the election fund disbursements were not properly audited for about three years. Therefore, the accounting for the 1994 Constituent Assembly elections was formally completed only after the 1996 elections.[15]

Table 2.1 Donor Contributions for Uganda's 1996 Elections

Donor	Amount (US$)
European Commission	2,368,572
NORAD	1,638,102
Netherlands	1,196,906
Japan	1,089,931
Sweden	985,000
DANIDA	522,050
UNDP	496,606
Austria	450,000
USAID	100,000
Ireland	56,716
Total	8,903,883

Source: Ugandan Interim Electoral Commission, *Uganda Presidential and Parliamentary Elections,* pp. 51–52.

Civic Education During the 1996 Elections

The electoral commission was required to arrange civic education programs for the 1996 elections. A consortium of NGOs under the commission's supervision, the Civic Education Joint Coordination Unit (CEJOCU),[16] created a joint civic education project proposal that was acceptable both to the commission and to the donor community. The commission asked the group to deliver civic education on its behalf. Other individual NGO members were also allowed to participate in election monitoring.

Civic education did bring about some improvement over the Constituent Assembly elections, as fewer invalid votes were recorded (3.5 percent in the 1993–1994 assembly elections versus 3.2 percent in the presidential and 1.12 percent in the parliamentary elections in 1996). However, several problems were reported. Time constraints limited the impact of civic education, because electoral laws were enacted late and because donor funds were disbursed in an irregular, unpredictable manner. The quality of civic educators and monitors was poor, and the training for them was also flawed. Civic educators were poorly paid for their work. Given the high level of illiteracy and low comprehension level for English, the program relied too heavily on written English manuals that were not translated into the local language.

Election Observation and Monitoring of the 1996 Elections

There were two reasons why the electoral commission believed election observation was necessary in the 1990s. First, "to enhance the credibility of the process as a whole," and second, as a means of securing badly needed international financial support.

The commission accredited both international observers and local monitors. The local monitors included over seventy NGOs. The international observers included the UNDP, which in May 1996 funded the Joint Secretariat for Support of International Observer Groups (JSSIOG), which coordinated the deployment and activities of the international observers.

The task of the monitors and observers was to verify the impartiality of the commission and the integrity of the voting process. All the observers gave the elections a positive assessment. The international observers stated that "the elections marked a further positive step within the transition process in Uganda."[17]

■ The 1997–1998 Local Council Elections

In 1997–1998 the Ugandan government spent approximately US$24.3 million (27 billion shillings) on the local council elections. The donors, with the assistance of the UNDP, spent US$3.6 million (4 billion shillings).[18] These funds came from the UNDP, SIDA, Norway, Austria, Belgium, and Ireland (as shown in Table 2.2), and subsidized civic/voter education activities, updating of the voter register, consultant fees, financial management, and auditing costs.

In choosing NGOs to conduct civic education programs, the electoral commission required the prospective organizations to have established departments and offices from the local to the city level, experienced and professional staff who could manage civic education efforts, sound finances, and a nonpartisan identity and history. However, none of the NGOs in Uganda that applied could fulfill all the requirements. The commission nonetheless accredited seven groups that met at least one of the requirements: NOCEM, the UJCC, the Association of Women Lawyers (FIDA), the National Association of Women's Organizations of Uganda (NAWOU), Action for Development (ACFODE), the Ugandan Media Women's Association (UMWA), and the Ugandan Journalists Safety Committee (UJSC). Most of these NGOs were directly funded by the international donors and worked independently of the electoral commission. But according to the commission, this "made it difficult to effectively supervise and regulate their activities."[19]

The 2000 Referendum on Political Systems

The referendum of June 29, 2000, was one of the most controversial votes to be held in Uganda. All the established and credible political parties and organizations questioned its legitimacy and all boycotted the exercise. Only the ruling Movement championed its cause. Groups that suddenly emerged to support the multiparty cause were suspected of being fronts for the government.

Table 2.2 Donor Contributions for Uganda's 1997–1998
Local Council Elections

Donor	Amount in Uganda Shillings	Amount (US$)
SIDA	1,189,473,030	1,052,631
Norway	944,290,150	835,655
Austria	894,960,000	792,200
UNDP	667,830,000	591,000
Belgium	331,305,804	293,191
Ireland	54,467,130	48,201
Total	4,082,326,114	3,612,878

Source: Ugandan Electoral Commission, *1997/98 Local Government's Councils Elections Report,* p. 23.

Indeed, some of the individuals on the so-called multiparty side were rewarded with state jobs after the referendum.

Conditions of the 2000 Referendum

The political parties all argued against holding the referendum, because it sought to take away fundamental rights of freedom of association and assembly. Much was written on the subject before the referendum.[20] The cases for and against the referendum were well argued.[21] It was also clear that while urban dwellers understood the issues, those in rural areas (over 80 percent of the total population) were not as well informed. The government enjoyed a considerable advantage over the multiparty side, given its access to state machinery and government institutions. Moreover, the Movement secretariat had been campaigning against multiparty politics and political pluralism since 1986. Finally, at a technical level, the electoral commission was not well prepared for the elections, because there were delays in passing the relevant laws, the government provided inadequate funding, and civic education was limited.

Constitutional and Legal Framework

The referendum arose from the constitutional provisions put in place by the Constituent Assembly in 1995, because the assembly could not agree on a future political system. Article 69 of the constitution provided for the people to choose a political system to govern them, from time to time, from three options: the Movement system, the multiparty system, or "any other representative and democratic system." Between 1995 and 2000 the assembly decided, without any further reference to the people of Uganda, that they were deemed to have chosen the Movement political system (Article 271[1]). However, the law also required that the first referendum on political systems had to be held in the fourth year of the term of parliament, which meant 2000 (given that the sixth parliament had started in 1996).

Referendum Act 9 of 2000 was passed hurriedly after an earlier act on the referendum and other provisions, of 1999, had been successfully challenged as unconstitutional (there was no quorum in parliament when it was passed). The new act required the electoral commission to organize, conduct, and supervise the referendum, but the minister was to refer the matter of the referendum on political systems "to the Chief Justice who shall appoint a panel of three Judges to frame the question in consultation with the sides to the referendum."

Establishing sides to argue for a yes or no vote on the question to be put in the referendum was a key aspect of the exercise. The law said that "any person or group of persons is free to canvass for support of any side in the referendum and may form a referendum committee or similar structure for that purpose."

But because the opposition political parties boycotted the referendum, there was no credible group putting forward the arguments in favor of a multiparty system. So, while the government side had all the organizational advantages of state authority and resources, an insignificant, artificially created group was fielded as "the multiparty side." While technically and legally a referendum did take place, there was effectively no genuine contest, because the real contestants did not appear in the race. Under such conditions, the referendum could not gauge popular support for the Movement or multiparty politics.

Donor Assistance for the Electoral Commission in the 2000 Referendum

The referendum was essentially funded by the government and not by donors. However, donors did give it considerable political support. They viewed it as part of the democratization process in Uganda, in spite of opposition from all genuine political organizations in the country. Indeed, the donors even declared benchmarks for determining the legitimacy of the vote.[22] Although the referendum itself was not directly funded, donors provided assistance for civic education and monitoring. The Ugandan government provided US$9.0 million (13.5 billion shillings), out of the US$12.4 million (18.6 billion shillings) requested by the electoral commission. The donors provided US$125,415 (188 million shillings) to the electoral commission, with US$57,224 provided by the UK Department for International Development (DFID) and US$35,000 from the Australian High Commission. A larger sum of money, US$2.91 million, was provided directly to NGOs to "carry out civic education and monitoring."[23]

Donor Assistance for Civic Education in the 2000 Referendum

The electoral commission organized a civic education program and developed manuals, brochures, pamphlets, and posters that were used by its officials and designated NGOs. The commission accredited thirty-seven NGOs to work in five areas: monitoring, materials development, civic education by parish civic educators, media, and women. Many NGOs were directly funded by the donor community: the UJCC, ACFODE, NAWOU, BEKA-FALEC, the Foundation for African Development (FAD), United Religious Initiative, Retrenched Manpower Service, FIDA, CASE International, UMWA, the Ugandan Project Implementation and Management Center, Wilksen Agencies, the UJSC, and the Ugandan Women's Network (UWONET).

However, the so-called civic education program was less than effective, and most voters boycotted or did not bother to turn out for the referendum. According to the electoral commission, there were four reasons for this: voter fatigue, voter apathy, the major political organizations' boycott of and campaign against the referendum, and inadequate voter education because of lack of funding.

The commission's explanation defies the facts and common sense. Voter turnout in elections before and after the referendum was substantial. Well-funded, elaborate civic education efforts were undertaken but could not overcome prevailing public skepticism. The government only had itself to blame for such a low turnout. The prohibition and discrimination against opposition political parties led to the boycott and to a widely held view among the public that the referendum was illegitimate. Table 2.3 compares voter turnout across Ugandan elections, from 1993 to 2001.

Election Monitoring During the 2000 Referendum

Referendum results showed that of more than 9.6 million people registered, only 4.9 million voted (51.1 percent), and that of these votes, 4.7 million (96 percent) were valid.[24] Apart from the problem of inflated voter registers in the period 1996–2001, the turnout for the referendum was indeed the lowest of all the elections in the past decade. Yet apart from the National Election Monitoring Group of Uganda (NEMGROUP-U), most of the observers judged the results as reflecting a free and fair election.

There were several problems with this positive assessment. Under the Other Political Systems Act of 2000, Ugandans were free in theory to put forward systems other than the Movement and multiparty systems. However,

Table 2.3 Voter Turnout in Uganda, Various Elections, 1993–2001

Election	Population	Registered Voters	Total Votes	Turnout (%)
Constituent Assembly, 1993–1994	15,671,705	7,186,164	6,225,150	87.7
Presidential elections, 1996	20,600,000[a]	8,492,231	6,193,816	72.9
Parliamentary elections, 1996	20,600,000[a]	8,498,382	4,780,586	60.7
Referendum, 2000	23,317,000	9,609,703	4,914,524	51.1
Presidential elections, 2001	24,400,000	10,775,836	7,511,746	69.7
Parliamentary elections, 2001	24,400,000	10,775,836	7,576,144	74.2

Sources: Ugandan Electoral Commission, *Report on the Referendum,* p. 11; Ugandan Electoral Commission, *Report on the Presidential Election,* p. 46; Ugandan Electoral Commission, *Parliamentary Election Report;* http://www.nationmaster.com/country/ug/democracy.
Note: a. Estimate.

those who wished to propose other political systems feared retribution if they openly displayed support for alternatives and avoided signing documents in the presence of commission staff.

The Referendum Support Group (RSG), a consortium of donors as well as NGOs, was also critical of the referendum. The RSG said that the campaign had not been conducted on a level playing field and that the resources available to those on the government side were substantially larger than those available to the multiparty advocates.[25] They did say that the referendum was held in a peaceful and orderly fashion "despite some minor irregularities." However, in spite of the referendum not measuring up to the declared benchmarks set by the donors, the RSG did little or nothing to encourage the further democratization and opening up of political space in the country.

According to NEMGROUP-U, although Ugandans were allowed to choose their political system, "the campaign fell short of being a fair contest."[26] They observed that senior civil servants, and the resident district commissioners in particular, did not appreciate the need to be neutral. In some districts they were seen campaigning for the Movement. Those with dissenting voices were not free to campaign throughout the country and some were unfairly barred by public officials and the police from expressing their views at meetings. The group judged the whole exercise as flawed and unfair.

The electoral commission noted with satisfaction that international observers gave a stamp of credibility to the referendum process, as "it enabled the Commission to get to know the strengths and weaknesses of the electoral process as reflected in their reports."[27] As a result, the funding for civic education and monitoring, as well as the international monitoring itself, helped lend legitimacy to a vote of dubious fairness and credibility.

■ The 2001 Presidential Elections

The presidential ballot of March 2001 was among the most controversial ever held in Uganda. The election was bitterly fought between the incumbent Y. K. Museveni and Kiiza Besigye, a retired colonel. The campaign was characterized by intimidation; the harassment of candidates' agents, voters, and supporters; abusive language; hooliganism; destruction of property; clashes; and the involvement of military and high-ranking government officials in the electoral process.[28] The electoral commission did not mention in its report that it was President Museveni's supporters and state employees (resident district commissioners, soldiers from the Presidential Protection Unit [PPU], Gumball internal security officers and district internal security officers, and the paramilitary Galangal Action Plan) who were responsible for most of these offenses and abuses.

After the election, the Supreme Court ruled with a five-to-nil vote that the electoral commission had failed to comply with some provisions of the law and that the principles of a free and fair election had been compromised.[29] However, the court concluded with a three-to-two vote that the omissions and abuses had not substantially affected the results of the election.

Donor Assistance for the 2001 Elections

The presidential and parliamentary elections cost US$19.3 million (33.8 billion shillings). The donor community funded neither the presidential nor the parliamentary elections, apparently because the donors believed it would be inappropriate to lend support in the absence of a liberal political parties act.[30]

Accordingly, all the activities of the electoral commission, including voter education, were managed and funded by the government. Election monitoring was the only activity that the donors chose to fund. The commission selected and accredited 66 institutions and NGOs out of the 530 that had applied to engage in civic education and election monitoring. The donors, however, chose only six organizations to monitor the elections (the UJCC, FIDA, the UJSC, UWONET, ACFODE, and CASE International). The meager funding for civic education created a number of problems. The selection of civic educators was tainted by rampant nepotism. A lack of funds meant that radio and television electoral programs were not aired. In addition, donors chose NGOs without guidance from the commission. However, the donors themselves were not competent to choose the most able and independent of NGOs for this purpose, the result of a lack of a nationally acceptable civic education program and the absence of a process of imparting this to Ugandan citizens.

Election Observation During the 2001 Elections

The electoral commission accredited a team of 166 election observers, both local and international, to monitor the presidential election. Some observers noted that there were no serious problems, while others found "minor" irregularities. Despite the evidence available, the observers concluded that the polls had been conducted fairly, correctly, and satisfactorily. In this view, they were considerably less critical than was the Supreme Court.

■ The 2001 Parliamentary Elections

The electoral commission designed civic education materials, including manuals translated into twenty local languages, brochures, and guidelines for election officials, to cover both parliamentary and presidential elections. For both elections, the Ministry of Finance scaled down the civic education budget from US$1.79 million (3.1 billion shillings) to US$451,430 (790 million shillings), but actually released only US$371,430 (650 million shillings).[31]

As a result, the electoral commission was not able to deploy any parish civic educators during the parliamentary elections. It only accredited a local NGO, the Ugandan Project Implementation and Management Center (UPI-MAC), which used vans to mobilize voters. Most voter education was conducted through radio programs on FM stations and television, as well as through road shows in mainly urban and trading centers. Out of the thirty-nine NGOs accredited by the commission to carry out civic education and monitor the elections, only six were selected by the donors for funding, as mentioned above. These NGOs were also only funded to monitor the elections.

The NGOs formed the umbrella organization NEMGROUP-U. The commission noted that "the decision by the donors not to fund civic education seriously hampered the Commission's effort in the conduct and delivery of this vital service to the people."[32]

■ The July 2005 Referendum on Change of the Political System

On July 28, 2005, Uganda held another referendum to decide whether the country should remain under the Movement system or should move to a multiparty system of government. In the referendum, the Ugandan population was asked to say yes or no to the following question: "Do you agree to open up the political space to allow those who wish to join different organizations/parties to do so to compete for political power?" More than 90 percent voted in favor of a return to multiparty politics. However, voter turnout was extremely low, originally estimated at 15–20 percent of registered voters, although the electoral commission later claimed that 47 percent of registered voters took part in the referendum.[33]

Because President Museveni and Movement leaders had campaigned so much against multipartyism since 1986, to many it came as a surprise that Museveni finally supported the yes campaign.[34] The opposition parties, on the other hand, boycotted the exercise, arguing that it was irrelevant and a waste of resources, since both sides agreed on the need to change the system.

Similar to the 2000 referendum, the international donor community did not fund this exercise either, and the government had to foot the entire bill.

◼ Impact Assessment of International Electoral Assistance

Impact on Free and Fair Elections

Until July 2005, political parties in Uganda were banned from taking part in the electoral political process. Election contests therefore tended to concentrate on clashes between individuals rather than between policies and ideologies. As a result, the presidential election contests have taken on increasingly religious, ethnic overtones. This is ironic, as the NRM/Movement government came to power on a platform opposing the politics of ethnicity and religious sectarianism.

The northern part of the country has consistently voted against President Museveni. The 1996 presidential elections were not a close contest, because the main contender against the president, P. K. Ssemogerere, was widely regarded as discredited by a number of earlier mistakes. Nonetheless, Ssemogerere was harassed and generally prevented from freely campaigning, especially in western Uganda.

In 2001, as the electoral commission itself acknowledged, the campaigns in the presidential contest were characterized by intimidation, use of the military (especially the PPU), unlawful campaigning by government agents, and partisan use of state media and public resources.[35] The Supreme Court in its ruling confirmed these irregularities and blamed President Museveni and his campaign team, the army, and state agents. Indeed, President Museveni only won the case by a three-to-two majority of the court judges. It is therefore clear that the 2001 presidential elections were less free than those of 1996.

Donors did not fund the 2001 parliamentary and presidential elections. While in 1996 there was international optimism for the electoral process in Uganda, by 2001 donors had grown skeptical about the conditions surrounding elections and only funded electoral observers. Even this activity was funded in a begrudging, nominal way. The electoral commission complained of this lack of international funding and blamed donors for shortcomings in civic education. Yet the earlier general funding for previous elections (Constituent Assembly and 1996 elections) had made the government and the electoral commission complacent. When it became clear that no international support would be forthcoming in 2001, the state was caught unprepared. The donors had in turn failed to provide the government with sufficient notice to adjust. Nevertheless, the central factor undermining the credibility of the presidential election was President Museveni's determination to win the elections by all means, fair or foul.

In parliamentary and local council elections, there was no marked difference in voter turnout or the role of civic education between the 1997–1998 and 2001 ballots. Despite considerable differences in the level of donor funding between the two elections, the verdict of the local and international observers was that both elections had been generally free and fair. However, several election petitions for constituent seats and women's seats in the 2001 parliamentary elections revealed instances of bribery, voter card buying, intimidation, double voting, and similar malpractices upon which many members of parliament were unseated.

The underlying weakness of parliamentary and local council elections is that political organizations have been systematically stifled and have not been developed. Instead, there has been a rise in antagonism between competing individual candidates, especially among Movement/NRM supporters. Losing an election thereby becomes a personal loss instead of a loss of a party or group. In addition, the individual-merit model is very expensive for the candidates, and many have been bankrupted by the system. So while the stakes in these elections are not as high as in the presidential elections, the level of freedom and fairness in each contest is much more difficult to measure, because it is not determined institutionally (by the electoral commission or general state machinery) but rather by the financial and other resources of the individual.

As in the presidential elections, international assistance has had little relevance to the electoral process. Voter education and election monitoring tend to serve as merely technical procedures concerned with mechanics, with little impact on the essential nature, character, and outcome of the elections. The political process is stunted because legitimate and contending political interests are excluded.

Impact on NGOs, Civic Education, and Election Monitoring

The NGO groupings, networks, or coordination bodies created since 1993 to carry out voter education and election monitoring were formed as a result of donor initiatives. The first, NOCEM, was set up with the support of USAID in 1993. CEJOCU was also set up simply to coordinate civic education and election monitoring. Both eventually dissolved or faded away after the expiration of donor support and as donors found new NGO groupings. Succeeding the previous NGO constellation, NEMGROUP-U was strongly encouraged by donors in the run-up to the controversial 2000 referendum on political systems. It was funded by the Referendum Support Group after the referendum. NEMGROUP-U also effectively replaced NOCEM, which appeared relatively more credible, as it had more substantive membership. NEMGROUP-U, on the other hand, was a network of only six organizations.

The verdict of these NGO civic educators and monitoring groups was always similar: that the elections were free and fair or generally reflected the will of the people, despite numerous election petitions overturning results. These NGO monitors served to lend legitimacy to the government's prohibition against political pluralism and viable parties.

Donor assistance to the NGOs in civic education and monitoring also failed to create sustainable organizations. The NGO networks were not grassroots, indigenous endeavors but rather ad hoc creations narrowly defined around elections. They had no long-term common vision, mission, or purpose. These groups would come together only to provide a technical type of voter education and to passively observe the elections. They failed to question the political and legal framework and philosophy of the electoral process and thus failed to contribute to the democratic process. This is one reason why networks for civic education have changed so frequently and have been characterized by the emergence of donor "favorites" that avoid challenging their designated apolitical role.

Impact on Political Party Formation

Political parties in Uganda have not been allowed to operate freely under the NRM government. Between 1986 and 1994 the Democratic Party and Conservative Party cooperated with the NRM, and two of their leaders were co-opted into the NRM government. However, the Democratic Party leader left in 1994 during Constituent Assembly proceedings when it became clear that the government was going to adopt articles in the 1995 constitution to proscribe freedom of association in political parties. The Conservative Party leader remained in government, but his party split, with one faction led by Secretary-General Ken Lukyamuzi refusing to cooperate with the NRM regime. The 1993 assembly law, the 1995 constitution, and subsequent electoral laws prohibited political parties from campaigning for any public political office, whether local government, parliamentary, or presidential.

By giving political support to the referendum process, the donors sent a message that taking away political rights from Ugandans was legitimate. Their actions seemed to betray their support for the view expressed by Madeleine Albright, former US secretary of state, that President Museveni was "a stabilizing force in the region."

Moreover, by funding the 1996 and 1997 presidential, parliamentary, and local council elections, the donor community lent credence to the individual-merit principle of the government, which disregards political pluralism and the role of organized political interests. Paradoxically, however, it was this absence of pluralism that led donors to dramatically reduce electoral assistance by 2001, providing funds only for election monitoring.

Donors generally have chosen not to support the organization and development of political parties in Uganda. They have instead formed an alliance with government and NGOs to buttress government-created obstacles to the operation of political parties. The direct impact of donor assistance to the monolithic no-party state in Uganda has been to prevent the emergence of new political parties and stifle the old existing parties such as the Democratic Party, the Ugandan People's Congress, and the Conservative Party. Emergent political groupings, such as The Free Movement (TFM), the Reform Agenda (RA), the National Democrats Forum (NDF), the Justice Forum (JF), and more recently the Forum for Democratic Change (FDC), have not been assisted by donor acquiescence with the existing repressive constitutional framework. One may conclude, therefore, that donor assistance for elections between 1993–1994 and 2001 has actually undermined political pluralism and the democratization process in Uganda.

Strengths and Weaknesses of International Electoral Assistance

Strengths

The donor assistance given to the electoral commission in the 1993–1994 and 1996 elections was within the context of a system that prohibits parties from competing in elections. Apart from this serious weakness, donors provided budget support that allowed the commission to conduct its administrative work, helping to ensure the elections went forward with adequate resources (but with some limitations on how the funds could be spent).

The donors' concept that civic education and election monitoring should be carried out by independent actors rather than directly by the state was a commendable approach. This strategy carried the potential to provide credible and objective civic education to the citizenry, even if this was not always the result.

Election monitoring by both independent local and international observers in a fragile political and constitutional environment did provide a degree of confidence in the electoral process, and carried the potential of discouraging obvious abuses and outright fraud. However, as this study has illustrated, it was insufficient to prevent widespread irregularities.

Weaknesses

International electoral assistance created a climate of complacency and dependency. Both the government and the electoral commission were taken aback when donors declined to lend financial support for the 2001 election. This meant the government had to cut back on other budgets to fund the election.

Funding an election where the fundamentals of a political system are still contested risks taking the side of the incumbent regime and aggravates local political disagreements. In particular, the donor support and funding for activities related to the 2000 referendum was regrettable, because rather than resolving prevailing political disagreements, it compounded them. While in the first ten years of NRM rule (1986–1995) it may have been necessary to try and build consensus as well as promote social and economic reconstruction,[36] it was necessary for donors from the 1996 elections onward to support opening up the political space, building democratic institutions, and planting the seeds of multiparty democracy. By not questioning the political system early enough, donors arguably reinforced the slide into the current undemocratic arrangements.

Supporting civic education through fledgling NGOs was problematic, because it was not conducted through well-established educational institutions. More important, the educational curriculum should have been agreed to on the basis of consensus. As a political organ appointed by the president, the electoral commission was not best-placed to design and oversee civic education efforts, though it is constitutionally and legally mandated to do so.

National and international observers have been discredited after having declared elections "free and fair" regardless of what abuses have occurred during the voting period. These observers are then seen as vehicles for legitimizing the current government. These declarations from observers conflict with the evidence in various election petitions and with what citizens know has taken place. Such declarations can undermine the public's faith in the election process and the democratic process in general.

Civic education of a purely technical nature and devoid of genuine political content is meaningless. In 1980, when there was no voter education program, and when more people were illiterate, Ugandans were able to vote for parties or leaders of their choice. The problem at the time was not voter ignorance, but election rigging by the military commission. Indeed, most citizens lacked enthusiasm for civic education in all the elections (1993–2001), because such efforts were perceived as irrelevant. Subsequently, one could also argue that, now, civic and voter education is not the key issue. The best civic and political education for voters may be provided by genuine, pluralistic political debate and competition.

Elections organized by what some see as a partisan electoral commission and electoral system cannot be credible. International electoral assistance, civic education, and monitoring have little chance of advancing the democratic process unless the ground rules for elections and the political process are agreed to by all political players in the country. This was not the case in Uganda until recently, when the 2005 referendum allowed parties to exist and operate throughout the country. However, the country's laws, institutions, and the government as a whole are still partisan, favoring Museveni and his NRM-O (National Resistance Movement–Organization) party.

Donor funding and support for elections has been based on the assumption that the Movement regime and President Museveni's leadership have been beneficial overall. He has been perceived for a long time as one of a "new breed" of promising African leaders, credited with overseeing Uganda's impressive economic growth in the 1990s, despite shortcomings in his government's democratic credentials. However, unqualified international support has undermined and delayed the emergence of viable independent democratic institutions in Uganda. The recent removal of term limits for the president, and the politically motivated charges against FDC leader Kiiza Besigye,[37] point to a need to review international support for President Museveni, as his continued leadership for more than twenty years is likely to be detrimental to Uganda's future fragile body politic.

Moreover, by funding merely the procedural aspects of democracy without promoting the rights of civil and political association, assembly, and dissent, international donors buttressed a monolithic system to the detriment of pluralistic multiparty democracy. It is hoped that as Uganda slowly moves to a multiparty political dispensation, future assistance will not simply benefit the government, but will also go to political parties, where necessary and if acceptable by them, as important players in Uganda's ongoing political transition.

Notes

1. This chapter relies on reports from successive election commissions, newspapers, unpublished papers, books by informed scholars, as well as interviews with representatives of nongovernmental organizations involved in election monitoring and voter education, human rights activists, and donor representatives. In addition, a stakeholder workshop was held on October 30, 2003, in Kampala that helped inform the chapter.

2. Abbink and Hesseling, *Election Observation and Democratization in Africa.*

3. Hearn, *Foreign Political Aid, Democratization, and Civil Society in Uganda in the 1990s.*

4. Ibid., p. 12.

5. Ibid., pp. 12–13.

6. NOCEM's membership includes the Ugandan Law Society (ULS), the Association of Women Lawyers (FIDA), Action for Development (ACFODE), the Foundation for Human Rights Initiative (FHRI), Ugandan Human Rights Activists (UHRA), Ugandan Community-Based Association for Child Welfare (UCOBAC), the Ugandan Muslim Supreme Council, the Ugandan Christian Prisoners Aid Association, the Youth Alliance for Development and Cooperation, the Makerere Law Society, the Ugandan Journalists Association (UJA), the Ugandan Newspaper Editors and Proprietors Association (UNEPA), the Ugandan Federation of Business and Professional Women, and the National Curriculum and Development Center.

7. This was the first time that technical, seemingly apolitical civic education had been provided, and the motives behind it were not clear to people.

8. UNDP and Ugandan Commission for the Constituent Assembly, *Placing the People First,* p. 25.

9. Ibid., p. 58.

10. Ibid., p. 328.

11. Ibid., p. 329.

12. Ibid., p. 340.

13. Ugandan Interim Electoral Commission, *The Uganda Presidential and Parliamentary Elections 1996,* pp. 50–52.

14. Ibid., p. 54.

15. Information from a UNDP official in Kampala.

16. CEJOCU consisted of NOCEM, the UJCC, ACFODE, the Ugandan Media Women's Association (UMWA), the National Association of Women's Organizations of Uganda (NAWOU), the Ugandan Civic Education Foundation (UGACEF), the Ugandan Muslim Youth Assembly (UMYA), the Organization of University Muslim Women of Uganda (OUMWU), the Evangelical Fellowship of Uganda (EFU), and the Technical Assistance Foundation for Rural Development (TAFFORD).

17. Ugandan Commission for the Constituent Assembly, *Report of the Constituent Assembly Elections 1993,* p. 65. This international team of observers included foreign ambassadors accredited to Uganda and staff from various foreign embassies, the Organization for African Unity (OAU), the Commonwealth Secretariat, the International Foundation for Election Systems (IFES), the African American Institute (AAI), the Ghanaian Electoral Commission, the Eritrea Electoral Commission, the Tanzania Electoral Commission, UNDP, the World Food Programme (WFP), USAID, and SIDA.

18. Ugandan Electoral Commission, *1997/98 Local Government's Councils Elections Report,* pp. 22–23.

19. Ibid., p. 14.

20. Mugaju and Oloka-Onyango, *No-Party Democracy in Uganda.*

21. Barya, "Political Parties, the Movement, and the Referendum on Political Systems in Uganda."

22. Benchmarks included a fair referendum law, a fair political parties act, framing the referendum question early, and a level playing field.

23. See Ugandan Electoral Commission, *Report on the Referendum 2000 on Political Systems in Uganda,* p. 13.

24. Ibid., pp. 18, 33.

25. *East African,* July 3, 2000.

26. *The Monitor,* July 5, 2000, p. 5.

27. Ugandan Electoral Commission, *Report on the Referendum 2000,* p. 20.

28. Ugandan Electoral Commission, *Report on the Presidential Election, March 2001.*

29. Election Petition no. 1/2001, Supreme Court.

30. See *East African,* November 6, 2000.

31. Ugandan Electoral Commission, *Parliamentary Election Report, June 2001,* p. 14.

32. Ibid., p. 15.

33. For the final results of the referendum vote, see the website of the Ugandan Electoral Commission, http://ec.or.ug/referendum/finalresults.pdf.

34. A combination of internal struggles and international pressure for more democracy was said to be responsible for this shift. BBC News, *Uganda "Backs" Multiparty Return,* July 29, 2005, http://news.bbc.co.uk/2/hi/africa/4726419.stm.

35. Ugandan Electoral Commission, *Report on the Presidential Election,* p. 38.

36. See Barya, *Popular Democracy and the Legitimacy of the Constitution,* wherein a proposal for a United Front was mooted.

37. In November 2005, three weeks after his return to Uganda from a four-year self-imposed exile after the 2001 elections, Kiiza Besigye, FDC opposition leader and main challenger to Museveni in the 2006 presidential elections, was arrested and charged with planning to overthrow the government.

3

Electoral Assistance and Democratic Transition in Ethiopia

Dessalegn Rahmato and Meheret Ayenew

Ethiopians have suffered through recurrent famines, political upheaval, and civil war over the past four decades. Under an authoritarian monarchy that ruled until 1971, parliamentary elections were held, though the emperor retained ultimate authority on all issues. Between 1974 and 1991, the despotic Derg (Committee) military dictatorship crushed all dissent and held sham elections that carried no meaning. Ethnic-based insurgents eventually defeated the Derg regime and inherited a country devastated by years of repression and disastrous land reform. The ruling Ethiopian People's Revolutionary Democratic Front (EPRDF), a coalition of ethnic-based groups, has held a series of elections since 1991. While civil society groups have flourished and some independent newspapers have emerged, the EPRDF has been accused of using state authority and state-owned media to undermine opposition parties and promote its candidates. Prospects for democratic and economic development were undermined further in 1998, when a border dispute triggered a two-year war between Ethiopia and Eritrea (a former province that had been allowed to secede seven years earlier).

As one of the world's most impoverished countries, Ethiopia has received significant international assistance since the fall of the Soviet-backed Derg regime. Foreign aid has been directed mainly toward humanitarian relief programs, while funding for the promotion of democracy has been relatively limited. Although a number of elections have been held since 1991, the political landscape continues to be dominated by the ruling EPRDF, with an absence of genuine debate and pluralism. Democratic institutions and opposition parties remain extremely weak.

This chapter focuses on international assistance for elections in Ethiopia since 1991. Such assistance includes support to strengthen the capacity of the National Election Board of Ethiopia (NEBE) to administer elections, aid, and advice for political parties, support for civic education efforts by civil society groups, and sponsoring for election observer teams. The chapter identifies political bias by the NEBE and weak political opposition as major problems plaguing the electoral sector. We provide insights and recommendations for delivering international assistance to strengthen Ethiopia's electoral process.

■ Historical Background

With a land area of 1.13 million square kilometers and a population of more than 70 million, Ethiopia is one of the largest and most populous countries in sub-Saharan Africa. As a result of earlier civil conflict, high population growth, degradation of natural resources, and regular famines, the country faces a permanent food crisis and mounting poverty.[1] This is exacerbated by Ethiopia's troubled political history, which has been colored by repression, civil war, and arbitrary land seizures and resettlement programs. From 1930 until today, the country has had three radically different political regimes involving dramatic economic, legal, and administrative change. Between 1930 and 1974, the country was ruled by an absolute monarchy, with political power concentrated in the hands of Emperor Haile Selassie, and economic power in the hands of a class of landed nobility and local gentry. Together, they controlled a preponderant share of the country's productive resources. Selassie's regime, interrupted by a brief period of Italian colonial rule (1935–1941), was relatively stable, and for the majority of the population this was a fairly peaceful period. In Eritrea, then a province of Ethiopia, an uprising erupted in the first half of the 1960s that the imperial regime was unable to put down. The regional conflict eventually turned into an established liberation struggle, though the daily lives of a majority of citizens were not affected.

The modernization of the state under Selassie's imperial regime contributed little to democratic development. Nevertheless, the emperor established a parliament, provided a written constitution (in 1931, revised in 1955), and introduced universal suffrage and a national electoral system. Although elections were held every five years from 1957 onward, political parties were prohibited and electoral seats were contested on an individual basis only. Moreover, parliament had little effective power and acted more as a sounding board for new legislation. The absolute monarchy did not tolerate dissent or criticism, and the constitution affirmed that the emperor ruled by divine right. Neither civil society organizations (other than customary self-help associations and burial societies) nor independent media were allowed.

In 1974, Colonel Mengistu Haile Mariam's Provisional Military Administrative Council (PMAC), also known as the Derg, overthrew the monarchy, shifting the country's diplomatic alliance to the Soviet bloc and embarking on a disastrous road of "socialization." The earliest reform that became the cornerstone of agricultural collectivization was the radical land reform of 1975. This effectively ended landlordism in the country, emancipating millions of peasants from the control of the propertied classes. From then on, land was to be state property, with peasants enjoying usufruct rights only. In the 1980s, partly as a response to devastating famine and environmental shocks, the Derg embarked on a massive program of resettlement involving millions of peasants. The popularity and goodwill that the regime had gained from the peasantry as a result of its effective measures against the propertied classes and the distribution of land evaporated as the Derg regime turned more and more toward hard-line Stalinist policies and practices.

In 1987 the Derg introduced a constitution that vested power in the National Assembly. However, in line with the accepted practice in Soviet-bloc countries, the Derg established a one-party model in the Leninist tradition, called the Serategnoch Party of Ethiopia (ESP). Behind this façade, effective power remained in the hands of Colonel Mengistu and a small coterie of advisers who were appointed as the leading officials of the party. Assembly elections were held, but the seats were contested only by ESP cadres, and the outcome was determined long before ballots were cast.

During the 1980s, Ethiopia was engulfed by violent conflicts that had their roots in earlier eras but escalated as a response to the unpopular policies of the Derg. Most of these conflicts were attempts at armed resistance against the Derg regime by the so-called counter-revolution. These included remnants of the propertied classes and their allies on the one hand, and radical opponents of the Derg regime on the other. Other conflicts included the war with neighboring Somalia, the Eritrean independence struggle, and the ethnically based insurgency, first in the northwest of the country by the Tigray People's Liberation Front (TPLF), and later in the rest of Ethiopia by the Afar Liberation Front (ALF) in the northeast, the Oromo Liberation Front (OLF) in the southwest, and an Islamic movement in the southeast of Ethiopia.

Most of these anti-Derg forces united into a coalition of ethnic parties called the Ethiopian People's Revolutionary Democratic Front, which was led by the TPLF. Toward the end of the 1980s, the EPRDF intensified its offensive against government forces, rapidly advancing on Addis Ababa. As the Derg army continued to disintegrate, and the military regime lost all of its popular support, particularly among the peasantry, the insurgents' offensive met with little resistance. In mid-May 1991, with the rebels almost at the gates of the capital, Colonel Mengistu fled the country for exile in Zimbabwe. The EPRDF forces finally entered Addis Ababa on May 28, with the Eritrean liberation forces capturing Asmara soon after.[2] This brought an end to a decade and a half of the Derg's brutal military dictatorship, perhaps the most repressive period in the country's history.

The EPRDF's immediate objective after seizing power was to bring about peace and public order. This soon evolved into a reform agenda, aimed at destroying the state institutions built up under the Derg, restructuring the country and its civil administration along ethnic lines, and establishing ethnicity as the defining principle of political, social, and economic policy. As part of this endeavor, a month after assuming power the EPRDF convened a "peace and democracy conference" in which twenty-nine ethnically based political groups, most of them hastily organized for the occasion a week or two earlier, participated. The conference, which was dominated by the EPRDF and, through it, the TPLF, endorsed a charter for the transitional period, and approved the establishment of the Transitional Government of Ethiopia (TGE). The TGE included an interim legislative body in which the TPLF and the OLF were heavily represented. It also approved the holding of a UN-supervised referendum in Eritrea to formalize its separation from Ethiopia.

Following the establishment of the transitional government, there were a number of important political developments. The country's administrative map was redrawn along ethnic lines and a "regional state" for each of the major nationalities was created. These regional states were given wide administrative and legislative power. The goal was devolution of power within a federal framework. This meant that all ethnic nationalities had the right to self-determination and were even allowed to secede, but the objective was the creation of a federal Ethiopia.[3]

▣ Postconflict Elections: A Brief Overview

On coming to power in 1991, the EPRDF made a public commitment to democracy, national reconciliation, and a broad-based government that would be inclusive of all groups that fought against the Derg regime. It carried out a series of elections, including interim elections in 1992, constituent assembly elections in 1994, national and regional elections in 1995 and 2000, local government elections in 2001, and another round of parliamentary and regional elections in May 2005.

The 1992 Interim Elections

Following the ousting of the Derg regime by the EPRDF in 1991, the country conducted its first interim national elections, leading to the establishment of the TGE in 1992. The TGE was set up in the wake of the London and Addis Ababa peace conferences and was entrusted with the task of administering the country on a provisional basis under a transitional charter. Under the charter, the TGE was committed to conducting regional and local elections within three months of its establishment, drafting a new constitution that required elections for a constituent assembly, and holding national elections under the new constitution within two and a half years.

The EPRDF conducted the 1992 elections at national, regional, and *woreda* (administrative district) levels to establish a transitional government that could fill the gap created by the Derg's departure. The elections took place in about 450 of the 600 *woredas*. Constituting Ethiopia's first post-Derg elections, the ballot was characterized by chaos and poor organization.[4] Election irregularities were widely reported. Most serious of all, the EPRDF-affiliated parties manipulated the elections in most of the constituencies to ensure complete victory.[5]

The Amhara National Democratic Movement (ANDM), the TPLF, the Oromo People's Democratic Movement (OPDM), and the South Ethiopia People's Democratic Coalition (SEPDC) constitute the core parties of the EPRDF. About forty-five other smaller, predominantly ethnic parties are supported by and work with the EPRDF coalition but are not member organizations of the front. Over the years, ethnic parties closely allied with the EPRDF emerged as single ruling parties in their respective regions, with little or no challenge posed by opposition parties. This eventually helped the EPRDF to consolidate its control over the country's major regions.

However, the attempt to establish a broad-based government following the 1992 elections was unsuccessful, because major political and ethnic groups boycotted the elections on grounds of "unfair and unequal conditions" orchestrated by the dominant EPRDF coalition.[6] Although disputed and flawed, the 1992 elections were important in setting the stage for the division of the country into ethnic regions controlled by parties closely affiliated to the EPRDF.

The 1994 Constituent Assembly Elections

In June 1994, Ethiopia held elections for a constituent assembly that was to discuss and ratify a draft constitution prepared earlier by a special commission in March of that year. Voter turnout for the 1994 elections was low compared with the earlier elections. According to data obtained from the NEBE, out of more than 25 million eligible voters, only about 15 million, or 60 percent of the eligible electorate, voted. The EPRDF again scored an overwhelming victory, winning 460 (90 percent) of the total 510 organized constituencies. This ensured its unrivaled hegemony in shaping the form and content of Ethiopia's post-Derg constitution. The result also set the stage for legitimizing two singularly important and core agendas of the dominant EPRDF for the future Ethiopian state—the division of the country along ethnolinguistic lines, and the constitutionally enshrined right of any nation or nationality to secede from the federation. While much of this exercise may have contributed to a peaceful transition, the inclusion of the controversial Article 39 of the constitution, which sanctions secession for any nationality or ethnic group, has continued to be a source of acrimony between the EPRDF and its critics.

The 1995 National Assembly Elections

The constitution that came into effect in 1995 provided for a national parliament, the House of People's Representatives, with up to 546 members elected on the basis of single-member constituencies on a first-past-the-post basis, as well as elected councils in each of the nine regional states. After nearly four years in power as a transitional authority, the EPRDF ruling group conducted the 1995 parliamentary elections to provide for a permanent government. These were largely peaceful and took place in a climate of relative political calm and order throughout much of the country. Nevertheless, many opposition groups and independent candidates boycotted the elections. Allegations of intimidation, imprisonment, and voting irregularities were widely reported.[7] In addition, the elections had other shortcomings, including insufficient civic education, apathy among the voting public, especially among the rural peasantry, inequitable access to the media, and the absence of a strong and united opposition that could provide an alternative.[8]

When the National Election Board announced the results of the 1995 elections, the EPRDF scored another massive victory, winning 89 percent of the parliamentary seats (491 out of 546).

The 2000 National Assembly Elections

After the expiration of its first five-year term as a permanent government, the EPRDF conducted the 2000 national and regional elections to provide a second term for itself. The elections took place at a time when relative peace and stability prevailed throughout much of the country. It was also a period of improved law and order, in sharp contrast to the 1992 and 1995 elections, when the EPRDF had not yet firmly established state authority. Nevertheless, it was also a time when the general public had not yet come to grips with the disastrous consequences of the 1998–2000 Ethiopian-Eritrean border war and the ensuing fragile cease-fire.

The 2000 elections provided the EPRDF with a second term. Despite the high number of independent candidates (412 out of a total of 1,156), the EPRDF won about 88 percent of the available parliamentary seats (see Table 3.1).

Of all the elections that the EPRDF conducted in the first decade of its rule, the 2000 national elections were by far the most important, better

Table 3.1 Results of Ethiopia's 2000 National Assembly Elections

Description	Number of Seats	Percentage of Total
Number of parliamentary seats won by the EPRDF and affiliated parties and uncontested seats	481	87.9
Number of parliamentary seats won by the opposition	53	9.6
Number of seats won by independents	13	2.3
Total number of parliamentary seats	547	99.8

Source: Author-compiled based on Berhanu and Meleskachew, *Report on the Media.*

organized, and showed a relative degree of competitiveness, especially in the southern region and some urban areas such as Addis Ababa and Dire Dawa. There was much more spirited public discussion of issues among candidates representing different parties, and the public followed the elections with a great deal of interest. For the first time, the government allowed limited access to the state-controlled media and airtime for campaigning by opposition and independent candidates. However, the ruling party still dominated the broadcast media. Out of a total of 608 minutes of airtime (divided equally between television and radio) used by various politicians, the opposition appeared for only 60 minutes. In contrast, the ruling party's politicians and officials received nearly 90 percent of the total airtime, giving it undue advantage in introducing its programs and plans to the electorate. The role of the electronic media, particularly radio, is critical in a country such as Ethiopia, where print media reaches only a small proportion of the people.

The 2001 Local Government Elections

Local government elections in 2001, held at different times of the year in different parts of the country, saw a return to the boycott politics of 1995. The practice is for *woreda* and zonal elections to be held on one Sunday and *kebele* elections (to the councils of the lowest level of local government) to be held on the following Sunday in the same locations. Based on their relative success in 2000, the opposition parties entered the elections with high hopes. At the same time, the ruling party approached the elections determined to win, a determination that sometimes translated into intimidation of opposition candidates and supporters and other electoral abuses. After performing poorly in the *woreda* elections, the opposition withdrew from *kebele* elections the following Sunday, leaving the ruling party to sweep the field in all except a few *kebeles* where word of the opposition boycott had not yet arrived.

The 2005 National and Regional Assembly Elections

In May 2005, Ethiopia conducted its third national and regional assembly elections, which were observed by election monitors from the Carter Center and the European Union's Election Observation Mission. Prior to the elections, the ruling EPRDF eased restrictions for opposition parties and independent candidates to freely campaign on radio and television. Allowing a forum for free and unrestrained discussion of national issues generated significant interest among the public and contributed to a high voter turnout. As a result of the opening up of the political process, a large number of opposition parties and independent candidates registered to compete in the elections. Table 3.2 provides data on the number of candidates and parties contesting the 2005 elections.

Table 3.2 Number of Parties and Candidates in Ethiopia's 2005 National Assembly Elections

Description	Number of Candidates	Percentage of Total
Independent candidates	353	19.1
EPRDF-affiliated parties	505	27.3
Opposition and non-EPRDF parties	990	53.6
Total	1,848	100.0

Source: NEBE, *Data on 2005 National Assembly Elections.*

Table 3.3 Number of Registered Voters in Ethiopia's 2005 National Assembly Elections

Region	Number of Registered Voters		
	Male	Female	Total
Oromiya	4,840,270	4,337,250	9,177,520
Amhara	3,649,292	3,621,480	7,270,772
Southern Nations, Nationalities, and Peoples Region	2,639,873	2,461,334	5,101,207
Tigray	745,365	815,915	1,561,280
Harar	35,083	32,035	67,118
Afar	474,541	293,310	767,851
Beshangul-Gumuz	127,168	109,132	236,300
Gambela	83,952	67,375	151,327
Addis Ababa City Administration	612,419	549,523	1,161,942
Dire Dawa City Administration	57,758	52,735	110,493
Total	13,265,721	12,340,089	25,605,810

Source: NEBE, *Data on 2005 National Assembly Elections.*

The number of voters who registered is a strong indication of the level of public participation in the electoral process. As can be observed in Table 3.3, more than 25 million Ethiopians were registered for the 2005 elections, representing a reasonably equal proportion of female and male voters. This attested to the growing interest in a genuinely democratic electoral process among the Ethiopian public.

Official results of the May 2005 elections by the NEBE indicate that the EPRDF received around 59.9 percent of the votes cast, translating into 327 seats in the House of People's Representatives (see table 3.4). Opposition political parties—consisting mainly of the Coalition for Unity and Democracy (CUD) and the United Ethiopian Democratic Forces (UEDF)—won 172 seats in the 547-seat parliament—quite an achievement over the previous record of only 12 seats before the elections. The EPRDF suffered its worst defeat in the capital Addis Ababa, where all the 25 seats were won by opposition parties.

Despite the substantial gains, however, the main opposition parties did not accept the official results of the May elections and accused the ruling EPRDF of extensive vote rigging and manipulation to preempt an imminent defeat in the polls. International observers from the Carter Center and the European Union agreed with the opposition in their assessment that the electoral process failed to meet international democratic standards for free and fair elections.[9] The ensuing row between the ruling EPRDF and opposition parties triggered civil unrest in which nearly a hundred demonstrators were killed by government security forces and thousands were jailed throughout the country. Moreover, the entire leadership of the CUD was

Table 3.4 Results of Ethiopia's 2005 National Assembly Elections

Party	Number of Seats	Percentage
EPRDF	327	59.9
CUD	109	19.9
UEDF	52	9.5
SPDP	24	4.4
OFDM	11	2.0
BGPDUF	8	1.5
ANDP	8	1.5
GPDM	3	0.5
SMPDUO	1	0.2
HNL	1	0.2
ANDO	1	0.2
Independent	1	0.2
Total	547	100.0

Source: NEBE, *Data on 2005 National Assembly Elections.*

incarcerated and faced treason charges for inciting violence and insurrection. Nor were the private press and civil society spared, as the government took steps to silence independent journalists and leaders of civil society organizations.

■ International Assistance

Ethiopia's postconflict elections coincided with heightened international interest in the early 1990s in electoral assistance and support for building democracy and better governance in previously undemocratic countries. Foreign assistance to the electoral process in Ethiopia has concentrated on the electoral system, political parties, civic education, and election observation.

Building the Electoral Administration

Support for building the capacity of the electoral administration has taken the form of technical assistance, financial support, and in-kind assistance (commodities). The Ethiopian government received a major infusion of international electoral assistance in the early 1990s, before the present NEBE was formally established. In 1991 a team from the US-based National Democratic Institute visited to advise on electoral arrangements. The local government elections of 1992, a pioneering effort conducted under a national election commission with members representing various parties, received substantial international support, including financial support (in the amount of US$1,281,450, from Canada, Denmark, Germany, the Netherlands, and Sweden) and contributions in kind valued at US$1,916,850. The latter included radios from Canada, printing and copying equipment from the European Economic Community, tents from Norway and Sweden, ink and staff from the United Kingdom, and radios, computers, and rations from the United States.[10]

Although the 1992 elections proceeded smoothly in some parts of the country, in many areas they did not. Substantial changes and improvements were achieved before the Constituent Assembly elections of June 1994 and the first national elections under the constitution in 1995.

By mid-1993 the National Election Board, responsible for the management of elections at federal, regional, and local levels, had been established in its present form. Unlike its predecessor, whose members represented various political parties, the NEBE's seven members (who are accountable to and appointed by the House of People's Representatives on the nomination of the executive branch of government) are recruited "in consideration of national representation, technical competence, integrity and experience." However, it was not until January 2005 that the electoral law was amended to stipulate that board members should also be appointed "on account of their allegiance to the Constitution, non-partisanship to any political organization and professional competence."[11]

The period between the 1992 and 1995 elections saw a procession of international experts coming to Ethiopia to assess developments and to advise the young NEBE. Some technical assistance was provided by the Australian government and also by the US Agency for International Development (USAID), through the International Foundation for Electoral Systems (IFES). However, the bulk of technical and other assistance during this period was given through the UN Development Programme (UNDP) under the project title "Assistance to the National Electoral Board of the Transitional Government of Ethiopia." This project amounted to more than US$14.9 million.

The UNDP grant was intended to assist the NEBE in preparing and carrying out the Constituent Assembly elections of 1994 and the national elections of 1995. In particular, the project was to assist in the planning of the elections and mobilization and coordination of external resources. It is also possible that some of the assistance was used in drafting the constitution and the legal provisions for elections. Given the chaotic situation and the level of disorganization at the time, it is difficult to assess how much aid was used for these purposes and what effect it may have had. The aid was intended to be used for the provision of computer systems, a wide range of materials, equipment, and support for civic education, training of workers at polling stations, supplies and materials in support of voter registration, and supplies for election-day activities. The current NEBE has little information on how the money was spent and it was unable to provide any useful documents that would serve as a basis for assessing the grant's impact. Neither could any other government agency, or the UNDP, provide any proper accounts showing how the funding was used. Hence, although the donation was significant and possibly represented a major contribution to the electoral process, the absence of relevant documentation has made it difficult to assess the full impact of this assistance.

For the 2000 national elections, donor support for building the capacity of Ethiopia's election system departed from the previous model. By this time the system was largely in place, and lessons learned from 1994 and 1995 had been incorporated into regulations and practice. As a result, there was comparatively little need for technical assistance. There was no umbrella UNDP project, but various donors renewed assistance similar to previous support for the NEBE, in response to NEBE requests. For example, USAID provided three vehicles, upgraded a previously supplied computer system, and sponsored the purchase of fifteen vehicle-mounted radios and a base station, amounting to a contribution of US$300,000. Norway and Sweden assisted with overhauling printing equipment previously supplied, Canada

again provided election materials, and the UNDP bought a paper counting
and bundling machine.

For the 2005 ballot, there was a reversion to the UNDP model, under
the program title "Multi-Donor Assistance for the 2005 National Elections
in Ethiopia," approved in December 2004. The total donor contribution
reached US$4 million, covering a range of needs, including training for
NEBE staff and polling-station workers. Funds were set aside to strengthen
the NEBE's public information capacity, including developing a comprehensive website and other materials.

Drawing on experiences in the past, electoral assistance for the 2005
elections appeared much more coordinated, targeting key areas that could
greatly assist the holding of orderly and transparent elections. Early on, for
example, the international assistance group in Addis Ababa set up a joint
donor basket group consisting of Austria, Canada, Finland, Italy, Ireland,
Japan, the Netherlands, Norway, Sweden, Switzerland, the United Kingdom, the United States, and the UNDP to channel assistance to categories
that could help pave the way for free and fair elections.

The early initiative of the donor basket group was to organize training
programs for election officers of the NEBE as well as members of the
police, prosecutors, and judges of ordinary courts. The goal was to enable
the trainees to learn about the roles of electoral institutions and appreciate
the need to uphold basic principles and democratic practices. Also, the
donor group and the Electoral Reform International Services (ERIS) jointly
supported training for members of the police and the judiciary on the handling of election disputes. This effort also helped launch a formula for
media access and monitoring of media coverage in cooperation with Addis
Ababa University. Apart from foreign governments, the National Democratic Institute (NDI) and the International Republican Institute (IRI), two
nonprofit organizations affiliated with the main political parties in the
United States, were also involved in civic and voter education programs. In
addition, the NDI and IRI were instrumental in preparing the code of conduct for political parties participating in the election campaign.

It would be premature to assess the impact of this latest round of international aid, though it is likely the effort has improved the electoral process
in a number of ways. Since 1992, international electoral assistance has
helped to create a system that is capable of conducting a technically credible
election at the national, regional, and local levels. Whether the system is
capable of conducting a democratically credible election is another question.

Financing of Elections

Postconflict elections can be costly affairs for poor nations such as Ethiopia.[12]
Table 3.5 presents data on election costs for selected African countries.

Table 3.5 Comparative Data on Cost of Elections in Selected African Countries

Country	Date of Election	Total Cost (US$ millions)	Number of Voters (millions)	Cost per Voter (US$)
Angola	1992	100.0	4.5	22.0
Botswana	1994	1.0	0.4	2.7
Ethiopia	1994 Constituent Assembly	8.2	14.7	0.6
	2000 national elections	3.5	18.7	0.2
Kenya	2002	45.5	5.9	7.8
Lesotho	1995	6.0	0.8	6.9
Malawi	1994	8.0	3.8	2.1
South Africa	1994	250.0	22.7	11.0
Tanzania	1995	23.8	n/a	7.9

Sources: Fambon, "The Funding of Elections and Political Parties"; NEBE, *Report to the House of Representatives.*
Notes: The calculations for Ethiopia were made using the Ethiopian government's budgetary allocations.
n/a = data not available.

Ethiopia's ballots have incurred surprisingly modest costs, especially given the country's vast territory and its lack of experience in running democratic elections. It is clear that Ethiopia, with US$0.6 and US$0.2 per voter for the 1994 Constituent Assembly and 2000 national elections respectively, has conducted the least-expensive elections among the countries sampled. This is a spectacular achievement when compared with Angola's US$22 and South Africa's US$11 per voter.

The international electoral assistance Ethiopia has received over the years might have been a significant factor in keeping the cost of elections low. The most critical factor, however, has probably been the NEBE's use of the huge state bureaucracy and the civil services at federal, regional, and local levels for the administration of elections. The use by the NEBE of existing government administrative structures and resources has kept costs down significantly. However, serious questions can be raised as to whether the elections are likely to be free and fair, given the fact that they are conducted through the state apparatus and public personnel, both of which are under the ruling party's strong influence. In other words, low electoral costs may come at a price.

When interviewed, the NEBE's chief executive insisted that a government must be able to cover the full cost of elections, because external funding could bring undue influence that could compromise the country's sovereignty and independence.[13] While he was prepared to accept international capacity-building support for the NEBE, he insisted that the running costs of elections should be covered from the country's own resources.

Political Party Support

Ethiopia has limited experience with organized political activity. The ruling EPRDF is strong and enjoys all the advantages of a party in power. Opposition political parties are weak, poor, badly organized, deeply divided among themselves, and largely confined to major urban centers, such as Addis Ababa, Bahir Dar, Nazareth, Jimma, and Dire Dawa. To transform Ethiopia into a true multiparty state, these parties would need to undertake sustained political campaigns among Ethiopia's vast rural constituency to provide a credible alternative program to the electorate. In recognition of this need for competitive democracy, international electoral assistance has also focused on political party support.

However, Ethiopian election legislation places limitations on the kind of international support parties can receive. Donations or grants from foreign nationals, foreign governments or political parties, welfare organizations and religious organizations, and prisoners of law are strictly prohibited.[14] Donors and recipients have found two ways around this obstacle. One is to provide capacity-building support in the form of training. A second method is to take advantage of a provision of the electoral law that allows parties to receive subsidies and grants from the government, using the NEBE as a government-approved conduit to pass support to the parties. The second approach has been more successful than the first.

The NDI initiated a political party strengthening program with USAID funding in July 1994, but found it a frustrating experience. Initial sessions were marred by walkouts by the intended beneficiaries. The NDI persisted in conducting training in the period up to the 1995 national elections, but after the elections it observed that

> most opposition parties, despite NDI's training programs in this area, still refuse to work with the existing process or to suggest specific improvements to that process. The reasons for this are complex and interrelated, including lack of access to the peasantry, lack of interest in the peasantry, lack of resources, lack of organization skills, and a cultural tradition that sees non-participation as the only honorable form of opposition.[15]

Shortly thereafter, the NDI was told to cease operations in Ethiopia until it had registered with the government. Eventually it registered, but in 1997 it withdrew from Ethiopia without renewing its party training.

Another form of international party assistance was the candidate support fund of US$318,625 that was given to the NEBE to be distributed to political parties during the 2000 elections. The purpose of this fund was to provide financial assistance through the board to legally registered political parties, enabling them to contest the general elections in a competitive manner. The support was used for transportation, communications, office space, access to the public media, and any other measures that might broaden participation for free and fair elections. The money was distributed to thirty-three registered political parties (using a formula based on the number of candidates nominated) through a committee chaired by the head of the NEBE. The disbursements ranged from US$35,798, which was awarded to the Oromo National Congress, to as little as US$586, which went to the Yem Nationality Democratic Movement. A number of European countries and the UNDP contributed to the fund. A breakdown of donor contributions is provided in Table 3.6.

In general, the establishment of this provisional fund was helpful in providing support to legitimate political parties and in fostering participation in the 2000 elections. This contributed to broad political participation in the elections and might have aided the democratization process. However, despite the positive contribution, there were some weaknesses in the distribution and use of the money. For example, the majority of the parties that benefited from the support have not provided complete financial reports as to how the funds were spent. Also, according to reports received from many political parties, the money was late in arriving, which might have reduced its effectiveness in assisting fair political competition. None of the donor governments have insisted on seeing reports detailing how the contributions were spent. The lack of transparency and effective monitoring has made it difficult to assess the full impact of this type of international assistance.

The UNDP program for the 2005 elections recognized the need for strengthening political parties, but did not propose a broad program similar to the effort undertaken by NDI in 1994–1995. In an attempt to ensure voters had access to the full range of parties and candidates for the election campaign, donors this time provided about US$550,000 to parties and independent candidates to cover a portion of their costs, including equipment

Table 3.6 Assistance to Registered Political Parties for Ethiopia's 2000 Elections

Donor	Amount (US$)
UNDP	58,685.44
Norway	56,383.22
Netherlands	56,989.97
Sweden	58,538.58
Ireland	29,342.72
United Kingdom	58,685.44
Total	318,625.37

Source: NEBE, *Overall Narrative and Financial Report.*

such as computers, photocopiers, and printers, airtime for radio and television, transport, and other campaign-related expenses.[16] Moreover, the program concentrated on training for political party agents who would represent candidates' interests at each polling station. The NDI, and its Republican counterpart, the IRI, returned to Ethiopia for work that involved parties in the approach to the 2005 elections. However, the groups failed to complete registration with the government and, in a reaction that was seen by many as a preemptive move by the Ethiopian government aimed at discouraging independent observers from monitoring the elections, their representatives were expelled from the country in March 2005. There were other party-oriented programs that focused on formulating codes of conduct for parties, improving communication among parties on election issues, and training women candidates. But there was no comprehensive program for party strengthening.

For the 2005 elections, donors were divided over whether to renew the candidate support fund. Eventually it was decided to provide support in kind rather than in cash. ERIS administered the program in close cooperation with the NEBE. Unlike previous efforts, the support extended to independent candidates as well as party nominees. EPRDF candidates, who were allowed access to the fund in 2000 but refrained from using it, also participated in the program this time.

The opposition parties found the 2000 program extremely useful in carrying out campaign work. They complained that the 2005 program was less useful and less flexible. For example, only 25 percent of a party's allocation could be used for transport, and that 25 percent was provided in the form of four-wheel-drive vehicle days. From the parties' point of view, sometimes the ability to purchase a number of bus fares from one rural center to another would have been of greater use than a four-wheel-drive vehicle.

Another serious limitation on political party support was that it concentrated on national elections. However, the need was equally great, or even greater, for local government elections, which involved tens of thousands of candidates in the more rural areas.

Civic Education

Since it first became involved in Ethiopia, the international community has acknowledged the importance of civic education, ranging from subjects such as the nature of democracy to the mechanics of registering and voting. Support has typically taken the form of funding the growing number of civil society organizations (CSOs), individually or through consortia, to engage in election-related programs employing a range of techniques and media.

As early as 1995, donors (Sweden, the Netherlands, Norway, Canada, and the NDI) funded a consortium of seven Ethiopian CSOs called the

Advocacy Network (AD-NET), taking its name from their common interest in advocacy. The group defined its objective as "familiarizing citizens with democratic election procedures and practices." The foundations laid in 1995 were built upon as the 2000 elections approached.

With international and bilateral electoral support, a number of CSOs were active in voter and civic education programs in the period leading up to the 2000 elections. These included the Addis Ababa Chamber of Commerce (AACC), the Ethiopian Women Lawyers Association (EWLA), the Confederation of Ethiopian Trade Unions (CETU), the Eneweyay Civic and Social Education Center (ECSEC), and the Society for the Advancement of Human Rights (SAHRE).

To improve coordination in voter and civic education, in early 1999 a group of six CSOs established the Ethiopian Nongovernmental Organizations Consortium for Elections (ENCONEL). The objectives of the consortium were "to develop standard and coherent teaching materials for voters' education; to determine target areas for voters' education among the constituent CSOs in order to avoid a geographical duplication of efforts as well as to maximize the use of scarce resources; and, finally, to apply a coordinated and structured approach towards the donors in the process of equitably using the limited available resources."[17]

Voter and civic education programs prior to the 2000 elections focused on human rights and law, good governance, Ethiopian electoral law, and election processes and procedures. Some of the programs initiated by CSOs either had targeted audiences or were intended to advance the cause of a particular constituency. For example, with assistance from the Friedrich Ebert Stiftung of Germany, the British Council in Addis Ababa, and the Canadian International Development Agency, EWLA's activities focused on increasing the participation of women in the elections. With assistance from USAID, CETU arranged public forums for political parties and individuals to introduce their programs to workers. It also encouraged workers to participate actively in the national elections. Through a project known as "Vote Addis," the AACC's efforts focused on encouraging the membership to vote for candidates that supported the business community's agenda. By buying airtime, the AACC also helped the media to cover the election in a fair and acceptable manner and serve as a bridge between candidates and voters.

The various civic education programs conducted in the run-up to the 2000 elections reached hundreds of thousands, if not millions, of people and were credited with creating an unprecedented level of debate in the country. However, the impact was not as great as it could have been. The organizations involved represented only a small part of the civil society community, and their outreach was limited because they could cover only Addis Ababa, Dire Dawa, and some cities in the south. In addition, many of them only started their work just before the elections and as a result did not have a serious impact.[18]

In 2003 the Irish embassy funded a conference to take stock of lessons learned in civic education in 2000 and to plan for 2005.[19] A donor representative spoke frankly on what the international community wanted to see from organizations it supported, including coherence in planning, improved monitoring and evaluation, and broader and more specifically targeted outreach. Seven organizations presented their experiences in 2000, and there were lively question-and-answer sessions. Frequent themes that emerged were the desirability of starting sooner, planning better, and funding earlier. However, these lessons seem to have been largely ignored in preparations for 2005, except in the case of organizations such as the Inter Africa Group and Initiative Africa, which had included election-related activities in their core funding.

The UNDP program for 2005 included support to national civil society and nongovernmental organizations for civic and voter education. The program document stressed the importance of civic education, particularly civic education targeted at women, if voter turnout were to be improved. However, the program document seemed to reveal a degree of ignorance of past civic education in the country, saying that "television commercials and discussions aired on radio . . . have been the conventional modes of communication and although they continue to be effective, supplementary and innovative approaches to reach out to the masses should be considered." A civic education bus tour, camel caravans, and street theater were given as examples of "possible avenues for outreach to rural masses."

The UNDP program supported the election-oriented civic education efforts of twenty-four CSOs. Contracts with each of these were signed on March 1, 2005. However, the period for voter registration had already ended in mid-February. By all reports, the CSO programs were not well coordinated and the civic education campaign materials were poorly prepared compared to 2000. Doubtless the effort had some effect, but it was not likely to be as great, and the donors were not so likely to get value for their money as would have been the case had the exercise started much sooner. However, one area of improvement was that the UNDP program implemented by ERIS looked beyond the national elections of 2005 toward the local government elections of 2006. In 2001, civic education before local government elections received minimal international support.

Election Monitoring

The international community has funded its own election monitoring efforts and supported domestic observers with Ethiopian civil society groups. The government has had decidedly mixed feelings about election monitoring, and its attitude toward observer teams has ebbed and flowed over time.

International monitoring has taken several forms. For the local government elections of 1992, the TGE invited international observers, attracting some 250 individuals from twenty-three foreign countries and ten international organizations at a cost of more than US$1.7 million. Reports issued after the election by international observers were highly critical, and the government responded angrily. For example, then-president Meles Zenawi told the NDI that its report was "unabashedly partisan and highly exaggerated."[20] Notwithstanding the government's dissatisfaction with their findings, international observers were invited for the 1994 and 1995 elections, although they returned in smaller numbers.

In 1995 the international community adopted a fresh approach to election monitoring. It created the Donor Election Unit (DEU) with its own senior adviser and administrative and logistical support. Starting in March, the DEU sent some fifty missions into the field to observe the election process in every region of the country. Reports from these missions were not made public, although findings were shared with the NEBE on a regular basis. At the end of the day, the DEU compiled a final analytic summary of the elections. But rather than issuing a public verdict on the election, the ambassadors of the countries involved sent their findings to the foreign minister, with a copy to the chairman of the NEBE.

For the 2000 national elections, the government let it be known that it would not be inviting international observers. In the absence of invitations, the only international observers from outside the country were a few researchers from the Norwegian Institute of Human Rights, which has taken a close interest in Ethiopia's elections from the beginning. At the same time, however, the government cooperated fully with monitoring conducted by members of the international community resident in Addis Ababa.

During the 2000 elections, many embassies and bilateral and multilateral aid agencies based in Addis Ababa organized election monitoring missions or sent representatives to observe the election process in various parts of the country. For example, the US embassy fielded seventeen observers and election monitors throughout the regions and Addis Ababa. The assessments that followed were largely positive and reflected a cautious sense of optimism. According to the report of the US Department of State's Bureau of Democracy, Human Rights, and Labor: "Most opposition political parties competed in the May election; however, due to lack of funds and often weak organization, opposition parties contested only 20 per cent of the seats to the federal parliament."[21]

One reason for the relative success of the 2000 elections was that the major aid providers were keen to see a democratic and competitive electoral process. The donor community in Addis Ababa coordinated aid to the elections and political parties, and closely monitored whether the elections would be fair and free. This joint platform helped the group to exchange information and express a common position to the Ethiopian government regarding any irregularities.

In our informal discussions with representatives of selected foreign embassies, it was emphasized that the intention of international election monitoring missions was not to influence or pressurize the government, but to see to it that elections in Ethiopia followed international standards and practices. That the donor community was paying such close attention to the election process might have helped to create a more level playing field for the elections than in the past, the representatives suggested.

The NEBE's chief executive criticized many international election monitors and observers for failing to provide constructive advice and suggestions on how to improve the electoral process. He also resented the fact that in many instances, inexperienced recruits with little knowledge and appreciation of Ethiopia's history and culture were appointed for monitoring the elections, and that this had resulted in superficial and highly impressionistic assessments of election processes and outcomes. More neutral observers, reasonably knowledgeable about the history and politics of the country, could make significant contributions to improving the system for future elections. In his opinion, it is also necessary that international monitors be deployed throughout the country well in advance of the actual elections in order to observe the entire process from the start, including campaigning, registration, voting, counting, and announcement of results.[22]

For their part, opposition parties generally welcome international election monitoring, seeing it as a means of exerting some pressure on the government and the ruling party to level the electoral playing field and as a kind of insurance in protecting supporters from the extremes of intimidation.

For 2005 the government decided to invite international observers again. The European Union organized an observer team of some 159 members at a reported cost of US$3.68 million. These were joined in the field by more than 40 medium or short-term observers from the Carter Center, as well as observers from other organizations and countries. The opposition parties are on record as saying that the international observer effort for 2005 was too little and too late, arguing that a few hundred international observers cannot effectively monitor what happens in more than 30,000 polling stations, and that the observation effort began too late in the process to make a difference.[23]

The other focus of international assistance has been election monitoring by domestic groups. In 1992, the international observers were supplemented by thirty-two local observers constituting the Ethiopian Free Election Observer Group, which received international support channeled through the

African American Institute. In 1995, the voter education consortium AD-NET created an internationally funded adjunct called E-95 for election monitoring. In 2000, attempts to mobilize an election monitoring coalition came too late for much to be accomplished. By the time the effort was launched, most donor funds had been committed. However, although there was no coordinated approach, several CSOs, most notably the Ethiopian Human Rights Council (EHRCO) and the Research Center for Civic and Human Rights Education, managed to carry out monitoring.

For the 2005 vote, the UNDP program anticipated no support whatsoever for domestic monitoring groups. Nevertheless, a consortium of some twenty civil society groups, led by the Organization for Social Justice in Ethiopia, organized itself to carry out monitoring in a coordinated fashion. Hopes that some support in this could be obtained from the IRI were dashed when the latter was expelled in March 2005. Some members of the consortium had adequate resources through their core funding, allowing some election monitoring to take place within the limits allowed by government authorities. The NEBE announced a policy of only providing monitoring credentials to organizations that have monitoring among the purposes declared in their registration papers.

◼ Impact of Electoral Assistance

Ethiopia has received substantial international electoral assistance to build the NEBE's institutional and logistical capacity to administer elections. In addition, donor assistance has also sought to establish or strengthen civil society organizations, develop and institutionalize political parties, hold public debates and discussions during and before elections, and conduct voter education and training. At one level, this assistance has had an effect to the extent that it has helped Ethiopia to create a system capable of administering a technically credible election. However, at a deeper level this assistance has not had any real impact on democratizing the electoral process.

It seems that elections have not led to more political pluralism. Bent on improving its image as a democratic government domestically and abroad, the EPRDF regime wanted to be seen to be opening up the country to multiparty competition. However, none of the elections it conducted were judged to be either free or competitive, because voting irregularities were widely reported and the main opposition parties boycotted.[24] What is more, voters were not given real choices, because the ruling party used state and bureaucratic resources to ensure landslide victories.[25] On the other hand, the nascent opposition remains institutionally weak and disorganized.

■ Lessons and Recommendations

Ethiopia has enjoyed relative peace following the series of elections held since 1992. The international community has provided considerable humanitarian assistance as well as a degree of democratization aid to help with the country's peaceful transition. However, elections in Ethiopia have failed to create genuine reconciliation among rival factions, because some important contending groups were excluded in the postinsurrection power structure.[26] The ruling party, though less repressive than its predecessor, has persisted in seeking to stifle dissent and public protest through arbitrary arrests and violence. To date, the electoral process in Ethiopia has been consistently dominated by and biased in favor of a single ruling party. State authorities have failed to provide fair conditions for competitive, free elections. Contrary to the expectations of bilateral and multilateral donors, Ethiopia's transition to peace and democracy has been fraught with problems, and considerable anxiety still exists about the country's long-term political stability and the lack of political pluralism.

Capacity and Role of the NEBE

In Ethiopia, national, regional, and local elections have been conducted with the assistance of a government-managed electoral authority that formally has statutory independence. In practice, however, this legal provision has failed to ensure the NEBE's functioning as a neutral body free from outside influence, especially from that of the executive branch. The biased manner in which the NEBE operates has given an overwhelming advantage to ruling party candidates and casts doubt on the legitimacy of electoral outcomes as "the true expression of the wish of the people."

The membership of the NEBE's executive body should be broadened to include independent civil society organizations and professional associations to enhance its autonomy. The international community, which has partly funded the NEBE's supervision activities, should use its leverage to support such reforms and other recent initiatives proposed by opposition parties to bolster the independence of the NEBE. Further funding for election supervision and logistics should be contingent on these reform measures.

Electoral System Framework

In several of our discussions with opposition parties, most have severely criticized the current single-member constituency system as an undemocratic model that heavily favors the ruling party. They have repeatedly called for changes to the constitution to allow for a system of proportional representation, which would make it possible to share parliamentary seats among different political forces in proportion to electoral strength. In principle, with proportional representation, no political force or section of public opinion retains a monopoly. At the same time, no party or faction is excluded from representation. International donors should lobby for proportional representation to allow a more diverse political climate to evolve.

Access to Media

One of the most serious obstacles to pluralism and democratic progress is the ruling EPRDF's virtual stranglehold on the airwaves. The international donor community should place pressure on the Ethiopian government to allow for private broadcasters as alternative voices to the state-owned electronic media. Opposition parties must also be granted fair access during campaigns to state radio and television, which has consistently promoted the ruling party at the expense of opposition candidates. While equitable access to media and the establishment of private stations should be guaranteed on a permanent basis, fair access is especially important during elections.

Increased Political Awareness but a Lack of Pluralism

In a country without a democratic tradition and a history of repression, public awareness and familiarity with elections and democratic practices has advanced over the past fifteen years to an unprecedented level. The burgeoning private print media and civil society sector has opened up some space for political debate and discussion, though the government remains reluctant to tolerate sharp criticism.

Donor assistance has produced valuable public discussions on national issues involving different political parties, especially in rural areas, where the substantial majority of the electorate live. International assistance has helped civic and voter education programs reach large numbers of citizens, who have registered and cast ballots in significant numbers. Opposition parties have also received international assistance to help them communicate with voters. Compared to the previous era under the Derg dictatorship, this represents a degree of progress. However, Ethiopia is still some distance away from securing a genuinely democratic climate and fair elections.

To promote pluralism, donors should place a higher priority on political party development, within the constraints of the electoral legislation. Without carefully balanced institutional support to the main opposition parties, these parties will remain institutionally weak, ensuring the EPRDF more lopsided victories.

Role of Civil Society

Civil society nongovernmental organizations have emerged as an important grassroots force that did not exist until the 1990s. International assistance has helped cultivate this fledgling sector, including aid for voter education efforts in the run-up to elections. These educational efforts need to be expanded to go beyond the technical aspects of elections to more fundamental principles of democracy and the rule of law, especially in rural areas.

International donors should invest in civil society organizations that can pursue civic education on a long-term basis with long-range strategies and approaches. Too often, aid efforts have been conceived and delivered too late in a campaign to be fully effective. At the same time, donor representatives believe nongovernmental organizations need to present more coherent projects with rigorous monitoring, financial accounting, and greater outreach. Aid recipients should be required to account for and report on the use of donor assistance, providing a full assessment of their work, including lessons learned.

Donors also should consider building up domestic competence in election monitoring. There is support among political parties for the idea that election monitoring should be undertaken by both local and international organizations. Assistance should be provided to civil society groups, in particular those already active in voter education, to engage in election monitoring. In addition, donors should promote partnership between international observers and local civil society organizations active in election monitoring.

Finally, despite all the good intentions of donor assistance, the post–May 2005 developments in Ethiopia point to the fragility of democracy under the EPRDF regime. It is not inconceivable that Ethiopia's nascent democracy might have been nipped in the bud following the government crackdown on opposition leaders, activists, as well as members of the private press and civil society organizations. More serious, however, is the fact that unrestrained government actions after the May 2005 elections have plunged Africa's second most populous nation into a period of instability that might risk future violent, political turmoil.

▮ Notes

1. Dessalegn, "Poverty and Agricultural Involution."
2. Just before the Derg's fall, there was an attempt to bring together all the rebel groups and the Derg at a London Peace Conference in early May 1991. The United States played an active role to broker a peace deal, but this failed mainly because the Derg was already in a state of collapse at that very moment. The main beneficiary of the aborted conference was the EPRDF, which gained Washington's support, thus acquiring a measure of legitimacy among Western powers.
3. TGE, *The Transitional Charter of Ethiopia.*
4. Harbeson, "Elections and Democratization in Post-Mengistu Ethiopia."
5. Vestal, *Ethiopia;* NDI and AAI, *An Evaluation of the June 21, 1992, Elections in Ethiopia.*

6. One of the major groups that boycotted these elections was the Oromo Liberation Front (OLF). For more information, see Pausewang and Tronvoll, *The Ethiopian 2000 Elections.*

7. Tronvoll and Aadland, *The Process of Democratization in Ethiopia;* Polhemus, *An Action Plan for Useful Donor Involvement in Ethiopia's 2005 National Elections.*

8. Pausewang and Tronvoll, *The Ethiopian 2000 Elections.*

9. European Union Election Observation Mission to Ethiopia, *Assessment of Vote Counting and Release of Electoral Results;* Carter Center, *Ethiopia Elections.*

10. Obtaining full information on international support for Ethiopia's elections has proven difficult. However, for the 1992 elections, comprehensive figures are to be found in "Contributions Received by NEC for June 21, 1992, Elections in Ethiopia," Appendix 18, in NDI and AAI, *Evaluation,* pp. 154–155.

11. Proclamation no. 438/2005.

12. Some argue that the cost of elections must not be too expensive for parties and individual candidates, because of their dampening effect on competitive politics. The experience of many African countries over the past two decades shows that the costs of elections have been escalating, and there is a grave danger that this might impede democracy and effective participation in election campaigns by several parties. In addition, there is also the argument that if elections become expensive, fundraising becomes a major preoccupation of politicians, thereby distracting them from policymaking and their role as trustees of the public interest. See Shugarman, "Combating Corruption"; and Oyugi, "The Link Between Resources and the Conduct of Elections in Africa."

13. Authors' interview with Assefa Birru, chief executive of the NEBE, July 28, 2003.

14. Proclamation no. 46/1993, pt. 5.

15. Quoted in Polhemus, *An Action Plan for Useful Donor Involvement in Ethiopia's 2005 National Elections,* p. 56.

16. NEBE, *Data on 2005 National Assembly Elections.*

17. CLCBS, "Civic Education in Ethiopia."

18. Ibid.

19. Ibid.

20. Quoted in Polhemus, *Action Plan,* p. 19.

21. US State Department, *Country Reports on Human Rights Practices.*

22. Authors' interview with Assefa Birru.

23. *Addis Tribune,* March 25, 2005, p. 1.

24. NDI and AAI, *Evaluation;* Aalen, *Ethnic Federalism in a Dominant Party State;* Pausewang, Tronvoll, and Aalen, *Ethiopia Since the Derg;* Polhemus, *Action Plan.*

25. Abbink, "The Organization and Observation of Elections in Federal Ethiopia."

26. Asnake, "Regime Transition and Problems of Democratization in Post-Insurgent African States."

4

Fostering Multiparty Politics in Mozambique

Marc de Tollenaere

After an eleven-year armed struggle for liberation, Mozambique secured independence from Portugal on June 25, 1975. The victorious Mozambican Liberation Front (FRELIMO) then established a single-party socialist system.

The leadership that secured military victory was not prepared for the challenge of running a country. The exodus of the Portuguese following independence left a vacuum that could not be adequately addressed. Despite significant improvements in education and health, the structural problems inherited from the colonial economy and international pressures from the Cold War helped plunge the country's agricultural sector, industry, public services, and administration into crisis.

The influence and even direct military interference of neighboring countries (the former Rhodesia until it became Zimbabwe in 1980; South Africa until the late 1980s) and mounting public dissatisfaction gave rise to civil war between the FRELIMO government and the Mozambican National Resistance (RENAMO).[1] The conflict lasted from 1976 to 1992. By the mid-1980s, the country was in a deep economic depression and it became apparent that the war could not be ended by military means.

Mozambican churches started pressing for negotiations. Talks took place first in Nairobi (1989–1990) and later in Rome (1990–1992). Finally, on October 4, 1992, a general peace agreement was signed by the president of the republic, Joaquim Chissano, and the president of RENAMO, Afonso Dhlakama. The war claimed 1 million lives. Some 1.5 million people fled to neighboring countries and 4 million people were internally displaced. More than 1 million mines lay scattered across the country. The country's economy and social infrastructure were decimated.

The general peace agreement paved the way for the organization of the first multiparty elections in October 1994. In ten years time, Mozambique held another two multiparty national elections (1999 and 2004) and two multiparty local elections (1998 and 2003).[2]

Since 1994, Mozambique's political system has been considered as fundamentally bipartisan.[3] Both FRELIMO and RENAMO monopolized political competition, with FRELIMO as the holder of executive and legislative power since independence and RENAMO as the only force capable of challenging the incumbent at the polls.

The December 2004 general elections, the fifth multiparty election since the general peace agreement, dealt a blow to this perception. While FRELIMO managed to uphold its 1999 result, RENAMO lost nearly half of its voters. FRELIMO is now close to securing a two-thirds majority in the parliament and RENAMO remains the only opposition parliamentary party. In addition, the anticipated breakthrough of a third force, Raoul Domingos's Party for Peace, Democracy, and Development (PDD), failed to materialize. This result points toward the end of the bipartisan era and confirms the consolidation of a single dominant power without serious political competition.

This chapter looks at how outside financial and technical support to parties influenced the political landscape and explores whether such international support contributed to building a multiparty democracy. It gauges the importance attached to political parties in the wider framework of democracy assistance, provides an overview of the various initiatives to strengthen parties, and assesses the effects both internally (within the parties) and on the political process in general.

■ Political Parties in Mozambique

The Impetus for Permitting Pluralism

The second postindependence constitution, of 1990, provided for the possibility to create political parties.[4] According to Article 77, "all citizens have the freedom to form and participate in political parties" and "party membership shall be voluntary, and shall derive from the freedom to achieve their specific objectives and to own assets in order to carry out their activities." The constitutional provision was regulated by a specific law on the existence and operation of political parties in 1991 (Law 7/91). The main provisions of this law were also adopted in the general peace agreement under Protocol II (1992).

The decision to move to a multiparty system was not rooted in a recognition of its virtues. With hindsight, former president Chissano explained that the FRELIMO leadership felt resistance within the country to the idea of a multiparty system during consultations in 1989. "The people could not perceive the existence of other political groupings within our society because

FRELIMO had always been open to different ideas within itself."[5] Allowing pluralism was not based on a vision of democratizing Mozambican society, but rather on a pragmatic decision to accommodate RENAMO as a political player. Establishing a multiparty model was part of the postwar settlement and did not grow out of a genuine conviction that a pluralist system would provide for a more democratic result.

FRELIMO and RENAMO

FRELIMO was a coalition or front set up in Tanzania in 1962 from a merger of three anticolonial movements—the Mozambican African National Union (MANU), based in Kenya and Tanzania; the National Democratic Union of Mozambique (UDENAMO), based in Zimbabwe; and the National African Union of Independent Mozambique (UNAMI), based in Malawi—plus a group of independent intellectuals living in exile (most in Paris).[6] FRELIMO waged an armed struggle against the colonial regime from 1964 to 1974. An agreement that secured independence was signed in Lusaka on September 7, 1974, and independence was proclaimed on June 25, 1975. The broad liberation front suffered from internal tensions and conflicts. The faction favoring socialist ideology prevailed in the end. The liberation front was transformed into a party in 1977 during the third FRELIMO congress. A monolithic party-state was established based on "democratic centralism," with the overarching goal of maintaining national unity. The state was considered the engine of development and therefore was granted authority to intervene directly in the economy. FRELIMO also stood for a clear separation between the state and religion.

Serious shortcomings in its policies and armed opposition gradually convinced FRELIMO to liberalize the economy and the political climate. The changes were confirmed in a new constitution approved in 1990. The party was separated from the state and the state underwent a separation of powers (executive, judicial, and legislative). The government withdrew gradually from the economy, but "ownership" was secured through the positioning of FRELIMO loyalists and cadres in key functions in the burgeoning private sector. The ruling party's ideological fervor faded in the face of economic crisis and military deadlock. FRELIMO evolved into a less ideological and more technocratic, pragmatic party. This shift was illustrated in the different style displayed by Mozambique's first president, Samora Machel, compared to his successor Joaquim Chissano. The charismatic Samora Machel personified the ideological line, while Chissano's primary concern was to find a pragmatic and diplomatic solution for the conflict and mounting economic difficulties.

Dependence on international support, and the policy conditions related to that support, must have pushed FRELIMO to opt for economic and political liberalization as the Cold War receded. But the change in course was certainly not merely a reaction to outside pressures. FRELIMO leaders had also realized that changes were required.[7]

FRELIMO's internal organization has been largely unchanged since independence. The party base is made up of an estimated 30,000 *células* (cells, smallest units of a political party), followed by *círculos* (circles, intermediate units), *zonas* (zones, largest units), and then district and provincial offices.[8] The party had about 40,000 members in 1989, 250,000 in 1991, 1 million in 1994, and 1.5 million today. Only an estimated 10 percent of the members effectively pay membership fees.

Drawing on state authority and resources, FRELIMO enjoys a distinct financial advantage over opposition parties. FRELIMO reportedly spent about US$10 million during the 2004 election campaign. Less than 10 percent of that amount was public money, and the total was about twenty times more than what the major opposition coalition spent. FRELIMO has access to state resources for its operations (as has been abundantly clear during electoral campaigns), because it dominates executive power at all levels. FRELIMO also receives monthly public funding according to its large representation in parliament, owns businesses and real estate, and is the only party that receives some income from membership fees, even if it is only a minority of the members who effectively pay. There are no confirmed cases where FRELIMO benefits as a party from kickbacks or corruption, but friendly parties are known to support FRELIMO during election campaigns (the Popular Movement for the Liberation of Angola, the Chinese Communist Party) with funds or in-kind contributions.

RENAMO was born out of discontent with FRELIMO's Marxist policies immediately after independence, including the centrally planned economy, collective production, and resettlement.[9] RENAMO received critical support from external forces, mainly from Ian Smith's regime in Rhodesia until its collapse in 1980 and the apartheid regime in South Africa during the 1980s (with particular intensity until 1986).[10] Outside support armed and trained RENAMO. Abduction was used as a standard recruitment method, yet in some areas the local population cooperated and assisted with RENAMO's operations. As the economic crisis deepened, RENAMO offered an alternative for desperate and frustrated young men, who voluntarily joined. In some cases there was also tacit or active support of the population, often based on historical animosities between groups that used RENAMO forces as temporary allies to settle old disputes among neighboring clans.[11] Public support seemed to be opportunistic or enforced, but that would not explain the level of electoral support expressed in 1994. RENAMO did manage to generate more genuine support than outsiders and FRELIMO itself ever expected. One of the major reasons for this support was that RENAMO reinstated traditional authorities in the areas under its control.

In the mid-1980s, RENAMO established a political wing and later, when peace negotiations began, started recruiting more diplomatic and more educated staff rather than relying on former military staff. This was often done with promises that the organization would fund further education. Through the peace agreement, RENAMO agreed to turn itself into a political party and officially registered as such in 1993. After the 1994 elections RENAMO restructured itself during a congress.

The party's internal governance remains heavily influenced by its military background. Party bodies (a national council of sixty elected during the 2002 congress, a small political commission, and a few advisory bodies) are only superficially institutionalized, and decisionmaking processes are concentrated in and around Afonso Dhlakama, who has been leading the organization for nearly thirty years. Financial accountability mechanisms are equally weak.

According to research on the party, RENAMO succeeded in the transformation to a political party because of adequate demobilization, the establishment of some core structures, and the expansion of its support base from rural to urban areas.[12] But it remains a strongly personalized and weakly organized party, struggling to accommodate internal differences. In this sense, the party has gone through a limited and uneven process of institutionalization.[13]

RENAMO's sole regular source of income has been public funding through its representation in parliament. That source of income has now dropped by an estimated 20 percent due to the result of the 2004 elections, and this could further weaken the party, particularly in the light of its ongoing lack of managerial acumen. Other parties have no regular sources of income and usually function on the basis of private contributions, mainly by the leadership.

Current Political Landscape

In 2005 there were thirty-nine registered parties. This relatively high number of parties in Mozambique reflects the country's complex history, ethnicity, and regionalism, the driving ambition for power among some individuals, and the result of financial disputes rather than policy preferences.[14]

The labels "liberal," "democracy," and "national unity" are the most frequently employed by the parties. However, the parties do not distinguish themselves by clear ideological divisions. There are no distinct visions on economic, social, or cultural development. There are no elaborate alternative visions set out, with the exception of one issue, federalism (promoted by the Liberal and Democratic Party of Mozambique [PALMO], the Democratic Party of Mozambique [PADEMO], the Mozambique People's Progress Party [PPPM], the Democratic Renewal Party [PRD], the United Democratic

Front [UDF], and the Mozambican National Union [UNAMO]). National unity remains the highest priority for FRELIMO, even superseding poverty reduction.

FRELIMO is a member of the Socialist International, and RENAMO of the Christian Conservative International. The PDD has joined the Liberal International, and the Labor Party has plans to join the Socialist International.

PALMO was the first opposition group to appear publicly, and UNAMO was the first to register officially (1991). Seven parties were registered by 1993. Twelve parties and two coalitions participated in the first multiparty elections in 1994. New parties continued to appear after 1994, mainly due to the emergence of new approaches (e.g., ecologists) or fresh divisions and rivalries. In 1999, nine parties and three coalitions competed for mandates in the National Assembly. In 2004, fifteen parties and five coalitions successfully registered for elections.[15]

Local elections allow participation of registered parties, coalitions, and "groups of citizens." The first multiparty local elections (1998) were boycotted by RENAMO and all smaller opposition parties, except one: the Labor Party. Ten "groups of citizens" or civic-political movements also participated. Four of those groups managed to win mandates in municipal assemblies and the Labor Party won seats in two municipalities.

The 2003 local elections went ahead without a boycott. Apart from FRELIMO, only RENAMO participated in all municipalities, with its Electoral Union coalition of ten smaller parties. Another eight smaller parties (the Labor Party, the Independent Party of Mozambique [PIMO], the Social Liberal Party, PALMO, UNAMO, the Democratic Congress Party, the Ecologist Party, and the Greens) competed. Some stood in only one of the thirty-three municipalities where elections were organized. The movements were clearly more successful than the parties: five of them managed to win seats in municipal assemblies, while only one smaller party managed to do so (PIMO in Cuamba, Nampula, and Angoche).

Based on participation in the 2004 elections, the existing parties can be classified into four groups:

1. The two dominating parties of the multiparty era: FRELIMO and RENAMO. Since 1999, RENAMO has contested elections with a coalition referred to as the Electoral Union, comprising the National Convention Party (PCN), the United Front of Mozambique (FUMO), the Mozambique National Movement (MONAMO), the Patriotic Action Front (FAP), the PRD, the Independent Alliance of Mozambique (ALIMO), the National Unity Party (PUN), the UDF, the PPPM, and the Ecological Party of Mozambique (PEMO).

2. Small parties present throughout the national territory: the Social Liberal Party and PIMO. PALMO, the Democratic Union, and the Labor Party used to be able to establish lists of candidates in all constituencies, but no longer succeeded doing that in 2004. The PDD, the Ecological Party–Land Movement (PEC-MT), the Green Party of Mozambique (PVM), the Democratic Reconciliation Party (PAREDE), and the Mozambique Social Broadening Party (PASOMO) are parties established after the 1999 elections that managed to submit lists in all constituencies. PASOMO ran in two constituencies in 1999 and in all constituencies in 2004, showing clear signs of improved internal organization. More recently established parties such as PDD seem to have more capacity to network and establish local representations.

3 Parties and coalitions that are only present in some constituencies: the Popular Democratic Party (PPD), the Party of Freedom and Solidarity (PAZS), the United Congress of Democrats (CDU), the Democratic Liberal Party of Mozambique (PADELIMO), the MBG (coalition of UNAMO and the Party of All Mozambican Nationalists [PARTONAMO]), the Union for the Salvation of Mozambique (USAMO; coalition of the Democratic Alliance and Social Renewal Party [PADRES], the Mozambique Socialist Party [PSM], and the Union for Change [UM]), and the Enlarged Opposition Front (FAO; coalition of the Liberal Front and the African Conservative Party [PAC]). This is also the case for many coalition partners that joined the Electoral Union with RENAMO.

4. Parties that never competed or no longer participate in elections: seventeen of the fifty-seven parties that were established since 1992 never ran in an election, and it is unclear to what extent these organizations are still active. The Democratic Congress Party and PADEMO are two parties that participated in the 1994 and 1999 elections but disappeared from the scene afterward.

Mozambican parties have yet to satisfactorily fulfill their role and responsibilities. Political programs rarely address social demands, and a wide gap remains between most parliamentarians and the electorate.[16] Some political staff members have gained knowledge and experience through their exposure to the electoral process, but this is almost exclusively limited to the two major parties. Parties do little to encourage or inspire democratic practices. Public threats of violence by senior politicians, mutual humiliation in parliament, and obstructive opposition tactics illustrate that democratic norms have yet to take root. Opposition parties tend to limit themselves to opposing the majority without presenting policy alternatives.

■ Overview of International Political Party Assistance

The Scope of External Support

Support to political parties became a focus for international assistance in the 1980s and expanded dramatically in the 1990s, pushed by transitions in Eastern Europe and Africa. Despite its growth, political party support has remained more contentious than other dimensions of democracy assistance. Drawing a distinct boundary between neutral support focusing on institutional development and advancement of political competition can be difficult. The latter implies efforts to level the playing field. This is an activity that cannot be carried out without a bias in favor of the opposition, subjecting a donor agency to possible criticism of partisanship, and interference in domestic politics.

After 1994, donors became reluctant to engage in political party support in Mozambique. From 1992 to 1994, external support to parties was considered an element of the peace agreement's implementation. The first multiparty elections concluded that phase and donors became wary of engaging in further party assistance. Party officials, particularly those of the smaller parties, complained that donors "finance everything that moves" except political parties. They said that donors want democracy, but don't bother to assist in introducing its most basic ingredient: political parties. Donors, from their side, generally consider political party support via official cooperation as political interference.

It is important to note that private foreign donations from international partisan organizations or supporters are not addressed in this chapter. The focus here is exclusively on assistance with a clear development orientation. Such external support is usually delivered by specialized organizations or foundations within the framework of democracy assistance, aiming to improve the quality of democracy in a given country rather than promote the advancement of one particular party.

Assistance to political parties falls into two stages in the case of Mozambique. During the first phase, support to political parties, particularly RENAMO, is considered crucial for multiparty elections marking the conclusion of the peace process. In the second stage, support to parties as a way of consolidating democracy is deemed a low priority.

After the 1994 elections, which were mandated by the peace accords, donors concluded that democratic development could be bolstered not through aid to political parties but instead through civic initiatives, the holding of local elections, and reform of the judiciary, the parliament, the police, and the media.

Political Party Assistance as Peacebuilding, 1992–1994

In December 1992, two months after the signing of the general peace agreement, RENAMO's leader, Dhlakama, threatened to withdraw from some of the commissions that oversaw the implementation of the agreement. He declared that financial support for RENAMO was promised by the international community in return for his acceptance of some agreement provisions at the last stages of the peace negotiations. But the international community failed to carry out its promise after the conclusion of the general peace agreement on October 4, 1992. Dhlakama was in a strong bargaining position, as the international community did not want to jeopardize a hard-fought peace agreement and there was already a consensus that RENAMO would need financial support for its transformation into a political party. In January 1993, one month after Dhlakama's threat to withdraw from the peace process, the Italian minister of foreign affairs requested that the UN establish a trust fund to channel financial support to RENAMO. A UN trust fund for the implementation of the peace agreement was then created. There are varying records as to how much money was finally raised (between US$13.6 and US$17 million). Italy covered about half the contributions. Other donors to the RENAMO trust fund included the Netherlands, France, Norway, Portugal, Sweden, Switzerland, and the United States.

The UN reporting on the trust fund implementation has been erratic, and for good reasons. UN trust funds are cumbersome bureaucratic vehicles, managed entirely from outside and not at the local level. This approach was impractical for RENAMO. In January 1994 the UN Secretary-General informed the international donor community that Dhlakama would need US$300,000 a month in cash handouts from January to October 1994 to "enable the RENAMO leader to meet the expectations of his supporters so as not to lose his authority and prestige and destabilize the whole process."[17] According to UN special representative Aldo Ajello, cash transfers only took place during the last four months before the elections. That would imply that over US$1 million was handed out in cash to RENAMO's leader. There are no other sources that confirm this, and neither can it be confirmed that all cash came from the trust fund account or from parallel contributions.[18]

The rest of the money was used to pay for office space, housing, communications, vehicles, and equipment. The money could not be used to hire consultants, which angered RENAMO.[19]

The RENAMO trust fund bent traditional donor financing rules, but it is widely considered to have played a crucial role in keeping RENAMO behind the peace process. The international cash "bolstered Dhlakama's leadership, permitted [RENAMO] to pay off military leaders and officials it could no longer use, helped to maintain loyalty and services of the party cadres and allowed it to attract new leaders and activists."[20] According to scholars Stephen Chan and Venancio Moises, the trust fund "allayed RENAMO's fears about competing with the more politically sophisticated FRELIMO regime."[21]

Although the short-term gain was positive, the external financial support also compounded the financial problems of RENAMO in the longer run. The money was not disbursed according to practical needs and priorities. RENAMO ordered goods and services expecting that these would be covered by the trust fund. The combination of an irregular and unpredictable financial flow, an absolute lack of experience with financial management, pressing needs, and some audacity about their bargaining power resulted in RENAMO running up expenses beyond the limits of the fund. The party could not manage such exceptional generosity and its future was jeopardized by its financial mismanagement. RENAMO incurred debts, but there is no verifiable information about the total amount. This became clear in late 1996, when the balance of the trust fund had to be settled. Over US$300,000 was left for RENAMO. In consultation with the participating donors, the UN Development Programme (UNDP) asked RENAMO for a list of creditors. All creditors were private companies from which RENAMO had ordered goods or services but had failed to pay in full. Some of the debts were settled through direct payments by the UNDP to selected creditors.

After the 1999 and 2004 elections, RENAMO threatened to boycott parliament but ended up withdrawing the threat. The reason for backing down was financial rather than political. The indebted party and party members needed the monthly income guaranteed according to RENAMO's level of representation in parliament.

Apart from the RENAMO trust fund, the donors also established a second trust fund for parties participating in the first elections. Again Italy was the largest contributor to this fund. The initial target was to raise US$3.5 million, which would be enough for a single installment of US$200,000 per party, as was initially agreed between the national electoral commission and the parties. A smaller amount was raised, however, and the donors did not accept the proposal to hand out a lump sum with few conditions attached. Instead, donors proposed two disbursements of US$50,000 for each participating party. The funds had to be spent on the campaign costs and not on cars, houses, or salaries.

While the assistance may have created a more level playing field for the elections, it also fostered a passive attitude that such generous support was customary and to be expected. Smaller parties complained bitterly during subsequent elections that donors had failed to renew this kind of support. The parties argued that donors undermined democracy by subsidizing elections and observers but refusing to pay for the main actor in the process: political parties.

▩ Political Party Assistance Since 1994

Donor agencies and organizations have provided a range of assistance to political parties since 1994, though at a lower level following the first elections held after the signing of the peace agreement. The assistance was often short-term in nature and sometimes only focused on one or a few parties. The aid addressed party organizational development, campaigning, women's participation, legislative work, and cross-party collaboration.

Organizational Development

In the sphere of party organization, the Friedrich Ebert Stiftung of Germany worked with RENAMO and FRELIMO during the peace process and later provided capacity building for locally elected politicians. But at no stage did it pursue a program designed to strengthen political parties.

The Konrad Adenauer Stiftung started operating in Mozambique in 2002 and has been providing institutional support to RENAMO, but no details have been made available.

The US-based National Democratic Institute (NDI) began working in Mozambique in 1991, focusing on voter education. In 1996 it conducted a six-month constituency outreach program for parliamentarians that could be considered as a form of indirect support to political parties. In September 1998 the NDI started implementing a program called "PARTIDO" to support the institutional capacity of political parties (FRELIMO, RENAMO, the Democratic Union, and the PCN) and four independent political movements.[22] The program was designed to strengthen sustainable democratic practices and institutional capabilities. The objectives included the encouragement of accountability, transparency, and responsiveness to members within political parties; increased organizational skills and capacities in political parties; the cultivation of linkages among parties and political organizations; and the renewal of constructive political dialogue between parties and civil society.

The British Conservative Party has been supporting RENAMO with funds from the Westminster Foundation for Democracy since the mid-1990s, prior to the four elections that took place since 1998. More detailed information is unavailable, but there are indications that support focused on both campaigning techniques and institutional development.

The Netherlands Institute for Multiparty Democracy (NIMD)—previously known as the Dutch Foundation for the New South Africa (NZA)—has conducted the most comprehensive program for support to political parties in Mozambique. It is distinctive compared to most other initiatives in three ways:

1. Part of the funds are transferred to and managed by the parties. Most donors do not transfer funds to parties, but pay service providers directly.

2. The program is more inclusive in the sense that it is open in a more systematic way to a higher number of parties.
3. The focus is clearly on long-term institutional and organizational development, while many other programs have shorter-term and more narrow objectives.

The NZA/NIMD started with a pilot program in Mozambique in 1998–1999 in which an annual US$7,500 was made available to the nineteen parties that participated during the 1994 elections and that demonstrated some activity afterward. Another US$300,000 was distributed annually and proportionally to the parties represented in parliament. The pilot program was extended until 2000, when an office was established and funding considerably increased under a three-year mandate (May 2000–August 2003).[23]

The new NIMD program had two main components: a bilateral fund based on a system of drawing rights, and a special fund for cross-party activities and support to independent groups. The bilateral fund was made up of a basic amount for each of the twenty-five parties that participated in the 1999 elections (US$6,590 in the first year and US$10,930 in the second year), with an extra sum based on the percentage of the votes obtained, with a threshold of 2 percent. In practice the basic amount represented 50 percent of the bilateral budget and the extra amounts the other half of the budget (total for first year circa US$325,240 increased to US$421,600 in the third year). The sum corresponded to the drawing right for each party. Parties could submit for that amount one or more proposals according to preset guidelines and criteria.

Bilateral projects were contracted with most of the political parties, varying from national congresses, regional meetings, and training of provincial and district delegates, to seminars on the role of opposition parties or the position of women in politics. Between 2000 and 2003, the NIMD approved fifty-six party proposals for a total of US$732,490, which was one-third of the amount originally foreseen for this component.[24] Five parties (RENAMO, PIMO, the Labor Party, the PRD, and PALMO) formulated strategic plans using these drawing rights.

The objective of the program was to build the capacity of political parties, bolstering organizational structure, staff skills, and democratic practices and attitudes. The short-term goals were to create stronger and better organized parties, improved financial administration, and better readiness for elections. The NIMD program has certainly been successful in achieving these short-term objectives, at least for those parties that demonstrated a willingness to learn and had a minimal capacity from the outset. The expected long-term results were to reduce political tension, generate broader participation of political parties in national decisionmaking, and expand activities at provincial and local levels. It is still too early to assess if these long-term goals have also been met, though it is likely the program has produced mixed results. There are indications that more parties participate in public debate and are active at the local level. However, participation by a wider array of parties in national decisionmaking is declining, and elections since 1994 have been plagued by heightened political tension.

Election Campaigns

European Parliamentarians for Africa (AWEPA) engaged in capacity building for political party staff for participation in the local and national elections and the training of poll monitors. Beginning in 1998, when the first local elections were held, AWEPA shifted its focus from the central to the local level, although it continued with a limited program to support the National Assembly. Since 1994, AWEPA has organized various seminars and sponsored publications on Mozambican governance and politics (most notably the *Mozambique Peace Process Bulletin,* later renamed the *Mozambique Political Process Bulletin,* which reports on political processes and elections). In preparation for the past two elections, AWEPA coordinated the training of political party poll monitors with NIMD and the International Republican Institute (IRI).

The NDI trained parties to improve campaigning with better organizational skills and issue-based campaign platforms in preparation for the 1999 elections.

The IRI implemented training activities in 1994–1995 that emphasized ballot-box security, political party consultation, and parliamentary training. The IRI then suspended its activities in Mozambique, only to start again in 2004 with a US$150,000 grant from the National Endowment for Democracy to support "all-party election readiness" in preparation for the third general elections. This six-month operation had three objectives: (1) to help political party leaders incorporate ethics and accountability issues into their programs and communications, (2) to help parties develop programs that are broad-based and incorporate the views of the electorate, and (3) to improve the organization of political parties, allowing them to compete effectively for voter support.

The goal of the intervention was to improve the conditions for fair political competition in an arena strongly biased in favor of FRELIMO. The project focused on improved interparty communications, financial management, policy and strategy development, leadership skills, and increased awareness of democratic methods. Support focused on FRELIMO and RENAMO, but also on qualifying smaller parties in the hope that one of them would reach the organizational capacity to surpass the 5 percent threshold.

The IRI coordinated its election-related training efforts with AWEPA, the NIMD, and two national nongovernmental organizations (the Center for the Study of Democracy and Development [CEDE] and the Mozambican Association for the Development of Democracy [AMODE]), and conducted several training sessions and demand-driven roundtables.

Participation of Women

Most parties have a women's league, but few activities were identified that targeted such women's groups directly. The exception to this was a seminar by the IRI in the run-up to the 2004 elections concentrating on the subject of women in politics, which included some 160 party workers. Most donors, though, would always stress the need to involve a maximum number of women in capacity-building activities. The NIMD organized a few sessions for party members about the importance of the involvement of women, but an evaluation of the program suggested that the objective to promote the participation of women was not realized during the first three-year program cycle.

Participation in Legislatures

Parties also received indirect support through capacity building of municipal assemblies and the national parliament, where staff members were trained in technical and legal matters. Indirect support does not aim for parties to perform better and therefore it is not further analyzed here, yet clearly such indirect support can have a positive collateral impact on a party's performance.

Multiparty Collaboration

Collaboration among political parties was supported indirectly through the funding of joint capacity-building activities. The NIMD's special fund for cross-party activities was the only initiative that pursued such joint activities systematically. The special fund was used for needs assessments and the organization of cross-party seminars on strategic planning, financial administration, and joint project formulation, often in collaboration with other international partners. Eleven cross-party projects were implemented between 2000 and 2003. Five of these projects were carried out in partnership with AWEPA or the NDI. The budget planned over the three years was US$384,830, of which US$224,740 was spent by mid-June 2003 (a sharp increase in expenditures took place in the run-up to the local elections of November 2003). Cross-party initiatives certainly proved to offer more value for money, particularly because some could be conducted with cofinancing from other agencies. These initiatives also enabled a fruitful discussion among parties and helped to build mutual trust.

Through this fund, the NIMD oversaw the negotiation and conclusion of a code of conduct for political parties for the 2004 general elections. This was a clearly demand-driven expression of unprecedented multiparty collaboration.

■ Effects of External Support to Political Parties

Electoral Competition

Electoral competition in Mozambique has improved in that the number of parties vying for parliamentary seats has increased markedly. The number of parties and coalitions running for national mandates more than doubled between 1994 and 2004: from seventeen to thirty-five. But smaller parties have seen their share of the vote decreasing. Also, the popular support won by smaller parties in elections decreased from 12.5 percent in 1994 and 1999 to only 8.5 percent in 2004.[25] The recently elected parliament is the most lopsided since 1994. FRELIMO has 160 members and RENAMO 90, of which only 4 come from smaller coalition partners. Smaller parties blame the 5 percent threshold for national elections,[26] but an analysis of the results shows that this is not the main obstacle. A projection of the results of the 1994 elections shows that without such a minimum threshold FRELIMO would have won 128 seats and RENAMO 110, respectively 1 and 2 fewer than they actually won with the 5 percent threshold. A hypothetical 2 percent threshold gives the same result as the 5 percent threshold. The figures for the 1999 elections show a similar picture, although with a higher number of smaller parties. Abolishing the threshold only moderately affects representation in parliament. Moreover, it would also stall attempts to form coalitions, though this remains probably the best option for smaller parties to play an effective role, particularly because differences are usually more personal than programmatic.

The key question is whether international support to political parties has contributed to the strengthening of democratic competition in Mozambique. Based on election results, it clearly has not. Initially, in 1999, a more bipartisan balance emerged in parliament. However, after the elections in 2004, parliament is now overwhelmingly dominated by one party (FRELIMO). During the 2004 electoral campaign, expectations were high that Raoul Domingos's PDD would manage to surpass the 5 percent threshold. However, the PDD ended up with a sobering 2 percent of the national vote, failing to garner high numbers among its supposed support base. International donor assistance has failed to improve the plurality of elected bodies, at both the national and the municipal level.

Formation of Coalitions

The relatively high threshold has had a positive side effect by stimulating coalition building. Parties sometimes decided to cooperate to secure 5 percent of the vote and a role in the parliament. The Democratic Union coalition managed to do this in 1994, but that achievement has been dismissed by some as rather accidental.[27] Still, a trend toward more coalitions is visible. In 1994, two coalitions participated, representing five parties; in 1999, three coalitions covering a total of sixteen parties emerged; and in 2004, five coalitions involving twenty parties stood in the election.

It is difficult to assess if international assistance played a positive role in influencing the formation of coalitions. In several cross-party sessions sponsored by donors, collaboration between parties was certainly discussed. This may have raised awareness and nurtured the trend. Also, the mere fact that regular cross-party activities took place may have resulted in an improved understanding and enhanced trust among party leaders, paving the way for collaboration. However, the formation of coalitions could only be "positive collateral," as it is unlikely ever to be a direct result of outside support. Moreover, promoting coalition building in an explicit way could easily be interpreted as political interference by donors.

Creation of Political Party Programs

An increasing number of political parties have begun to demonstrate responsibility and leadership in their public actions and attitudes, presenting party platforms and engaging in public discussion. The preparation of Agenda 2025, a comprehensive vision on national development in which parties and civil society actively collaborated, illustrates this trend. Political parties are now more visible in the public debate and act with greater self-awareness. This indicates that some parties now have a better internal organization and a better-trained leadership. However, most opposition parties still lack a political program that carries the support of a broad enough constituency. Small parties are not rooted in social processes, rarely have a specific target group, and have few credible volunteers who can mobilize support at the local level. Moreover, none have managed to come up with a message that has an appeal to the wider electorate. Despite these shortcomings, international assistance undoubtedly helped at least a handful of parties to formulate programs and communicate their ideas to the public.

Institutional Development

The effects of international support to political parties are most visible in the area of institutional development:

- International aid has enabled various parties to organize national meetings or congresses.
- Party activists are now more aware of how a multiparty democracy should operate.
- Internal democracy has improved in some parties and links between the leadership and the rank and file have been strengthened. Donor assistance has played a critical role, as it has sponsored national and regional party meetings where central leadership could be made accountable as well as congresses in which party leaders could be elected.
- Some parties have enhanced their capacity to plan and implement initiatives.
- Party staff have learned how to communicate more effectively with the media.
- Some parties have significantly improved their electoral "readiness."
- Some parties now have more effective administrative and financial systems, and are more aware of their capacities and limitations.
- Five parties now have a strategic vision on how they want to develop further.[28]
- Parties have pursued collaboration and exchanges of ideas.

It is clear that international assistance has had a positive effect on the institutional development of parties with organizational potential.

■ Strengths and Weaknesses of Political Party Assistance

Before the first elections, party assistance had a distinctive and short-term goal: to ensure multiparty elections could take place. If that goal required political party support, then it would be provided. After 1994, most donors concluded that there was no longer a strategic objective for party support. With the exception of NIMD programs, party support has been erratic, hasty, or opportunistic, and has tended to concentrate on the months preceding elections. The lack of a long-term vision for political parties by both the donors and party leaders has undermined the potential of international assistance.

A second weakness is that the supply-driven launch of multiparty politics set a precedent for an unhealthy money-driven relationship between parties and donors. Based on the experience of 1994, opposition parties assumed it routine that donors would subsidize their activities and electoral costs without question. Party leaders tended to focus on attracting international assistance instead of mobilizing resources and support locally.

A third weakness was a bias for the national level and limiting aid to officially registered parties, leading to the exclusion of ad hoc "groups of citizens" that often proved to be more successful in national elections.

However, international assistance and the administrative demands that inevitably accompany it have led to the emergence of "leaders and stragglers." In particular, the focus and organization required to draw on the NIMD fund provided an insight into the skills and dedication of the parties. The best performers in assistance programs coincided with those that featured most prominently in the public debate. International assistance has confronted poorly organized parties with their weaknesses.

Efforts designed to build capacity usually addressed relevant topics and needs, but for many years these projects were pursued without coordination, resulting in the duplication of efforts and the inefficient use of already scarce resources. The NIMD has played a positive role in trying to boost coordination, and worked effectively together with AWEPA and national nongovernmental organizations during the 2004 election campaign. In contrast, smaller agencies tended to fall back on a certain routine, conducting training that was not always adequately adapted to the Mozambican setting.

■ Lessons and Recommendations

There are two distinct phases in terms of international support to political parties: before and after 1994. The support offered before 1994 (dominated by the two trust funds) was not directed primarily at the parties but focused on the country's peace process.[29] Support offered after 1994 concentrated on electoral readiness, but gradually evolved toward institutional development (in particular the PARTIDO and NIMD programs).

Within democracy assistance efforts to Mozambique, support to political parties has never been a priority. In financial terms political party support has been a marginal activity. Other areas of democracy assistance covering elections, parliament, media, police, civil society, or anticorruption campaigns could count on far larger financial and technical support since 1994. Donors invested US$150 million in the past five elections. The amount invested in building up the organizational structure of political parties was only about US$1.5 million. In the run-up to the elections, another US$5–6 million was invested in electoral readiness (campaigning, training of party monitors). The comparison with international support for organizing elections demonstrates that aid and advice for political parties has remained at a modest scale.

Political parties could count on moderate donor support since 1994, but the question is whether more generous assistance would be justified. FRELIMO is interested in some technical support that can help to fine-tune its party machinery, but can basically operate without outside aid. RENAMO needs financial support, but lacks the internal structures and organizational culture to make use of such assistance. Most smaller parties are in dire need of outside help, but there are doubts about the legitimacy of such support given the declining electoral support for such parties. The smaller parties together garnered only 8 percent of the vote in the 2004 elections, and individually each party received an average of 10,000 votes nationwide.[30]

The Mozambican experience shows that creating a political party is not automatically a contribution to democracy and a merit in and of itself that justifies donor support. To avoid encouraging the artificial creation of parties to attract donor aid, perhaps it would be better to involve smaller parties in multiparty capacity-building activities. Parties should also be encouraged to engage in debate with civil society organizations instead of considering themselves to be playing in a separate league.

There is no doubt that some parties have improved their organizational structure, and that many party activists are now more aware of democratic norms and practices. The number of parties has been growing steadily since 1991, but collaboration has also improved, visible in an increasing number of coalitions. International assistance has contributed to those positive trends. However, evidence on whether political parties in Mozambique are perceived and supported as useful organizations furthering the country's democratic progress is both scarce and contradictory.[31] International assistance can help political parties prepare meaningful contributions to the public debate on policies, but the mobilization of voters is mainly up to motivated party activists and volunteers at the local level. This critical dimension of building up legitimacy and credibility is perhaps beyond the reach of donor aid.

When it comes to national elections, most political parties face a bleak future. Local elections seem to offer a more feasible prospect. The successes recorded by several "groups of citizens" lists in local elections show that skillful mobilization of candidates and voters coupled with a local focus can yield solid results. International donors have so far focused mainly on the national arena, but municipal elections show that a more local approach is worth considering. Donors should also consider assisting the "groups of citizens" that participate in local elections, and not only formally registered political parties.

The potential return of capacity building is also constrained by a short-sighted perception of skills as a possible "threat to leadership" rather than added value. The ousting or marginalization of senior RENAMO members over the past years can be considered an expression of this attitude. Culturally embedded views on hierarchy determine to a large extent the "chief-oriented" structure of parties. Changing the basic nature of the parties will remain difficult.[32]

In short, international assistance has certainly influenced, albeit to a limited extent, the political landscape in Mozambique. Without international assistance, various smaller parties would not have been able to develop their internal organization and staff. Yet this support failed to produce greater pluralism in elected bodies. The opposition still faces a critical challenge to collaborate more and to improve their internal communication and organizational skills.

But although electoral prospects are severely limited for most parties, it is clear that, even without formal representation, parties can play a role in the democratic process. Parties can be channels to stimulate public debate via publications, the press, and seminars. Parties can be instrumental in establishing dialogue on political issues of a local, national, regional, and global nature. Parties should therefore not receive support primarily based on electoral potential, but rather based on their potential to stimulate debate and constructive political activity. The Labor Party, for example, had a dismal result in the 2004 elections, but played a key role in formulating a joint code of conduct for all parties and was an active participant in various public discussions.

Drawing on Mozambique's experience, the following are recommendations for future international assistance to political parties:

- Increase focus on long-term institutional development of parties.
- Focus on the role of parties as democratic actors and stakeholders rather than mere instruments of electoral competition.
- Focus on multiactor activities, not only between parties (national and international), but also between parties and civil society, the private sector, the international community, and other actors.
- Focus on the local level, which provides more of a chance for parties to gain formal participation and gain experience.
- Open up support to "groups of citizens," focusing on political actors rather than parties only.
- Provide incentives for interparty cooperation, including coalition building.

Too often, political parties have been overlooked by donors, and Mozambique is no exception. For international assistance to be effective, it is crucial that donors attach a high priority to providing aid to political parties, treating them as building blocks of democracy.

◼ Notes

1. Dissatisfaction was generated by the imposition of certain economic policies (such as collective production) and by FRELIMO's rejection of traditional authorities.

FRELIMO wanted a modern society and considered traditional authorities as obstacles to modernization. Part of FRELIMO's attitude was also due to the perception that traditional authorities allegedly collaborated with past colonial rulers.

2. Local elections are held in thirty-three municipalities and are strongly urban based. These municipalities represent about 30 percent of the national electorate.

3. See Carbone, *Emerging Pluralist Politics in Mozambique.*

4. The 1990 constitution has been altered at various times; a more fundamental revision was approved in 2004.

5. SARDC, *Peace and Reconstruction,* p. 4. There was no genuine conviction that a multiparty system would enrich governance and advance democracy. It was a pragmatic decision that created a necessary condition for peace by making it possible for RENAMO to turn into a political party.

6. Lundin, "Political Parties," pp. 417–424.

7. The first economic reform program was a FRELIMO plan; only later did the influence of the Washington Consensus become more obvious.

8. Carbone, *Emerging Pluralist Politics,* p. 10.

9. See Manning, "Constructing Opposition in Mozambique"; Vines, *RENAMO;* and Lundin, "Political Parties."

10. Ian Smith had an interest in destabilizing the FRELIMO regime, because Mozambique supported Mugabe's military insurgency to oust Smith's white minority rule. Moreover, RENAMO had its power base in areas where FRELIMO provided shelter for the Zimbabwean liberation forces and could thus also complicate their operations. After Mugabe's victory in 1979, South Africa took an interest in supporting RENAMO, again with the aim to destabilize Mozambique because it supported the African National Congress.

11. This is described in detail in Geffray, *La Cause des Armes au Mozambique.*

12. Lalá and Ostheimer, *How to Remove the Stains on Mozambique's Democratic Track Record,* p. 24.

13. Randall and Svåsand, "Party Institutionalization in New Democracies," p. 8.

14. Lundin, "Political Parties," p. 128.

15. A number of smaller parties are described in Hanlon, *Mozambican Peace Process Bulletin,* supp. 10/1993; Lundin, "Political Parties," pp. 430–447; and EISA, *Election Update 2004.*

16. This may be reinforced by the closed list proportional system that reduces the incentive of candidates to cultivate a connection with the electorate.

17. UN, *The UN and Mozambique, 1992–1995,* p. 215.

18. A letter of March 4, 1994, from the president of the Council of Ministers of Italy to the UN Secretary-General indicates a contribution of US$500,000 outside the trust fund, apparently to accelerate the demobilization of RENAMO troops. See UN, *UN and Mozambique,* p. 230.

19. Chan and Moises, *War and Peace in Mozambique,* pp. 56–57.

20. Manning, *The Politics of Peace in Mozambique,* p. 103.

21. Chan and Moises, *War and Peace in Mozambique.*

22. The PARTIDO program was part of a broader USAID-financed "democratic governance" program that lasted until 2003. With the end of the program, the NDI also closed its Mozambique office.

23. The initial budget was US$3,433,245 for programs, staff, and operational costs.

24. This fairly low disbursement rate was due to overoptimistic planning. The capacity of parties to formulate and manage projects was less than anticipated.

25. While FRELIMO received nearly 1.9 million votes in the 2004 ballot, all small parties combined received only a little more than 200,000 votes.

26. The electoral legislation determines that a party needs to receive at least 5 percent of the votes nationwide, although electoral districts coincide with an administrative province.

27. It is believed that the Democratic Union's last place on the parliamentary ballot, just as Joaquim Chissano's spot on the presidential ballot, may have won them the most votes.

28. RENAMO, the PRD, PALMO, the PDD, and PIMO.

29. Carbone, *Emerging Pluralist Politics,* p. 13.

30. The total electorate was estimated at about 8 million in 2004, but only 35 percent voted.

31. Carbone, *Emerging Pluralist Politics,* p. 15.

32. Carothers, *Aiding Democracy Abroad,* p. 153.

PART 2

Human Rights

5

Strengthening Human Rights in Guatemala

Dinorah Azpuru

Guatemala is the most populated country in Central America and one of the richest in natural resources. It arguably has the most complex society in the region, with a political history plagued by coups d'état, authoritarian governments, and violence. Guatemala gained independence from Spain in 1821, but for decades it failed to overcome intense social divisions to become a more inclusive and democratic country.

The discrimination of the indigenous community (of Mayan descent), which comprises about 45 percent of the population, and the uneven distribution of wealth, have always been latent sources of social conflict in Guatemala. Historically, however, military dictatorships resorted to repression to suppress dissent and maintain the status quo. This tension, together with the lack of political space for opposition forces, led to an armed conflict that lasted thirty-six years (1960–1996) and left a death toll of over 200,000. The main actors in the conflict were the Guatemalan army and the guerrillas, which in 1982 united in the so-called Guatemalan National Revolutionary Unity (URNG). It is important to highlight that the Guatemalan civil war did not originate as a result of interethnic conflict. It was instead an ideologically based conflict that developed in the framework of the Cold War. The army was especially ruthless with the Mayan population, however, and this gave the conflict an ethnic dimension.

The war has been considered one of the bloodiest conflicts in the Western Hemisphere, with human rights violations on a vast scale. For that very reason, human rights received a top priority during the peace negotiations that began in 1991. Concern over human rights abuses also drew the attention of the international community, which became involved in the conflict, the peace negotiations, and particularly in the implementation of the peace accords. Outside governments and international organizations delivered significant assistance to projects and organizations in the human rights sphere.

The central issue addressed in this chapter is how international assistance contributed to efforts to defend and bolster human rights in Guatemala. It describes the overall human rights situation in Guatemala during the conflict and the main human rights institutions in the country, explains what sort of assistance the international community has provided to Guatemala, and assesses the impact the international community had on the human rights situation in the country.

■ From War to Peace: A Long, Difficult Road

The Guatemalan armed conflict began in 1960 when a small group of young army officers rebelled against the military government, accusing it of corruption. The rebellion was put down, and the young officers fled to the mountains of eastern Guatemala, where they began a guerrilla war. These guerrillas soon turned into a Marxist movement whose objective was to overthrow the government and take power. The conflict took place in the context of the Cold War, with leftist guerrillas receiving aid from Cuba and other revolutionary governments. The United States, on the other hand, for many years supported Guatemala's successive right-wing military dictatorships in an effort to keep the communist threat and Cuban influence at bay.

The intensity and geography of the war varied throughout its thirty-six years. The first phase took place in the eastern part of Guatemala, where most of the population is nonindigenous. The conflict also affected the capital city at that time. The army's counterinsurgency campaign succeeded in forcing the guerrillas to retreat. In the late 1970s and early 1980s the guerrillas changed their strategy and moved to the western highlands, where they recruited the indigenous population to support their movement. The army responded with a ruthless counterinsurgency campaign that included brutal attacks on the civil population. Massacres, the razing of entire villages, and the decimation of social leadership were key elements of the military strategy, which also included organizing rural men into civil defense patrols. The army also attempted to gain the support of the rural population by providing them with food and shelter in so-called model villages, which many have equated with concentration camps. This counterinsurgency campaign attained its military objectives, and the guerrillas were again pushed back although not totally annihilated.

By the mid-1980s the military effort was winding down for a variety of reasons. While the guerrillas had been dealt a serious blow, they had not been totally defeated. At the same time, the economic elite of the country began to withhold its traditional support for the military, and US government administrations were increasingly reluctant to give open support to the Guatemalan army because of its appalling human rights record and its use of fraudulent elections and coups to remain in power. In the wake of the new wave of democratization in Latin America, international pressure was mounting on Guatemala's military to hold free elections. These and other factors led the army to allow a democratic opening. Between 1984 and 1985 a new Constituent Assembly was elected, a new constitution and new election laws were drafted, and an independent electoral tribunal was appointed.

The first free elections in decades took place, and a civilian from the Christian Democratic Party, Vinicio Cerezo, was elected. He took office in January 1986. Although many expected that the new civilian government would be able to start peace negotiations with the guerrillas, the army still held important power within the government and was opposed to any kind of negotiations if the guerrillas did not first lay down their weapons. This condition was not acceptable to the insurgents.

It is important to recall that Guatemala's civil war was only one of several armed struggles taking place in Central America. By the mid-1980s, a guerrilla movement known as the Sandinistas had succeeded in establishing a revolutionary government in Nicaragua, and in El Salvador the Farabundo Martí National Liberation Front (FMLN) was threatening to do the same. There were also tensions between the various countries of the region, in particular between Nicaragua's Sandinista government and the right-wing governments of El Salvador, Guatemala, and Honduras.

In this context, President Oscar Arias of Costa Rica presented a proposal for a Central American peace plan, which resulted in the signing of the Esquipulas I and Esquipulas II Accords in 1986 and 1987 by the presidents of all Central American countries. These accords included measures to reduce the tensions between countries, but also contained provisions to start negotiations between the respective government and guerrilla groups within each country. The Esquipulas II Accords had an especially positive impact on the Guatemalan peace process. Prominent leaders from various social sectors, in an effort to foster dialogue between government and guerrilla groups, formed the National Reconciliation Commission (NRC). After a couple of failed attempts, an important meeting between the NRC, the URNG, and government representatives took place in Oslo, Norway, in March 1990. The agreement that resulted from this meeting established the concept of negotiations and the procedures for holding them.

Unlike other societies in conflict, in Guatemala democratization developed separately from the peace process, though in a parallel fashion. In an important step forward for the cause of democracy, Guatemala's second civilian president, Jorge Serrano, was elected in 1990. Shortly after taking office in January 1991, Serrano appointed a governmental peace commission that included representatives from his administration (military and civilians), and he agreed to begin negotiations even before the guerrillas disarmed. Formal negotiations with the URNG guerrillas began in April 1991 and continued until the signing of the "Final Accords for a Firm and Lasting Peace" in December 1996.

The major actors in the peace negotiations were successive civilian governments and the guerrilla groups united in the URNG.[1] However, a variety of civil society groups and international actors were instrumental in the process. Civil society groups came together in the Civil Society Assembly and presented proposals to the negotiators. The international community played several major roles. The United Nations acted as moderator of the peace talks, while the "Group of Friends of the Guatemalan Peace Process"— comprising the governments of Norway, Spain, Mexico, Venezuela, Colombia, and the United States—provided important political support.[2] The UN Verification Mission in Guatemala (MINUGUA) was established in 1994, almost two years before the signing of the peace accords.

Throughout five years of peace negotiations, several substantive and operational peace agreements were signed covering a wide range of issues, from the return of refugees from Mexico to increasing the percentage of the national budget allocated to education. The most important peace accords are presented in Table 5.1.

Guatemala's peace process is often compared with that of its neighbor, El Salvador. Both are considered second-generation, multidisciplinary peace operations (i.e., those that go beyond a cease-fire to include socioeconomic

Table 5.1 Peace Accords Signed in Guatemala, 1991–1996

Title	Date Signed
Substantive Accords	
Accord on Democratization	July 1991
Framework Accord	January 1994
Comprehensive Accord on Human Rights	March 1994
Resettlement of Population Uprooted by Armed Conflict	June 1994
Historical Clarification Commission	June 1994
Identity and Rights of Indigenous Peoples	March 1995
Social and Economic Aspects and Agrarian Situation	May 1996
Strengthening of Civilian Power and Role of the Armed Forces in a Democratic Society	September 1996
Final Accord for a Firm and Lasting Peace	December 1996
Operational Accords	
Definite Cease-Fire	December 1996
Constitutional Reforms and the Electoral Regime	December 1996
Basis for the Legal Reintegration of the URNG	December 1996
Timetable for the Peace Accords	December 1996

aspects, human rights, electoral and institutional reforms, and humanitarian assistance). There are a few important differences, however.[3] The peace accords in El Salvador intended only to establish the mechanisms through which disagreements and social demands could be channeled—free and fair elections, rules for the appointment of impartial judges, a police organization that respects citizen rights, and restricting the army's role to the defense of national sovereignty. The assumption in El Salvador was that the parties involved could then proceed on a more equal footing to resolve economic and social problems.

In Guatemala, however, the assumption was that the peacebuilding process itself should try to resolve the underlying political, social, and economic problems in order to avoid renewed violence. As a result, the agenda for peace achieved in Guatemala is one of the most comprehensive ever signed. It goes far beyond a traditional cease-fire and even beyond mere democratization measures. Some authors have described the Guatemalan accords as unusually broad in their identification of key national issues, but weak in terms of providing specific measures to be implemented.[4] The Guatemalan peace accords addressed a variety of subjects, but failed to sufficiently tackle key issues, like demilitarization, that have to be resolved in order to build a stable, working democracy. The Salvadoran peace accords, in contrast, went in-depth into the issues of democratization and demilitarization. There are strengths and weaknesses to each approach. However, the scope and complexity of the Guatemalan peace accords—and their some 200 provisions—have made implementation an almost insurmountable task.

In 1999, a few years after the signing of the accords, a right-wing government linked to former counterinsurgency elements was voted into power. As a result, the peace process suffered a major setback and was essentially stalled for the next four years during the administration of the Guatemalan Republican Front (FRG) (2000–2003). In the November 9, 2003, elections, however, the FRG party and its presidential candidate, former dictator Efraín Ríos Montt, were defeated. The 2003 election campaign was marred by political violence as well as the incumbent party's mobilization of former counterinsurgency groups such as civil defense patrols.

The new government of Oscar Berger, which took office in January 2004, highlighted the importance of continuing to work for the implementation of the peace accords. Also in 2004, the remaining members of MINUGUA left the country after completing a ten-year mandate.

■ Human Rights: The Backbone of the Peace Accords

In view of the atrocities that occurred during the Guatemalan armed conflict, human rights issues have been considered a decisive aspect of the peace accords. The accords called for the formation of a UN Commission for Historical Clarification (CEH), to be charged with writing a report that would present information about human rights abuses during the armed conflict. That report, made public in 1999, asserts that the vast majority of the victims of state violence were not soldiers or members from guerrilla groups, but mostly civilians. Out of the total of 61,648 violations registered by the CEH, arbitrary executions accounted for 38 percent of the cases, restrictions of liberty for 22 percent, torture for 19 percent, forced disappearances for 10 percent, and sexual violence 2 percent.[5]

The CEH report concludes that over 200,000 Guatemalans were killed or disappeared from 1960 to 1996.[6] After studying different cases and testimonies, the report notes that about 83 percent of the victims of political violence were indigenous Mayans, and that "acts of genocide had been committed in Guatemala" in the period from 1981 to 1983. Of the 626 massacres, 400 (64 percent) were carried out by the army or government-related forces.[7] During the bloodiest years of the conflict, most violations occurred in the northern and northwestern departments of Guatemala, which have the highest percentage of Mayan population.

Violence forced about 150,000 refugees to flee to Mexico, and many others were displaced within Guatemalan territory. It is estimated that there were about 1.5 million internally displaced people in the early 1980s. About 70 percent of them returned to their place of origin toward the end of 1983, when "amnesty" was declared; another 30,000 stayed in the mountains; and the rest settled in urban centers.[8]

During the armed conflict, counterinsurgency strategies used by the government included the development of civil defense patrols in rural areas that served as paramilitary organizations within the local communities. The arming of civilians resulted in the polarization of rural society and the destruction of traditional structures and cultural values in Mayan villages.

The democratic opening of 1985 and the new constitution reestablished judicial power and the basic institutions of the state in Guatemala. The new constitution created the Office of the Human Rights Ombudsman (PDH), one of the first institutions of this type in Latin America. The PDH grew in importance as the democratization process advanced, in particular when Ramiro de León was appointed as ombudsman. Although human rights violations continued, this democratic opening permitted the emergence of local human rights organizations and a more active role for international human rights groups.

When the peace talks began in 1991, it was quickly recognized that the human rights situation had to improve before any further accomplishments could be made. Therefore, in order to protect the civilian population as soon as possible, one of the first accords signed by the Guatemalan government and the URNG was a comprehensive agreement on human rights, in

March 1994. This accord included important provisions on the rule of law and established immediate on-site verification of rights violations. The PDH played an important role in denouncing human rights violations. However, the ombudsman himself and his staff had been threatened, and it soon became clear that an international presence would be necessary to go beyond denouncing violations, to actually guaranteeing a basic respect for human rights.[9]

In mid-1994, therefore, MINUGUA began operating in Guatemala. The presence of international observers on-site had a significant impact. Gradually, the human rights situation began to improve and continued progress was made at the negotiating table. The dismantling of civilian counterinsurgency structures in early 1996 also contributed to an improved climate. Human rights violations thereafter ceased to be a systematic "state policy," although some serious violations continued and some remain to date.

The 1994 human rights accord specified that no measures should be adopted to "prevent the prosecution and punishment of persons responsible for human rights violations," and both parties agreed "on the need for firm action against impunity."[10] But the accord did not create war crime tribunals, and in 1996, only a few days before the ratification of the final peace accords, the Guatemalan congress approved an amnesty law known as the Law of National Reconciliation. The amnesty law indicated that, generally, only political crimes could be subject to this immunity and amnesty. However, the law also listed certain crimes that could not be considered for the application of immunity: genocide, torture, forced disappearance, and all crimes that do not allow the "extinction of penal responsibility" according to other internal laws or international treaties ratified by Guatemala. For this reason, when the CEH declared that genocide, torture, and other crimes had occurred during the armed conflict, the legal door was opened for prosecuting these crimes. In practice, however, it proved difficult to bring to justice those responsible for even the worst human rights violations.[11] Within Guatemala, a few relatives and survivors of the massacres have reached friendly settlements with the government and have been compensated, but these are exceptional cases. Overall, it can be said that some progress has been achieved in establishing the truth about human rights violations in Guatemala, but little has been achieved in terms of bringing responsible parties to justice.

■ International Human Rights Assistance

The involvement of the international community in the peace process in Guatemala has been wide and varied. Human rights has been one of the areas where most actors have sought to provide assistance during the conflict and postconflict period. The Inter-American Development Bank (IADB) estimated that a total of US$9.3 million in foreign aid was donated to Guatemala in human rights assistance during 1998–2003, along with US$78.2 million in assistance for administration of justice and security.[12]

The European Union provided assistance for many human rights projects (US$6 million), followed by bilateral donors such as the United States (US$1.7 million) and the Netherlands (US$1.2 million). In the areas of justice and security, the World Bank contributed US$46.5 million, the IADB gave US$14.6 million, Norway gave US$7.5 million, and the United States gave US$5 million.[13] Other major donor countries, though not necessarily only within the area of human rights, were Germany, Japan, Sweden, Canada, and Denmark.[14] In addition, thousands of dollars have been provided for different projects by international nongovernmental human rights organizations (NGOs), churches of diverse denominations, and other international actors.

The international community has shown great interest in human rights protection in Guatemala through on-site international verification missions, support given to human rights NGOs, and political pressure exerted on the various government administrations.

Human Rights Observation and Advisory Services

International observer missions have played an important role in the verification of the human rights situation. MINUGUA was established in 1994 and, after several revisions to its mandate, finally closed down its operations at the end of 2004. Two specific periods can be distinguished:

- *1994–1996.* MINUGUA arrived in Guatemala just a few months after the signing of the March 1994 human rights accord and quickly opened twelve regional offices and suboffices to provide easier access for the local population to report human rights abuses.[15]
- *1997–2004.* When the final peace accords and agreements for implementation were signed in December 1996, MINUGUA expanded its original mission to include the verification of the implementation of all the peace accords. MINUGUA pursued institution-building activities, with particular emphasis on the justice system, public security, the promotion of a multicultural, multilingual, and multiethnic educational system, the promotion and dissemination of the content of the peace accords, and support for the creation of a culture of respect for human rights in Guatemala.

In addition, from January to May 1997, a United Nations peacekeeping mission was established as part of MINUGUA in order to ensure the peaceful demobilization of former army and guerrilla soldiers and take care of demining activities.[16] This military mission was made up of 188 uniformed personnel from eighteen countries, at a cost of approximately US$4,570,800.[17] Its mandate ended after the former combatants turned in their arms and the lists of destroyed explosive devices were finalized. This demobilization phase was concluded successfully.[18]

MINUGUA had the complex task of verifying compliance with the hundreds of provisions contained in the peace accords, not only human rights issues as in its original mandate. The timetable, which aimed to complete its mission at the end of 2000, proved to be unrealistic and the mandate was extended several times. In 2004, MINUGUA gradually reduced its staff size, and began a process of transferring its duties and activities to local organizations, such as the PDH, that would take over the monitoring of implementation of the peace accords. At the end of 2004, MINUGUA withdrew completely from Guatemala.

On January 11, 2005, however, an agreement was signed between the UN Office of the High Commissioner for Human Rights (OHCHR) and the government of Guatemala. When the agreement came into force following its ratification by the Guatemalan congress, the OHCHR opened an office in Guatemala on July 13, 2005, to monitor how human rights are promoted and protected in the country. In addition, it advises the government as well as civil society organizations on the overall definition and implementation of human rights policies. It is supposed to inform the competent authorities on human rights violations and other abuses in cases where it believes that domestic legal procedures applied by the national authorities are not consistent with those set forth in international agreements. In such a case, the OHCHR would formulate recommendations on possible preventive or remedial action by national authorities. The agreement also provides for the High Commissioner to report to the UN Commission on Human Rights on the activities of the office. In contrast to MINUGUA, and other observer missions or individuals that have been assigned to Guatemala before, this new mission will have an advisory role only, not an official human rights monitoring function.

Other Observer Groups

Short-term visits by human rights experts from the United Nations and the Inter-American Human Rights Commission of the Organization of American States (OAS) were another form of human rights monitoring in Guatemala throughout the years, particularly during authoritarian regimes. The role of these experts was to gather information on the country's human rights situation and disseminate their findings throughout the international community. Though Guatemala could not be forced to comply with their recommendations, the political impact of noncompliance was significant at the international level. In addition, these visits gave local NGOs the opportunity to establish official contact with international representatives and to be heard and supported in their efforts to protect human rights and promote the enforcement of the rule of law.

During the period of military rule, the OHCHR considered Guatemala to be a country where human rights were systematically violated. UN rapporteurs went to the country periodically to investigate the human rights situation. Such on-site visits were also carried out by representatives from the Inter-American Human Rights Commission of the OAS. After the signing of the peace accords, Guatemala was removed from the list of countries under observation by UN rapporteurs. In 1998 the Inter-American Commission made a similar step and concluded that Guatemala's human rights situation had improved significantly. Later, during the FRG government (2000–2003), reports from national and international organizations warned that the situation had deteriorated again and rapporteurs with specific missions were sent to examine the situation. This kind of international monitoring was an important way of pressuring the military governments and helped to create conditions for the democratic opening of 1985.

Support to the Truth Commission

Political, technical, and financial support for the Commission for Historical Clarification, Guatemala's equivalent body to a truth commission, was another form of international human rights assistance. The CEH was formed as a result of a June 1994 agreement between the Guatemalan government and the URNG guerrillas. It had the following main purposes:

- To establish—objectively, fairly, and impartially—the human rights violations that took place during the war.
- To produce a report containing the results of the investigation.
- To make recommendations to preserve the memory of the victims, to foster a culture of respect for human rights, and to strengthen the democratic process.

The CEH had three commissioners: a person appointed by the Secretary-General of the United Nations, a Guatemalan citizen of "irreproachable conduct," and an academic from a list proposed by the chancellors of Guatemala's main universities. These appointments were filled by Christian Tomuschat, a UN human rights expert who had served as human rights rapporteur in Guatemala on several occasions during the armed conflict; Otilia Lux de Cotí, a Mayan woman and educator; and Alfredo Balsells Tojo, a renowned lawyer.

Contributions and technical assistance from international donors enabled the CEH to begin its work on July 31, 1997, with a budget of US$9,796,167 for implementing its mandate.[19] The three commissioners were assisted by a support office at the CEH that at one point had a total of 273 professionals, including 142 Guatemalans and 131 international staff from thirty-one different countries. Because of the broad scope of the work, the original deadline of six months had to be extended.

The work done by the CEH finally resulted in a report, titled *Memoria del Silencio* (The Memory of Silence), made public in early 1999 both in Guatemala and abroad. The members of the CEH recognized in the report that without the political, moral, and financial support from the international community, they would not have been able to complete the complex task, which had a tremendous effect in Guatemala.[20] The United Nations contributed experts and materials that helped offset the financial needs of the CEH.[21] The UN human rights mission provided crucial logistical support for the commission's operations. Finally, the CEH benefited from the help of international NGOs that offered technical assistance, enabled the gathering of information, publicized the commission's work, and made valuable efforts to obtain information from other governments.[22]

Assistance to the Ombudsman's Office

In order to help institutionalize human rights monitoring and protection, the international community strongly supported the establishment of an independent human rights body in Guatemala. The Office of the Human Rights Ombudsman (PDH) is now the most important human rights institution in Guatemala. Since its creation in 1985, the PDH has played a crucial role in denouncing human rights violations and monitoring the actions of the central government. It is headed by an ombudsman who is appointed by congress for a period of five years. According to the constitution, the ombudsman is congress's commissioner for the defense of human rights, and therefore has the same privileges as any congressman. The ombudsman's tasks are:

- To ensure a full respect for human rights in all government activities.
- To investigate and denounce any government actions against the interests of the people.
- To investigate any information on human rights abuses.
- To recommend to public officials changes in their operational behavior.
- To publicly censure actions or behaviors that violate constitutional rights.
- To take legal or administrative actions on specific cases as necessary.

Currently the PDH has approximately 300 staff, 200 of whom are in the Guatemala City headquarters. The rest are in regional offices across the country. The countryside offices include *auxiliaturas* (support offices) and *defensorías* (project offices) in charge of specific topics, including the rights of indigenous peoples and women. The annual budget for the PDH is approved and granted by congress. However, according to the PDH's Department of International Relations, the actual needs far exceed the amount that government allocates. In 2003, for instance, the PDH had requested some US$20 million, but the Guatemalan congress only granted US$5 million. For that reason, the ombudsman's office has always relied heavily on international assistance, using it even to cover salaries for some staff members, especially those who are working in the *auxiliaturas* and *defensorías* throughout the country. However, once assistance is withdrawn, the PDH's budget does not allow the organization to absorb the new positions that were created with funds from international donors.

Some projects are also short-lived, and last only as long as international assistance is available. In the past few years, however, the office has received an average of less than US$2 million annually from the international community. During 2003, fourteen projects were implemented directly with international funding.

One of the main institution-building goals of MINUGUA was to strengthen the PDH, which was already working by the time the UN human rights verification mission arrived in Guatemala in 1994. This process, however, was not totally successful, especially because two of the ombudsmen appointed by congress during the peacebuilding period were reluctant to work with international donors. This limited the scope of joint activities between MINUGUA and the PDH.

Assistance to the Presidential Commission for Human Rights

The executive equivalent of the PDH has received significantly less international attention. The Presidential Commission for the Coordination of Human Rights Policies (COPREDEH) was created in 1991. It is a high-level commission that works directly under the president of Guatemala. Its members include the ministers of foreign affairs, defense, and interior, as well as the attorney general and a representative of the executive.

One of its main objectives is to coordinate the work of the various human rights–related institutions of the executive, legislative, and judicial branches of government. Another objective is to coordinate the human rights policies of ministries and government offices. In addition, COPREDEH compiles information about human rights violations and establishes mechanisms to follow-up on human rights investigations. It makes regular reports to international human rights bodies using the latest research and studies. The commission also promotes and distributes information on human rights and prepares legislative proposals for the president to present to congress. Finally, COPREDEH is the official representative of the Guatemalan government at periodic meetings of the UN Human Rights Commission in Geneva, the UN General Assembly in New York, and the Inter-American Human Rights Court of the OAS.

COPREDEH has not received much international assistance, though some support was provided for the creation of the Special Office for the Defense of Indigenous Women.[23] COPREDEH did not succeed in negotiating further international financing during the FRG administration, probably because of the appalling human rights record of the main leader of that party. However, COPREDEH was part of the so-called Roundtables of Intersectoral Dialogue, which were promoted by the OAS and the UN Development Programme (UNDP) in 2003. It formed part of the Roundtable on Human Rights, Justice, and Security.

With the new administration of Oscar Berger and the appointment of one of Guatemala's main human rights activists as president of COPREDEH, it is expected that international assistance to the institution will improve. The website of the institution in late 2004 indicated that COPREDEH was involved in the project called Culture of Peace, with support from the UN Educational, Scientific, and Cultural Organization (UNESCO) and the UNDP. The website itself is sponsored by the Danish Program for Human Rights in Central America.

Human Rights Education

Although most of the human rights projects supported by the international community have an educational component, the Cultura de Paz (Culture of Peace) program by UNESCO deserves special mention here. The CEH invited UNESCO to assist the process of transforming Guatemalan society from an authoritarian and violent environment to a culture of mutual respect and peace. The project has been implemented through the Ministry of Education in three phases.

The first was developed in 2000. It introduced human rights, democracy, and social justice education into school curricula. Actions were also taken targeting teachers, youth movement monitors, and social workers. The second phase, from June to December 2001, focused on the development of the educational aspect, especially on curricular reforms. This phase also sought to involve civil society in the process of national reconciliation and in ending intolerant and authoritarian attitudes. Hosts of popular and indigenous radio programs also received such training. The third phase, which began in January 2004, includes two parts: education (teaching reform and civic education) and "social impact" (i.e., overcoming sociocultural problems that hinder the development of a trusting relationship between citizens and institutions, and between the state and civil society).

Extending beyond the capital to several departments of Guatemala, this new phase of the project has been made possible, as were the previous phases, by Italy's donation of US$873,682.[24]

Assistance for Judicial Reform

Two new judicial sector institutions have emerged from the 1996 peace accords: the Public Defender's Office in Criminal Matters, and the Office for Attention to the Public, the latter of which is part of the Public Prosecutor's Office. Other existing institutions have also been improved through the expansion of court services nationwide and the renovation of the School of Judicial Studies and the Public Prosecutor's Center for Training.

Though international assistance to the judicial system is more common today, such support dates back to 1993, when the US Agency for International Development (USAID) began financing activities to try to improve the rule of law in Guatemala. Since then, with varying emphases, USAID has supported activities such as assistance and training to establish the Victims' Assistance Office of the Public Ministry; access to justice, with focus on rural areas and indigenous people; legal education and training of justice sector personnel working in different institutions; civil society advocacy programs, especially for the Institute of Comparative Studies in Criminal Sciences and the Mayan Defense Office.

Police Reform

With the aim of demilitarizing and raising the professional standards of Guatemala's law enforcement institutions, the international community supported several activities in the field of police reform. The "Accord on the Strengthening of Civilian Power and the Role of the Armed Forces in a Democratic Society," signed in September 1996 in Mexico City, redefined the concept of security and stressed that a distinction must be made between external security (protection against external armed threats) and internal security (protection against threats to the public order). Internal security matters were to be taken care of by the new National Civilian Police (PNC), whereas the army was to limit itself to external security issues. This marked an important change from the situation during the armed conflict, when the army controlled the police and citizen security, and had often used its power to violate human rights in the name of national security.[25]

On February 25, 1997, the Guatemalan congress approved Decree 11-97, the law regulating the PNC. With a planned transition period of a year, the new institution was designed to take over human and material resources from the former National Police and the Treasury Police. The new law set out the role and functions of the PNC and established that it functioned under the authority of the Ministry of Interior. Once the PNC had been established, the international community helped in different ways.

The Spanish Civil Guard began to provide financial and technical assistance to the PNC in February 1997. However, it soon became apparent that members of Guatemala's former National Police and Treasury Police had been "recycled" and allowed back into the new National Civilian Police. In February and March 2000, two new decrees were issued with the intention of stopping this practice.

In August 1998 the European Union took over the financing of the police academy project.[26] Additionally, the International Criminal Investigative Training Assistance Program supported the academy and the Criminal Investigation Service. According to a MINUGUA report issued in 2001, some advances were made, but other aspects still needed improvement.[27]

In December 2001 the PNC finally reached the peace accords' goal of training 20,000 police officers. By August 2003 it had a total of 20,689 officers, with 52 percent of them working in the capital or in special services, and the remaining 48 percent working outside the metropolitan area. In terms of gender representation, in 2001 about 11 percent of all police were women, most of whom, 94 percent, had the rank of police officer. Women continued to be highly underrepresented in the higher ranks, from subinspector up to subcommissioner. In terms of cultural representation, in 2001 only 14 percent of the new police force was indigenous. Of these, 23 percent were Kiché, 19 percent were Kaqchikeles, 15 percent were Achi, 11 percent were Q'eqchi, and 11 percent were Mam. Though improved compared to the past, the police force is still far from accurately reflecting the ethnic diversity of the country, as required by law.

In October 2003 the PNC stated that about 44 percent of its staff had been "recycled" from the former National Police or the Treasury Police. The remaining 56 percent were new members without history in any of the former police institutions. Most of the people who occupied high-ranking positions, however, were still linked to former police bodies. Of the highest-ranking officers (10 percent of staff), only 17 percent were new.

Assistance to Nongovernmental Human Rights Organizations

Nongovernmental organizations have played a significant role in the human rights field in Guatemala. Over the years, most of them have received various forms of international assistance. The most important human rights NGOs can be grouped as follows:[28]

- *Organizations focusing on impunity.* These include the Alliance Against Impunity (ACI), the Center for Human Rights Legal Action (CALDH), and the Myrna Mack Foundation (FMM). Their activities range from informing the public and judicial reform to pursuing the prosecution of human rights violations in national and international courts.

- *Human rights groups founded by relatives of the disappeared.* Among them are the Mutual Support Group (GAM) and the Relatives of the Detained and Disappeared of Guatemala (FAMDEGUA). These organizations focus primarily on documenting human rights violations, searching for remains of relatives, and supporting the exhumations of mass graves.
- *Roman Catholic organizations.* The best-known is the Human Rights Office of the Archbishop (ODHA). This organization launched a nationwide program to gather data about human rights violations during the armed conflict. Its April 1998 report, titled *Guatemala Nunca Más* (Guatemala Never Again), contributed to the UN's Commission for Historical Clarification.
- *Indigenous rights organizations.* These include the Rigoberta Menchú Tum Foundation (FRMT), the Council of Ethnic Communities—"We Are All Equal" (CERJ), New Dawn, the Mayan Defense Network, and the National Coordination of Guatemalan Widows (CONAVIGUA).
- *The National Coordination for Human Rights in Guatemala* (CONADEHGUA). This organization coordinates the work of various human rights organizations. Diverse sectors of Guatemalan society participated in the Civil Society Assembly (ASC), established during the peace negotiation period, which presented proposals to the two parties at the negotiating table. Human rights NGOs that participated in the ASC were members of CONADEHGUA.[29]

Since human rights NGOs are not registered or coordinated by any government office in Guatemala, it is difficult to determine exactly how many exist. Even the human rights organizations themselves do not have figures related to the growth of this sector in recent years. It is important, however, to point out the difference between the "older" NGOs such as GAM, the Commission on Human Rights in Guatemala (CDHG), and others, which were founded during the war (in the 1980s), and the "new" human rights NGOs, established at the beginning of the 1990s. Some of the latter emerged to protest the 500th anniversary celebration of the conquest of the Americas and tend to work more on indigenous rights. Other organizations that emerged in the 1990s specialize in topics such as women's rights, the rights of handicapped persons, or the fight against common crime and kidnappings.

NGOs vary greatly in their level of organization and scope. The more professional organizations with a national voice (such as the Myrna Mack

Foundation, CALDH, or ODHA) are the ones capable of presenting legislative proposals, carrying out lobbying activities, and influencing political life in Guatemala. Many other NGOs are known only at the local or grassroots level.

Civil society organizations, and especially human rights NGOs, depend heavily on external sources for financing. Both the Myrna Mack Foundation and GAM, for instance, are completely dependent on international assistance. The level of international support varies according to outside perceptions about the state of the human rights situation in Guatemala. In addition to financial support, the international community provides training for staff and political support. ODHA is funded by several donors. Some of them include religious NGOs, such as Diakonia (Denmark) or Misereor (Germany).

■ Impact of International Human Rights Assistance

Impact on the Human Rights Situation

It is difficult to empirically prove a causal link between international assistance and improvement in the state of human rights. International assistance is one of the many variables in the equation. Still, in combination with domestic and regional political developments and grassroots initiatives, international assistance and pressure have undoubtedly played an important role in the cause of defending and strengthening human rights in Guatemala.

According to interviews with several human rights experts, there is a consensus that Guatemala has seen an improvement in fundamental rights such as freedom of association, expression, and assembly as well as voting rights and candidacy rules. There is also general recognition that elections are largely free and that citizen participation has increased at both the local and the national level, the latter mainly thanks to the opening up of public debate and greater tolerance between rival ideological groups.

If we use as a parameter one of the main indicators of democracy and civil liberties used in the world today, the Freedom House Index, we find that Guatemala was rated "not free" during the hardest years of the internal armed conflict, especially 1981–1982 and 1983–1984. When the country began its democratization process in 1985, the ratings improved and Guatemala was again considered a "partly free" democracy. By 2005, almost ten years after the signing of the peace accords, Guatemala was still considered only "partly free" by Freedom House standards.[30]

Figure 5.1 shows the variations in the Freedom House scores for Guatemala since 1990. It can be observed that the values have remained generally stable in the postconflict period (since 1997). To understand the graph, we

116

Figure 5.1 Freedom House Index for Guatemala, 1990–2005

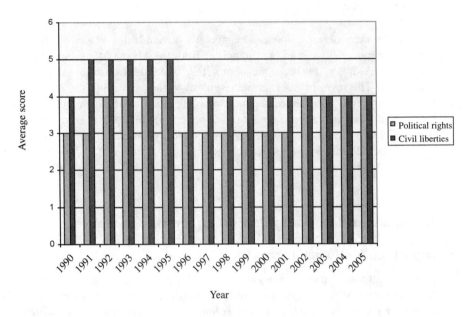

Year

Source: Freedom House, *Freedom in the World Country Ratings, 1990–2005.*

Table 5.2 Complaints Received by MINUGUA, 1995–2002

Complaint	1995	1996	1997	1998	1999	2000	2001	2002
Political rights	20	5	1	3	12	3	2	8
Freedom of association	142	39	16	18	14	12	34	8
Freedom of expression	12	4	0	3	4	8	19	3
Right to due process	349	318	210	243	288	328	260	182
Right to personal liberty and security	921	494	145	129	136	156	240	129
Freedom of movement and freedom to choose residence	48	24	21	2	18	3	5	2
Right to life	232	148	58	39	42	42	43	35
Right to personal integrity and safety	170	151	72	83	85	78	120	72
Total	1,894	1,183	523	520	599	630	723	439

Source: MINUGUA, *Décimotercer Informe Sobre Derechos Humanos.*

must remember that Freedom House ratings begin at the lower end of the scale; therefore the countries that are closer to zero are those that most respect civil and political rights. In the figure, it is clear that political rights show more improvement than civil rights, particularly since the peace accords were signed and the former guerrilla movement (URNG) became a political party in the late 1990s. However, from 2002 onward there was a setback in the ratings, partly reflecting the fact that the 2003 elections were marred by more violence than in previous years.

MINUGUA is a more specific source of information on human rights trends in Guatemala. Table 5.2 shows the violations reported to all MINUGUA delegations throughout the country between 1995 and 2002. It is important to note that MINUGUA gradually reduced its personnel from 549 in 2000 to 289 in 2002. This reduction of MINUGUA staff and offices meant that there were fewer sources to report human rights abuses.

From the information presented in Table 5.2, it is evident that 1996 was a better year than 1995. However, 1997 showed a more notable improvement in human rights. In the specific case of political rights, it is interesting to note that the number of complaints peak during election years (1995 and 1999). The assessments by Freedom House and MINUGUA seem to correspond with other reports by Guatemalan organizations, such as the PDH, GAM, and the Association of Investigation and Social Studies (ASIES), and international organizations such as Amnesty International, Americas Watch, and the US State Department. All reports agree that in the years immediately following the signing of the peace accords, the human rights situation improved. However, the situation eventually worsened again in several areas, especially under the FRG administration in 2000–2003. MINUGUA concluded that the deterioration was related to the stagnation of the accord implementation process and the persistence of ethnic discrimination and social inequality. According to the July 2002–June 2003 MINUGUA report, human rights during that period declined in the following five areas as compared to the previous year:

- Unsafe environment and lynching of alleged criminals by vigilantes.
- Threats against members of the judicial system and human rights defenders.
- Impunity.
- Lack of efficiency of the police, the attorney general, and the judiciary.
- Continued existence of illegal groups and clandestine security units.[31]

Overall, despite the human rights problems still facing Guatemala and occasional setbacks, there has been clear progress since the end of the civil war. International political pressure and assistance have undoubtedly played a role in calling attention to abuses, supporting efforts to stop those abuses, and establishing safeguards for human rights.

Impact on Civil Society

Support from the international community has been vital for Guatemala's broad group of civil society organizations. Not only did international assistance provide the much-needed financial resources for already existing organizations, but it also enabled many new nongovernmental organizations to emerge.

All these human rights NGOs have played an important role in improving the human rights situation in Guatemala. Since their emergence, even during the civil strife, they have acted as vigilant monitors of state actions. Some of them have moved from merely denouncing violations to making constructive proposals for change, including drafting laws to be presented for discussion in the Guatemalan congress. A recent achievement of the NGO human rights community is congress's election of an independent human rights ombudsman in 2002. Though there is no legally established role for civil society to have an influence in this matter, Guatemalan human rights organizations, unions, and others took the initiative to present their own list of three candidates for heading the ombudsman's office. Congress took the proposals into account, and one of the candidates proposed by civil society groups was chosen. Another recent result of the work by the human rights movement is the appointment of one of its most prominent leaders as the president of the Presidential Commission for the Coordination of Human Rights Policies.

Nevertheless, human rights NGOs face a number of problems. One is precisely the fact that human rights NGOs are highly dependent on international assistance. Without the economic resources of the donors, it is not likely that these organizations could have accomplished so much, or even survived. In some cases, this dependence has caused a competition for funds among NGOs.

Some NGOs suffer from leaders who try to advance their personal agendas through their organizations. A few of them make themselves a name with international donors and thereafter use human rights as an instrument rather than a goal. In addition, since more and more people have come to depend on NGOs as a source of income, the focus on NGO survival has become stronger. As a result, there may be some organizations that are tempted to misrepresent reality, manipulate data, or exaggerate human rights abuses to keep the money coming in. Although there is no concrete evidence to prove this last assertion, it did come up frequently in interviews.

In terms of the organization of the work, it seems that the increase in the number of human rights groups (especially those that work on specific issues) undermines potential coordination among the NGOs. Though some major human rights NGOs have worked together in recent years in temporary coalitions that seek a particular outcome, such as the election of the human rights ombudsman and the 2003 opposition to the presidential candidacy of Efraín Ríos Montt, the human rights movement has become increasingly fragmented in recent years. Currently, the major human rights organizations are trying to coordinate a national human rights movement to address this problem.

Another challenge for NGOs is that some are still unable to evolve beyond the civil war era. These groups display a confrontational mentality of denunciation and antagonism against the government, rather than a more conciliatory approach that undertakes constructive, concrete proposals.

Impact of the Commission for Historical Clarification

When in February 1999 the CEH published its report, the drafting of which was made possible only because of international financial assistance and political support, the Guatemalan political landscape was shaken.[32] Although there were no immediate legal repercussions from the report's conclusions, the mere acknowledgment of the human rights violations and the Guatemalan army's responsibility for an overwhelming majority of those violations had a major impact on Guatemalan society.

The reports of the CEH and ODHA were the first public and national acknowledgments of the crude reality of the civil conflict. During the years of the authoritarian governments, and even during the first years of the democratic opening, the subject was a taboo that few people—including the media—dared to address publicly. The publication of these reports, however, opened up breathing room in the media and elsewhere to discuss the war and related issues, such as the recent exhumations of mass graves. The recommendations of the CEH's report have been only partially followed, but the guidelines are clear. In 2004 several organizations, with international assistance, mounted a campaign to disseminate the results of the report. It is now up to the government as to whether the CEH's recommendations will be vigorously pursued.

Multiplier Effect of International Assistance

It is difficult to measure the precise relationship between international assistance and the improving human rights situation in Guatemala. However, it is widely accepted that such progress would not have taken place without the support of international actors. The structures of repression were deeply rooted in the country, and by 1994 the Office of the Human Rights Ombudsman had reached the limit of its own possibilities to effect change. It was not until the first MINUGUA mission arrived in 1994 that the situation started to improve significantly. Although the signing of the peace agreements and the end of the armed conflict helped ease tensions, it is likely that violence would have continued if not for the presence of international organizations, financial assistance to the ombudsman's office and human rights organizations, and international political pressure placed on government administrations.

■ Limitations of International Assistance

The impact of international assistance in Guatemala has also been limited by several factors. In recent years there have been violent attacks on several human rights NGOs, threats to leaders, burglaries, and other incidents. Although improvements have been achieved in other areas, neither the democratization process nor peace has brought true rule of law to Guatemala. Impunity is probably the worst legacy of the civil war, and it has undoubtedly encouraged the troublesome new practice of vigilante or mob lynchings, caused by the popular belief that the judiciary is incapable of dealing promptly with criminals. The most high-profile cases of impunity include the 1990 assassination of anthropologist Myrna Mack, the 1993 assassination of politician Jorge Carpio, the 1994 assassination of president of the Constitutional Court Epaminondas González, the 1995 massacre in Xamán, and the 1998 assassination of Bishop Juan Gerardi.

Since 1994, MINUGUA has pointed out that the Guatemalan government does not have the capacity to respond to criminal offenses in a timely and effective manner. According to MINUGUA data, the government's own noncompliance in its duties of crime prevention, investigation, and sanction accounted for 53 percent of all human rights violations in the period June 2000–July 2001.

Impunity is also linked to the existence of so-called parallel groups (or hidden powers) of former military members and others who, in alliance with drug-trafficking and contraband mafias, have made efforts to penetrate political parties and state structures at various levels. These entrenched authoritarian groups have proven difficult to dismantle, continuing to pose a barrier to civil rights efforts and sustaining a culture of impunity. A range of international actors, including the United States and the Netherlands, supported the creation of a commission to investigate the parallel groups. This initiative was to be coordinated by the United Nations and the Organization of American States. In January 2004 an agreement between the government and the United Nations, and supported by the Office of the Human Rights Ombudsman and several human rights organizations, was signed, establishing the Commission for the Investigation of Illegal Bodies and

Clandestine Security Groups (CICIACS). However, in August 2004 the Constitutional Court ruled that the commission contained articles that violated the current Guatemalan constitution. In response, the government of Oscar Berger declared that it would look for alternative mechanisms. Regrettably, as of early 2005, the project appeared to have stalled.

As in other countries, personality clashes and battles for bureaucratic control have hindered assistance efforts in Guatemala despite well-informed planning and analysis by donors. The former human rights ombudsman proved unwilling to work closely with international donors. The experience of the UN human rights mission with the former ombudsman shows that personality issues can sometimes disrupt institution-building plans. MINUGUA was supposed to strengthen the ombudsman's office, but the problematic relationship between the ombudsman and MINUGUA prevented this from happening for four years. Part of the problem was that the ombudsman saw MINUGUA as a competitor, rather than a supporter of the institution.

A focus group conducted with representatives from Guatemalan human rights NGOs also pointed to some weaknesses in international assistance itself. Those interviewed mentioned that coordination among donors, for example, is still lacking in some areas. According to the participants in the focus group, the imposition of conditions, paternalism, and the adoption of foreign models, agendas, methodologies, and "fashionable topics" remain common. A lack of in-depth knowledge about Guatemalan history or society, especially when it comes to the role played by different actors in the human rights community, was cited as another weakness of international assistance.

In some cases, Guatemalans had different priorities in the human rights field than did international donors. While international donors and MINUGUA mostly focus on political rights and civil liberties, the average Guatemalan experiences the increase of common crime as the biggest problem. This different approach to priorities seems to have had a negative effect on the perceived legitimacy of human rights issues and international assistance. Some surveys have shown that, in fact, over half of Guatemalans consider that "human rights" is an issue that has benefited the criminal at the expense of the common citizen.[33] Few efforts have been made over the years by local or international organizations to reach out to that common citizen and try to explain and legitimize the concept of human rights for all.

■ Lessons and Recommendations

The large amount of human rights assistance to Guatemala, covering a wide range of activities, makes the country an important case study. Reflections on the Guatemalan experience can be grouped into the following categories:

addressing weak state institutions and sustainability questions, collaborating with human rights NGOs, evaluating the effect of aid, and educating the wider public about human rights.

Building State Institutions and Sustainability

Like other postconflict societies, Guatemala has weak and unstable government bureaucracies. Many of the projects supported by international assistance are not sustainable because the government does not set aside necessary funding. This has been the case with the Office of the Human Rights Ombudsman, which has lacked adequate state financing. International donors should devote part of their funding to building institutional capacity before launching a project, making efforts to ensure that long-term state funding is available. This would allow the gradual phasing out of international assistance and transferring the responsibility to local authorities.

Institution building can be hindered by many factors, some of them as simple and mundane as difficult personal relations between some donor representatives and local leaders. The experience of MINUGUA with the former human rights ombudsman in Guatemala shows that personality clashes can sometimes disrupt institution-building plans. While MINUGUA was assigned the task of bolstering the ombudsman's office, the troubled relationship between the two bodies made it virtually impossible. The ombudsman viewed the UN human rights mission as a rival, instead of a potential partner that could provide assistance. These situations are not necessarily the fault of donors and sometimes cannot be avoided. Nevertheless, international donors should seek to learn about the conditions prevailing in a recipient organization or society, making efforts to adapt as appropriate and to reassure national institutions or officials that any aid is designed as a help and not a takeover. Similarly, donors should create and cultivate good relationships with middle managers to guarantee the continuity of projects and minimize potential conflict with high-ranking officers who may be skeptical of outside assistance.

Selective Funding: Supporting Human Rights NGOs

International funding for human rights is readily available for postconflict societies like Guatemala. This has caused competition among recipient institutions, especially civil society groups. Donors should understand that not all NGOs have the same strengths or the same degree of commitment to human rights. Some of them may be opportunistic groups that seek funding for their own benefit. International donors should undertake a comprehensive analysis of all the governmental and nongovernmental organizations that work on human rights in order to identify the most effective groups. Such a survey must include thematic, jurisdictional, and moral considerations.

Human rights NGOs may have a limited impact on the political system if they remain unwilling to cooperate with each other and with political parties. The international community should work to help unify the human rights movement and encourage better communication between civil society and political actors. Overall, in a postconflict society, human rights NGOs need to go beyond denouncing human rights abuses and develop a more constructive and long-term approach.

Most NGOs have headquarters in urban centers and little communication with ordinary citizens. Because they do not have a broad base of support, their impact is limited. International assistance should be focused on covering the country geographically, supporting local grassroots organizations, and requiring urban NGOs to extend their work to rural areas.

Evaluation and Assessment

Donors working in the human rights sector find themselves in a dilemma: if the overall human rights situation in a given country improves, then there is a tendency to consider that a program was successful and to subsequently scale back funding for human rights projects. Yet this may force human rights organizations to overemphasize problems and setbacks to keep the flow of aid money coming. Instead, donors should seek to provide long-term funding that ensures progress is embedded and that aid recipients offer honest assessments of the rights situation.

At the same time, donors have a right to expect concrete results. Each project supported by the international community should be evaluated, and there should be an attempt to measure its effect, although donors should be aware that the impact can be difficult to establish.

Educating the Public About Human Rights

At the end of the day, in order for human rights to be respected and take hold in postconflict societies, all of the population—or at least the majority of citizens—must be aware of and acknowledge the importance of human rights. Surveys have shown that many Guatemalans perceive that human rights issues do not benefit them and that, furthermore, human rights issues benefit the wrong people: criminals. Coinciding with this public distrust of human rights activism is a resurgence of authoritarian elements. These developments illustrate a need for the international community to assist with educational programs that could improve public understanding of civil and political rights. These programs should not be limited to the victims of human rights abuses or the organizations that are active in this field. Other stakeholders in society, apart from the small community of rights groups, need to be engaged and persuaded on this issue. New programs should be targeted at the general population to show how a culture of respect for human rights can contribute to a stable democracy and benefit everyone in society.

■ Conclusion: Human Rights Deserve Top International Priority

Before withdrawing from Guatemala in late 2004, MINUGUA organized an international congress called "Construyendo la Paz: Guatemala Desde un Enfoque Comparado" (Building Peace: Guatemala from a Comparative Perspective). Different sectors of Guatemalan society were invited to reflect on the legacy of international assistance and the pending tasks related to the implementation of the peace accords. Among other issues, participants in the congress concluded that MINUGUA and the international community had made an important contribution to Guatemalan society in the past decade, but urged them not to abandon the ongoing peacebuilding and democratization processes.[34]

International assistance for human rights has undoubtedly been one of the major contributions. Guatemala has made important progress from the days of the civil war and its immediate aftermath, progress that has come in part because of robust international support and assistance for the cause of human rights. Donors have employed a range of tools that reinforce each other: vigorously monitoring and protesting rights abuses, financing a UN human rights mission, lending experts to new, independent state institutions, helping with training a new police force, and supporting domestic NGOs engaged in human rights work. Since the signing of the peace accords in 1996, state-sponsored violence has receded, human rights issues receive greater scrutiny, and political debate has become more open and tolerant. Political dissent and free elections have replaced a climate of overwhelming fear and terror.

The challenges the country now faces are partially a reflection of this progress, challenges that will require extensive public education about civil rights, long-term reforms of the judiciary, an end to impunity for egregious political violence, the dismantling of "parallel groups," and more responsible, efficient governance. Addressing and implementing indigenous rights will be a major part of the human rights agenda in the years to come.

To address these significant challenges, continued international assistance—designed carefully in cooperation with the most effective Guatemalan partners—will be crucial. Donor governments and organizations have rightly attached a high priority to human rights, and have followed through with political support and substantial aid. The Guatemalan experience should provide a useful model to other donors and societies facing similar legacies.

Notes

I would like to thank Carlos Mendoza and Wolfgang Krenmyer, who helped gather valuable information for this chapter.

1. Three different government administrations were involved in the peace negotiations: those of Jorge Serrano (1991–1993), Ramiro de León (1993–1995), and Alvaro Arzú (1996–1999).

2. Because of its geographic location, Guatemala has always been in the US sphere of influence, and the United States has played an important role in its political life as it has in the rest of Central America. US involvement in the Guatemalan civil war and peace negotiations was significant, but not as extensive as it was in El Salvador.

3. See Pásara, *Ilusión y Cambio en Guatemala.*

4. See Stanley and Holiday, "Broad Participation, Diffuse Responsibility."

5. CEH, *Guatemala,* para. 1733.

6. Ibid., p. 73.

7. For methodological reasons and corresponding to the common Guatemalan expression, the Commission for Historical Clarification defined a massacre as the arbitrary execution of five or more persons.

8. CEH, *Guatemala,* paras. 4449 ff.

9. See Azpuru, "Peace and Democratization in Guatemala," p. 111.

10. UN, *The Guatemala Peace Agreements,* p. 25.

11. The assassination cases of Bishop Juan Gerardi and anthropologist Myrna Mack both went to trial in Guatemala. Those deemed immediately responsible for the murders were condemned to prison, but the masterminds behind the crime were not. Both cases are still being appealed. Other cases have been taken to the Inter-American Commission on Human Rights. Guatemalan Nobel Peace Prize laureate Rigoberta Menchú is also seeking to try several Guatemalan military officers in Spanish courts on charges of genocide.

12. IADB, *Guatemala,* p. 4 and appendix, pp. 2,3.

13. Ibid.

14. This other group of donors contributed US$10 million or more from 1997 to 2002.

15. MINUGUA, *First Report of the Director,* paras. 6 ff.

16. UN Security Council, Resolution 1094, January 20, 1997.

17. UN Doc. A/51/815, March 3, 1997.

18. In April 1997 the governments of Sweden, Switzerland, and the United States made a total of nearly US$3.5 million available for the work of MINUGUA. An additional amount of US$6 million was being negotiated from the governments of Belgium, Denmark, the Netherlands, Norway, and the United States. MINUGUA, *Compendio General Sobre el Proceso de Paz de Guatemala,* p. 34, para. 68.

19. CEH, *Guatemala,* para. 22, p. 30.

20. Austria, Belgium, Canada, Denmark, Germany, Italy, Japan, the Netherlands, Norway, Sweden, Switzerland, Great Britain, the United States, Argentina, and the European Union delivered the funds that allowed the CEH to do its work.

The US government helped by declassifying vital documents that helped the CEH work.

21. The UN Secretary-General, the UN High Commissioner for Refugees (UNHCR), the UN Children's Fund (UNICEF), the UN Office for Project Services (UNOPS), the UN Development Programme (UNDP), and the International Criminal Tribunal for the Former Yugoslavia (ICTY) all contributed by lending experts to the commission.

22. Examples include the appointment of an expert from the American Association for the Advancement of Science, financial contributions from the Ford Foundation, and the loan of vehicles by the Soros Foundation.

23. One of the projects, called "Everyone for Peace," aimed at promoting respect for human rights among the population; the other one focused on promoting the peace accords. Both were carried out in 1998 and 1999 with funds from the European Union.

24. See http://portal.unesco.org/en/ev.php-url_id=17410&url_do=do_topic&url_section=201.html.

25. This change limiting the role of the army to external security matters was supposed to be included in a series of constitutional changes that were to be made shortly after signing the final peace accords. This was part of twelve constitutional reforms linked to the peace accords. However, after two years of discussions, the Guatemalan congress added thirty-eight reforms, to make an overall "package" of fifty reforms; the package was rejected by voters in a referendum in May of 1999. For further discussion of this event, see Arnson, *The Popular Referendum and the Future of the Peace Accords in Guatemala.*

26. It was not possible to obtain any official statement from the Spanish Cooperation about why assistance had not been renewed for cooperation between the Spanish Civil Guard and the PNC. One reason may be that at a certain point during the FRG administration, new police were coming from the army; this remilitarizing might have been seen by some international donors as an obstacle to the building of the new institution, especially in terms of human rights.

27. MINUGUA, *Twelfth Report on Human Rights.*

28. Kulldorff, *Organizations in Guatemala.*

29. These include the CDHG, CERJ, the Center of Human Rights Investigation, Studies, and Promotion (CIEPRODH), CONAVIGUA, the National Council of Guatemalan Displaced People (CONDEG), and GAM. After the signing of the final peace accords, the ASC was weakened, because there was no specific role for it in the implementation phase. However, the organizations within the ASC did work together on preparing for the May 1999 referendum on the planned constitutional reforms and in the discussions around the fiscal pact.

30. The problem with the Freedom House survey methodology is that it shows overall trends, but hides short-term changes. Although consistent scores of 3 for political rights, and 4 in the case of civil liberties between 1996–2002 indicate that almost nothing happened, in fact some indicators improved while others deteriorated.

31. MINUGUA, *Décimotercer Informe Sobre Derechos Humanos,* p. 19.

32. Stanley and Holiday, "Broad Participation," p. 456.

33. See Azpuru, *La Cultura Democrática de los Guatemaltecos en el Nuevo Siglo.*

34. See MINUGUA and PROPAZ, *Paz y Democracia en Guatemala.*

6

Human Rights Challenges in Postconflict Cambodia

Sorpong Peou

This chapter examines the role of international aid in building human rights institutions in postconflict Cambodia. An underlying premise of this analysis is that domestic institutions can help promote political rights and civil liberties and that donors can contribute to this process. International donor attention, coupled with a history of repression, makes Cambodia a useful case study for examining how human rights institutions can be built and nurtured.

The country has endured outside intervention, political repression, violence, and armed conflict for centuries. Following the end of the Khmer Empire in 1431, several foreign powers, including Thailand and Vietnam, Spain (late sixteenth century), and France (1863–1953), invaded and sought to assert control over the country. From 1953, when Cambodia secured independence from France, to the end of the 1960s, Prince Norodom Sihanouk's paternalistic authoritarian rule prevailed. From 1970 to 1978 the dictatorial Khmer Republican and ruthless Khmer Rouge regimes carried out unprecedented repression and genocidal violence. The Khmer Rouge launched a vast, brutal program of social engineering, forcibly relocating city residents to rural areas. An estimated 2 million people were killed in the process. During the 1980s, Cambodia remained in the tight grip of socialist dictatorial rule.

In 1991, four warring factions—the State of Cambodia (SOC), the Khmer Rouge (officially known as Democratic Kampuchea [DK]), the Khmer People's National Liberation Front (KPNLF), and the royalist party, known as the National United Front for an Independent, Neutral, Peaceful, and Cooperative Cambodia (FUNCINPEC)—signed the Paris peace agreement on October 23, agreeing to move their armed conflict from the battlefield to the ballot box. The United Nations, on the invitation of the four armed signatories, launched a mission to organize a national election, which took place in May 1993.

Cambodia subsequently emerged as one of the most aid-dependent countries in the world. Donors, both bilateral and multilateral, have shown varying degrees of interest in promoting human rights and democracy in the country. The total volume of their assistance in various areas, including human rights, over the past decade has been substantial, though perhaps insufficient for a country torn apart by war for so long. Between 1992 and 2000, donors collectively pledged over US$5 billion at the first three meetings of the International Committee on the Reconstruction of Cambodia (ICORC) and the subsequent five Consultative Group (CG) meetings. By 2001 the total disbursement amounted to more than US$4 billion, representing 73.3 percent of the overall amount pledged by donors.[1]

International aid has had a positive effect on the overall human rights situation in Cambodia. But after more than a decade, the process of building rights institutions remains fragile. The country enjoys only nominal freedom despite improvement in political rights and civil liberties. Governmental and nongovernmental human rights organizations remain structurally weak, vulnerable to political control, and financially unsustainable. In the years to come, these institutions will remain anemic unless appropriate measures and actions are taken.

■ Human Rights Context, 1982–2004

This section briefly examines the overall trend in human rights over the past two decades, covering a period that began with the People's Republic of Kampuchea (PRK) regime in 1982 and ended in 2004 with the Cambodian People's Party (CPP) still in power. The purpose here is to establish how human rights evolved prior to and following the delivery of international assistance.

Political Rights

Before the deployment of the UN Transitional Authority in Cambodia (UNTAC) after the signing of the 1991 Paris agreements, serious human rights abuses persisted, though there had been clear progress since the Pol Pot years. The PRK/SOC regime was far less repressive than the fanatical Khmer Rouge regime, led by Pol Pot, and the PRK adopted a national constitution in 1981 that contained some provisions for political rights and civil liberties. These rights were not clearly defined or specified, however.

The electoral process itself was exclusionary. Only candidates from the communist CPP could be elected, instead of being elected by the people in multiparty competitive elections. True to the spirit of "socialism," the electoral process barred citizens from forming rival political parties that might challenge the CPP. This one-party system was designed to prevent opposition groups from competing in the political arena.[2]

During the period following the UN intervention, respect and protection of political rights improved. Plurality in the media sector began to emerge, and political violence and intimidation against journalists declined. Multiparty elections became more competitive, particularly the 1993 election. Opposition parties published their own newsletters and bulletins,[3] and some twenty political parties were registered to take part in the electoral process. There was a healthy element of uncertainty before polling day. The CPP could not be sure that it would garner all the votes, and did not seem invincible. But after the 1997 coup that reversed the 1993 election outcome, the CPP successfully consolidated its power. Subsequent government leaders were elected in 1998 and 2003, but these national elections were generally less free than the 1993 vote. The CPP-dominated coalition governments formed after the 1993, 1998, and 2003 elections failed to operate in an accountable, open manner though the military and security apparatuses never directly controlled the state.

Civil Liberties

Civil liberties improved over the period 1992–2004, but remained subject to abuse and prohibitions. Before this period, freedom of expression and belief had been severely restricted. Under the PRK/SOC regime, Buddhism flourished but remained under state control. Independent media were prohibited, academic freedom was extremely circumscribed, and political organization outside official state channels was banned. Local human rights organizations were not permitted to operate inside the country.

Since 1992, freedom of expression has improved to a relative degree. Some 100 newspapers are now privately owned and tend to be allied with different political parties. The government continues to dominate broadcast media, which is the main source of information for the largely rural population. The government has denied a radio broadcast license to the main opposition party, the Sam Rainsy Party (SRP). News organizations operate in a climate of fear. Journalists who issue critical reports face potentially lethal risks. A deputy editor of a radio station allied with the opposition FUNCINPEC was shot dead in 2003.

Freedom of assembly has fluctuated since 1992 but worsened in recent years, with greater restrictions imposed after early 2003. After 1991, this right was guaranteed by the constitution and the International Treaty on Human Rights, ratified by Cambodia, but limits persisted in practice. Those organizations perceived as a threat to the regime have been denied official recognition, such as the Students Movement for Democracy Organization. Political rallies and marches, demonstrations and strikes, meetings and seminars have been officially permitted, but numerous constraints and pressures still apply. The March 1997 grenade attack on an opposition party demonstration provides a clear example of the risks attached to open dissent. Local nongovernmental human rights organizations are allowed to exist but face intimidation and threats. In January 2003, new restrictions were imposed on freedom of assembly, with the government citing vague threats to national security and public order. Throughout 2004, police violently dispersed at least twenty public demonstrations.[4]

Minority rights have improved, but many problems and challenges remain. Although better represented in government, women remain underrepresented in all branches of government. By the end of the twentieth century, two women were serving as cabinet ministers (minister of women's and veterans' affairs, and minister of culture and fine arts) among the twenty-five ministries, compared to none in the period 1993–1997. Ethnic minorities enjoy more freedom than previously, but still face repression. Some 200,000 to 500,000 Vietnamese often suffer from racial discrimination by both political officials and throughout mainstream society, especially during election periods.

Individual economic freedom has improved since the early 1990s, though violations continue. Since the early 1990s, the right to private property, particularly to own land, has been revived and improved. However, military and police officers often illegally confiscate lands, and land disputes are not resolved in a legal manner. According to a UN report, the absence of a proper land-title registration system and corruption by vested interests are to blame.

Deep inequalities, with a small wealthy elite living among an impoverished majority, continue and are worsening. According to the UN Development Programme (UNDP) in its 2004 Human Development Report, Cambodia remains one of the world's poorest nations, ranking 130th out of 177 countries. The number of people living below the poverty line (US50¢ per day) increased from about 36 percent in the late 1990s to about 43 percent (about 5.6 million) in 2002.

The UN Special Representative for Human Rights repeated his calls on the Cambodian government to address problems of meager and slow disbursement of national budget allocations, citing the negative effect on health, education, and judicial reform. He cited an example of the total health budget for 2003, of which only 10 percent had been released for the first half of the year.[5] Government indifference to poverty and corruption remains endemic. The World Bank has issued scathing reports describing rampant corruption.

The Fragile Rule of Law

The judiciary under the PRK/SOC regime in the 1980s was rudimentary and lacked independence. The rule of law did not prevail in civil and criminal matters. Not only was the court system newly established, but it also faced a severe shortage of professionally trained staff. Judges, prosecutors, and defense lawyers had "a very limited legal background."[6] Judicial decisions were mainly settled through conciliation mechanisms, and the courts lacked the capacity to handle numerous cases efficiently.

Other public organizations that could ensure the protection of human rights were extremely weak and highly politicized. The security apparatus was far more powerful than the judiciary. At the time of the 1991 Paris agreements, the SOC claimed to have a 47,000-strong police force, whose members were as heavily armed as soldiers, but barely trained for professional duties. According to Amnesty International, the regime employed long-term detention of political prisoners (including prisoners of conscience) without charge or trial, summary use of the death penalty, and systematic torture. Some political detainees died under dubious circumstances while in custody.

The UNTAC mission led efforts to introduce the rule of law in a country with no democratic tradition. Until 1991 the country had been at war, and the state faced challenges from resistance movements seeking to undermine its authority. In the months leading up to the 1993 election, human rights violations included the senseless slaughter of ethnic Vietnamese, abuse of prisoners, and incidents of politically motivated murder. Although the number of extrajudicial executions decreased to two in 1995, the human rights situation worsened in 1996 and deteriorated rapidly in 1997, when four people died as a result of torture and at least twenty-seven people, including six children, were arbitrarily executed. During and after the coup in 1997, scores of FUNCINPEC members were extrajudicially executed, while hundreds of others were detained without charge or trial. By the end of 2003, none of the perpetrators of these crimes had been brought to justice. Prisoners are often placed in overcrowded cells and given inadequate food with little or no nutrition. According to a UN report, "over-crowding is terrible—people are like sardines, and there are prisons where they can't lie at the same time, so they do it in turns. While some sleep, others have to stand up."[7] The situation worsened in 2004, with the number of prisoners increasing by 30 percent to a total of 7,840, aggravating overcrowding problems. In addition, rampant corruption persists among prison officials.[8]

■ International Assistance for Human Rights, 1992–2003

Bilateral and multilateral donors involved in the promotion of human rights in Cambodia included outside governments, multilateral organizations, and international nongovernmental organizations (NGOs). The United States, Australia, and Japan were among the main bilateral donors providing such assistance. A leading multilateral donor was the European Commission (EC), which made efforts to promote human rights through a variety of strategies. When it began its trade negotiation with Cambodia in 1996, the EC stated that the agreement would be conditional on the latter's respect for human rights. On November 7 of that year, a joint declaration was made, stating that the agreement could be suspended in the event of serious human rights violations. International NGOs, such as Human Rights Watch and Amnesty International, also played an influential role. Above all, the United Nations represented the most important actor in human rights. Apart from the UNTAC mission, stationed in the country between 1992 and 1993, the UNDP's office in Cambodia and the Cambodian Office of the High Commissioner for Human Rights (COHCHR) also led efforts to protect human rights.

Regulatory Reforms

The Paris agreements laid a foundation for promoting human rights in Cambodia, based on the recognition that the country's "tragic recent past requires special measures to assure protection of human rights, and the non-return to the policies and practices of the past."

The human rights component of UNTAC played a crucial role in providing international assistance to help protect political rights and civil liberties in general. The component consisted of a small group of specialists on human rights, including international lawyers, charged with monitoring and investigating human rights issues as well as providing training, education programs, and information. The office adopted regulations relating to the judiciary and criminal law procedures during the transitional period before the election of the Constituent Assembly. It also established the Prisons Control Commission, leading to the release of political prisoners and prisoners detained without trials, improved jail conditions, and enrolled prisoners to vote. As part of the long-term objective to protect human rights, UNTAC established the UN Human Rights Trust Fund, which was used to support international and regional nongovernmental organizations working with Cambodian counterparts in a variety of education and training activities.

Foreign governments provided further assistance for specific legal projects. Beginning in 1999, for instance, Japanese legal experts worked on drafts of a civil code and a civil procedure code. French legal experts also worked on preliminary drafts of the penal code and the criminal procedural code and completed them in September 2000.

Legal Training and Judicial-System Reform

UNTAC pursued an ambitious agenda for judicial reform. Its human rights component conducted training courses for judges, defense lawyers, and public prosecutors. UNTAC once considered the possibility of importing foreign judges and lawyers, but this idea was never put into practice. UNTAC also assisted in the process of translating the various human rights instruments from English into Khmer and distributing them to government officials and human rights activists. In addition, UNTAC provided assistance to Cambodia's Supreme National Council (SNC) in accepting seven international human rights instruments, including the Convention Against Torture and Other Forms of Cruel, Inhuman, and Degrading Treatment or Punishment; the Convention on the Elimination of All Forms of Discrimination Against Women; the Convention on the Rights of the Child; and the Convention Relating to the Status of Refugees and its protocol.[9] Unfortunately, most of the judicial reform initiatives by UNTAC were considered unsuccessful, due in part to the limited time frame, political disputes among the four Cambodian signatories, and the complexity of the task at hand.

Following UNTAC's departure shortly after the 1993 elections, donors showed a heightened interest in promoting human rights. They pressed for judicial reform at various annual Consultative Group meetings and pledged assistance for human rights. In March 2000, Japan pledged up to US$20 million. In Paris in May 2000, donors expressed continued concern about human rights abuses and the culture of impunity in Cambodia. The European Union (EU) offered a US$5.2 million grant set aside for judicial and administrative reform. Efforts by donors to promote human rights were also directed at building relevant local organizations.

Assistance for State-Run Human Rights Institutions

At the state level, efforts were made to promote enforcement of human rights through building institutions in the executive, legislative, and judicial branches of government. The UNDP, while focusing mainly on economic development, sponsored training for judges and court staff to assist the judiciary and the courts to act independently, uphold the rule of law, and ensure equity and access to justice. Key projects sponsored by the UNDP included the "Human Rights Training Project" and "Education on Human Rights." It also gave support to the Cambodian Human Rights Action Committee (CHRRCC), a national human rights network that monitors rights abuses and provides training for rights activists. The COHCHR worked on human rights issues in cooperation with government ministries and agencies, parliamentary commissions, law professors, and the prosecutor general's office.

International NGOs also played an active role in efforts to bolster human rights. The International Human Rights Law Group provided technical training to judges, prosecutors, clerks, prison authorities, civilian and military police, and local officials on human rights, domestic law, and the role of the judiciary. Human Rights Watch/Asia consistently lobbied donors to insist on accountability and transparency in Cambodia's judicial system.

Establishing the Khmer Rouge Tribunal

Donors also put pressure on Cambodia to establish an international criminal tribunal with the aim of bringing Khmer Rouge leaders to justice for their crimes against humanity. Among the international actors, the UN was the most active in lobbying Cambodia to establish the tribunal. After several setbacks, the UN and the CPP government finally signed an agreement on June 6, 2003, to establish extraordinary chambers capable of exercising jurisdiction in accordance with international standards of justice.

The European Parliament was among the international bodies pushing for justice against Khmer Rouge leaders. In April 1999 it passed a resolution condemning the Cambodian government for any attempts to prevent the establishment of such a tribunal and calling on EU member states and the European Council to support the cause.

Countries such as the United States, Japan, and Australia as well as major international organizations took the lead in pushing for action on the tribunal's establishment. During his visit to Cambodia in 2000, Australian foreign minister Alexander Downer urged Cambodia to meet international judicial standards and announced that his government would offer a two-year US$20.8 million (Aus$28 million) aid package including funding for a criminal judicial assistance project. On a visit to Cambodia in January 2000, Japanese prime minister Keizo Obuchi also told government representatives that his government would not lend support to any tribunal lacking an endorsement by the UN, and urged Cambodia to cooperate fully with the world organization.

As of early 2006, the international community is still expected to provide financial assistance to the tribunal (made up of Cambodian and foreign judges, prosecutors, and staff), covering the bulk of the estimated total cost of US$57 million. For its part, the Cambodian government is required to contribute US$13.5 million to these costs.

Assistance for Human Rights NGOs

International donors delivered financial, technical, and political assistance to numerous local nongovernmental organizations working in the sphere of human rights. In 1997 the Swedish International Development Agency (SIDA) approached the Swedish NGOs Diakonia and Forum Syd with the aim of funding local NGOs. As a result, Diakonia and Forum Syd provided financial assistance to support the annual budgets and activities of various Cambodian human rights groups.[10] In July 1999 the US government announced an aid package of US$3.4 million to Cambodia's local human rights NGOs. The Asia Foundation also played a crucial role by mobilizing citizens to monitor human rights abuses, improving investigation and legal representation, and bolstering advocacy efforts aimed at securing the Cambodian government's commitment to protecting human rights. The foundation worked in partnership with the Cambodian Health and Human Rights Alliance and the Cambodian League for the Promotion and Defense of Human Rights (LICADHO). It funded other local human rights NGOs, such as the Cambodian Defenders Project and Legal Aid of Cambodia, both active in providing legal representation to poor Cambodians. The Japanese Federation of Bar Associations also provided assistance for legal training to law graduates.

Several other international organizations helped build, protect, and strengthen human rights NGOs in Cambodia. Some organizations, such as Forum Asia and Amnesty International, focused on monitoring human rights in Cambodia. Others, such as the COHCHR, cooperated closely with Cambodian human rights NGOs and other civil society groups to help promote national policies and practices consistent with Cambodia's international obligations. Its staff also took part in regular meetings held by the Human Rights Action Committee (a coalition of eighteen local NGOs that met and coordinated work on human rights).

■ The Impact of Assistance and Remaining Challenges

How would Cambodia have evolved without international donor assistance? One good indicator is to look at its former socialist allies in the region, Laos and Vietnam. Both remain repressed, one-party states. It is hard to imagine multiparty elections, the emergence of indigenous human rights organizations, and other relative progress since 1991 in Cambodia without the support and presence of international donors.

International assistance for human rights over the past decade clearly has contributed to the promotion of human rights norms in the country. Moreover, the number of human rights organizations grew during the 1990s and played a positive role in protecting as well as promoting human rights. However, the overall impact of international assistance has failed to meet expectations. Human rights institutions remain fragile and require long-term attention.

Institutional Growth of Human Rights Institutions

The emergence of new human rights NGOs represents one of the positive legacies left by the Paris agreements and UNTAC. In 1992 the Cambodian Human Rights Action Committee had only four founding members but subsequently expanded to eighteen.[11] In 2000 the total number of NGOs that focused on human rights issues had increased to approximately forty.[12] This was a remarkable achievement, as none existed before 1991.

Human rights NGOs undoubtedly made a positive contribution to the protection and promotion of human rights norms, engaging in monitoring, advocacy, education, and training efforts. In the capital, Phnom Penh, human rights education also had an impact on government officials. LICADHO reported that its training and education initiatives helped raise awareness among civil servants about human rights. Such awareness resulted in the improvement of legal procedures and decreased incidents of torture in prison. Other organizations helped train government staff on political rights and civil liberties, due process and procedure, and substantive and procedural law.

Official Recognition of Human Rights

Even if it has failed to build and strengthen human rights, the Cambodian regime has at least formally recognized their importance. The National Assembly established its own human rights commission, and the Senate has one as well. The Council of Ministers' Administrative Reform sought to protect government employees from arbitrary prosecution. The Ministry of Justice created a human rights committee, overseen by Prime Minster Hun Sen's senior adviser, Om Yenthieng. The primary function of the committee is to provide remedy for legal issues involving the government and its agencies.[13] The Ministry of Women's and Veterans' Affairs (MWVA) also has a unit created to address gender discrimination through advocacy and outreach activities.

Legal institution building in other areas also has continued. Several state-run institutions were recently established, including the Center for Training of Lawyers (which began at the end of October 2002) and the Royal School for Training Judges and Prosecutors. Criminal justice has been pursued, if halfheartedly. On April 11, 2002, Cambodia ratified the Rome Statute of the International Criminal Court (ICC). By the end of 2004, it was one of only two countries in East Asia, the other being Timor-Leste, to have ratified the statute. The Khmer Rouge tribunal marked an attempt by Cambodia to promote justice, albeit under considerable pressure from the international community. The tribunal is seen by proponents of human rights and opposition party leaders as one way to help end the persistence of impunity. By late 2005, however, the entire process was still at the early stage: only the director and deputy director of administration had been appointed; the process of selecting judges and prosecutors remained unfinished. It was unclear how the process would eventually contribute to institution building in the justice sector. This looked like a missed opportunity.

Persistence of Corruption and Impunity

Apart from the positive effects of international assistance, a number of challenges relating to the efficacy and conduct of state institutions have yet to be adequately addressed by donors. Corruption, for example, remains endemic in Cambodian society. Despite numerous assistance and training programs, the judicial system remains corrupt and subservient to powerful interests. The UN Special Representative for Human Rights in Cambodia has stated that "justice is not the same for people who are rich and powerful, and people who are poor and weak."[14] In his view, "impunity lies at the centre of problems in the administration of justice." He added that "impunity for those responsible for human rights violations, especially the police and military and those in positions of political and economic influence, remains a serious problem."[15] King Sihanouk also mourned: "In today's Cambodia, the God of impunity reigns side by side with the King of corruption."[16] Even the prison system is highly corrupt. Some families are required to pay prison guards for lawful access to prisoners, according to a UN report.

The state spends a paltry amount on the judicial and penal systems. The Ministry of Justice's 2003 budget was only US$2.4 million (0.3 percent of the US$707.4 million national budget). According to a 2002 UN report, "This already inadequate amount is often not even fully paid to the Ministry of Justice and the courts. When other ministries overspend their allocated budgets, funds are diverted from the Ministry of Justice to compensate."

In addition, the three human rights commissions within the Ministry of Justice, the National Assembly, and the Senate lack independence and are virtually incapable of addressing complaints involving human rights abuses. Even the National Assembly's human rights commission was kept politically weak and subordinate to the interests of powerful individual politicians within the ruling party. With the exception of budget allocations for a few institutions, such as the Supreme Council of Magistracy, the Supreme Court, and the Appeal Court, the budget earmarked for the judiciary remained under the control of the Ministry of Justice.

Politicization of Human Rights Institutions

Closely related to the problem of impunity and corruption is the tendency of most governmental human rights institutions to defer to the dominant political party, respond to issues in a passive manner, and slavishly defend government policies. The government's human rights committee was mandated to investigate political killings during and after the violent coup in 1997, but did little to bring those responsible to justice. Details of some investigations were documented, but only three people involved in two cases of extrajudicial killings were tried, convicted, and sentenced to jail terms. No details of the trials were divulged, however.

Other government institutions designed to promote human rights also lacked real political influence. Judicial rulings are subject to interference, especially when dealing with politically powerful individuals. In August 2001, for instance, a provincial court's refusal to comply with the governor's instruction led to a public demonstration that intimidated the court and eventually forced it to comply with the governor's wishes. In December 1999, Prime Minister Hun Sen ordered the rearrest of prisoners released by courts. The Ministry of Justice then suspended two senior judges.

The judiciary is deeply politicized and clearly subservient to the ruling party. Judges have been quick to punish members of opposition parties, impoverished criminal suspects, and other powerless individuals, while avoiding prosecuting suspects loyal to the ruling party. In April 2002, for instance, a judge found guilty a journalist who was working for an opposition newspaper, fined him US$18,000, and then threatened to put him in jail if he failed to pay. The ruling came after the journalist reported that two former Khmer Rouge generals and a wealthy pro-CPP businessman were involved in illegal logging.[17] In contrast, judges have convicted few of those suspected of killing opposition party members, and have almost always argued that such killings lacked any political motivation or context. Judges remain inadequately trained and have also been appointed on a partisan basis, mostly by the CPP. Even the Supreme Court avoided considering cases related to political rights.

The Supreme Council of Magistracy is plagued by a lack of transparency. A draft bill to amend legislation on the magistracy's organization and functioning has been blocked. According to a UN report, "COHCHR has provided comments on the draft Bill. A group of NGO leaders . . . forwarded comments with recommendations for larger reform of the Council. However, the lack of transparency that dogs most draft laws means that no public discussion has yet taken place despite the repeated commitments of the Government to encourage public consultations in the law making process."[18]

With strong links to the Ministry of Justice, the Supreme Council of Magistracy, entrusted by the constitution (through Articles 132–134) with the task of helping the king ensure judicial independence and disciplining judges and prosecutors, is far from independent. According to a report in August 2003 from the UN Special Representative for Human Rights, the Council "is largely ineffectual, effectively leaving Cambodia without an institution to discipline its judges," while the executive remains reluctant to empower the judiciary.

Limited Influence and
Institutional Weakness of Cambodian NGOs

Domestic human rights NGOs are plagued by a number of weaknesses. Despite the rise in the absolute number of human rights NGOs during the mid-1990s, the number of genuinely independent human rights NGOs decreased over time. Few maintain high degrees of political independence, institutional accountability (through effectively functioning boards of directors), or transparency. Most lack significant influence. Political leaders choose to ignore their requests for action or investigation and even threaten NGO activists. Following the grenade attack on an opposition party rally in March 1997 and the violent coup of July 1997, human rights NGOs encountered greater open hostility from authorities and scaled back their activities, fearing government reprisals. According to Sara Colm of Human Rights Watch, human rights NGOs in Cambodia face "an uncertain future," even if human rights workers developed a sense of courage and optimism. She indicated that most local human rights groups hesitate to confront the state, hoping to avoid political retaliation. In her words, "most rights groups [did] not employ activist tactics such as conducting demonstrations or organizing communities affected by a problem to advocate for change."[19]

By 2004, most local human rights NGOs scarcely functioned. Only a few could now be said to have a promising future: the Documentation Center of Cambodia (DC-CAM), LICADHO, and the Cambodian Human Rights and Development Association (ADHOC). However, only two, LICADHO and ADHOC, seem ready to perform regular human rights duties. However, both organizations lack adequate institutional resources, and heavy reliance on international assistance presents a long-term challenge. Perhaps most worrying, however, is that some in the human rights NGO community say morale is declining and that the sector is "losing heart."[20]

▪ Limiting Factors

There are a number of factors that explain why the impact of international assistance on human rights has been so limited in Cambodia. These limitations can be described as domestic challenges, regional influences, and shortcomings of donor assistance.

Domestic Challenges: Culture, Politics, and the Economy

Cambodia's cultural values have made it difficult to promote a new liberal culture of accountability and transparency based on the concept of human rights. Respect for individual human rights has never been part of the country's political culture. Traditionally, the concept of "divine rights" associated with the idea of a "god king" with spiritual links to the Hindu god Shiva dominated Cambodian society for many centuries. This traditional concept was later replaced by a more liberal model of individual rights after Prince Sihanouk was ousted from power in 1970. But individual rights soon gave way to republican authoritarianism under the leadership of President Lon Nol and then to collective obligations under the socialist-oriented regimes of the Khmer Rouge and the PRK/SOC.

Ignorance about human rights principles also naturally hampered its development. Education efforts failed to reach much of the rural population. Approximately 85 percent of the population knew little about individual political rights and civil liberties. The average citizen had inadequate access to international and local rights organizations. Even if access was possible, most were not encouraged to register complaints due to the fear of political reprisals. This lack of public participation and awareness held back the advance of human rights and related organizations.

The dominance of one political party at the expense of pluralism posed another serious challenge to the development of human rights. When the CPP and FUNCINPEC dominated the first coalition government after the 1993 election with no serious opposition, the parties increasingly resisted international efforts to pursue judicial reform. While still prime minister, Prince Ranariddh adopted an indifferent stance to the idea of making the judiciary independent from the CPP and the Ministry of Justice.

Following the 1998 election, when it emerged as the country's dominant party and successfully consolidated its political, military, and economic power, the CPP strongly opposed reforms meant to make the judiciary more accountable, transparent, independent, and sustainable. Moreover, in June 1998 the government sought, albeit unsuccessfully, to tighten control over human rights NGOs by drafting a new law that complicated registration requirements, prohibited international assistance, and barred international associations from receiving any government funding. While the security atmosphere beginning in 2000 improved compared to previous years (as the war had ended in 1998), "public officials issued strongly worded warnings to NGOs," according to Human Rights Watch.[21]

As the CPP grew more powerful, it also grew more resistant to international pressure on human rights issues. In August 1999, Prime Minister Hun Sen called for the closure of the Office of the UN Secretary-General's Special Representative in Cambodia when his mandate expired in January 2000. In addition, Cambodia sent no delegation to the examination by the UN Committee Against Torture of Cambodia's initial report in April 2003. The UN Special Representative for Human Rights in late 2003 noted recent efforts, apparently by Cambodian government officials, to describe the UN involvement in human rights as "a kind of harassment" and to "reduce the UN involvement" in this area.[22]

Depressed economic conditions have hindered efforts to promote human rights and to make human rights organizations sustainable. There has been some modest increase in funding judicial reform and training. Judges and prosecutors recently received increased allowances, and training schools for judges, prosecutors, and legal practitioners also began to operate. However, courts remain poorly funded and often have to borrow money from local authorities to pay for basic necessities such as electricity. Widespread poverty has made it all the more difficult for Cambodians to build, strengthen, and sustain human rights organizations. Impoverished citizens concerned with daily survival could not provide active support to human rights organizations or afford to buy publications produced by human rights organizations. ADHOC, for example, was forced to adopt a policy to cancel sales of its biweekly magazine to recover costs. As a result, the association continued to depend entirely on international assistance.

Cambodian leaders also have sought to hold back human rights activities by justifying undemocratic behavior on grounds that they need to focus first on providing food and basic needs to the population, even though they have not done much in this regard. Economic development has been presented as a higher priority than promoting political rights and civil liberties. The Cambodian leadership has employed the argument that rights should be defined in economic rather than in political terms. According to the political leadership, grinding poverty justifies state-sponsored violence as a tool to restore or maintain order. The state, citing poor economic conditions, has made no effort to provide funding for the bar association and the few NGOs active in providing Cambodians with legal representation and advice.

Regional Challenges

States in the region have had a negative influence on the limited respect for human rights of Cambodia's government. Instead of promoting human rights, regional governments have actively discouraged human rights protection and dismissed reports of widespread abuses. China, Vietnam, and Myanmar (Burma) remain undemocratic states and have never sought to defend human rights at home or abroad. These countries exert real influence over Cambodia and have maintained close bilateral ties with the country. Although both the French government and the Australian federal police ran training or "cooperation" projects with Cambodian police, the Cambodian government also continued to send the majority of its security forces to Vietnam for training.[23] Until the early 2000s, the Association of Southeast Asian Nations (ASEAN) had little to say about human rights and made no attempt to raise concerns. Malaysia has opposed intervention in the affairs of other states, even if a regime clearly violates human rights. In 2002, when asked if his country would intervene in another country controlled by a notorious figure such as Pol Pot, Malaysian prime minister Mahathir Mohamad replied, "There will be ways of intervening that don't amount to actually interfering with their administration."[24] When asked a similar question, Singaporean prime minister Goh Chok Tong said: "The principle idea is not to comment or interfere in someone else's domestic affairs."[25] The most democratic state in ASEAN, the Philippines, never adopted a policy to promote human rights outside the UN system.[26]

ASEAN leaders have maintained that human rights values defined in individualistic terms are based on Western culture and ideas and cannot be universally applied. They have embraced the notion of cultural "relativism" and "particularism" to defend their stance. ASEAN even admitted Cambodia into the regional group as a member in 1999 after its government had seriously violated human rights norms. Within ASEAN, there was no formal requirement for a government to display accountability.

China defended the Cambodian regime throughout the 1990s. Beijing "was the most consistent and outspoken opponent of an internationally managed or supervised tribunal for former Khmer Rouge leaders," based on the defense that any "internationally controlled tribunal would infringe upon Cambodia's national sovereignty."[27] Beijing was known for being "unwilling to support a Security Council resolution under Chapter VII of the U.N. Charter"[28] to bring surviving Khmer Rouge leaders to justice. As Sino-Cambodian ties expanded, the CPP regime exhibited a growing opposition to human rights efforts.

Donor Limitations

Donors seemed unable to promote accountability and transparency in Cambodia. UNTAC was criticized by international human rights organizations, such as Human Rights Watch, for tolerating the bombing of opposition party offices during the period leading up to the 1993 election, for encouraging Khmer Rouge leaders to take part in the election, and for failing to stem the climate of impunity.

In the post-UNTAC period, donors used "carrots" rather than "sticks" to encourage the Cambodian government to promote human rights. The UN Special Representative for Human Rights was among the few outspoken international officials who demanded that Cambodian leaders end the prevailing impunity and introduce accountability. For many other donors, human rights issues were not high on their agenda.

In the mid-1990s, most donors had continued to pledge their faithful support for the Cambodian government. At the 1996 Consultative Group meeting, the main donors promised to provide Cambodia US$501 million in unconditional aid. Even after the grenade attack on an opposition party rally in March 1997, the European Parliament's Committee on Development and Cooperation recommended approval of a proposed cooperation agreement with the Cambodian government. At the July 1–2, 1997, CG meeting, the donor community pledged to give Cambodia an additional US$450 million. As Cambodia's largest donor, Japan protested Hun Sen's call for the closure of the COHCHR in April 1995, but always maintained "a low profile on human rights issues." After Cambodia joined ASEAN in 1999, Japan avoided linking aid to human rights progress and instead focused on the restoration of political stability. Until recently, Japan tiptoed around the issue of Khmer Rouge trials, apparently because it wanted to avoid tensions with China and the United States. Officially, the United States seemed active in promoting justice in Cambodia, but the reality was not as straightforward. At the end of 2004, the United States chose not to join three countries—Australia, France, and Japan—that pledged financial support for the planned Khmer Rouge tribunal. Even the three pledging countries offered only small amounts that fell far short of the US$57 million that the tribunal would need: France with US$1 million, Australia with US$2 million, and Japan with US$3 million.

In recent years, the donor community has begun to express more public concern about human rights abuses and indignation at the climate of impunity. Donor governments have agreed to set up a working group to focus on judicial reform and corruption. In July 2004 the World Bank led a group of donors on good governance, which comprised the United States, the EU, Germany, Britain, the UNDP, the Asian Development Bank (ADB), and the COHCHR. Overall, however, the United States has remained "ambivalent" about Khmer Rouge trials, apparently because of its involvement in the Cambodian war in the 1970s and the indirect support provided to the Khmer Rouge movement during the 1980s.[29] Moreover, the United States likely would prefer to avoid angering China on this issue, especially since the beginning of the war on terrorism in autumn 2001. The George W. Bush administration's opposition to the International Criminal Court also did not help in this regard.[30]

Donors have tended to attach a lower priority to promoting more accountable management within human rights NGOs. Although generous, the donors have been accused of failing to exercise proper oversight over human rights NGOs and accounting for the assistance granted. "Shame on the donors that condone these practices and do not investigate the organizations they give money to," one researcher wrote in 2002.[31] Donors chose not to encourage reform in the NGO sector: "Sponsors knew all along that some rotten apples existed, yet this did not affect their funding practices."[32]

Part of the problem was that donors lacked effective international coordination. Donor governments often funded human rights NGOs with similar activities without setting out a clear division of labor. Diakonia, Novib, Oxfam America, Oxfam Belgium, Oxfam Great Britain, Oxfam Hong Kong, the British embassy, the Australian embassy, CIDA Canada, and the Asia Foundation all funded ADHOC, while most of these donors also funded LICADHO. This aid was delivered even though several of ADHOC's and LICADHO's programs and target groups were similar and overlapping. Donors haphazardly supported whatever programs they admired rather than adopting a complementary, long-term approach.

■ The Future of Human Rights in Cambodia

Prospects for the development of human rights are mixed, at best. Regional developments, the attitude of international actors, and economic conditions will help shape how human rights evolve. The regime's political will to promote human rights has never been strong and may weaken further given the ruling party's increasingly dominant position. The tendency for human rights NGOs to rely on charismatic leadership instead of more efficient and accountable management will have to change if these organizations are to survive and thrive.

It remains unclear what kind of impact the global economy will have on Cambodia and human rights promotion efforts. The UN Special Representative for Human Rights in Cambodia has already expressed concern that Cambodia's recent entry into the World Trade Organization (WTO) could influence the human rights situation. Together with Nepal, Cambodia is the first least-developed member of the organization. Landlessness, which has become a growing source of social conflict and human rights violations, might be exacerbated. While WTO membership might bring benefits from trade liberalization, it might also adversely affect a majority of the population and increase the burden of human rights NGOs, in that they would have to address more rights cases related to healthcare systems, rural lifestyles, rural employment, and food security.[33]

With human rights NGOs remaining weak and the ruling party growing stronger, the government will likely face no immediate pressure to answer for rights abuses or to explain its actions. Local human rights activists have even grown somewhat pessimistic about the future of their organizations. As noted earlier, directors of human rights NGOs appear to be losing momentum and hope. If this attitude becomes entrenched, the future of local human rights activism could be jeopardized. The role of international donors will be a crucial factor in the development—or deterioration—of human rights.

▮ Lessons and Recommendations

Given Cambodia's tragic past, it is not surprising that the rule of law has yet to take root and that efforts to protect and promote human rights face numerous obstacles and difficulties. Some of these obstacles reinforce each other. The first barrier grows out of cultural attitudes and historical experience that places little value on human rights. Authoritarian, undemocratic practices throughout the region provide an additional destructive influence. The stifling of political pluralism and democratic competition among different parties places human rights organizations and institutions in a perilous situation, vulnerable to state manipulation and coercion. International pressure has become less effective as Cambodia's dominant party has consolidated its power and felt less of a need to display a cooperative attitude. Deeply rooted poverty and social inequality make it difficult for human rights organizations to become self-sufficient. Once reliant on international aid, these organizations are likely to stay dependent on such assistance. Poverty itself is cited by the regime as a rationale for delaying and devaluing the protection of human rights.

Still, some obstacles are more easily addressed than others. The following are constructive suggestions as to how donors and domestic actors might build human rights institutions in a more effective manner.

Toward More Effective, Better-Managed Human Rights NGOs

There has been an ongoing debate in Cambodia as to whether local human rights NGOs should adopt a confrontational or a low-profile approach toward the state. This debate is unhelpful and seems to miss the point. Either of these approaches runs the risk of weakening the power of human rights activism. The nonconfrontational approach could weaken the legitimacy of human rights NGOs, as it could be seen as bowing to government pressure. On the other hand, the confrontational approach has its limits, especially when it threatens the very existence of human rights NGOs.

Local human rights NGOs need to focus on practical steps that could make their organizations more effective. Instead of relying on improvisation and personal charisma, these NGOs need to improve their internal organization and management. These NGOs should themselves practice the values they preach: accountability, democracy, and transparency. Too often, leading activists perform their duties based on personal popularity that results from their resentment of the state or from pleasing donors. Some operate on a humanitarian basis, but do not have the faintest idea how to build effective and influential institutions. For long-term sustainability, human rights NGOs need to give thought to staff development and leadership succession. Human rights NGOs may also need to improve their division of labor to avoid duplication and wasted effort.

Donors could play a constructive role by providing incentives to NGOs for more professional, accountable management. Donors should continue to demand that human rights NGOs promote internal management reforms, administrative accountability, and operational transparency from boards of directors down to lower-level staff. Future funding should be based on NGOs' willingness or commitment to submit self-evaluation reports and concrete future plans about long-term institutional development. Adopting a firmer stance with the NGOs on accountability issues need not be perceived as taking away their policy initiative or institutional autonomy.

Donors should only fund human rights NGOs that can attract public support, thus ensuring institutional legitimacy and long-term sustainability. Without a solid social foundation, human rights institutions cannot be influential or effectively sustained.

The Need for a National Human Rights Commission

Better coordination among independent human rights NGOs remains an important challenge of domestic human rights activism. Nevertheless, there is still a genuine need for a nationwide human rights commission that will promote effective dialogue and mutual understanding between the state-run human rights committee and local as well as international human rights NGOs. It was understandable that leading local human rights NGOs wished to keep a healthy distance from the state, largely because of the legitimate belief that working with the latter would compromise their activities. But a national commission for human rights might benefit Cambodia if it would also officially associate with the UN Commission for Human Rights and other international human rights organizations. The government might not show any interest in this initiative, as it once rejected LICADHO's proposal and showed no interest after late 1997. Still, it would be useful to explore the possibility and examine the potential benefits.

The Necessity of International Pressure

Donors should not naively assume that Cambodia will sooner or later become "enlightened" to the extent that it will respect human rights and uphold the rule of law. The cultural, political, and socioeconomic conditions within Cambodia and the region as a whole will ensure that any Cambodian government will avoid a voluntary embrace of human rights. Strong and constant pressure on the Cambodian state from donors is absolutely necessary. Unless there is an effective system of checks and balances, any personal promises by political leaders to promote human rights and uphold the rule of law will be easily broken.

Improving Donor Coordination

Donors need to speak with one voice on human rights issues and to agree on a clear division of labor. Although they may have expressed concerns about the problems of impunity and lack of judicial reform, they have proven unable to coordinate their activities effectively.

Coordination in judicial reform remains essential for improving the judiciary as a whole. Cooperation among donors should focus on the prevention of duplication and overlapping projects. It makes no sense to fund local organizations with similar or identical programs and activities. Donors need to be clear on what those local organizations plan to achieve and whether those tasks are complementary.

With better coordination, donors can strengthen their collective demands that local partners undertake specialized tasks in the field of human rights and cooperate rather than compete with each other. The time has come for donors to help consolidate the few remaining domestic human rights organizations that still have potential.

In Cambodia as in other postconflict societies, it is crucial that donors adopt a comprehensive, long-term approach to building human rights institutions. As part of a successful strategy, donors must place sustained pressure on the Cambodian government, especially at a time when one party rules to the exclusion of other political factions and open debate. Donors should also ensure that recipients of human rights assistance promote internal democratic governance as well as work toward successfully constraining the state's abuses of civil liberties. Building respect for human rights is a long, arduous process in a country that has experienced such traumatic repression and violence. It is vital that donors and rights activists retain their determination to persevere and to gradually establish a more solid foundation for human rights.

▓ Notes

1. Council for the Development of Cambodia, *Development Cooperation Report 2001*, p. 11. For an analysis of pledging-disbursement gaps, see Peou with Yamada, "Cambodia."

2. Political opposition to the ruling party was not permitted until after the Paris agreements were signed. In May 1990, a number of government officials were detained without any charges or trials. They were arrested after making an attempt to publish the charter of a new political party. Amnesty International, "Cambodia" (1991), p. 54.

148   *Human Rights*

3. FUNCINPEC had a significant media system. It must be acknowledged that the media sector was far from independent; it operated freely along party lines. For more detailed analysis, see Marston, "Cambodia News Media in the UNTAC Period and After."

4. ADHOC, *Human Rights Situation Report 2004,* pp. 1, 9.

5. UN Doc. A/58/317, August 22, 2003, paras. 44–45. This chapter draws on UN reports, documents, and press releases on Cambodia that are too numerous to cite in detail.

6. UN, *Report of the United Nations Fact-Finding Mission on Present Structures and Practices of Administration in Cambodia,* p. 114.

7. Cited in *Phnom Penh Post,* November 22–December 5, 2002, p. 6.

8. ADHOC, *Human Rights Situation Report 2004,* pp. 17–18; LICADHO, *Cambodia Human Rights Report 2004,* pp. 12–13.

9. Duffy, "Toward a Culture of Human Rights in Cambodia," pp. 273–274.

10. For detailed background, see Karistedt, *Cambodian Human Rights and Democracy Organizations.*

11. The eighteen human rights NGOs that composed the Cambodian Human Rights Action Committee included the Cambodian Human Rights and Development Association, the Cambodian Center for the Protection of Children's Rights, the Cambodian Defenders Project, the Coalition of Human Rights Advocates for the Khmer Muslims in Cambodia, the Cambodian Health and Human Rights Alliance, the Cambodian Women's Crisis Center, the Mission of Generous Cambodian Alliance, the Indradevi Association, the Khmer Human Rights and Against Corruption Association, the Khmer Institute of Democracy, the Khmer Kampuchea Krom Human Rights Association, the Khmer Students Association, the Khmer Youth Association, Legal Aid of Cambodia, the Cambodian League for the Promotion and Defense of Human Rights, the Cambodian Human Rights Task Force, and Human Rights Vigilance of Cambodia.

12. Neou, *Human Rights in Action,* p. 17.

13. After the violent incident in 1997, Hun Sen accused the UNHCHR of false reports and announced that he would set up his own human rights committee to investigate abuses.

14. Cited in *Phnom Penh Post,* December 20–January 2, 2003, p. 15.

15. UN Doc. A/58/317, August 22, 2003, para. 27.

16. Cited in *Phnom Penh Post,* July 19–August 1, 2002, p. 10.

17. *Phnom Penh Post,* April 12–25, 2002, p. 5.

18. Cambodian Office of the High Commissioner for Human Rights, "Note on Legal and Judicial Reform for the Mid-Term Consultative Group of Donors Meeting, January 2003" (undated manuscript).

19. Colm, *Cambodia,* p. 13.

20. Author interview with Kek Galabru, president of LICADHO, August 30, 2003.

21. Human Rights Watch, "Cambodia," p. 203.

22. UN Press Release GA/SHC/3762, November 10, 2003.

23. According to the *Phnom Penh Post,* "the majority of police training seems to come from Vietnam, whose law enforcement instructors work in the [Ministry of the Interior]'s Department of Training. Around 30 high-ranking officers travel annually to Vietnam for police training." *Phnom Penh Post,* February 28–March 13, 2003, p. 7.

24. "ASEAN 2002," *Cambodia Daily,* November 4, 2002, p. 29.

25. Ibid., p. 52.

26. President Gloria Macapagal Arroyo, for instance, commented the following: "As a leader of a democratic country, I feel that all countries are ready for democracy. But whether I would interfere and impose my values on another country outside the UN system is another thing. ASEAN has different cultures, different political systems, different histories, different religions, and different social organizations. And one country cannot impose its system on another." "ASEAN 2002," *Cambodia Daily,* November 4, 2002, p. 26.

27. Ciorciari, "Great-Power Posturing and the Khmer Rouge Tribunal," p. 1.

28. Marks, "Elusive Justice for the Victims of the Khmer Rouge," p. 713.

29. Drachman, "The War in Cambodia and the Case for Judicial Enforcement of Human Rights Conditions on Foreign Aid."

30. See Ciorciari, "Great-Power Posturing," p. 3.

31. See *Phnom Penh Post,* April 26–May 9, 2002, p. 10.

32. Vijghen, "Guilty by Association," p. 9.

33. UN Doc. A/58/317, August 22, 2003, paras. 65–68.

7

Human Rights Assistance to Sierra Leone

Mohamed Gibril Sesay and Charlie Hughes

After a decade of civil war, the people of Sierra Leone yearn for democratic rule and lasting peace. International assistance will play a crucial role in moving the country toward that goal. Aid and advice for the promotion of human rights is at the heart of the international and domestic effort to build democracy and the rule of law. This chapter describes and assesses international support for human rights protection in Sierra Leone, exploring possible lessons to be drawn from the experience.

Beginning with an exploration of the human rights situation prior to and during the civil war, the chapter examines the nature and scope of past violations and abuses, the pervasiveness of impunity, and the governance and security environment, and also looks at key actors involved in rights violations and existing organizations engaged in human rights protection. The chapter then outlines international assistance for state institutions and civil society organizations since the signing of the Lomé peace accords in 1999. It analyzes and evaluates the impact of such assistance on local institutions and on the general human rights situation, identifying strengths and weaknesses. The chapter ends with a look at the challenges remaining and possible lessons learned.

■ Human Rights Context

Declining Respect for Human Rights After Independence

The abuses and atrocities that occurred during Sierra Leone's 1991–1999 war have prompted unprecedented international attention to human rights issues in the country. Respect for human rights, however, has been lacking for many years. Restrictions on political activity and predatory maneuvers at both the national and local level created the conditions that ultimately encouraged some to seek change through war in 1991.[1]

With its open system of multiparty politics, Sierra Leone was an exceptional case among newly independent African states in the period between 1961 and 1966 and was relatively accountable and representative.[2] The British-model parliamentary arrangement may not have been perfect, but political leaders did not set out to deliberately sabotage it. Executive intrusions into civil and political liberties began when Sir Albert Margai became prime minister following the death of independence leader Sir Milton Margai in 1964. Parliament passed the Public Order Act in 1965, seriously compromising freedom of expression by making libel a criminal offense. In 1966 an absenteeism law was adopted that led to the expulsion of four opposition members from parliament. Although Sir Albert failed in his attempt to make Sierra Leone a one-party state, this personal meddling in governing institutions persisted under the rule of Siaka Stevens's All People's Congress (APC), which came to power in 1969.

Political repression became the order of the day as Stevens and his ruling APC party sought hegemonic control over the country. State agents and politicians frequently engaged in arbitrary arrest, unlawful detention, torture, and suppression of freedom of speech. Some of the excesses committed by the rebels in the war years were earlier practiced, albeit on a smaller scale, by the APC.[3] Although there has been no conclusive proof, Stevens's APC has long been suspected of assassinating certain influential members of opposition groups. There is no doubt that the APC frequently resorted to violence in quelling student protests, especially during elections. The state of civil liberties deteriorated further in 1978 when Sierra Leone became a one-party state.

Corrupt, Co-opted Judiciary

Institutions that were meant to protect citizens were progressively impaired and undermined. The judiciary was "co-opted and domesticated" to serve the whim of political leaders.[4] Laws in the 1971 republican constitution and the 1978 one-party constitution on judges' tenure of office served as a leash with which the government held the judiciary in check.[5] The 1978 one-party constitution, for instance, required a judge to retire after attaining the age of fifty-five. Even without the deliberate weakening of the judiciary by the executive, many judges willingly acquiesced to the culture of corruption that was engulfing public office. "Disputes of little political relevance became the cash cows of judges and colluding lawyers."[6]

Apart from executive intrusions and pervasive corruption in the courts, the judiciary was also weakened by low salaries and a chronic shortage of administrative resources. The state struggled to meet the judiciary's financial and logistical needs. With fewer people willing to work for low wages in an institution that lacked basic infrastructure, there were huge delays in cases. It was not uncommon for suspects to be held on remand for years awaiting trial or for litigants to simply quit cases that had dragged on interminably.

Police and Prisons: Accomplices in Human Rights Abuse

If the judges were there to "play" with the law for the government's self-serving interest, the police and the prison service sought to physically punish those who fell foul of the state. Many of the violent attacks on publishing houses in the 1980s were the work of the police following orders from their political masters.[7] An illustrative example of how the police served merely as an instrument in the hands of the state was Siaka Stevens's appointment to parliament of the police force's chief. Through the police the regime exerted control over recruitment into the armed auxiliary group—the Special Security Division. This was the force that was used to violently break up demonstrations against the state and to attack political opponents. Prisons became torture centers. Prisons such as Mafanta in the Tonkolili district were notorious as detention centers for political opponents.

Violations of human rights resulted from deliberate actions of politicians, police officers, and government officials. However, years of bad governance had pushed the economy into decline and severely weakened state institutions. The police force and prison system lacked basic resources. When making statements at police stations, complainants had to provide their own stationery. Citizens who brought cases to the police had to cover the cost of the investigating officers' transport fares. And because demanding money for bail was a source of illegal income for poorly paid police officers, arbitrary arrest was common. Prison guards would even steal food, medical, and other supplies meant for inmates.

Dictatorship of Customary Chieftaincy Rule

In rural Sierra Leone, where most of the population lives, customary rule under "paramount chieftaincy" was responsible for major human rights abuses.[8] Only those from families designated during the colonial era as members of "ruling houses" could be elected as paramount chiefs. Franchise in paramount chieftaincy elections was not universal. Only chiefdom counselors (representatives of groups of taxpayers) could vote in elections. Court chairmen and clerks had no knowledge of law beyond customary practice. Customary law was not codified, and there were no unified rules for court procedure. State supervision of the native administration courts was dysfunctional, giving chiefs and court officials a clear field for graft,

patronage, and administrative abuses. Moreover, customary law systemi-
cally discriminated against women in areas such as inheritance, marriage,
and property rights.

Customary rule, in varying degrees, was simply a dictatorship of a
rural gerontocracy. Forced labor, arbitrary fines, banishments, and discrimination against women and young people were part of everyday life. The
chiefs themselves were not exempt from suppression by the central government, however. They could be dethroned, suspended, or banished from their
chiefdoms.

The War and Extreme Human Rights Abuses

It was against this backdrop of executive excesses, judicial and institutional
impotence, and legislative weakening that war broke out in 1991. The conflict has been described as one of the most brutal and deadliest in recent
times. A defining mark of Sierra Leone's war was that appalling human
rights violations were a "devilishly well-calculated" instrument of warfare.[9]

The eleven-year war claimed more than 75,000 lives. One single two-
week attack on the capital city in January 1999 alone killed an estimated
6,000 people. Half of the country's 4.5 million people were displaced, and
as many as half a million people sought refuge in other countries. Tens of
thousands of women and young girls were raped or sexually enslaved.
Amputation was employed as a method of murder and terror. The number
of survivors of amputations has been estimated at around 1,000. And these
survivors likely represent only a quarter of those who suffered amputations.

The abuse of human rights as a method of warfare should be understood
in context. On March 23, 1991, the Revolutionary United Front (RUF)
launched war in Sierra Leone with the declared aim of ousting the APC's
one-party regime, ending political corruption, and creating social justice
and equal opportunities. Excepting the few people who benefited from the
corruption and misrule of the times, a majority favored the fall of the
regime. However, this did not necessarily translate into affection for the
RUF's war agenda. The RUF began by relying heavily on both Sierra
Leonean and Liberian men brought over from the war in neighboring
Liberia. These first RUF recruits deliberately targeted and killed civilians,
and looted and pillaged property.

The RUF only belatedly attempted to drum up civilian support for a
common cause of overthrowing the despotism and misrule of the regime.
Lacking a clear ideology as a rallying point and without any ethnic or religious agenda, brute force became the instrument by which the RUF sought
to convince civilians of its power and to negotiate recognition. As part of
this reliance on terror and reckless violence, civilians were gang-raped,
amputated, tortured, and maimed, and villages and towns razed.

In some cases, human rights abuses served a direct military goal. The RUF abducted civilians, especially children, to replenish its fighting ranks. Amnesty International estimates that more than 5,000 children under the age of eighteen fought as combatants in the war. Given the difficulty the RUF faced in recruiting volunteers, it turned to frequent abductions of civilians. Others have argued that the gruesome atrocities were part of a way of life for drug-addicted and psychologically disturbed young men. The question as to why the war was conducted with such brutality and cruelty has yet to be answered.

Rebel forces bear the overwhelming responsibility for human rights abuses during the war, but progovernment Civil Defense Forces (CDF) were also culpable on a "significantly smaller scale," according to Amnesty International. In addition to murder and torture, members of the CDF were blamed for obstructing humanitarian assistance and recruiting child soldiers. Finally, the national army itself was involved in human rights abuses. Soldiers rarely kept prisoners of war alive and would arbitrarily punish civilians, seizing civilian property without cause. When junior officers of the national army overthrew the civilian government of President Joseph Momoh and established the National Provisional Ruling Council (NPRC), the human rights situation deteriorated further: arbitrary arrest, torture, and confiscation of property became routine. In 1992 the NPRC executed twenty-four people for allegedly plotting to violently overthrow the government. There were strong suspicions that those executed were never tried in any court.[10]

Limited Civil Society Involvement in Human Rights Protection

Through the efforts of Amnesty International, human rights abuses were monitored and reported internationally. However, domestic nongovernmental groups made no significant attempt to address human rights issues in a comprehensive and programmatic way. The void was filled by the efforts of individual lawyers who took up the cases of victims of human rights abuse. At the height of the despotic one-party rule of the APC in the mid-1980s, when human rights violations were rampant, lawyers such as George Banda-Thomas and Suliaman Banja Tejan-Sie represented journalists and ordinary citizens who fell foul of the state. Newspapers also complemented human rights work by investigating and exposing abuses. In 1990 the publisher and journalists of *For Di People* newspaper formed the National League for Democracy and Human Rights.[11] The organization, through *For Di People,* investigated and reported cases of human rights abuse.

A lull in the war in 1995 enabled popular pressure to force the NPRC to return the country to multiparty civilian rule. Many domestic and international organizations with a human rights agenda emerged at this moment to support the democratic transition. The NPRC itself had established the National Commission for Democracy to carry out civic education, organize citizens' discussions of public interest issues, and initiate other activities to support the democratization process. The Forum for Democratic Initiatives (FORDI) was established in 1995 with a mission to contribute to the process of building democracy in Sierra Leone. The Campaign for Good Governance (CGG) was formed in 1996 to activate meaningful citizens' participation in the democratization process. A number of development or faith-based organizations that were already in existence, like the Network Movement for Justice and Development (NMJD) and the Council of Churches in Sierra Leone (CCSL), revived their advocacy work, incorporating human rights issues.

rise of interest groups

This emergent and promising environment for democracy and human rights activism was violently disrupted by the military coup of May 25, 1997. The period between the coup and May 8, 2000, was a defining moment for human rights in Sierra Leone. The worst abuses occurred during this period. Torture, mass killing, rape, wholesale burning of communities, and amputations had been common during the war, but these abuses were carried out with extraordinary intensity during this period. The Armed Forces Ruling Council (AFRC) government that the soldiers had formed was not granted recognition by the international community or the citizenry. Instead, the council turned to the RUF to try to govern the country. For nine months the coup leaders and the RUF unleashed willful terror to enforce submission to their rule. With the elected government in exile and the AFRC unable to assert recognized authority, there was effectively no governing authority. Every drug-taking, armed man was a law unto himself, unrestrained by any legal, social, or moral consideration. Renegade soldiers and rebels raided the countryside and walked the streets of Freetown maiming civilians, forcefully recruiting young boys, sexually enslaving girls, and looting property. In other wars in Africa civilians have been deliberately targeted, but it has been mainly on account of ethnic, religious, or ideological loyalties. In Sierra Leone there was no such motivation for the terror and atrocities, which were carried out in a wholly arbitrary, anarchic atmosphere.

In February 1999, military forces with the Economic Community of West African States Cease-Fire Monitoring Group (ECOMOG) drove the AFRC/RUF alliance out of Freetown. The ousted civilian government was restored. Local groups were again able to return to human rights work. Some, such as the CGG, the NMJD, the CCSL, and FORDI, put human rights at the center of their work.

In 1999 the National Forum for Human Rights (NFHR) was formed as an umbrella organization of local groups involved in the human rights field. Nearly all of the NFHR's founding organizations had been formed between 1995 and 1999, or else had assumed a human rights mandate in direct response to the excesses of the war. The human rights work of the local nongovernmental organizations (NGOs) was limited mainly to collecting information on violations and ad hoc community meetings on human rights. It is important to note, however, that information collected by these local groups contributed in no small measure to the impressive reports of many international organizations on Sierra Leone. Regrettably, local activists believe their contributions were rarely acknowledged.

■ International Human Rights Assistance

Between 1997 and 2000 the international community's involvement in human rights in Sierra Leone developed at a level never witnessed in the country before. Since then, the international community has tried to protect and promote human rights in Sierra Leone in various ways. This included human rights observation; police, justice, penal, and military reforms; assistance for native administration courts, the National Commission for Democracy and Human Rights, and the human rights ombudsman; and support to nongovernmental human rights organizations.

International Human Rights Observer Missions

Observer missions have been critical elements in international efforts designed to tackle Sierra Leone's human rights challenges. These missions became active in Sierra Leone in the period immediately following the signing of the Lomé peace accord in 1999. Hostilities had not ceased entirely; rebels were still armed and controlling large parts of the country. This environment provided an opportunity for international missions to come in on short visits to document the human rights situation.

Following the ousting of the AFRC in February 1998, and the restoration to power of President Ahmed Tejan Kabbah in July, the UN Security Council established the UN Observer Mission in Sierra Leone (UNOMSIL). The mission was assigned the task of advising on efforts at disarmament and at restructuring the security sector. UNOMSIL also documented human rights violations. Following the signing of the Lomé peace accord a year later, the Security Council, through Resolution 1270, established the UN Mission in Sierra Leone (UNAMSIL) on October 22, 1999, to assist with the implementation of the accord. With a much wider mandate than the observer mission, and an authorized strength of 13,000 military personnel and more than 400 hundred international and local staff, UNAMSIL became the largest UN peacekeeping mission ever (eventually growing to 17,500 personnel).

UNAMSIL had a human rights section that monitored, documented, and reported violations of human rights and international humanitarian law.

In an attempt to build a framework for continuing respect for human rights, the section also supported local human rights groups. This support included many training seminars and workshops around the country, representing the first opportunity the emergent human rights community had for training in such basic skills as monitoring, documentation, and reporting. UNAMSIL's human rights section also organized fortnightly meetings of human rights organizations as a forum for interaction and exchange of information and views. In support of building national human rights capacity, UNAMSIL also provided assistance and advice to state-level institutions, including, in particular, the Truth and Reconciliation Commission (TRC), the Special Court for Sierra Leone (SCSL), the police, and the judiciary. In mid-2003 the mission completed draft legislation for the establishment of a national human rights commission.

In addition to the work of the permanent human rights section of UNAMSIL, the UN's engagement in human rights also consisted of "visiting missions." Although some of the missions were for general situation assessments, most were focused on human rights. In June 1999, then–UN High Commissioner for Human Rights Mary Robinson visited Sierra Leone. An eleven-man Security Council delegation led by Ambassador Jeremy Greenstock visited Sierra Leone from October 9 to October 12, 2000, to hold talks with leaders of the Economic Community of West African States (ECOWAS) and look into ways of fully applying UN resolutions. Earlier in September the Under-Secretary-General for Peacekeeping Operations, Jean-Marie Guehenno, had visited UN operations in the country. The Deputy Secretary-General, Louise Frechette, in April 2001 paid a three-day visit to Sierra Leone on a general assessment mission. That same year, the Special Representative of the Secretary-General (SRSG) for Children and Armed Conflict, Ambassador Olara Otunnu, visited Sierra Leone. The UN Special Rapporteur on Violence Against Women, Radhika Coomaraswamy, came to Sierra Leone in August 2001 to ensure women's issues received a priority in the peace process, recognizing the human rights abuses that women suffered during the war. In December 2001 the Secretary-General of the UN himself came to Freetown.

These missions were the source of some important recommendations on policy or action. For instance, after hearing what women had suffered throughout the war, the UN Special Rapporteur on Violence Against Women made an appeal for women to be included on the Special Court bench and in other positions of high office. During her visit to Sierra Leone, Mary Robinson joined UNOMSIL, the National Commission for Democracy and Human Rights (NCDHR), and the NFHR in signing a human rights manifesto, a pledge to uphold human rights in Sierra Leone. The establishment of the National Commission for War-Affected Children, which took place in 2003, had been recommended by SRSG Olara Otunnu after his visit to Sierra Leone.

International NGOs have also used short-term visits to address the human rights situation in the country. In March 2000 a three-member team from the US-based organization Physicians for Human Rights conducted preliminary investigations into war-related sexual violence. The organization sent a team again in early 2001 to complete its research. The report of that research was eventually published and presented in the United States in 2002 as the most comprehensive study of rape and sexual violence as an instrument of war. Another important short visit by an international organization was that by the International Human Rights Law Group in August 1999. Although the visits by the group were originally connected with preparatory work for the establishment of the TRC, the organization, seeing the need to engage in Sierra Leone on a long-term basis, eventually opened its country office in 2001.

Assistance to Law Enforcement Agencies

The law enforcement sector suffered immense damage during the course of the war. Before the signing of the Lomé peace agreement in July 1999, with half of the country under rebel control, the courts in Freetown, a couple of police stations, and irregular sittings of the magistrates and high courts in the provincial towns of Bo and Kenema were all that remained of the country's judicial and police services. Before the outbreak of the war, the judiciary and police had been seriously compromised by corruption, political interference, and a dearth of resources. When the rebels deliberately torched police stations and prisons across the country, they were merely administering the final blow to what was already a moribund institution. After the war, reviving the law enforcement machinery became a critical element of efforts to promote national recovery and to consolidate peace.[12]

Police

Consistent with the need to reestablish government authority throughout the country after the war, the government first focused on the police when it began to reconstruct the law enforcement bureaucracy. With infrastructure, equipment, and records deliberately targeted for destruction by rebels, the police had serious problems that the cash-pressed government could not adequately handle without external support.

International assistance to the police started with the appointment in July 1998 of Keith Biddle by the UK's Department for International Development (DFID) to head the Commonwealth Police Development Task Force to Sierra Leone. The British-born officer's responsibility was to advise government on policing issues and to direct the restructuring of the Sierra Leone Police (SLP). Since the security environment has stabilized and the SLP's needs have become broader, the DFID has pursued a more comprehensive program of support related to institution building and criminal justice. Its assistance for longer-term training and advice to the SLP has been channeled mainly through the Commonwealth Community Safety and Security Project (CCSSP), with a budget of US$22 million, and a permanent country team. The DFID's support has enabled the acquisition of more than 400 vehicles for the SLP, logistical equipment for riot control, communication equipment, and uniforms.

In addition to assistance with logistics, another major component of the DFID's support to the police has been training. Many senior police officers from Sierra Leone have been to Britain on training courses, and there has also been a great deal of in-country training. Although most of these training courses overseas or in-country have been on such core policing issues as criminal justice, border security, public order, and intelligence, some attention has also been given to capacity building in such areas as administration, financial management, and policy planning.[13]

UNAMSIL, through its Civilian Police (CIVPOL) section, has also provided assistance to the police to complement the DFID's effort. CIVPOL's support began with providing advice and encouraging the deployment of the SLP so that after disarmament it could cover the whole country.[14] Broader support came to include "mentoring," by which CIVPOL police officers were placed at each police division to work directly with divisional heads. CIVPOL mentors actually carried out policing work themselves, so as to provide local police with a direct demonstration of best practice. CIVPOL also had advisers for five key areas: training, diamond-mine policing, airport policing, cross-border policing, and policy planning. It assisted the SLP in recruitment and training to help the force achieve a target personnel strength of 9,500 by the end of 2003. Lack of police stations was a major problem that the SLP faced when it started expanding its presence across the country at the end of hostilities, and CIVPOL took the lead in addressing this issue. Through a UN trust fund and a UN/DFID stopgap project, between June 2001 and the end of June 2003, CIVPOL constructed or rehabilitated fifteen police stations across the country.

In addition to bolstering the police presence across the country and enhancing operational capabilities, attention was also devoted to helping the police set up new services. This saw such innovative changes as the establishment of the Complaints, Discipline, and Internal Investigations Department (CDIID), the Family Support Unit (FSU), and the Media and Public Relations Unit (MPRU). The CDIID receives and investigates complaints made by individuals against police personnel. Prior to the establishment of this unit there was no clear-cut mechanism for individuals seeking redress for police abuses. The FSU settles intrafamily "quarrels" through advice and mediation, and handles matters involving women and children. The MPRU was set up to build a new, positive image for the police and communicate the force's work to the public and media. Another important innovation is "community policing," which brings local communities and the police together to identify local community needs and work out solutions. The CCSSP and CIVPOL also helped with improving institutional management in personnel, finance, management, and general administration.

Judiciary

Before the war, the judiciary had already been progressively weakened under successive one-party and military regimes. As noted earlier, Sierra Leone erupted into conflict partly because of the judiciary's steady ethical corrosion. The judiciary was widely seen as inefficient and ineffective because of corruption, and underresourced in terms of equipment, personnel, and facilities. Attempts to rebuild the judiciary can be traced back to the 1991 constitution, which had provisions for the guarantee of independence and tenure for judges.[15] This constitution had been written for Sierra Leone's return to multiparty politics. However, the outbreak of war that year and a military coup the following year meant that the intended judicial reform could not be carried out with the necessary training, equipment, and facilities.

The eleven-year conflict took a tremendous toll on the judiciary by destroying or damaging court infrastructure and creating chaotic conditions that undermined the judiciary's work. In many parts of the country, court facilities had been destroyed. The number of judges and magistrates was grossly insufficient. Records management had collapsed. The only library for the judiciary in Freetown was understocked with outdated books. In the capital there was only one car to take judges to and from work, which meant that they were nearly always late for court sittings.

In 2000 the DFID launched a three-year project on law development to revive the ailing judiciary and court system. With a budget of US$3.8 million (£2.2 million), the project sought to address the whole range of problems facing the judicial system. To restore infrastructure, the main lawcourts building in the capital was renovated, and new court facilities and residences for judges were built in the eastern and southern regional headquarters towns of Bo and Kenema. Equipment needs were met with the supply of tape recorders, computers, and stationery to the judiciary, the bar association, and the law school. In the area of technical support the project provided a draftsman for the attorney general's office, and assistance in archiving and record-keeping in the administrator and registrar-general's office. Training was also a major component of the DFID's project and, in addition to seminars on legal issues, courses were run for various categories of personnel in the sector, including police prosecutors, bailiffs, registrars, and undersheriffs. Judges were even trained in the use of computers. A compilation of all conventions and treaties signed by the government of Sierra Leone was undertaken, and law reporting, which had ceased for over two decades, began once again. The project on law development ended in

2003. In December 2004 the DFID and the government of Sierra Leone signed a US$43.4 million (£25 million) grant agreement in support of a larger project on state security and access to justice. The project will encompass the police, judiciary, and prisons.[16]

Penal System

At the time of the signing of the Lomé peace accord in mid-1998, only one prison—the Pademba Road Central Prisons in Freetown—was running effectively. The rest had been either completely razed or extensively damaged. Prisons, like police stations, were deliberate targets of the rebels. Major prisons such as Mafanta in the Tonkolili district, Masanki in the Moyamba district, Kono, Pujehun, and Kailahun district prisons, and the New England Camp in the capital were torched. In 2001 the charred remnants of the Prison Officers Training School and the yard of the New England Camp were handed over to the Special Court for Sierra Leone by the government, for the construction of court and detention facilities. The Prison Service lost its entire network of barracks across the country.

The prison system has received less international assistance than the police and judiciary. Since the signing of the Lomé peace accord in 1998, the only international support for prisons has come from the UN Office for Project Services (UNOPS), which collaborated with the National Commission for Social Action (NACSA) to build the Kono and Kambia district prisons, and rehabilitate the Bo and Bombali district prisons. The Bonthe and Pujehun district prisons were rebuilt with government resources. This means that only about half of the prewar prison facilities are back in use.

However, the postwar problems encountered by the Prison Service have not gone entirely unnoticed by the international community. In 2002 the UN Development Programme (UNDP) conducted an assessment of the Prison Service in Sierra Leone and in May that same year the International Committee of the Red Cross (ICRC) published a report on the health and sanitation situation in Sierra Leonean prisons. These assessments did not lead to any commitment on the part of the international community to provide assistance to this sector. However, the DFID, as the major donor agency supporting law enforcement in Sierra Leone, started discussions with the Prison Service in May 2003 and agreed to begin construction of barracks for prison officers in a number of districts later that year.

Military Reforms

The military also bore responsibility for human rights violations and abuses during the war. Yet international human rights assistance was not extended to the armed forces. Ministry of Defense officials have been quick to point out that the army is being rebuilt mainly to meet its obligation to defend the territorial boundaries of Sierra Leone. The military largely disintegrated at the height of the war and the ministry says it wants to revive the army as an institution. The International Military Assistance Training Team (IMATT), which is overseeing British support to the military, is concerned mainly with recruitment, training, logistical support, and institutional reorganization. Little attention has been paid to the military's human rights obligations, beyond routine training in international humanitarian law or the law of war. UNAMSIL's human rights section in December 2000 ran a ten-day training course in broader human rights for 1,000 army recruits. This type of training does not form a regular part of IMATT's military rebuilding efforts, however.

Assistance for Chiefdom Governance and Native Administration Courts

Since the majority of Sierra Leoneans live in rural areas, chiefdom governance is their usual reference point for justice. The war, which was mainly fought in the countryside, took a heavy toll on chiefdom governance and its native administration courts. Court "barrays" were destroyed, and court staff and chiefs killed or displaced.[17] In those areas that were not controlled by the government, rebel factions and the CDF replaced the established customary justice system with their own administration of justice. At the end of the war, people returned to live in villages and communities that had no structured systems for justice, other than the customary mediation efforts of elders.

In restoring chiefdom governance and native administration courts the key challenges to be addressed were appointing court chairmen, rebuilding court barrays and lockups, and training chiefdom functionaries. Under the government's national recovery strategy, paramount chiefs who had left their chiefdoms as a result of the war were to be returned.

Chiefdom governance has been one of the components of the DFID's support to governance reform since 2001. Support through the Governance Reform Secretariat mainly sought to restore paramount chieftaincy rule in all 149 chiefdoms in Sierra Leone. To this end, consultations were held in all chiefdoms to facilitate interaction between chiefs and their people.[18] Houses were also built for paramount chiefs to enable their return to the chiefdoms. At the end of 2002, sixty-three paramount chief vacancies had been filled through elections funded by the DFID.

The government, for its part, appointed court chairmen for all the chiefdoms. Out of 287 court barrays in the country, the government was able to reconstruct 36 by the end of 2002.[19] The government also had plans to rebuild court barrays in 50 chiefdoms by the end of 2003. Training chiefdom functionaries, a key objective in government efforts to revive chiefdom administration, was not undertaken, however.

During consultations aimed at improving communication between the chiefs and other citizens, issues of accountability and administration of chiefdom courts emerged as a serious concern. As a result, the Governance Reform Secretariat wrote a project proposal for chiefdom courts reform. Although the reform project had yet to be funded in mid-2003, it provided the basis for the DFID to contract a local consultant to look at customary law reform.

Assistance for the NCDHR and Office of the Ombudsman

In 1995 a national democracy commission was established by the NPRC in support of a program to return Sierra Leone to constitutional order. The succeeding civilian government adopted Parliamentary Act no. 3 in 1996, which added human rights to the commission's mandate. A new organization, known as the National Commission for Democracy and Human Rights, was established. The NCDHR undertakes civic education to cultivate democratic citizenship, and also seeks to protect the human rights of all Sierra Leone citizens. It carries out its human rights mandate through popular education and a legal advice service, initiating platforms for civil society discussion of political issues to inform government decisions or policy.

The commission is entirely dependent on meager government funding, and these funds have been used largely for general administration. Although the NCDHR is free to solicit external assistance, it has not had much success in doing so. In 1999 it received small grants from agencies such as World Vision International to run conferences and workshops in connection with the Lomé peace process. The largest amount of international aid has come from the UNDP for a national awareness-raising program.[20] This project was to run for three years, from November 1998, but was abruptly ended by the UNDP in March 2000. The NCDHR has also received a small grant of US$10,000 from the Office of the High Commissioner for Human Rights (OHCHR) for a TRC-related activity.

The 1999 Lomé peace accord provided for the establishment of a national human rights commission as an autonomous quasi-judicial organization, fulfilling a pledge by the parties to uphold and promote human rights. This body was to be established ninety days after the signing of the peace accord,[21] but it was not until early 2003 that the human rights section of UNAMSIL produced the relevant draft legislation for discussion. It is not clear what will happen to the existing NCDHR once the new human rights commission is established.

The Office of the Ombudsman, provided for in the 1991 constitution, was one of the institutions that had been foreseen during Sierra Leone's earlier preparations for multiparty democracy. The escalation of the war, however, prevented its establishment. In 1997, Ombudsman Act no. 2 was passed into law, setting out the mandate and procedural and other operational details of the office. In February 2000, Sierra Leone's first ombudsman was appointed. The ombudsman's functions are to investigate complaints of injustice and human rights abuse brought by members of the public against holders of office in government institutions or statutory authorities.

It was not until 2002 that the office began effective work, after the government had secured the necessary financial support. The ombudsman's office is entirely financed from government funds, although the Chinese embassy donated some office equipment. In 2003 the government provided it with one four-wheel-drive vehicle and an annual budget of US$100,000.

According to the Office of the Ombudsman, the only international assistance it received (until the end of 2003) was funding for attendance at two annual Commonwealth training seminars and at ombudsman conferences in Senegal, Gambia, Seychelles, South Africa, East Timor, and Trinidad and Tobago.

Assistance for Nongovernmental Human Rights Organizations

Local NGOs are now a vital component of the human rights landscape in Sierra Leone. Human rights work on a nongovernmental institutional platform, as noted earlier, was rare or totally lacking before the war. The sector grew dramatically in response to the circumstances of the war and the post-conflict democratic transition. Assistance from abroad has been crucial in shaping and sustaining the work of local human rights NGOs.

In 1996 and 1999, World Vision International, funded by the US Agency for International Development (USAID) under its Transition Initiatives Program, provided one of the earliest opportunities for Sierra Leonean NGOs to engage in human rights work. It gave grants ranging from US$500 to US$10,000 to a number of local civic groups to undertake small and short-term programs addressing the transition challenges of the day. Many organizations, with the help of even the smallest grants, were able to carry out activities such as community-level human rights awareness, monitoring, and documentation, surveys of prison conditions, and training seminars.

Since the signing of the Lomé peace accord, a number of foundations and international organizations have emerged that serve as a resource for local NGOs. Indeed, they are almost the only source of assistance for these local human rights groups. In general, two types of assistance can be distinguished: grants from major, permanent organizations that promote democracy and human rights, and time-limited special funds. In the first category, the biggest providers of direct assistance, in terms of both number and volume of grants, have been the US-based National Endowment for Democracy (NED), the Open Society Initiative for West Africa (OSIWA), and the Canadian Catholic Organization for Development and Peace (D&P). Table 7.1 provides

Table 7.1 International Grants to Sierra Leonean Human Rights NGOs, 2000–2003

Year	Donor Organization	Beneficiary	Budget	Project/Activity
2000	NED	Campaign Against Violation Events (CAVE)	US$20,000	Motivation of young people and strengthening of community values
2000	NED	Campaign for Good Governance (CGG)	US$40,000	Monitoring of human rights
2000	D&P	Network Movement for Justice and Development (NMJD)	US$131,700	Development, education, and socioeconomic justice
2001	NED	Forum for Democratic Initiatives	US$24,800	Civic education
2001	NED	National Forum for Human Rights (NFHR)	US$30,000	Work on human rights and Lomé peace process
2001	OSIWA	NFHR	US$10,000	Education of paramount chiefs and traditional rulers about truth and reconciliation
2001	NED	Center for Democracy and Human Rights (CDHR)	US$20,000	Workshops on electoral systems, voter education, local laws, and child labor
2001	D&P	NMJD	US$131,700	Development, education, and socioeconomic justice
2002	Ford Foundation	Forum of Conscience (FOC)	Unknown	Truth and reconciliation activities
2002	NED	CGG	US$40,000	Human rights education, campaign monitoring, and advocacy

(continues)

Table 7.1 Continued

Year	Donor Organization	Beneficiary	Budget	Project/Activity
2002	NED	Forum for Democratic Initiatives (FORDI)	US$25,000	Production of civic education handbooks on police, constitution, and courts
2002	NED	CAVE	US$20,000	Human rights education and monitoring
2002	NED	NFHR	US$32,000	Human rights education and monitoring
2002	D&P	Civil Society Movement (CSM)	US$87,800	Strengthening of civil society
2002	OSIWA	CGG	Unknown	Purchase of digital cameras, television receivers, tape recorders, and computers
2002	OSIWA	FORDI	Unknown	Civic education activities
2002	OSIWA	NFHR	US$20,000	Small grants for community-based groups
2002	OSIWA	FOC	Unknown	Access to information
2002	OSIWA	Postconflict Reintegration Initiative for Development and Empowerment (PRIDE)	Unknown	Consultations with former combatants on education about the TRC and SCSL
2003	D&P	FORDI	US$26,330	Access to public service for disadvantaged citizens
2003	D&P	NFHR	US$17,550	Monitoring of the TRC and SCSL
2003	NED	FORDI	US$27,000	Schools Democracy and Peace Club project

Source: Various interviews with representatives of donor and recipient organizations, June–September 2003.

an overview of some assistance flows from foreign grant organizations between 2000 and 2003.

The second category of support—the time-limited special funds—has included USAID's Transition Initiatives Program, the US embassy's Democracy and Human Rights Fund, the Canadian Fund for Local Initiatives, and the funds managed by the OHCHR for the Truth and Reconciliation Commission. Grants in this category have averaged between US$500 and US$15,000. These funds have been directed toward short-term objectives or activities.

USAID's Transition Initiatives Program was aimed at restarting civic activism in the period immediately after the war, and for this purpose it gave small grants to various civic groups to undertake programs promoting democracy and human rights. Similarly, the OHCHR has given funds to local organizations to carry out activities related to the work of the truth and reconciliation process. In 2001 it gave a grant to Manifesto 99, to undertake research on traditional methods of reconciliation among the various ethnic groups in the country. The OHCHR also gave US$10,000 to the NFHR to carry out education work on the truth and reconciliation process. The Forum of Conscience (FOC) benefited from a grant of US$15,000 from the Canadian Fund for Local Initiatives, in order to "take human rights education to law-enforcement agencies."[22] In support of the general elections in 2002, the US embassy gave a US$15,000 grant to FORDI to establish a Political Parties Resource Center for the elections. The NFHR also received grant support from the embassy to conduct institution-building workshops for human rights organizations. The Postconflict Reintegration Initiative for Development and Empowerment (PRIDE) received support that same year from the International Center for Transitional Justice (ICTJ) to do research on the views of former combatants on the TRC and Special Court. In 2003, FORDI again received a US$17,000 grant from the US embassy to establish a resource center for artisan organizations and youth groups.

Of the more than thirty organizations claiming involvement in human rights work, the CGG, the NMJD, FORDI, the FOC, the CCSL, and the NFHR have received the most international support. Assistance for core program work has come mainly from the NED and OSIWA. The Center for Democracy and Human Rights (CDHR), in the northern town of Makeni, was the only human rights organization based outside the capital to get a grant (US$20,000 from the NED).

Apart from financial support, local human rights groups have also received international assistance in the form of training. A handful of human rights activists have benefited from, for example, the International Human Rights Law Group's annual Bridge program, the annual human rights training programs of Columbia University and the Canadian Human Rights

Foundation, the meetings of the African Commission on Human and People's Rights, the Transitional Justice Training program of the International Center for Transitional Justice, and Pretoria University's Masters in Law program. UNAMSIL's human rights section conducted a dozen human rights training workshops for local activists by 2004. Human rights activists have also attended a number of relevant international conferences and seminars.

▪ Contributions to Human Rights Protection

The signing of a peace accord represented a first step in Sierra Leone's emergence from an appalling period of atrocities. But much more was required to reengineer and consolidate a comprehensive environment for human rights protection. International assistance has played a pivotal role in the effort to construct a foundation for human rights. Whether in the form of small grants, large-scale funding, training, partnership, or program conceptualization, this assistance has been a lifeline for nonprofit organizations and for state-level institutions engaged in human rights work. The array of human rights organizations now operating in Sierra Leone and the legal processes under way are certainly impressive. With a war crime court, a truth and reconciliation process, a national democracy and human rights commission, and dozens of local NGOs and judicial and police reforms launched, Sierra Leone has employed a full range of activities designed to reshape human rights in a society torn asunder by conflict.

A true measure of the impact of international assistance, however, is the extent to which it has dealt with the past, halted the culture of impunity, addressed problems with access to justice, and left local organizations with a longer-term institutional capacity. The US-based democracy monitoring organization, Freedom House, ranked Sierra Leone as "partly free" in its 2004 *Freedom in the World* report. Central to Freedom House's calculations are issues of political rights and civil liberties. This is certainly impressive for a country that, according to Freedom House, "once had one of Africa's worst human rights records." At the same time, major human rights problems remain.

Indispensability of International Financial Support

International human rights assistance provided valuable financial resources that could never have been generated by the local authorities. Emerging from war with a shattered economy, there was no way that the Sierra Leonean state would have been able to pick up the bill for the institutionalization of human rights. No matter how strongly Sierra Leoneans may have felt about bringing to book those who bore the greatest responsibility for war atrocities, the establishment of the Special Court, costing an estimated

US$58 million, would have been impossible without international assistance. The TRC, at an estimated cost of US$4.5 million, could not have been secured, however much the public yearned to validate their memory of war for the sake of national healing and reconciliation. Rebuilding the police has cost US$22 million. In addition, there have been small grants from foundations given to civic organizations involved in human rights work. Apart from financial aid, Sierra Leone had no possibility of finding indigenous personnel with the necessary professional and technical capacities to confront the country's human rights challenges. Institutions such as the Special Court and TRC, for instance, were directly created by international technical support. International assistance has also provided technical expertise to provide on-site support to the Special Court, TRC, and police.

Timeliness of International Support

The international community responded relatively promptly to challenges as they emerged, including the initial challenge of bringing the appalling human rights situation to the world's attention. As the war ebbed, organizations such as Amnesty International, Human Rights Watch, and others informed the world about the human rights tragedy in Sierra Leone, and called for justice. Immediately after hostilities ended, USAID was quick to help build the capacity of local civic groups to respond through human rights education, monitoring, documentation, and reporting. The study by Physicians for Human Rights in 2001 and the video documentary *Witness,* on rape and sexual enslavement as an instrument of war, are other examples of valuable assistance.

Conveying Legitimacy on Domestic Human Rights Efforts

International assistance has also engendered credibility, dignity, and acceptability for local human rights efforts. In three decades of one-party and military rule, the police had become an instrument of the state and had lost respectability in the eyes of the people. International assistance in rebuilding "decent" police stations, restoring barracks, and providing uniforms and vehicles not only has been a question of addressing policing needs, but also has had the effect of reshaping society's perceptions of the force. It is to this end that practical assistance has been complemented by symbolic steps such as the drafting of a "new statement of vision," a policing charter, and a catchy slogan—"A Force for Good." The appointment of British-born Keith Biddle as inspector-general of police was appreciated by the public not only because of his expertise, but also because he was seen as someone who could bring the necessary credibility to the force.

Similarly, international assistance has granted credibility to civil society groups engaged in human rights work. By sharing platforms with international organizations and personalities to declare their position on human rights issues, local organizations have earned a greater degree of respect and acceptance from the general population. This was particularly needed, given the postconflict climate of factionalism, cynicism, and disillusionment.

Police Reform: Not There Yet

The police force has received the largest proportion of the international assistance given to the three components of law enforcement. Given the level of destruction that the institution suffered, senior officers have cautiously expressed satisfaction with how much the police force has recovered.

In September 2003 the new, Sierra Leonean–born inspector-general completed 100 days in office, providing an opportunity for the public to assess whether the police force had changed for the better. One newspaper, the *Salone Times,* wrote in an editorial on September 19, 2003, that "the legacy of foreign intervention has considerably bolstered efficiency in the police." Police officers themselves have pointed to innovations such as the Family Support Unit (FSU), control of armed robbery, and community policing as proof that real improvements have been made with concrete results.

The effect of international assistance on the police should not be overstated, however. The aid and advice have helped the force to demonstrate its potential, but many critical gaps remain to be filled. Petty corruption, such as taking bribes from commercial vehicle drivers and demanding money to make an arrest or grant bail, still persist at intolerable levels. In one attempt to tackle some of these problems, the inspector-general in June 2003 issued instructions that no officer on road-traffic duty should have more than 1,000 leones (about US50¢) on him. Since its establishment, the Complaints, Discipline, and Internal Investigations Department has received and acted on several complaints of police corruption or abuse of power brought by members of the public. Senior police officers have warned, however, that the force can never achieve the highest ethical and professional standards while there are extremely low wages and poor living conditions.

Although the police force has increased its presence around the country, the police were still short some 3,000 officers in July 2003, well below the personnel target of 9,000 in uniform. Police officers agree that this shortage of manpower undermines the rationale behind expanding the force across the country. Many outposts and stations in remote parts of the country are staffed by only a couple of policemen, making it difficult to operate with speed and efficiency. In addition, the inspector-general has pointed out that the force has a problem with the quality of personnel, declaring that only 4,000 could be called "real policemen."[23] The rest are illiterate or only semiliterate. Moreover, police cells are overcrowded with suspects because of the slowness of the prosecution process.

Increased Justice Capacity, but Problematic Local Access

Justice delivery in prewar Sierra Leone was notoriously compromised under successive one-party and military regimes. At the height of the war the judiciary collapsed to the point that it had relevance only in Freetown. Magistrates' courts and high courts in other parts of the country have been rebuilt thanks to international assistance.

Beyond that, the critical test of the impact of international assistance for the judiciary is the extent to which it has addressed delays in hearings, difficult access to courts, and corruption. In these areas, international assistance has had only a very limited effect. Trials still take an inordinate amount of time. "For such cases as murder, or armed robbery for which bail is not granted easily, suspects have languished in jail for years," said Melron Nicol-Wilson, whose organization, the Lawyers Center for Legal Assistance (LAWCLA), carried out a project on prisoners' access to justice.[24] It is still common for complainants to drop cases because of long delays in their coming to trial. Senior law enforcement officials, including the inspector-general of police in newspaper interviews, and the ombudsman in his 2002 annual report, have bemoaned the persistent problem of delays in completing cases.

The "quality" of verdicts and rulings of the courts also remains troubling. It was a common perception in the past that rulings and verdicts were easily influenced by such considerations as politics, money, or other forms of corruption. If articles in newspapers are an indication of public opinion, then the perception still holds. In an interview, international human rights award-winner and journalist Paul Kamara did not mince words in describing Sierra Leone's judiciary as "the worst in the world, a bastion of injustice and a den of corruption."[25]

The limited effect of international assistance on judicial reform can be attributed to two factors. First, the assistance did not address the personnel problem, particularly the insufficient number of judges and magistrates available to sit on cases. A notable exception to this was the UNDP's training and deployment of "justices of the peace" to sit in magistrates' courts. And in September 2003, the Commonwealth Secretariat provided a judge to handle anticorruption cases. Second, international assistance failed to address questions of corruption, misbehavior, or abuse of office by judicial officials—an issue that is central to citizens' concerns about the courts. No matter how many computers are purchased or court houses renovated, if judges continue to be able to mete out arbitrary, dubious rulings without constraint, nothing is achieved.

Little Attention for the Prison System

As indicated earlier, the prison service has received little international attention. While the government has made a priority of completing improvements to the prisons infrastructure, many critical problems remain unresolved. The institution lacks basic transport facilities. In addition, administrative systems need overhauling to modernize the management of penal institutions. Furthermore, there is a serious lack of trained manpower, as the last time any local officer had overseas training was in 1979.[26] Finally, overcrowding has already emerged as a serious problem. The country's largest prison, the Pademba Road Central prison in Freetown, built in 1914 to accommodate 324 prisoners, held 659 prisoners in May 2003.

The Unattended Challenge of Legal Reform

In three decades of one-party rule and military rule, Sierra Leone has adopted numerous antidemocratic laws. Citizenship laws in the 1961 constitution discriminate against women by not automatically granting citizenship to any offspring of a Sierra Leonean woman and a man of non-African Negroid descent. The Provinces Land Act, which bars certain Sierra Leoneans from acquiring freehold land in the provinces, could also be regarded as undemocratic and reactionary.[27] The Noncitizens Trade Act of 1965 excludes foreigners from retail trade. The Public Order Act, cited earlier, compromises free speech by making libel a criminal offense. Finally, although there are constitutional guarantees of equal rights for men and women, traditional practices and customary law continue to discriminate against women in such areas as divorce, inheritance, and property rights.

Human rights protection cannot be fully realized with these antidemocratic laws still in force. Most of these laws still exist because little attention has been paid to legislative advocacy and legal reform, not only by the Sierra Leonean government but also by the donor community.

Limited Support for State Human Rights Institutions

In addition to law enforcement bodies, other state-level institutions designed for the protection of human rights in Sierra Leone are the National Commission for Democracy and Human Rights, and the Office of the Ombudsman, as described earlier. These two institutions, relying entirely on the government for funding, have unfortunately played an insignificant role in the human rights field.

The NCDHR has no permanent lawyer for the legal aid service it runs in the capital; only a volunteer lawyer, who is available twice a week for advice. In 2000 the NCDHR had to lay off staff and close two regional offices in the south and east of the country, following the termination of the UNDP's awareness-raising project. Between 2001 and 2004 the NCDHR ran no more than three workshops, as and when small grants were available.[28] The commission's work has been restricted to civic education on radio and television, benefiting only people in the capital.

The ombudsman has demonstrated potential as a vital component of the country's human rights network. In its first year of operation, the ombuds-Sman's office handled 570 cases; 430 were successfully investigated and settled.[29] Without the ombudsman many of these cases would have found their way into the courts, with all the delays and cost implications. The speed with which the ombudsman is able to attend to complaints without cost to the complainant represents a major strength in a situation where the judiciary is weak and the majority of the population is poor. However, due to limited resources, the ombudsman's office exists basically as a capital city institution. As a result, citizens in the rest of the country lack access to this important legal mechanism.

Explosive Growth of Human Rights NGOs, but with Mixed Results

The number of civil society–based human rights organizations in Sierra Leone today is quite impressive. Compared to the prewar era, when human rights work was understood only in terms of the on-and-off engagement of volunteer lawyers and journalists, Sierra Leone today can list about forty organizations claiming involvement in human rights work. Many of these are small and based in Freetown or else in local communities. Groups such as the CGG, FORDI, the NMJD, and LAWCLA, however, have acquired national stature in their work.

However, civil society organizations have depended entirely on the international assistance they have received. Activists interviewed around the country were generally unimpressed with the volume of assistance given to local organizations. It is worth noting, for instance, that the grant given by the National Endowment for Democracy to the American Federation of Labor for democracy-promotion work in Sierra Leone in 2000 was US$103,430. This is half of all the grants that the NED gave to local organizations for 2001 and 2002. Moreover, even the little that has been received from international foundations has been devoted to related democracy and peacebuilding activities instead of core human rights work. As a result, the scope of conventional human rights work remained limited.

The number of human rights NGOs that have emerged in Sierra Leone might be regarded as impressive, but the majority of them have not evolved into effective institutions or major organizations. The majority of NGOs lack a coherent mandate, functional boundaries, autonomy, and managerial and programmatic procedures that are understood and followed.[30] Many organizations remain one-person setups or have unclear objectives and are willing to do anything for which funding is available. Most of the organizations we visited lacked clear procedures for financial and administrative management. Donors are aware of this state of affairs, pointing out that there is little financial accountability in many local organizations.[31] But at the same time, donor agencies have taken little action to improve matters.

Limited Reach of Domestic Monitoring Activities

Much of the work undertaken by local organizations is geared to monitoring, reporting, and grassroots education. The impact of these efforts on the human rights situation has been limited, however. Human Rights Watch has been categorical in saying that local groups have done little human rights monitoring over the years. For instance, in their monitoring efforts the majority of local organizations did not operate nationwide but were confined to big towns. Again, until mid-2002 there was no real governmental control over at least one-third of the country, further limiting the reach of indigenous organizations. The thin spread of these groups and their restricted reach meant that the human rights situation across the country was not adequately monitored.

Weaknesses in reporting methods further diminished the effectiveness of the monitoring activities of local organizations. The CCSL's Child Rights Violation Network had a regular newsletter informing the public about child rights issues. The NFHR's annual report and occasional press releases represented another reporting channel. However, other human rights organizations reported their monitoring findings only through periodic reports to donors.[32] It is worth noting that even the Campaign for Good Governance, with the largest monitoring network across the country, issued no report for public consumption. There were therefore no regular channels for disseminating the findings of local human rights monitoring to the broader public. Organizations predominantly followed human rights issues to back up advocacy efforts and shape international policy. However, one could argue that their advocacy role is lost if the sole purpose of monitoring is to report only to donors.

Human Rights Education Useful, but Too Little

The little grassroots education carried out by local organizations has had a positive impact, given that it has been the only source of knowledge about human rights for ordinary citizens unaccustomed to the concept. There is no human rights education in schools, and intermediary international NGOs are paying no attention to popularizing human rights through education. It is local organizations that are providing education about human rights, through radio, posters, handbooks, and community meetings. Grassroots education efforts of local organizations have involved popularizing themes and issues contained in international instruments such as the Universal Declaration of Human Rights, the Convention for the Elimination of All Forms of Discrimination Against Women, and the Convention on the Rights of the Child, as well as the human rights provisions of the Sierra Leonean constitution.

It is difficult to ascertain how many people have been reached by these human rights education efforts. But it is fair to assume that with few people owning radios, illiteracy at 70 percent of the population, and the presence of local organizations limited to towns, the majority of Sierra Leoneans who live in rural areas have not been touched by human rights education. However, urban populations who have benefited from popular human rights education are now able to utilize services such as the police force's Family Support Unit, the Office of the Ombudsman, and legal assistance offered by NGOs.

The Lawyers Center for Legal Assistance, one of the newest human rights organizations in the country, has demonstrated what opportunities there are for effective human rights work beyond monitoring, reporting, and education. Established in 2001, the organization claims that 2,500 individuals sought its legal advice and assistance in the first eighteen months of operating. As a result, LAWCLA opened 800 case files.[33] The majority of cases related to labor issues, sexual offenses, assault, disputes between landlords and tenants, and theft. LAWCLA has also solved cases without recourse to litigation. Its Juvenile Justice Unit, for instance, has addressed matters of child maintenance, neglect, and guardianship through legal correspondence.

LAWCLA, like all other civil society organizations, relies heavily on international assistance to maintain the organization and to run programs. However, it has received no funding for its core—and most effective— human rights work, its pro bono legal aid. Voluntary work by its member lawyers, and resources received for related human rights work, have kept the legal-aid program alive, according to the organization's executive director. In 2002 the organization was contracted by the DFID to undertake a prisoner rights survey. The only grant support it has received has been from the Open Society Initiative for West Africa, for a prisoner rights project. This has enabled LAWCLA to extend its operations to the four regional headquarters towns. The Office of the High Commissioner for Human Rights in 2003 also provided funds to enable the organization to buy furniture for its headquarters office. In addition, LAWCLA has informal partnership arrangements with such organizations as the International Human Rights Law Group, the Greater Boston Legal Services, and UNAMSIL. These contacts have not translated into significant financial or technical assistance, however.

Local Governance Challenges Unaddressed

Donors have paid inadequate attention to reviving judicial services in rural communities. In this respect, nothing has progressed in the chiefdoms beyond the building of court barrays and the filling of vacant paramount chieftaincies. Critical challenges that faced chiefdom governance and native administration courts before the war have remain unaddressed. Court officials are still untrained in basic law and court administration; rules of court procedure remain uneven; customary law has yet to be codified. Moreover, with the old appellate system in place, people in rural areas still find it difficult to appeal against rulings from the native administration courts.[34] Additionally, it has been argued that the election of paramount chiefs for life, in elections not based on universal suffrage, is out of tune with the concept of democracy. As Patrick Zombo, project officer in the Governance Reform Secretariat, said in an interview, "In restoring chiefdom governance the opportunity was not seized [by the international community] to address this debate."[35]

◾ Lessons and Recommendations

The scale and nature of wartime atrocities in Sierra Leone prompted a wide range of responses from a myriad of international actors. Consolidating the fragile peace by restoring government authority throughout the country had the overriding priority in all the efforts by the Sierra Leonean government and the international community. This also determined the level of support given to institutions such as the police, judiciary, prisons, and local government. Due in large part to this assistance, major violations have receded, human rights institutions have been created with substantial resources, education efforts have begun, a network of indigenous organizations has emerged, and law enforcement reforms have been launched. Yet, as this chapter has shown, serious problems have remained unaddressed. If the mixed impact is to be improved, certain things have to change in the future international human rights approach toward Sierra Leone.

Institutionalizing Human Rights Through Domestic Ownership

Until now, international donors have set the agenda and priorities for human rights efforts after the war. The fate of every human rights initiative or process has hinged on the attitude of the international donors, for better or worse. As one local activist told us: "This explains why the Special Court, a one-time institution that will try about two dozen people, will consume

US$58 million while the Office of the Ombudsman, a permanent state-level institution that many more citizens relate with regularly for human rights protection, has not received a thousand dollars from the international community."[36] This view is shared by many people in Sierra Leone.

Agenda-setting in international human rights assistance also had a great bearing on what programs local organizations could pursue. In some instances it entailed the imposition of programs, as many resource-starved local organizations could not afford to decline any aid on offer. Donor agendas were even more binding on state-level institutions, with donors determining training and equipment needs, issues to be addressed, and institutional reforms to be undertaken.

To ensure the protection and institutionalization of respect for human rights in the country itself, it will be crucial to enhance the role of national staff in the public and NGO sector. Donors will need to begin transferring substantial responsibility over to the citizens of Sierra Leone in the human rights field. As part of this transition, local organizations should be chosen as partners of international intermediaries, allowing local staff to learn skills and techniques from their international counterparts. Donors could start this process by making such "twinning" partnerships a condition for aid. In case there are good reasons to work through international intermediary organizations, donor agencies may at least consider twinning these organizations with local NGOs.

Developing a Strategic Framework for Human Rights

Another weakness of international assistance has been the lack of a strategic framework for rebuilding human rights protection in Sierra Leone. Such a framework would mean that government, civil society, and the international community would agree on priorities, objectives, benchmarks, and the sequence of activities. In the absence of an agreed framework, the process of supporting human rights became arbitrary, inconsistent, and chaotic. Every organization did what it wanted to do. There was no purposeful coordination of efforts among organizations, or between organizations and state authorities.

To address this uneven approach, international donors should first conduct an audit on human rights protection. This exercise could identify issues that have been overlooked or addressed haphazardly in past assistance programs, laying the foundation for a more coherent donor strategy. Donors should also bear in mind how prospective projects may reinforce or complement other efforts. Such linkages should play an important role in formulating a strategy for international human rights assistance, preferably based on a multiyear engagement.

A Different Assistance Approach to Institution Building

There has been a dualist approach that promotes institution building for state-level human rights institutions while paying little attention to institution building for civil society organizations. Assistance to the police and judiciary, for instance, has included support for infrastructure, equipment, and personnel training. For NGOs, however, there has been no assistance for building institutional strength in the areas of finance, management, and administration. Support to civil society organizations has focused almost entirely on programs, and international foundations have ruled out support in the form of training or infrastructure and many kinds of equipment. An aid official in a bilateral institution in Freetown put it bluntly, saying that taxpayers in Europe and the United States were more interested in the number of victims served than the number of institutions built.[37]

International assistance can have greater impact if the local organizations through which it is delivered are institutionally strong. International donors therefore should begin to incorporate an institution-building dimension into their support for local human rights work. The emphasis on short-term activities like workshops should be dropped in favor of a minimum set of institution-building initiatives, including financial and organizational management, operational procedures, and administration.

Prioritizing Rural Access to Justice and Confidence-Building Mechanisms

Because the majority of Sierra Leoneans live in the rural areas, any attempts to promote justice delivery and law enforcement for democratic consolidation should prioritize direct support to the native administration courts. In addition to the rebuilding of courthouses, personnel must be quickly restored and trained in basic law, and in administration. Consideration should also be given to streamlining the relationship between the native administration courts and the higher courts. Harmonizing rules of court procedure and codifying customary law should be prioritized in this connection.

However, rebuilding of the judiciary, also at the local level, has to go beyond constitutional guarantees of security of tenure for judges, improved conditions of service, infrastructure rehabilitation, equipment support, and training. There is an additional need to create a national mechanism for checking misbehavior as well as abuse of power and privilege by judges, magistrates, and native courts' staff. An internal unit for the judiciary similar to the police's Complaints, Discipline, and Internal Investigations Department is needed if citizens are to retain trust in the judicial system.

Fostering Real Institutional Change Through Consultation and Benchmark Mechanisms

Human rights institutions that have been reliant entirely on government commitment have not fared well. The government has failed to establish a national human rights commission as provided for in the Lomé peace agreement. The work of the ombudsman and the NCDHR is still confined to Freetown. These facts are illustrative of the government's lack of commitment to institutional change.

Therefore, it is recommended that the government's commitment to institutional change be purposively incorporated into international assistance for human rights activities. One way to go about this could be to set benchmarks of government commitment as conditions for continued assistance to human rights at the state level.

Finally, there should be a mechanism for consultations among donors and consultations between donors and government. In supporting national recovery processes and in the preparation of the 2003 general elections, the international community did have such a mechanism that provided an opportunity to discuss the problems of project duplication, benchmarks to check progress in project implementation, and funding priorities. Future international human rights assistance should adopt a similar consultative process to address remaining problems highlighted in this chapter.

▓ Notes

1. See Richards, *Fighting for the Rain Forest.*
2. Dunn, *West African States;* Koroma, *Agony of a Nation.*
3. In 1978 a woman testified at a commission of inquiry that the wife of a government minister enlisted the help of men to hold her legs apart so that she (the minister's wife) could smear her private parts with pepper. Kandeh, "Ransoming the State."
4. Sesay, "Paradise Lost and Regained?"
5. Ibid.
6. Mahony, *Access to Justice for the Ordinary Citizen in Sierra Leone.*
7. Author interview with Pios Foray, publisher of the newspaper *Tablet* in the 1980s, February 16, 2003.
8. In Sierra Leone, customary law prevails in the countryside, while English common law is upheld in cities and towns.
9. Richards, *Fighting for the Rain Forest,* p. xvi.
10. At a TRC public hearing in Freetown in May 2003, retired brigadier Kelly Conteh said there had been no proper trials.
11. Author interviews with Paul Kamara, Joseph Rahall, and Sallieu Kamara, Freetown, May–June 2003.
12. In its *National Recovery Strategy 2002–2003,* under "Restoration of State Authority," the government set benchmarks for establishing magistrates' courts in

all twelve districts with sitting magistrates and justices of the peace, and for rehabilitating prisons and increasing prison personnel.

13. Some of these details are from author interviews in June and July 2003 with senior police officers and with Ian Stuart of the DFID.

14. Author interview with Francis N. Muhoro, CIVPOL (UNAMSIL) deputy force commander, July 21, 2003.

15. *The 1991 Constitution of Sierra Leone,* sec. 120, pp. 135–140.

16. Details of the DFID's support to the judiciary are drawn from an author interview with Rowland Wright on August 1, 2003, and an interview with Honor Flannigan, deputy director of the British Council, Freetown, on May 21, 2003.

17. "Barray" is the local name for a village courthouse.

18. According to an official of the Governance Reform Secretariat, community quarrels associated with the war meant that external parties had to mediate the return of some chiefs to their chiefdoms.

19. *National Recovery Strategy 2002–2003.*

20. In an author interview, the NCDHR's executive secretary said she believed that the total grant was US$2 million.

21. Article XXV of the peace agreement between the government of Sierra Leone and the Revolutionary United Front of Sierra Leone.

22. Author interview with John Caulker, director of the FOC, October 6, 2003.

23. Interview with inspector-general of police, *Awoko Newspaper,* September 15, 2003.

24. Author interview with Melron Nicol-Wilson, executive director of LAWCLA, June 21, 2003.

25. Author interview with Paul Kamara, September 23, 2003.

26. Author interview with Moses Showers, deputy director of prisons, June 23, 2003.

27. Citizens from the capital city and its environs cannot acquire freehold land in the rest of the country.

28. Author interview with the NCDHR's executive secretary, June 14, 2003.

29. Republic of Sierra Leone, Office of the Ombudsman, *1st Annual Report 2002,* January 1, 2002–December 31, 2002.

30. Diamond, *Developing Democracy.*

31. Author interviews with DFID, EC, and USAID officials, Freetown, June–July 2003.

32. This was confirmed at all four focus-group meetings in July 2003.

33. LAWCLA, *Twenty-one Month Report.*

34. Author interview with Emmanuel Gaima, governance specialist of the UNDP, October 3, 2003.

35. Author interview with Patrick Zombo, October 3, 2003.

36. Author interview with Sheku Lahai, executive director of the NFHR, June 13, 2003.

37. Author interview, June 24, 2003.

8

Transitional Justice in Sierra Leone

Marieke Wierda

In an attempt to address and heal the violent legacy of Sierra Leone's civil war, the international community has assisted in the implementation of two separate transitional justice initiatives. The first is the establishment of the Truth and Reconciliation Commission (TRC) as provided for in the Lomé peace accord, which ended hostilities between the government of Sierra Leone and the Revolutionary United Front (RUF) in 1999. The second is the creation of the Special Court for Sierra Leone (SCSL) by agreement between the United Nations and the government in January 2002. Although it may be too early to evaluate the overall impact of these institutions, this chapter seeks to analyze the role that international actors have played in shaping each institution.

Sierra Leone's difficult history is described elsewhere, including vast economic inequality, consistent political disenfranchisement, and violations of civil and political rights by successive governments. This formed the background to the eruption of war and widespread atrocities that were perpetrated at the hands of all the main fighting factions, including the RUF, the Armed Forces Ruling Council (AFRC), the Civil Defense Forces (CDF), and even the forces of the Economic Community of West African States Cease-Fire Monitoring Group (ECOMOG). Confronted by the consequences of a civil war marked by appalling atrocities, the government and international community chose to implement a multifaceted transitional justice strategy, including both a truth commission and a special court. Both institutions have drawn significantly on international assistance, both in planning and implementation, and in terms of staff, judges, and commissioners. This approach has been heralded as an advance in the field, but has not been without complications. This chapter will seek to explore the origins of the mandates for these two distinct initiatives, including the operations and the main sources of international support; the respective achievements of and challenges faced by these initiatives; and the application of transitional justice in the context of Sierra Leone.

■ The Truth and Reconciliation Commission

Establishment, Mandate, and Operations

The establishment of the Truth and Reconciliation Commission in Sierra Leone was strongly supported by civil society activists as a way to ensure a measure of accountability in a peace agreement that was otherwise favorable to former combatants, particularly the RUF. The Lomé peace accord contained a comprehensive amnesty provision, which granted "absolute and free pardon and reprieve to all combatants and collaborators in respect of anything done by them in pursuit of their objectives, up to the time of the signing of the present Agreement."[1]

In the legislation governing its establishment, the TRC was mandated to "create an impartial historical record of violations and abuses of human rights and international humanitarian law related to the armed conflict in Sierra Leone; . . . to address impunity, to respond to the needs of the victims, to promote healing and reconciliation, and to prevent a repetition of the violations and abuses suffered."[2] Some of its tasks and authorities were similar to those of truth commissions elsewhere, such as the power to conduct investigations both of the violations and the context surrounding them; to carry out a record of statements and testimony, including the ability to take statements in confidence; to hold public hearings (a regular feature of truth commissions since South Africa's); and to produce a report with public recommendations to the government. The commission was afforded discretion to decide whether to name names of perpetrators.[3]

Other notable features of the TRC included provision for a "hybrid" composition, with a slight predominance of national commissioners (four, as opposed to three international commissioners), to ensure what was deemed to be a blend of impartiality and local legitimacy;[4] and provisions for the involvement of traditional leaders in the processes of the commission at the community level,[5] and for "constructive interchanges" between perpetrators and victims.[6] Although the Truth and Reconciliation Act specified that the TRC was to look at events from the outbreak of the conflict in 1991 until the conclusion of the Lomé peace accord in 1999, its mandate also required it to explore "to the fullest degree possible, including their antecedents, the context in which the violations and abuses occurred."[7]

The Truth and Reconciliation Act was adopted by Sierra Leone's parliament in February 2000, not long after the conclusion of the Lomé process. It was envisaged that the passage of the act would give rise to a series of preparatory activities in partnership with the government and civil society that would enable the prompt establishment of the TRC. However, this period was interrupted by a resumption of hostilities in Freetown in May 2000, and only resumed in late March 2001, with the commencement of the process for disarmament, demobilization, and reintegration (DDR).

As a consequence, an interim secretariat was only established in March 2002. The terms of reference for the secretariat included a host of tasks that would have ensured that the TRC, once inaugurated, could launch straight into its activities. However, the interim secretariat soon proved to be plagued with severe mismanagement and administrative difficulties, including the hiring of unqualified staff through recruitment processes that were less than transparent.[8] As a result, many of its activities were left incomplete and the reputation of the TRC suffered during a time when it would have been crucial to cultivate an image both domestically and among donors that it was an institution worth supporting.

Nonetheless, the TRC was formally inaugurated on July 5, 2002. It then launched into a preparatory phase of three months, to be followed by a launch of official operations. The preparatory phase essentially was consumed by many of the tasks that should have been carried out by the interim secretariat. In September 2002 the TRC engaged in a number of public awareness-raising activities, including town-hall meetings in each of Sierra Leone's twelve provinces. The statement-taking process was launched in November 2002. About 7,000 statements were gathered through this process.

This was followed by a period of public hearings, held in both Freetown and each of the provinces, from April until August 2003, encompassing hearings on representative cases, particular events, and thematic and institutional hearings.[9] After the conclusion of the hearings, the TRC launched its report-writing phase, and requested two extensions in order to finish its work. Even then, it went beyond its originally designated time limit of eighteen months before finally handing over an extensive report of five volumes to the government in a ceremony on October 5, 2004.

However, this was not the end of the TRC's difficulties. It soon emerged that the few report copies that were available were riddled with editing errors, and commissioners requested that the reports be returned to run a clean print-run. Although an electronic version had briefly been made available on the Internet, few people in Sierra Leone were able to access it before it was removed after a few days.[10] The unavailability of the report to the wider public generated much disappointment, and a sense that the report was not intended for the "ordinary person" in Sierra Leone but for foreigners and elites. The government responded with a white paper in June 2005, before the TRC report was finally made publicly available in August 2005. The white paper was brief and was considered by many commentators to be substandard, and to demonstrate a lack of serious engagement with the TRC findings and recommendations.

International Assistance to the TRC

International assistance to the TRC came from the UN Development Programme (UNDP), the UN Mission in Sierra Leone (UNAMSIL), foreign governments, and nongovernmental organizations (NGOs). The main international partner for the TRC, particularly in its preparatory and operational phase, was the UN Office of the High Commissioner for Human Rights (OHCHR).

Planning and support functions. The relationship between the OHCHR and the TRC stems from a visit by Mary Robinson, then High Commissioner, to Sierra Leone in June 1999, during which she committed her office to assisting the development of human rights institutions and standards in Sierra Leone. In the months prior to the conclusion of the Lomé process, the OHCHR had organized a working group of human rights organizations, where the concept of a truth commission first emerged. After Lomé, the OHCHR hired two international consultants to travel to Freetown to assess the interest in a truth commission, and to identify what form such a commission might take. The consultants undertook a broad array of consultative meetings, concluding not only that there was strong interest in and support for a truth commission, but also that there were a number of potentially unique elements that could be incorporated. On the basis of their consultations, they produced draft legislation. Several national workshops were hosted by local civil society groups and by the UN Children's Fund (UNICEF) to discuss the proposed terms of reference.

Further activities carried out with the support of the OHCHR assisted with the establishment of the TRC and its planned work. Preparatory funds were made available to local groups for raising public awareness and conducting outreach in the period prior to the actual establishment of the commission. Also, a "mapping exercise" was carried out, which sought to gather testimonies in order to develop an overview of the types, frequency, and patterns of violations. The OHCHR also commissioned research on traditional methods of conflict resolution and reconciliation, and enlisted technical support in devising mechanisms for engaging with children. Finally, the OHCHR encouraged discussions on the relationship between the TRC and the Special Court.

Operational direction and management. More controversial is the role that the OHCHR played in providing operational direction to the TRC once it was established. The TRC was designated as a project of Geneva, and the

OHCHR assumed a significant role in planning the commission's work, as well as an exclusive role in fundraising. This role split core decisionmaking powers between Geneva and the TRC in ways that were detrimental to the commission in its ability to pursue its own initiatives.

The OHCHR did not match its substantial direction of the TRC process with a field presence; neither did it choose to consult closely with potential partners. It was therefore vulnerable to the criticism that its directives were out of touch with realities on the ground. For instance, through a political maneuver before the selection panel, a highly qualified international candidate, an Italian priest who had spent decades working in Makeni and who had the confidence of RUF leadership, was excluded from the commission. This was harmful to the perceived impartiality of the TRC, but the OHCHR, which was supposed to play a decisive role in the selection of international commissioners, did nothing to prevent it. Arrangements to allow international commissioners to spend limited time in-country caused tension with their national colleagues. The result was a distinct lack of solidarity and esprit de corps among commissioners. This continued to plague the TRC throughout its lifespan. The question of how to integrate international representatives as commissioners poses difficulties and policymakers will continue to grapple with it. At the same time, the recruitment of international senior staff by the OHCHR brought a number of qualified experts into the commission who would prove indispensable to its work.

Moreover, the OHCHR's oversight of operations was also problematic. In spite of lacking prior experience in working with truth commissions, the OHCHR exercised considerable control over the workings of the TRC and oversaw all major planning and operations. The OHCHR drafted a detailed one-year operational plan, dividing the work of the commission into three distinct phases: statement-taking, public hearings, and report-writing. Each of these phases was allocated four months. Research and investigations were scheduled to operate throughout the statement-taking and public hearings phase, as were units on reconciliation and protection, media and public education, and the legal unit (which was combined with reconciliation and protection).

The reason given for this unusual and rigid approach was mainly budgetary. It would enable the TRC to retain a flexible staff structure, in which staff with certain skills, such as statement-takers, would only be retained for the time required by the particular phase. In practice, the rigidity of the work plan meant that each phase became a "going through the motions" exercise, where the emphasis at any given time was on the successful completion of the phase in question. Instead, a more integrated and strategic approach should have been designed to enable the TRC to fulfill its mandate in the best manner. This approach also did little to develop capacities of national staff beyond the narrow functions in which they were employed;

tasks were compartmentalized and segregated, detracting from the ability of staff to be vested in the process as a whole. Finally, this approach did not allow for a thorough and ongoing analysis. The research and investigations functions of the commission were underemphasized. While statement-taking or public hearings were under way, researchers were asked to help with the preparation of hearings.[11] The result of this was that much of the analysis of materials gathered by the commission was delayed until the report-writing phase, exceeding the scheduled deadline and by which time many staff were fatigued and demoralized from continuous work.

Much of the operational planning of the TRC reflected efforts to remain within budget. An original budget had been drafted by the OHCHR in February 2002 for roughly US$10 million, not an excessive figure for truth commissions. But both the OHCHR and donors (mostly governments) expressed pessimism that this amount could be raised. The budget was therefore revised downward by the TRC to US$6.6 million in July 2002. However, in the meantime donors had witnessed some of the difficulties under the interim secretariat, and when the OHCHR finally launched its funding appeal in August 2002, financial assistance was trickling in at a slow pace. This effectively left the TRC without a budget for its operations in the first few months, during its outreach activities in the provinces. Staff volunteered to accompany the commission during this time, as one of many examples of their level of dedication.[12]

The role played by Geneva in funding effectively meant that commissioners chose not to assume any responsibility for raising funds. This deprived the TRC and donors from bilateral contact essential for building trust and enthusiasm for the endeavor. Conversely, the indirect link between donors and the commission led to a more distant relationship in which funding failed to flow freely. Problems with funding continued to hamper the TRC throughout its work. The eventual budget of the TRC was probably around $4.5 million, though financial information on the commission was not readily available. Major donors included the United States, the United Kingdom, and the European Union (all contributing between US$500,000 and US$1 million), as well as Denmark, Norway, and Sweden.[13] The Sierra Leonean government made an in-kind donation of premises. As a result of the tenuous funding situation, staff levels were kept at a minimum, and staff members were continuously overstretched. A haphazard approach to extending the TRC's tenure also led to poor planning, overworked personnel, and persistent uncertainty about employment and salaries that damaged morale.

The UNDP had been designated to control the financial oversight of the TRC. This arrangement was designed to allow the commission to avoid replicating a department of its own for finance and to augment donor confidence. Nonetheless, donors retained an ambivalence with regard to the commission. Some have suggested that this was because the funding contributed to the TRC came into direct competition with that pledged to the Special Court, and that the latter diminished the enthusiasm of donor governments to contribute to the TRC.[14] It is difficult to gauge whether this supposed rivalry for funding played a role or not. The indirect relationship between the TRC and the international community, the lack of tools to cultivate that relationship, and the absence of an outreach strategy by the commission all contributed to a certain reluctance and ambivalence among donors. There also were some allegations of mismanagement of funds. An external audit was suggested but never took place, and the suspicion of mismanagement, although unverified, lingered.

Networking and partnerships. The United Nations and various NGOs collaborated with the TRC in some areas, though potentially useful partnerships were not fully explored or exploited. At the height of its operations, the local peacekeeping mission, UNAMSIL, had twenty staff members working in its human rights section. Although UNAMSIL might therefore have been considered a natural partner to the TRC, this role was resisted by the OHCHR, and the role of UNAMSIL during the actual operations of the TRC remained limited to closely monitoring the commission's proceedings and providing some forms of expertise.[15] Some have subsequently commented that with the resources available to UNAMSIL, a closer collaboration would have helped the TRC.[16]

A limited but otherwise more successful partnership was the TRC's joint project with the UNDP to support the formation of district reconciliation commissions. This project was designed to foster informal reconciliation activities at the community level, training officers to run and oversee reconciliation activities.[17]

International NGOs also partnered with the TRC, and concentrated on the following:

1. Training for commissioners and staff, because no such program had been organized by the OHCHR.[18]
2. Providing policy advice in technical areas, such as the relationship with the Special Court.
3. Enabling interactions between local NGOs and the TRC.
4. Promoting specialist consultancies to the TRC. Consultancies funded by the International Center for Transitional Justice (ICTJ) included advice on the database of violations (with the American Association for the Advancement of Science [AAAS]), psychological aspects of the violence (with Handicap International), analysis of the reparations issue, assistance on the relationship with former combatants (with Postconflict Reintegration Initiative for Development and

Empowerment [PRIDE]), and a campaign to solicit creative contributions on a vision for the future of Sierra Leone (the National Vision Project).

5. Producing a video version of the final report (by WITNESS), and a children's version (by UNICEF).

Relationships between the TRC and the NGO community fluctuated and were often complicated. As mentioned, many local NGOs were originally supportive of the concept of a truth commission at the outset and contributed actively to an information campaign. But by the time the TRC was established, many were skeptical that it would happen at all or had moved to implement other programs. Funding for outreach activities had run out. The TRC maintained an arm's-length relationship with NGOs, but did little to explore indirect means of engagement. As a result, NGO interest in the commission waned to an unfortunate extent and resulted in missed opportunities to mobilize advocacy on human rights issues. Also, international assistance to the TRC process was not closely evaluated or reexamined during the course of the process. Instead, international NGOs concentrated largely on propping up the TRC process with ancillary specialist consultancies. This may have prevented the emergence of new strategies external to the commission that could have assisted its work.

Assessment of the TRC

It may be too early to evaluate the legacy of the TRC. Individual phases of the commission's work enjoyed a certain measure of success, including the statement-taking process and the provincial hearings. However, the TRC failed to make an impact on national public debate on a scale equal to similar institutions in South Africa, Guatemala, or Peru.

Lack of public engagement. There was a general lack of momentum and public engagement with the TRC's work, which exhibited itself in low numbers of people attending the hearings in Freetown (although attendance in the provincial hearings was far better). Even victim testimony on occasion seemed uninvolved and stunted. A number of commentators have speculated on the reasons why the public did not engage more with the TRC. One factor may have been the great divide between a largely illiterate and rural-based population and policymakers (governmental and nongovernmental) in Freetown. Also, the lack of adequate information about the TRC, or confusion between the TRC and the Special Court, aggravated this situation. The TRC, for example, never established a permanent regional presence. Some commentators also cite cultural habits or traditions for the lack of interest, arguing that the TRC's approach to truth-telling as a way to bring healing failed to resonate, because it was not in keeping with local customary practices in dealing with the past.[19] Certainly these customary practices probably were not sufficiently explored prior to the establishment of the TRC.

Reintegration conducted without coordination with the TRC. Due to the numerous delays that plagued the TRC, reintegration of former combatants through disarmament, demobilization, and reintegration, as well as informal processes, was already substantially complete when the TRC started its work. In a study by PRIDE, an NGO based in Freetown, former combatants had expressed hope that the TRC would assist them with reintegration.[20] The disconnect between the operations of the TRC and the DDR process or informal forms of reintegration meant that there were few obvious incentives for former combatants to engage with the commission (since they already benefited from a comprehensive amnesty). Some were probably fearful that their testimony might be shared with the Special Court. Many citizens refer to the continued presence of perpetrators in their communities.[21] These perpetrators will not be processed by the TRC or the Special Court, and have been reintegrated into local communities without consideration of their past crimes.

Insufficient political support from the government. The relationship between the TRC and the government was problematic. The government was outwardly supportive of the TRC process, but in practice it remained unresponsive particularly to requests for information. A number of senior government officials failed to show up to testify, and although the president did, he refused to accept responsibility for any aspect of the war, including the actions of the CDF. The white paper that was finally produced and presented as the government's official response, according to many, demonstrated a lack of serious engagement with the TRC's findings and recommendations.

Perceived lack of independence. Even though the government maintained a distance from the TRC's operations, the commission still had trouble shaking a perception that it lacked political independence. On a much publicized occasion, the chairman of the TRC supported the country's president in his refusal to apologize. The perceived lack of independence may have had a chilling effect, particularly as public trust in the government is still weak in much of the country given the state's inability to deliver basic social services in the aftermath of the conflict.

Relationship with the Special Court. Much of the debate prior to the establishment of the TRC and the Special Court focused on whether the TRC should be compelled to disclose information taken in confidence to the Special Court and if so, in what circumstances. This debate prompted several position papers by major NGOs and dominated the convening of an expert group discussion at the UN.[22] Moreover, this debate triggered strong public opinions and received so much attention because it had an ideological dimension, and because supporters of the TRC feared that such authority could fatally undermine the whole reconciliation process. Supporters of the Special Court tended to put the emphasis on its legal status and the supremacy of international over domestic law.[23] In practice, the scope for conflict on this issue was greatly reduced by a commitment from the prosecutor early on that he would not seek information from the TRC, and a memorandum of understanding was never concluded.

However, public confusion about the respective roles of the two institutions remained, as did competition between the respective advocates of each institution internationally and domestically. The situation deteriorated when the TRC requested access to persons held in detention of the Special Court, particularly Chief Hinga Norman. The TRC first asked for a confidential interview session, and later requested access with the view to holding a public hearing.[24] This gave rise to extensive negotiations between the two institutions, followed by litigation before the judges of the Special Court. The Special Court denied the request for a public hearing, although it left the TRC with the option to conduct controlled interviews, which was not pursued. The TRC therefore was not able to interview certain key stakeholders, although this probably would not have changed any of its main findings. Opinions will probably vary for some time to come on the inherent compatibility of these processes, but both carried out the main tasks at hand without fatally undermining the other.

* * *

The TRC's final report may end up defining an important legacy. The commission's broad interpretation of its mandate enabled it to produce a report that tackles many of the most pertinent issues relevant to Sierra Leone. It rejected a commonly held view that the war was a fight over diamonds, and goes beyond the actual perpetration of violations to identify causes for the conflict. Among the causes, the report cites Sierra Leone's history of abuse of civil and political rights (such as arbitrary detentions and unfair trials and executions); corruption and misuse of public assets, including the country's wealth of natural resources; the lack of political accountability and the collapse of state institutions; the alienation of youth and women from political processes; absence of the rule of law; and other fundamental flaws in governance. The report is robust in assigning responsibility for these failures in governance as well as for wartime atrocities.[25] The TRC made detailed recommendations as to how to remedy some of these issues and included a proposal for a reparations program for victims. The TRC's report will usefully serve as a yardstick against which future progress can be measured. Although the white paper has not been encouraging, civil society, in a domestic and international collaboration, is continuing to mount pressure for implementation, especially of the imperative recommendations.[26]

The Special Court for Sierra Leone

Establishment, Mandate, and Operations

The request to the United Nations for assistance in establishing the Special Court for Sierra Leone constituted a significant shift in government policy after the Lomé Accord. A number of intervening events brought about this dramatic reversal. The RUF had violated the cessation of hostilities agreed to at Lomé, and had perpetrated further attacks, including the killing of demonstrators at Foday Sankoh's house in May 2000, and the hostage-taking of hundreds of UN peacekeepers by the AFRC's infamous "West Side Boys." The war now threatened to involve Guinea, alerting the UN to a renewed threat to international peace and security. These events triggered a military intervention by the United Kingdom, defeating the West Side Boys and finally bringing a permanent peace.

It was during this time, in October 2000, that President Ahmed Tejan Kabbah invited the United Nations to assist Sierra Leone in the establishment of the Special Court, originally intended to try the RUF. The UN accepted,[27] passing Resolution 1315, and commencing the process of negotiating an agreement with the government, appending a statute to regulate the jurisdiction and proceedings of the Special Court. However, the UN Security Council and the UN Secretariat took strongly opposing views on how this should be done. UN member states were keenly aware that previously established international tribunals, one for the former Yugoslavia and one for Rwanda, had become a financial drain on UN resources.

- The UN Secretariat supported assessed funding, arguing that voluntary contributions would be dangerously uncertain, while the Security Council insisted the opposite.
- The UN Secretariat argued in favor of granting the Special Court Chapter VII enforcement powers while the Security Council opposed this.
- The UN Secretariat wanted personal jurisdiction to include "those most responsible," as opposed to the narrower jurisdiction proposed by the Security Council, over "those who bear the greatest responsibility."

Eventually it was agreed that the SCSL be established by treaty rather than by resolution, so that it could proceed without committing UN members to funding it. The Special Court would function independently of the

UN bureaucracy, would be subjected to the oversight of a "management committee," and would be required to raise its own funds rather than work off assessed contributions. With this financial compromise, the SCSL's operation was significantly scaled down, and the Security Council subsequently prevailed on each of the above points of disagreement.[28] Discussions on the Special Court's statute were largely to the exclusion of Sierra Leonean actors other than the government. This has led to a perception, which remains, that the Special Court is more of an international than a domestic institution.

The SCSL has several unique features:

1. It is the first international tribunal since Nuremberg to sit in the country where the crimes occurred.
2. Since it was established by an agreement with the UN, rather than through a Security Council resolution (unlike the International Criminal Tribunal for the Former Yugoslavia [ICTY] and the International Criminal Tribunal for Rwanda [ICTR]), the Special Court lacks the Security Council's Chapter VII enforcement powers, which could be used to oblige states other than Sierra Leone to grant cooperation.
3. It has a mixed composition, with a predominance of international judges (there are currently nine judges from outside Sierra Leone and two from Sierra Leone, and both the prosecutor and the registrar of the Special Court are internationals). Currently, 57.5 percent of the Special Court's staff are Sierra Leonean and 65.4 percent are from outside the country. Many of the Special Court's senior positions continue to be filled by foreigners.[29]
4. The crimes enumerated in the Special Court's statute are a blend of international and domestic provisions, although the indictments focus on international crimes (war crimes and crimes against humanity).
5. The Special Court has a limited temporal jurisdiction, starting from November 1996, five years after the war began in the provinces of Sierra Leone, but including much of the violence that affected Freetown.[30] The reasoning given for this limitation was mainly that it would be more expensive and more difficult in evidentiary terms to look at crimes that occurred earlier in the war. However, this approach presents a public relations challenge for the Special Court, playing into existing divisions and rivalries between the capital Freetown and the provinces.

Three months after the signing of the agreement establishing the SCSL in January 2002, the Secretary-General appointed Robin Vincent from the

United Kingdom as registrar and David Crane of the United States as prosecutor. The prosecutor and registrar arrived in Freetown in late summer and began setting up offices. The Special Court would require an entire site of its own to be built and construction quickly started. On July 26 the Secretary-General announced the appointments for the three trial and five appellate judges, three of whom were appointed by the government of Sierra Leone.

The prosecutor deployed quickly and started working toward the production of the SCSL's first indictments, which were issued on March 10, 2003, some nine months after the Special Court had begun operations. In a quick operation, the Special Court was able to arrest five indictees, including the then–minister of interior, Sam Hinga Norman, alleged head of the CDF. Foday Sankoh, former leader of the RUF, was already in custody, and two other accused, Sam Bockarie from the RUF and Johnny Paul Koroma from the AFRC, were missing and presumed to have escaped to Liberia. Three other accused were arrested on a subsequent date. However, during that time the SCSL had not yet fully finished its building site and it was still lacking a permanent detention center.

Among the indictments was a sealed file that only became public when Charles Taylor, president of Liberia, chose to attend the Liberian peace talks held in Accra on June 4, 2003. Instead of arresting him, the Ghanaian authorities assisted Taylor in his expedited return to Liberia, and the SCSL was criticized by some international policymakers for disrupting the peace talks and potentially delaying a peaceful solution to the conflict in Liberia. That issue subsequently became moot when Taylor accepted asylum in Nigeria on August 11, 2003, under the condition that he was to leave Liberian politics forever.

The period following the indictments was consumed with finishing the building of the SCSL, organizing its innovative defense office, and allowing defense teams to commence their own investigations and file preliminary motions to challenge the jurisdiction of the Special Court. Upon a motion for joining the various indictments, the trial chamber decided that there should be three trials: for the RUF, the CDF, and the AFRC. Trials finally began on June 3, 2004. The Special Court had requested a second trial chamber in March 2004, to enable it to finish its work within the three-year period, but there were extensive delays in the recruitment of new judges by the UN Secretariat, and the second trial chamber was only sworn in a year later, in March 2005.

International Assistance to the Special Court

The Special Court for Sierra Leone mainly derives its support from individual states and from the United Nations. Table 8.1 lists the main donors.

Table 8.1 Main Donors to the Special Court for Sierra Leone

Donor	Year 1 Contributions (2002–2003, US$)	Year 2 Contributions (2003–2004, US$)	Year 3 Contributions (2004–2005, US$)
United States	5,000,000.00	10,000,000.00	7,000,000.00
Netherlands	3,994,173.46	5,255,682.60	5,347,316.87
United Kingdom	3,609,300.00	3,556,000.00	3,556,000.00
Canada	654,063.95	696,880.12	766,239.62
Denmark	237,792.34	145,074.71	674,465.59
Sweden	337,448.99	491,979.99	671,456.39
Ireland	112,030.00	250,951.04	604,968.97
Germany	500,000.00	584,854.00	—
Norway	500,000.00	499,970.00	—
Finland	297,332.97	320,000.00	—
Japan	500,000.00	—	—

Source: Special Court for Sierra Leone.
Note: Other donors, for smaller amounts, include Australia, Belgium, Chile, Cyprus, the Czech Republic, Greece, Israel, Italy, Lesotho, Liechtenstein, Malaysia, Mali, Mauritius, Mexico, Nigeria, Oman, the Philippines, Senegal, Singapore, South Africa, and Spain.

Planning and oversight. The SCSL represented an exception in UN practice, as the Security Council decided to fund the Special Court through voluntary contributions, a decision that the Secretary-General opposed on the grounds of viability. However, this approach left open the question of what would take the place of the UN Secretariat for the administration of the contributions. This led to the establishment of the management committee. The formation of the committee was proposed by the legal counsel of a "Group of Interested States," an informal gathering of states that were contributors to the Special Court (in funds or in kind).

The management committee was to fulfill several functions, including assisting the Secretary-General in fundraising for the SCSL, providing advice and policy direction on all nonjudicial aspects of the Special Court's operations, and overseeing the Special Court's annual budget and other financially related reports. It was also meant to rally political support for the SCSL. The management committee was originally meant to be composed of "important contributors," including the United States, the United Kingdom, Canada, and the Netherlands, but this was interpreted broadly so as also to allow for the participation of Lesotho and Nigeria and the government of Sierra Leone itself (which had not previously been included), as well as the UN Secretariat.

The flexibility to operate without cumbersome UN bureaucracy and regulations has allowed the SCSL to operate with greater efficiency upon its launch. On the other hand, the departure from ordinary rules and regulations created difficulties among those attempting to work under the new structure.

Disputes caused several months of delay in the startup phase of the Special Court. Second, there was disagreement about the composition of the management committee (and the Group of Interested States). Most of the members attending on a regular basis had legal but no financial or administrative training. Also, many were mid-ranking diplomats with insufficient political weight to rally support for the Special Court. As a result, the management committee increasingly became a mere oversight mechanism, unable to rally necessary support.

In early 2004, after the SCSL had borrowed against pledges for its third year of operations to complete its second year of work, the situation became critical.[31] This was not because the Special Court had not kept within budget but rather because voluntary contributions had been insufficient and even pledges had not matched the budget. It took a warning in late 2003 by the registrar as to the grave financial situation of the SCSL, resulting in an intervention and meeting between the Secretary-General and permanent representatives of the UN, to secure a "subvention grant" from assessed contributions to allow the Special Court to finance its third year of operations. In mid-2005 the Special Court had only received $54.9 million of the $104 million needed for four years of operations, with no assurances of funds beyond the end of 2005.[32]

Operational assistance, including logistics and security. Another consequence of the SCSL operating on the fringes of the UN family meant that it could not be assured of cooperation from UNAMSIL, then the largest peacekeeping force in the world, with 16,000 troops and over 1,000 civilians. During the planning mission in January 2002, Special Court officials were assured that UNAMSIL assistance was forthcoming, provided UNAMSIL was mandated by the Security Council to do so. This led the Special Court to frame its proposed first-year budget and work plan with substantial reliance on UNAMSIL, particularly in areas such as human resources, finance, and procurement.

The Security Council adopted Resolution 1400 in March 2002, which stated that the Security Council "endorses UNAMSIL's providing, *without prejudice to its capabilities to perform its specified mandate,* administrative and related support to the Special Court on a cost-reimbursable basis."[33] However, this text left room for interpretation, thus allowing the UNAMSIL leadership to adopt the position that the SCSL posed a potential threat to Sierra Leone's fragile peace process, so that giving it assistance would be contrary to the mandate of UNAMSIL. The result of this was that the Special Court lost months and millions of dollars in having to replicate existing structures in UNAMSIL.

However, with time and due to the express support of the Secretary-General for the SCSL, the relationship between UNAMSIL and the Special

Court improved. A notable exception from the outset had been UNAMSIL's force commander, who gave a great deal of crucial logistical support to the SCSL during the investigative stages of its work. Likewise, the British inspector-general of police gave valuable assistance in the form of seconded policemen. The Special Court was heavily reliant on UNAMSIL security and logistical support, and had to negotiate a new arrangement for a small UN military unit to remain when UNAMSIL's mandate finished in late 2005.

Training needs and technical assistance. The SCSL has enjoyed close relations with a number of international NGOs. These are some of the areas in which international NGOs have been active apart from the obvious areas of advocacy and monitoring:

- *Technical assistance to the government.* No Peace Without Justice, an NGO with offices in Europe and the United States, was active in assisting the government throughout the negotiating process, and also in granting it technical assistance for drafting the implementing legislation. An Argentine forensic team provided assistance in exhumations. Many NGOs also advised on the relationship between the TRC and the Special Court.
- *Outreach.* No Peace Without Justice also organized a series of other activities, such as training on the rules of procedure with the local legal community, the compilation of a resource center, and the development of outreach materials. Other groups also produced outreach material.
- *Conflict mapping.* No Peace Without Justice undertook an extensive research exercise to map command structures of the main warring factions, providing much useful information to the Special Court.
- *Seminars for judges and the local media.* The ICTJ also organized, in partnership with the University of California–Berkeley's Human Rights Center and War Crimes Studies Center, training for judges of the Special Court and for local journalists covering it. More recently, some crucial seminars on gender were offered by the Women's Coalition for Gender Justice.

Networking and partnerships. International NGO attention to the SCSL has exceeded that to the TRC, but still cannot be described as sustained, because all of the relevant organizations lack a permanent field presence in Sierra Leone. Moreover, rather than working in an alliance and trying to combine efforts, international NGOs have often operated in a disjointed way and in a slightly competitive manner. Efforts to build the capacity of local NGOs in respect to the Special Court have been limited. The nongovernmental organization No Peace Without Justice engaged in early efforts to build a coalition around the Special Court. The ICTJ has invested in building a project for national monitors that produces a newsletter and radio commentary on the trials. The Special Court itself hosts a monthly interactive forum to receive feedback from NGOs.

Another example of networking from which the SCSL has benefited has been the Intertribunal Cooperation Project. The prosecutors and registrars of the International Criminal Tribunal for the Former Yugoslavia, the International Criminal Tribunal for Rwanda, the International Criminal Court, and the SCSL meet regularly to share experiences and explore cooperation. At a recent meeting the group decided to prepare a manual for best practice.

Assessment of the Special Court

As for the impact of the SCSL, it is too early to reach a conclusion, with trials still under way. To have come this far the Special Court has overcome considerable challenges, both logistical and political, to advance the basic elements of its mandate. Activists in Sierra Leone have praised the Special Court for raising awareness of human rights, crimes against children, and the suffering of women due to rape, forced marriage, and other abuses. It will clearly serve as a useful example for future tribunals, both for its successes and for its shortcomings.

However, the SCSL, more so than the TRC, has two different audiences to satisfy: the affected population, and the international policymakers who helped to create it and view it as a potential model to replicate elsewhere. Meeting both sets of expectations inevitably leads to tensions. On the one hand, the support it receives from the international community is entirely contingent on performance, including mainly efficiency and the conclusion of work within a limited time frame. On the other hand, support from the Sierra Leonean public is contingent on the Special Court demonstrating that it is responsive to their needs and that it will be an institution with an impact that goes beyond the trials of a few individuals.

A conference on victims' issues organized by the SCSL in March 2005 shed light on local expectations of the Special Court. In a country where many of the national institutions are dysfunctional and inaccessible, the SCSL has to some extent become a lightning rod for expectations from the international community, in much the same way as the TRC became a venue for voicing expectations and frustrations vis-à-vis the government. Although the importance of putting prominent individuals on trial for war crimes and crimes against humanity should not be underestimated, many Sierra Leoneans still question why the Special Court's jurisdiction is so limited, when many mid-level perpetrators continue to roam free in their communities.[34] This is particularly because four of the most high-profile indictees, Charles Taylor, Foday Sankoh, Sam Bockarie, and Johnny Paul

Koroma, have all eluded the SCSL, and this has raised questions as to whether the Special Court is still able to fulfill its mission. On the other hand, the indictee left in custody with the highest profile (Sam Hinga Norman) is also one of the most popular public figures in the country.

While effective and targeted outreach by the SCSL has assisted in managing some of these expectations, others are difficult to manage by means of information alone. For instance, the Special Court has received numerous informal requests to explore some kind of reparations or to concretely assist the situation in particular villages by rebuilding schools, roads, or clinics. For observers who have watched the construction of the SCSL from the ground up on a deserted plot of land in the middle of Freetown, within a matter of months, the Special Court has become a tangible symbol for what the international community is able to do when the will is there. In the meantime, so much remains to be done in terms of reconstruction in Sierra Leone. Ironically, the Special Court may serve as a reminder of the inactivity of government and the international community in this regard. Activists and experts in Sierra Leone are also concerned that the Special Court will fail to leave a tangible, meaningful legacy, especially outside the capital.[35]

Within Sierra Leone, there is a real question, largely outside the control of the SCSL, about its relevance in an environment where there continues to be enormous deprivation of basic rights, including particularly social and economic rights, and where the national legal system has made no significant progress toward recovery since the end of the conflict.[36] Perhaps it is this factor that has kept overall attendance in the public gallery low. Moreover, with its predominance of international representatives in representative positions, the Special Court is still in danger of being perceived as an international, foreign institution that mainly benefits the internationals who work there and that will quickly fade away. This perception is aggravated by the fact that the government has placed international representatives in positions that could have been occupied by prominent Sierra Leonean lawyers and jurists. The "face" of the SCSL is therefore invariably international. This perception of the transient nature of the Special Court, sometimes referred to as the "space ship phenomenon," may harm its ability to have long-term impact on restoring trust in the rule of law, in that it may be seen as an anomaly that is unlikely to be repeated.

On the other hand, at the international level, policymakers are more likely to judge the SCSL by its ability to finish trials promptly. Although the Special Court will not have concluded its work in the three years originally anticipated, it may manage to try all its cases in the first instance by mid-2006.[37] It will have cost less over that time period than the International Criminal Tribunal for the Former Yugoslavia currently costs in a single year. The trials at the SCSL to date are not necessarily being concluded much faster than at the ICTY, but the prosecutorial strategy has been more focused, with a net result of allowing an earlier and more deliberate completion strategy. Also, the trials are generally perceived as meeting international standards in spite of the lower costs. This in itself is likely to be heralded as a success by the international community. However, evaluation criteria on the international level have shifted. For instance, while originally there was resistance to the concept of "legacy" among donors, and an emphasis on pursuing the "core mandate" of the SCSL rather than what were perceived as ancillary activities, the Special Court is sometimes criticized for its inability to have an impact on the domestic legal system or for usurping more funds than are available to that system. On the other hand, this criticism neglects the value that the "demonstration effect" of the Special Court may have had on domestic rule of law actors, particularly in its treatment of witnesses and terms of allowing for a full and adequate defense.

Other reflections on the SCSL model from the international perspective include the fact that the Special Court remained quite isolated both from the UN system and from regional organizations, and has had to fight its own political battles with insufficient backup and funding support from those that created it. For instance, it has lacked an adequate political (and legal) framework to resort to for securing cooperation from states other than Sierra Leone, particularly in its pursuit of Charles Taylor. Also, the Special Court lacks negotiating power on issues such as enforcement of sentences and witness relocation. Many of the problems that have arisen reflect the challenges that arise when operating outside the UN structure. But this has to be weighed against the gains made in efficiency from allowing the SCSL to operate outside of UN regulations particularly on recruitment. Therefore, future tribunals and courts will need to examine the Special Court's experience and try to anticipate the problems it has encountered.

■ Lessons and Recommendations

Although it is too early to pronounce a verdict on the Truth and Reconciliation Commission and the Special Court for Sierra Leone, a few observations can be made.

Lack of Coordination of Different Policies

Sierra Leone has suffered from a lack of coordination in its strategy to address injustice and crimes committed during the war. Several issue have arisen. First, postconflict stability and justice have often been presented as conflicting rather than complementary policy goals. Second, at the time the TRC became operational, informal reintegration of combatants had already taken place in many communities. As a result, the TRC had to combat the perception that the government is doing more to provide for former combatants than for victims, a sentiment that was expressed by the Amputee Association during the work of the TRC but that continues in its aftermath. Third, the rapid growth and operations of the SCSL stand in sharp contrast to the lack of progress in rebuilding domestic legal institutions, a much more onerous task. Fourth, there were some contradictions that arose in the simultaneous pursuit of criminal justice along with a TRC. Due to the numerous political actors active in this realm it is difficult to envisage a forum in which these conflicts could be addressed. For instance, there was no obvious independent platform to resolve the earlier dispute between the Special Court and the TRC on public hearings.

Importance of Domestic Ownership in Designing Policies and Projects

The experience of establishing the SCSL shows the importance of consultation and identifying local interlocutors among the legal profession and civil society at the formative stages, rather than engaging exclusively with government officials. This would have increased the sense of ownership among Sierra Leone's population and would have possibly resulted in a more positive relationship with the local legal community. In contrast, the drafting of the Truth and Reconciliation Act was a more successful collaboration between international and national actors, which has since been replicated in Liberia. Also, international assistance to the TRC that amounted to support of well-defined preparatory projects tended to be effective. It may be assumed that this is because such projects left ownership and decisionmaking in the hands of local organizations.

Impact on Sierra Leone's Legal Framework

Both institutions, the TRC and the SCSL, carry the potential for impacting the reshaping of the country's legal framework. The TRC, for instance, has suggested immediate changes to domestic laws, including abolishing the death penalty and laws allowing for "safe custody detention" and the declaration of public emergencies. It has also suggested a wide variety of other measures to tackle some of Sierra Leone's most immediate problems of corruption and abuse of political power, discrimination against women, and disaffection of youth, as well as implementing a program on reparations.[38] Under the Truth and Reconciliation Act, the government is legally bound to implement these recommendations under the observation of a follow-up committee.

As for the contribution of the SCSL, its direct effect on Sierra Leone's legal framework is likely to remain limited as it operates outside the domestic framework. Nonetheless, it may serve as a model for aspects of the criminal justice system, with its detention unit, witness protection program, and defense counsel unit. Also, the Special Court's jurisprudence is bound to have influence, particularly in its treatment of crimes against women. Its presence may also have spurred the commitment of additional resources to legal reform efforts, in terms of drafting revised laws on criminal procedures and gender issues. But the extent of any of these contributions over time remains to be seen.

Another concern is the continued absence of collaboration and exchange between the government and civil society representatives. Many opportunities for local civil society organizations to develop and learn from the TRC and the SCSL projects have been missed. International actors should seek to encourage cooperation between the government and civil society NGOs for joint policy formulation.

Legacy and Effect on Domestic Legal System

Significant improvements to the domestic legal system will require a commitment of time and resources beyond the tenure of the SCSL. Its work has underscored shortcomings in the current judiciary and helped shape the thinking of a younger generation of legal professionals. It will also leave behind new buildings and offices for the domestic courts.

Expectations in this regard will have to be adjusted. Improving and reforming the judiciary is a much longer-term task and one that will need more support from donor governments. Also, parallel initiatives to develop capacity in the domestic legal system must be locally initiated and driven. An uneasy relationship between the Special Court and the domestic legal profession has hindered potential reform efforts. The SCSL and its work have been received better by nonlawyers, such as police investigators, prison guards, and even the workers who constructed the courthouse.

To raise public awareness and bolster the perception of the rule of law, donor governments should have provided ample funding to allow the SCSL to carry out outreach efforts. Explaining the Special Court's work to the public should be considered an integral part of a tribunal's mandate. This part of the SCSL's work has not been funded from the core budget. The European Union has been the main supporter of such activities, and has donated funds for an internship program and the production of audiovisual materials. Ideally, this educational side of the Special Court's work should have been incorporated into the original design of a hybrid tribunal instead of treated as an ancillary activity.

A potentially serious impediment to the legacy of both the TRC and the SCSL is that the international community may have gone too far in assuming responsibilities that in fact should fall to the state. This has allowed the government to keep its distance from policies that may be perceived as controversial or politically sensitive. Apart from its presence on the SCSL's management committee, the government has publicly distanced itself from the Special Court and senior government officials imply that any involvement with it would harm its independence. However, in so doing, the government may also have disassociated itself from the goals behind the creation of both the TRC and the SCSL. These goals and principles need to be affirmed by Sierra Leonean leadership to ensure that the Special Court's contribution will be lasting.

Effect of Policies on National Reconciliation

In examining the question of postwar reconciliation in Sierra Leone, it is important to bear in mind that the government prevailed in the conflict and that the RUF and AFRC were utterly defeated. In this sense, the political transition has followed a course of presidential and other elections and decentralization of government without any attempt to pursue reconciliation with the government's former enemies or rivals. The ruling Sierra Leone People's Party (SLPP) has rapidly consolidated its hold on power, and Sierra Leone could soon slide back into a one-party system, posing potential dangers to democratic development.

There are obvious limits on the ability of the TRC or the SCSL to deliver the drastic change needed to reform governance and ensure that Sierra Leone's fragile peace takes root. As mentioned, the TRC was able to implement some reconciliation programs in local communities. But much of what has happened in terms of reintegration has been informal, and Sierra Leoneans continue to be uneasy with the presence of perpetrators in their communities. Both institutions have provided a limited platform for victims, though the situation of many of those most affected by the war remains dire. In short, both institutions are helping mark a break with the past. However, neither has fundamentally affected the political culture, nor should these institutions necessarily be expected to do so. Perhaps the Truth and Reconciliation Commission and the Special Court will be remembered as the beginning of a new era in Sierra Leone, but it is far too early to say. In any case, it is not reasonable for donors or Sierra Leoneans to place the burden of the country's future on these two temporary institutions. Altering and redefining the political landscape in a way that ensures the advance of democratic reform is a monumental task that will take years of commitment and dedicated effort, first and foremost by national actors themselves.

■ Notes

This chapter does not necessarily represent the views of the International Center for Transitional Justice (ICTJ), where I am based.

1. *Lomé Peace Accord,* signed between the government of Sierra Leone and the RUF, July 7, 1999, art. 9.

2. *Truth and Reconciliation Commission Act 2000,* sec. 6(1).

3. The act states that the TRC has the power to investigate the context in which the violations and abuses occurred, including "the question of, whether those violations and abuses were the result of deliberate planning, policy, or authorization by any government, group, or individual." *TRC Act 2000,* sec. 6(2)(a)(1).

4. The national commissioners were Bishop Joseph Humper (chair), John Kamara, Laura Marcus-Jones, and Sylvanus Torto, each of whom hailed from one of the four regions of Sierra Leone. The international commissioners were William Schabas from Ireland, Yasmin Sooka from South Africa, and Ajaaratou Satang Jow from Gambia.

5. *TRC Act 2000,* sec. 7(2): "The Commission may seek assistance from traditional and religious leaders to facilitate its public sessions and in resolving local conflicts arising from past violations or abuses or in support of healing and reconciliation."

6. According to *TRC Act 2000,* sec. 6(2)(b), the commission should have the purpose of "creating a climate which fosters constructive interchange between victims and perpetrators."

7. *TRC Act 2000,* sec. 6(2)(a)(1).

8. These difficulties are chronicled in ICG, *Sierra Leone's Truth and Reconciliation Commission.*

9. About 350 people testified in the public hearings. Thematic hearings included sessions on good governance, the role of civil society, management of mineral resources and corruption, women and girls, and children and youth. Institutional hearings looked at the roles of the armed forces, police, media, political parties, and the like. There were also specific hearings dealing with the 1992 and 1997 coups, the attack on Freetown in January 1999, and the taking of peacekeepers as hostages in 2000.

10. The TRC's findings and recommendations continue to be available, but due to the length, the material is not easily downloaded and printed in Sierra Leone, where electricity is not readily available to most people.

11. In the interim, researchers were required to explore themes such as the military and political history of the conflict; the role of external actors; the use of mineral resources; issues relating to women, youth, and children; issues of governance; the relationship between the TRC and the Special Court; and forward-looking themes such as reconciliation, reparations, and a national vision for Sierra Leone.

12. Some staff also volunteered toward the end of the process, during report-writing, when salaries were no longer forthcoming.

13. Germany and the United States pledged US$200,000 to US$400,000 to successor institutions. See Hayner, *The Sierra Leone Truth and Reconciliation Commission.*

14. See ICG, *Sierra Leone's Truth and Reconciliation Commission,* p. 9.

15. It submitted testimony and gave technical assistance in certain specific areas, such as on interaction with children or with the Amputee Association. UNAMSIL also gave some logistical support to the TRC, as well as granting it access to its database on human rights violations. Finally, it made plans for report production and dissemination.

16. Pettersson, *Postconflict Reconciliation in Sierra Leone.*

17. This project was implemented by the Inter-Religious Council, and enabled the TRC to extend its activities at the community level. The project was significant, because the commission had not succeeded in establishing much of a regional presence, with the exception of one week of public hearings in each province. These provincial hearings had been very well received and each one ended with a day of

traditional reconciliation ceremonies. There was demand to extend the hearings phase, to allow for more provincial hearings, but this was ruled out because of cited financial constraints.

18. No trainings were organized by the OHCHR, and even the trainings provided by the ICTJ were very limited. There was also an opportunity for TRC commissioners to meet with senior staff of other truth commissions, organized in Freetown in November 2003.

19. Shaw, *Rethinking Truth and Reconciliation Commissions.* Further work in this area has been done by Tim Kelsall.

20. PRIDE and ICTJ, *Views of Ex-Combatants on the Truth and Reconciliation Commission and the Special Court.*

21. This was an issue raised at the National Victim Commemoration Conference, organized by the Special Court in Freetown on March 1–2, 2005. Delegates recommended the establishment of reconciliation panels and the establishment and use of mosques, churches, recreational centers, and trauma-healing centers as places of reconciliation. They also recommended that civil society and community-based organizations should receive assistance to carry out reconciliation activities, and suggested that a national commemoration day should be instituted.

22. ICTJ, *Exploring the Relationship Between the Special Court and the Truth and Reconciliation Commission for Sierra Leone.*

23. The situation was not clear-cut in legal terms, as the legal instruments creating both institutions were silent on the matter.

24. Chief Hinga Norman had been the alleged head of the CDF and is revered by many as a war hero.

25. The TRC assigned responsibility for atrocities to all the factions in the conflict, using its empirical research to make conclusions on who was primarily responsible, and concluding that the RUF committed the most atrocities, followed by the AFRC, and finally the CDF. The TRC also named those in senior offices in each of these factions during the conflict, implicating persons including senior members of the current government.

26. These efforts have included a presentation of the report in parliament in November 2005, to be followed by the presentation of a draft omnibus bill on TRC implementation put together by a small team of lawyers, which is supported in parliament by the human rights committee as well as UNAMSIL's human rights section. The team of drafters was funded by WITNESS and the ICTJ.

27. The UN deemed that it was not bound by the amnesty in the Lomé agreement, as its representative had appended a reservation, stating that the UN would not recognize an amnesty granted for genocide, crimes against humanity, war crimes, and other serious violations of international law.

28. Dougherty, "Right-Sizing International Criminal Justice."

29. These statistics were provided by the registry of the Special Court. With the departure of David Crane, the prosecutor, Desmond da Silva, the deputy prosecutor, has taken his place. There are senior Sierra Leonean trial attorneys, but the chiefs of prosecution, investigations, and operations are all internationals. One of the section chiefs in the registry is a Sierra Leonean (Binta Mansaray, chief of outreach).

30. A subsequent plea from the government of Sierra Leone in August 2001 to have the temporal jurisdiction of the Special Court extended back to 1991 was rejected.

31. In-kind contributions included personnel from Canada and Switzerland, and furniture from China. See Special Court for Sierra Leone, *Annual Report 2002/2003.*

32. "Statement of President of Special Court for Sierra Leone to the Security Council," May 24, 2005.

33. UN Security Council, Resolution 1400, March 2002. Italics added.

34. To date, the Special Court has indicted thirteen individuals from all three warring factions: the RUF, the CDF, and the AFRC. Many of the delegates at a recent conference hosted by the Special Court felt that this was too limited, and that the mandate of the SCSL should be extended to lower-level perpetrators.

35. In terms of the SCSL's legacy, national delegates at the conference identified the following as some of the areas on which they think the Special Court has had an impact: promotion of women's issues, including rape and forced marriage; restoration of dignity of children; increased awareness of international law, human rights, and international humanitarian law in Sierra Leone; awareness of witness protection; and job opportunities for Sierra Leoneans. However, delegates made the following recommendations: that the outreach program be expanded; that the visibility of the Special Court and accessibility be increased; and that trials be held in different parts of the country.

36. A significant DFID-funded justice sector development program, which will cost US$43.4 million (£25 million) over five years, has only recently begun to operate under the auspices of the British Council.

37. See identical letters dated May 26, 2005, from the Secretary-General addressed to the President of the General Assembly and the President of the Security Council, May 27, 2005, UN Doc. A/59/816-S/2005/350, *Annexing Special Court for Sierra Leone Completion Strategy,* May 18, 2005.

38. These include repealing constitutional provisions allowing for discrimination against women; instituting a code of conduct for judges and magistrates and other public sector officials; transparency for contributions to political campaigns; provision of protection for whistle-blowers exposing corruption; noninterference with prosecution of corruption cases; quotas for youth and women in participation of political parties; repealing of provisions in legislation that link prosecution of sexual offenses to the moral character of the complainant; abolishing customary practices of compelling rape victims to marry the offender; enacting a children's rights bill; and more transparency in the handling of mineral resources.

PART 3

Media

9

Media Assistance
to Postgenocide Rwanda

Christopher Kayumba and Jean-Paul Kimonyo

The tragic scale of the 1994 genocide in Rwanda is difficult to convey. An estimated 1 million people were killed. Another 1–2 million were driven from their homes, fleeing to states across the Great Lakes region of Central Africa. Amid rising political tensions and violent clashes between government and rebel-backed forces, in April 1994 Hutu extremists launched a campaign of murder against Tutsis, moderate Hutus, and the Twa minority. Despite clear warnings from UN agencies, aid workers, and others, the international community hesitated and utterly failed to take adequate action. The killing spree ended three months later when the Rwandan Patriotic Front (RPF), led by Rwanda's current president, Paul Kagame, defeated forces loyal to the former Rwandan government and took control of the country's capital, Kigali.

A transitional government dominated by the RPF was formed in July 1994. The Arusha Accord, the peace agreement that had been in place before the genocide, was adopted as a constitutional foundation though power-sharing rules were altered. Members of the former ruling National Revolutionary Movement for Development (MRND) and others deemed to have participated in the genocide were banned from holding office. The RPF was awarded the presidency and vice presidency, justifying its powerful position by arguing it had stopped the mass murder and had a duty to secure order. The RPF has continued to dominate political life while amassing a poor human rights record, winning elections in 2003 with the help of fraud, arrests, and appeals to ethnic fears. The International Criminal Tribunal for Rwanda (ICTR), established under the auspices of the UN Security Council and based in Arusha (Tanzania), has tried and convicted prominent figures who helped orchestrate the genocide. Yet the events of 1994 still cast a shadow over all aspects of Rwandan society.

Before, during, and after the 1994 genocide, Rwandan media played an instrumental role in inciting ethnic hatred and violence. Yet there are no comprehensive studies about developments in the Rwandan media sector since the 1994 genocide. This chapter tries to fill that void and to ascertain the role of international assistance in strengthening media organizations as part of broader peacebuilding and democratization efforts in the aftermath of the 1994 genocide.

After describing the media's role in the genocide and how the sector has evolved since 1994, the chapter offers an overview of international media assistance and its effect. The impact of outside aid has been mixed, with donors lacking a coherent, coordinated strategy and the government often seeking to stifle journalistic inquiry. Still, there have been positive developments, including training for a significant number of journalists, reform of media legislation, diplomatic pressure for media freedom, and an expansion of pluralistic debate.

▓ The Rwandan Media Before the Genocide

From State Control . . .

Until the late 1980s, the Rwandan government monopolized the mass media and tolerated no dissent. The 1991 *World Report* of the UK-based media nongovernmental organization (NGO) Article 19 observed that "the MRND is the sole political organization, outside of which no political views can be expressed or political activity exercised and to which all Rwandan citizens, including infants, automatically belong." President Juvenal Habyarimana's regime controlled both print and electronic media. It owned and operated the only radio station in the country, the national Radio Rwanda. It also owned a national television station (mainly targeting the urban elite and the international community) as well as two news journals called *Imvaho Nshya* (New Undisputed Truth) and *La Nouvelle Relève*. The bimonthly and moderately critical Catholic Church journal *Kinyamateka* (The Newspaper), begun in 1933, was a notable exception to complete state control over the media.

Radio Rwanda covered the whole country on FM and shortwave. It broadcast in French, Swahili, and Kinyarwanda (the national language), reaching as far as Kabale in southwestern Uganda and parts of the Democratic Republic of Congo (DRC) and Burundi. Because Rwanda is mainly an agrarian peasant economy, with more than 90 percent of the population living in rural areas and illiteracy levels above 60 percent, Radio Rwanda was a powerful medium of communication and influence in the country.[1] However, "until 1992, Radio Rwanda was very much the voice of the government and of the President himself." Many times, especially during the war, the radio broadcast false information. Since there was no other reliable source to verify the information, its word became the "Gospel truth."[2]

Télévision Nationale du Rwanda (TVR), Rwanda's national television, had less influence and a smaller audience. Established in 1992, it broadcast only twice a week and primarily reached the city of Kigali. In addition, the impact of the print media was small and its circulation was also limited to Kigali, where it reached an already politically aware, literate elite.[3]

. . . To Independent Media . . .

The first crack in the armor of state-controlled media occurred in 1987 with the birth of an independent, critical journal called *Kanguka*. In subsequent years, with the collapse of communism and the end of the Cold War, new global trends brought further changes to Rwanda. During the late 1980s, international donor pressure on the Rwandan government increased and a strong, vocal internal opposition emerged. War broke out in the northern and northeastern areas of the country, forcing President Habyarimana to move toward democratization.

The idea of an independent media continued to gather strength during the democratization experiment and rebirth of political pluralism in 1990–1991, gaining even more currency immediately after the signing of the Arusha peace accord in August 1993. In 1990, eight new newspapers began publishing. In 1991, a new constitution guaranteed freedom of the press and freedom of expression and opinion. A press law passed in November 1991 further ensured freedom of the press and resulted in the establishment of independent newspapers, radio, and television stations. In 1991 alone, forty-five newspapers and journals were founded, while more than sixty were created between 1991 and 1993.[4]

A number of the newspapers and journals that emerged in the early 1990s, especially *Kanguka* and *Rwanda Rushya* (The New Rwanda), were genuinely interested in meaningful political change and political pluralism. However, a strong polarization began to take shape between those that supported the status quo and those that advocated change and sympathized more with opposition groups. Human Rights Watch reported that eleven of the forty-five journals founded in 1991 were linked to the powerful Akazu group of the Habyarimana regime.[5] Journals like *Rwanda Rw'Ejo* (Rwanda for Tomorrow), *Rwanda Rushya, Le Tribun du Peuple,* and *Le Flambeau* sympathized with the Rwandan Patriotic Front, while the other opposition political parties in the country each had their own journal. The divide led to a confrontational kind of journalism, with newspapers defending their political patrons and attacking their rivals. Soon the media was exploited by extremists as a tool to aggravate ethnic divisions and hatred.

Some opposition and moderate politicians were aware of and concerned about a media saturated with hateful propaganda. As early as November 17,

1991, the major opposition parties (the Liberals, the Social Democrats, and the Democratic Republican Movement) sent a joint memorandum to President Habyarimana complaining that the use of state radio and television for MRND propaganda was standing in the way of democratization.[6] Habyarimana's response was to accuse his critics of hypocrisy: on the one hand pressuring him to democratize and liberalize and on the other asking him to limit this new press freedom. He was often quoted as telling donors: "This is what you wanted—democracy and freedom of speech."

Political-ethnic polarization spread to the radio sector as well, with dire consequences. In late 1991 the RPF opened Radio Muhabura (The Beacon), which it used to appeal to the patriotism of its listeners and to praise RPF combatants. Initially the station's coverage was small and the population was afraid to listen to it for fear of reprisals. By 1992, however, its audience had increased steadily. According to Human Rights Watch, whereas Radio Muhabura "glorified the RPF, it did so in a nationalistic rather than an ethnic context, consistent with the general RPF emphasis of minimizing differences between Hutu and Tutsi."[7]

. . . To Hate Media

Against the backdrop of increasing political uncertainty and ethnic polarization, the extremist Radio Télévision Libre des Mille Collines (RTLM) was founded in August 1993, aided by the staff and facilities of the official government-owned station. RTLM was probably established to fill a vacuum created by changes at the national Radio Rwanda, which had been banned from partisan reporting and directed to accommodate all political voices—including that of the RPF. RTLM used nationally owned transmitters around the country to relay its programs,[8] and was funded primarily by Felicien Kabuga (a wealthy businessman whose daughter was married to Habyarimana's son) and Alphonse Ntilivamunda (the son-in-law of the president). It was also supported by other members of the political inner circle—the Akazu.

Though RTLM claimed it would uphold democracy and journalistic ethics, it utterly failed to adhere to these principles in practice. The station's strategy was to use the new political space to resist the democratization process. It demonized the opposition and did its best to undermine the Arusha peace process as well as denounce moderate members of the ruling circle. It used a mixture of popular music, street slang, and popular expressions to awaken the "great mass" (of Hutus) who were, once again, facing perceived threats from their traditional enemies, the Tutsis.[9]

In the early days of April 1994, various media began to broadcast messages indicating that something sinister was being organized. On April 3, RTLM announced: "On the 3rd, 4th, and 5th, heads will get heated up. On the

6th of April, there will be a respite, but a small thing will happen. Then on the 7th and 8th and other days in April, you will see something."[10] *La Médaille Nyiramacibiri,* a journal allied with the MRND, wrote in its February 1994 issue, "By the way, the Tutsi race could be extinguished." Hassan Ngeze's *Kangura* magazine wrote cold-bloodedly in its January 1994 issue no. 55 that the president would die in March and asked, "Who will survive the March War?"[11] On April 6, something happened indeed. Habyarimana's presidential jet was shot down, and the following day the RTLM hate media openly called for avenging his death.

According to a wide range of experts, RTLM was an important factor in the spread of genocide, especially with its broadcasts after President Habyarimana's death. During the three months of genocide, RTLM often made explicit calls to the Hutu to participate in the killings. At one point it announced: "You have missed some of the enemies in this or that place. Some are still alive. You must go back there and finish them off. The graves are not yet quite full. Who is going to do the good work and help us fill them completely?"[12]

The role of the media in the Rwandan conflict cannot be overestimated. For the genocide, it was tantamount to "the match that started the fire."[13] And even when the genocidal regime was routed out of Kigali in July 1994, RTLM was only off the air for a week. It continued to broadcast propaganda with mobile FM transmitters, calling on the Hutu masses to flee from the "invading cockroaches," the RPF, and by extension, the Tutsis.

The diverse media that emerged in the early 1990s suffered from a severe lack of professionalism, journalistic ethics, and most important, editorial independence. In the end, extremist media with generous political and financial sponsorship overpowered other voices and paved the way for a murderous agenda. Analysts of the genocide have noted that the international community ignored articles in the newspaper *Kangura* and hate-speech broadcasts by RTLM that represented early warnings of imminent genocide. All of this has had enormous implications for the media in postgenocide Rwanda.

■ The Media Sector After 1994

The genocide and war had a devastating effect on the media sector, both physically and psychologically. Given the pernicious role played by RTLM in inciting ethnic assault in 1994, public trust in the media was severely damaged. As a result, the current RPF-dominated government has exerted a near monopoly over the media since 1994, with radio and television under its exclusive control. Promising new legislation adopted in 2002 and 2003 has opened the possibility for more private, independent news outlets to emerge. Foreign radio services also provide quality news coverage for a large Rwandan audience and now offer programming in the Kinyarwanda and Kirundi languages. Journalistic standards remain poor, but international donors have sought to improve professional skills through training courses and a new school of journalism at the National University of Rwanda. Media outlets still struggle to achieve profitability due to a limited advertising market and a largely state-run economy. The number of newspapers has dwindled over the past decade and only two enjoy genuine editorial independence. In addition, there are a few publications owned and operated by various human rights or civil society organizations.

Editors or reporters who have broadcast or published critical stories have suffered harassment and intimidation by the government, forcing several to flee the country and causing their colleagues to engage in self-censorship. The government has sought to justify its hostility to independent media by citing the role of radio in the genocide. The concept of media freedom is often misunderstood in Rwanda, both by the political leadership and by working journalists. Media outlets tend to fall into progovernment or opposition categories, failing to provide balanced coverage of important issues. Nevertheless, a degree of pluralism and more open debate has begun to develop though it remains tenuous.

◼ Overview of International Media Assistance

This section examines international assistance for the development and rehabilitation of Rwanda's media sector. In comparison with other forms of aid, overall assistance to the media has been rather limited. The small number of media projects by the international community had different objectives. Five categories of assistance can be distinguished. First, international donors established "alternative" media to counteract Rwanda's hate media and to inform refugees and internally displaced persons. Second, there has been support to international and Rwandan media outlets. Third, international media assistance has targeted the training of journalists and other media professionals. Fourth, international support was given to reform the legal and regulatory media framework. Finally, the international community has provided substantial political and moral support for media freedom. Table 9.1 outlines some of the international media development projects from 1992 to 2003, without reference to contributions in kind.

Establishment of Alternative Media: Radio Agatashya

Even after the defeat of the MRND government, which was responsible for carrying out the genocide, Rwanda's hate radio, RTLM, continued to broadcast

Table 9.1 International Assistance for the Rwandan Media Sector, 1992–2003

Period	Amount	Donor	Beneficiary	Expected Purpose
1992–1997	US$7,621,837	GTZ	ORINFOR/radio	Build Kalisimbi antennae, rehabilitation, training, equipment
1992	US$500,000	French Cooperation	ORINFOR/ television	Start a national television station
1994	US$300,000	UNICEF	ORINFOR/radio	Logistical and technical support
2001	US$44,462	Netherlands Embassy	RIMEG/newspaper *Umuseso*	Strengthen the independent media
2000–2002	US$11,737,380	Netherlands Embassy	EJC	Equip school laboratories with computers and Internet connections
2002	US$17,032	DFID	*Umuseso*	Cover printing costs, rent, salaries
2002–2003	US$1,089,261	Netherlands Embassy	Internews	Produce videos of proceedings at the ICTR in order to increase profile, consultancy
2003	US$1,019,900	Netherlands Embassy	Radio Benevolencija	Counteract trauma
2003	US$15,905	CIDA	*Umuseso*	Cover printing costs, rent, salaries, equipment
Total	US$22,345,777			

Source: Various documents.

Note: The table excludes assistance from UNESCO, one of the major donors in the field of media assistance. In addition, some small projects from various foreign embassies and nongovernmental organizations have been omitted, where either the contribution could not be readily clarified or the beneficiary was unwilling to disclose information.

genocidal messages and urged the Hutu population to flee the country. This led to increased fear among the population and caused hundreds of thousands to flee into neighboring countries, especially the DRC, Tanzania, and Burundi. The mass movement of refugees helped trigger long overdue international action. On May 24, 1994, more than a month into the genocide, Philippe Dahinden addressed the UN Commission of Human Rights on behalf of Reporters Without Borders (RSF) and proposed the creation of a "free radio station" that would "allow Rwandans to receive honest and independent information"[14] to counter propaganda that was worsening the refugee crisis and deepening the conflict. Thus, RSF International gave its Swiss division the mandate of creating a radio station that would serve humanitarian ends and fight the damaging effects of RTLM and its related propaganda.

Authorized by the then–DRC government in Kinshasa and with assistance from the UN, the UN High Commissioner for Refugees (UNHCR), and the Swiss government, Radio Agatashya was created with offices in Bukavu (DRC).[15] This was the first international attempt to neutralize Rwanda's hate media. Its first broadcast was on August 4, 1994, in both Kinyarwanda and French, later widening its horizon to Swahili and English. In September–November, RSF set up a Radio Agatashya office in Kigali. In March 1995 the Swiss NGO Fondation Hirondelle took over the management and operation of this radio station. At that time, the station had installed transmitters in Goma, Bukavu, and Uvira, with the new capacity helping to reach as far as Bujumbura in Burundi, eastern DRC, and northwestern Tanzania.

In July 1995, Fondation Hirondelle signed an agreement with the UNHCR to produce radio information magazines as part of a voluntary refugee repatriation program. The magazines were broadcast to several transmitters in the region, including Radio Rwanda, Radio Agatashya, Radio Nationale Burundaise, Radio UNAMIR, and Radio Kwizera (in neighboring Burundi). It widened its coverage to include broadcasts in Burundi and daily news coverage of trials at the International Criminal Tribunal for Rwanda in Arusha. Broadcasting eight hours a day and reaching about 4 million listeners, including 1 million refugees, Radio Agatashya served both humanitarian needs and offered unbiased news and information to refugees. However, broadcasting ceased on October 27, 1996, due to the outbreak of hostilities in the DRC.

Assistance to Radio UNAMIR and Other Foreign Radio Stations

The UN Assistance Mission to Rwanda (UNAMIR) did not have a radio station of its own when it arrived in Rwanda in October 1993. In July 1994, with permission from the Rwandan government, it used Radio Rwanda to broadcast its programs. On February 16, 1995, Radio UNAMIR began FM broadcasting in Kigali. It broadcast four hours a day with programs in English, French, and Kinyarwanda. When the UNAMIR mission ended in March 1996, the radio station closed down as well.

Neither the British Broadcasting Corporation (BBC) nor Voice of America (VOA) had Kinyarwanda- or Kirundi-language services before 1994. However, after the genocide, both started broadcasting on FM in these languages. The BBC began with the broadcast of a fifteen-minute program in both Kinyarwanda and Kirundi in late 1994. The program offered regional news and refugee-related information. With increased demand and worsening conflict in the region, the program was expanded to thirty minutes and covered news on health, agriculture, and political developments in the region. The BBC also started a thirty-minute program called *Imvo N'Imvaho* (The Origin), focusing on political, social, economic, and cultural issues. A consortium of British organizations and the UNHCR funded these programs.

As the conflict expanded to eastern DRC, the VOA also started a thirty-minute program in both Kinyarwanda and Kirundi languages on July 15, 1996. A grant from the US Agency for International Development (USAID) was used to create a hotline program broadcasting the whereabouts of refugees, which has helped reunite an estimated 500 families. Later, as the conflict in the DRC worsened, an additional sixty-minute program was initiated, broadcasting on Saturdays and Sundays. These programs covered regional news, conflict resolution programs, features on political developments, and democratization-related programs in both Rwanda and Burundi. In 2005, both the BBC and the VOA still broadcast on FM. Research indicates that the two foreign radio stations enjoy a high level of trust and credibility across the country.

Support to Media Outlets and Organizations

The Rwandan Information Office (ORINFOR) is the government office in charge of media, managing the national radio, television, and two newspapers. It was one of the first media organizations to receive international support, and it probably received more assistance than any other media outlet or organization in the country. In 1992, German Technical Cooperation (GTZ) and the government of Rwanda cofinanced the construction of the Kalisimbi antennae, with GTZ contributing US$1.2 million of the total US$2.4 million needed. In December 1992, the French government offered US$500,000 for construction and equipment of the national television network (TVR). They also provided studio equipment and an outside broadcasting van. Belgium helped with the housing for the station and studio. Unfortunately, this project was not completed due to the war and the 1994 genocide.[16]

After the genocide in September 1994, the UN Children's Fund (UNICEF) promised US$300,000 to meet logistical and technical needs of Radio Rwanda. In 1996–1997, GTZ funded the US$914,571 rehabilitation of the principal Jali antennae. In 1997 it gave an additional US$4.9 million for buying equipment and training of personnel. The aid provided training for journalists, managers, and administrators and also enabled the reconstruction of buildings, housing both the broadcast administration and two studios. Explicit conditions for this assistance included a commitment from the Rwandan government to support an open media with divergent opinions, setting out clear regulations for ORINFOR, and embarking on reforms that would lead to the enactment of a democratic press law.[17]

In 1995, RSF provided some financial support to independent newspapers in Kigali for printing costs. The assistance amounted to US$1,000 given to individual editors. Between ten to twenty editors are said to have received funds enabling them to publish at least five issues of their respective newspapers. Later, in 1999, RSF had to pay legal fees for the news editor of *Rwanda Newsline,* who had been accused, detained, and arraigned in court for publishing a story that implicated a senior military officer in the corrupt purchasing of military helicopters. The editor was released after six months without being formally charged.

The UN Educational, Scientific, and Cultural Organization (UNESCO) has been one of the major providers of assistance to media outlets and organizations after the genocide. In October 1994, following an international conference on the media in South Africa, it opened a resident office in Kigali at the request of the Rwandan Ministry of Information. UNESCO began its work in 1995 by advising local journalists to set up a press house aimed at bringing together all media organizations within the country to facilitate assistance and strengthen the sector. The Press House was created in 1996, following the establishment of the Association of Rwandan Journalists (ARJ) in 1995. UNESCO equipped the Press House with a library and documentation center complete with chairs, printers, computers, telephone and fax machines, a restaurant, and café. This not only gave media staff a meeting place of their own, but also allowed the organization to provide print production services to newspapers, journalists, and editors at subsidized rates. UNESCO provided almost all the equipment and paid rent for both the Press House and the ARJ from 1996 until 2001, after which it phased out its "Project Rwanda Media." UNESCO also provided funds to twelve independent newspapers, including the journal *Ukuri* (The Truth) and *Rwanda Newsline* to produce at least five issues. To ease transportation problems, UNESCO provided ORINFOR with twelve four-wheel-drive vehicles in 1995. Foreign embassies also donated equipment and modest funding to various publications.

The British embassy, through its "Small Grants Scheme," funded one of the Press House's major projects, *Le Messager* (The Messenger). This project established kiosks in all the provinces throughout the country to sell newspapers, journals, and magazines to encourage sales, while also catering to the needs of readers and improving the culture of reading in the country. The British embassy also provided assistance by covering printing costs for the now defunct *Rwanda Newsline,* and the UK's Department for International Development (DFID) provided similar support for the *Rwanda Herald.*[18]

USAID is another organization that provided assistance to the media sector. Its aid focused on publicizing the work of the newly created ICTR by helping the NGO Internews to produce a video about the tribunal's proceedings. The videos are now shown in Rwanda as a way of increasing awareness about the tribunal and its work. Later, this assistance included coverage of the traditional, communal *Gacaca* courts. USAID also paid for the subsistence costs of ORINFOR journalists who reported on proceedings at the ICTR in Arusha.

The Royal Netherlands embassy in Kigali has been the biggest contributor to the development of an independent media sector in the country, in both financial and political terms. In March 2001 the embassy provided financial support totaling US$44,118 to the Rwandan Independent Media Group (RIMEG). Since January 2003 it has spent US$286,184 to support Internews consultants who are working on a project with the DFID and the Rwandan Ministry of Local Government, Information, and Social Welfare aimed at establishing strategies for creating an independent media in the country. In January 2003 the embassy agreed to contribute US$1 million toward the startup and operation of Radio Benevolencija, established to serve victims of trauma. For the "Media for Justice" initiative, the Netherlands also donated US$1.1 million to Internews between 2002 and 2003. In addition, the Netherlands had plans to spend US$476,930 in 2004 and US$178,912 in 2005 on various media projects.

Finally, in 2003 the Canadian International Development Agency (CIDA) provided US$19,111 to the newspaper *Umuseso* (Dawn), assisting with printing costs, rent, salaries, and the acquisition of a generator. *Umuseso* also received some assistance in the form of computers and other equipment from the German and British embassies. The DFID provided US$17,381 to *Umuseso* as a way of helping it meet printing costs, rent, and salaries.

Training of Media Professionals

Prior to 1994, GTZ had provided regional training to journalists through the Community of Great Lakes Countries (CPGL), a regional body that includes Rwanda, Burundi, and the former Zaire (now the DRC). At a time when Rwandan universities offered no courses in journalism, this project helped to train journalists working for the national station Radio Rwanda from 1986 to 1992.

Belgium also provided training to sixty Rwandan journalists (thirty in Rwanda and thirty in Belgium). Through its offices in Arusha, Fondation Hirondelle has provided annual training in international law and court reporting to selected journalists from both public and private media organizations covering the ICTR. The training emphasizes legal terminology and journalistic skills needed to cover tribunal proceedings, genocide-specific cases in the country, and any related judicial proceedings. The French government also provided training for three Rwandan television journalists.

In 1997, GTZ provided US$548,849 for training Radio Rwanda journalists and technicians on topics such as digital programming and editing. It also provided a consultancy to Radio Rwanda managers aimed at restructuring and improving the quality of programs to make them more attractive and helpful to audiences.

Through the ARJ and the Press House, UNESCO funded the training of journalists both inside and outside the country, including the funding of selected journalists to attend a diploma course in journalism in Uganda. Egypt and Sweden also sponsored journalist training through the Swedish International Development Agency (SIDA). In 2002, SIDA initiated a regional fund for a diploma program in environmental journalism.

Care International financed the training of twenty Radio Rwanda journalists, two at Cardiff University in Wales. The German international broadcasting agency Deutsche Welle trained four journalists from Radio Rwanda in 1996 and 1997, and Israel offers two scholarships every year.

Assistance to the School of Journalism and Communication (EJC) is also worth noting. The school was established in 1995 with major support from UNESCO. Between 2000 and 2002 the Royal Netherlands embassy in Kigali provided US$62,011, which helped the school to construct its own laboratory complete with Internet connection and computers. Various international educational institutions have also formed relations with the school in order to help build its capacity. The University of Lille in France, for example, signed a three-year partnership agreement aimed at training journalists and students and sending lecturers to Rwanda. US journalism schools have contributed through the Fulbright and Knight fellowship programs.

Assistance for Legal and Regulatory Reforms

The genocide in Rwanda not only derailed the democratization process, it also destroyed the media infrastructure put in place between 1991 and 1993. After the war, the press had to start virtually from scratch. In addition, it had to face the population's mistrust, given the media's role in the genocide.

Although limited, there was some international technical and financial support for reforming the regulatory media framework. In 1997 the assistance program to Radio Rwanda by GTZ was also specifically targeted to promote legal reforms that would enable a more democratic press law.

However, the RPF leadership in the transition government sought to block the growth of independent media and was reluctant to guarantee freedom of the press. As a result, the new press law was stalled until early 2002. However, by May 2003 the government had changed its position somewhat and finally promulgated the national constitution that guaranteed freedom of the press and expression.

Political and Moral Support

Research indicates that independent-minded newspapers facing government pressure received crucial international political support. Newspapers such as *Rwanda Newsline* (now closed due to financial and managerial problems), *Umuseso,* and *Indorerwamo* (The Mirror) would probably have been shut down and journalists imprisoned were it not for protests raised by foreign missions, international media, and human rights organizations. Political support came mainly from the Royal Netherlands embassy, with some "behind the scenes" discreet diplomacy by the British and German embassies as well.

■ Contribution of Media Assistance

It is difficult to gauge the long-term impact of assistance to the media sector during 2001–2003, as distinguished from assistance during the emergency phase of 1994–1999. The new progressive press law and constitution were passed after the emergency phase and selected independent media organizations then started receiving some support from government. Additionally, in 2003, some development partners (especially the UK's DFID and the Netherlands) began working in partnership with the Ministry of Information and other stakeholders to devise a media assistance strategy, including the funding of independent radio stations. While more recent international support may produce more dramatic progress, it is clear that past assistance efforts have already made several important contributions to Rwanda's media sector.

Enabling Radio Broadcasting

The reconstruction of the state radio service provides one of the most visible examples of the effect of international assistance. Substantial assistance helped rebuild and strengthen the editorial quality of state-owned media, particularly the national radio. Charles Nahayo, the head of the technical section at Radio Rwanda, describing the state of the radio situation after war and genocide, said in an interview: "We could not broadcast. On July 19, 1994, when the transitional government was sworn in, we had to install an antenna on a tree for the broadcast to be heard."[19] Faustin Karangira, former director of Radio Rwanda and now director of national television, agreed, saying that without international assistance it would have been hard for the station to recover. Now the studios have been reequipped, ORINFOR and radio buildings have been renovated, journalists and administrators have been trained, and the quality of the programming has improved—at least in some cases. Karangira estimates that before assistance, the radio was operating at about 50 percent of its capacity. Now it is nearing 100 percent, as studios for government-supported community radio stations are being built and opened in provinces such as Butare and Gisenyi. Others are planned for Kibungo and Umutara.

Improved Journalism Standards

The former director of Radio Rwanda, Faustin Karangira, acknowledged that Radio Rwanda is still inclined toward official thinking, but he insisted that training has left journalists and radio and television programs far better off than they were in 1994. Programs have also become more varied. Two popular, quality programs that are a direct result of international assistance are Sunday's television and radio live broadcast of *Kubaza Bitera Kumenya* (Asking Is the Source of Knowledge) and *Radio Mubaturage* (Radio Among Citizens).

Father Dominique Karekezi, the president of the Press House and director of the newspaper *Kinyamateka,* said that journalism training has had an enormous impact, although sloppy reporting and low professionalism remain a problem. This confidence in training as the hope for a future vibrant media was also expressed by 93 percent of respondents to an informal survey conducted by Internews.[20] However, despite international support since 1994, 53 percent of the same respondents thought that the poor quality of Rwandan media was due to a lack of training and education. This view illustrates that inadequate training remains one of the major obstacles to building a higher-quality media, despite the various education projects undertaken so far.

Creation of the School of Journalism and Communication

As part of the training and education effort, international donors have contributed significant assistance to the School of Journalism and Communication at the National University of Rwanda. The school houses television and radio studios and an Internet laboratory, all of which have improved the quality of education. The school plans to launch an FM community radio station, with the help of the European Union through UNESCO. This is expected to further improve the skills of journalism graduates, contribute to free debate, and expand the flow of news and information. With substantial assistance from UNESCO, the school has trained close to a hundred journalists in "license" (bachelor of arts) programs. Graduates are now employed by state or private media agencies and organizations. Karangira, the national television director, said in an interview: "Of course they are better. It is very easy to train them, and they understand very fast. They have had a very positive impact on our television, radio, and print mediums."[21] At the end of 2003, there were over sixty students of journalism in their first to fourth years at the school. Twenty-two of them entered the job market in late 2004. Although this has been achieved in partnership with the Rwandan government, international support was vital.

Building Domestic Media Institutions, Promoting Journalistic Solidarity

To promote journalistic solidarity, UNESCO came up with the idea of the Press House, a place where media professionals could meet and that eventually gave rise to a journalists' association. UNESCO funded the organization until 2001, when it ended its "Rwanda Media Project." Currently, the Press House does not have a building of its own due to lack of funds. However, it still has computers, scanners, and printers that are used by interested journalists and editors to write stories, typeset newspapers, and print various documents at subsidized rates. It also continues to be the meeting place of journalists (both national and international). There is a general consensus that without international assistance, it would have been difficult for Rwandan journalists to form and run an umbrella organization that brings together the country's journalists and newspapers.

At the same time, assistance failed to fulfill the goal of making the organization self-sustaining. The kiosks selling newspapers, the journals and periodicals, as well as the cafeteria and the print production services were all part of the plan for sustainability. These services failed to generate sufficient income for the Press House, however. The cafeteria closed down due to mismanagement, while the kiosks focus more on selling soft drinks and beer than on selling newspapers. Photocopying, printing, layout, and scanning services are still provided, but the income from these services is minimal compared to what is needed to sustain the organization.

Observers agree that both international organizations and Rwandans themselves are to blame for the failure of the organization to achieve sustainability. The donors are criticized for their direct personal contacts with the Press House's first executive secretary, which allegedly led to mismanagement and embezzlement of funds. In addition, the donors decided to assist with rent payments over five years, instead of building permanent offices on land that was offered by the president.

However, the members of the Press House themselves are also responsible for missed opportunities. They failed to prove that the executive director did, indeed, embezzle funds, and it is up to them to improve the organization's condition since the departure of the executive director in 2000.

The Rwandan Independent Media Group and specifically the independent newspaper *Umuseso* have also been major beneficiaries of international assistance aimed at building and strengthening the nascent independent press. Unfortunately, assistance failed to strengthen RIMEG, and in some respects even contributed to unraveling it. Early mismanagement led to wrangles and internal divisions between the seven founding members. The split was caused in part because donors allowed money to be transferred to a personal account. In 2003, only one of the original seven was a member (in exile). When a second round of assistance was made available, the new team also fought and became divided over the funding in the same manner. Allegations of financial mismanagement and embezzlement arose, once again, by the transfer of funds to a personal account. The matter was taken to the police and the group eventually dissolved.

Umuseso has served as a bold, critical voice in Rwanda, representing one of the biggest successes of donor assistance to the media sector. While certainly a credit to media donors, it might have been more effective to share this support and assistance with other independent newspapers such as *Ukuri, Ukuri Gacaca,* and *Ubumwe* (Unity). A broader approach might have created a more lasting effect beyond a single newspaper.

Fledgling Pluralism and Opening Public Debate

Despite restrictions imposed on journalists by the authorities, a more open public debate appears to have emerged in recent years. This opening, however, falls far short of the public's expectations for a critical discussion on important issues that affect their lives. Land distribution and alleged corruption among government officials are topics of great interest that are often ignored in the country's media. This unsatisfied demand for a more open political climate helps explain the popularity of *Umuseso,* the only newspaper that has not refrained from reporting on more sensitive issues like corruption.

While radio still tends to toe the government line without asking hard questions or considering critical views, it has improved somewhat due to international attention. However, concerns persist that the radio still fails to convey accurate, statistically supported information. Jean Pierre Gatsinzi, director of the School of Journalism and Communication at the National University of Rwanda, argues that radio programs fail to reflect genuine reporting or audience interest. The last known survey of the radio audience was conducted in 1968. One survey carried out by the Thomson Foundation in 1999 was never published or distributed to the appropriate managers. ORINFOR continues to operate under an inflexible mandate and remains under the tight grip of government officials in violation of conditions set out by international donors demanding more autonomy, efficiency, and professionalism.

As for print media, international assistance has been significant for only a few of the thirty-seven newspapers, journals, and periodicals formally registered with the government. These are the newspapers owned and run by human rights organizations (*Amani, Le Verdict, Umukindo,* and *Haguruka*) and the two independent newspapers, *Umuseso* and *Indorerwamo.* The latter two have served as a litmus test for the impact of international assistance. *Umuseso* and *Indorerwamo* are not any more accurate, balanced, impartial, or professional than other publications, but they have managed to retain a degree of editorial independence from the government. Without support from the international community, these papers would likely have gone out of business.

Positive Influence of Foreign Radio

The British Broadcasting Corporation and Voice of America have enabled a greater degree of dissent, rendering the authorities more tolerant of divergent views. This has in turn benefited both ordinary citizens and the local media. Both international radio services provide airtime to government officials as well as opposition politicians.

Government officials seem more willing and available to talk to the BBC and VOA than to the independent media in the country. The information is quoted locally, without the risk that people will be accused of spreading rumors and false news, and it has added variety to what is written in the local press. The informal Internews survey referred to earlier indicated that among the 66 percent of the sixty-one respondents who cited radio as their primary source of news, 43 percent of them mentioned the BBC as their favorite, followed by 20 percent for VOA. Radio Rwanda was the favorite for only 12 percent of those surveyed.

Both the BBC and VOA have been, and continue to be, instrumental in the joint Rwandan government and UNHCR's program of repatriating Rwandan refugees from neighboring countries. The high degree of trust enjoyed by the radio services has contributed to the return of many refugees since 1996.

However, radio sponsored by outside governments cannot be relied on entirely to promote an open debate on important public issues.

International Political and
Moral Support for Media Freedom

According to journalists and other observers, political and moral support for media freedom in Rwanda has proven to be the most valuable assistance offered by donor governments and agencies. Yet such diplomatic support carries virtually no financial cost, unlike the equipment and training courses provided by donors. Editors at *Umuseso* believe that many journalists would be in prison were it not for international scrutiny and protests. A diplomat in Kigali agreed, saying that while *Umuseso* may not be the best newspaper, it is a lone voice outside the government-controlled media. The Royal Netherlands embassy has been a vocal advocate for journalists who were arrested and illegally detained. Other organizations such as Human Rights Watch, Amnesty International, Reporters Without Borders, and the International Federation of Journalists (IFJ) have also denounced the arrest and illegal detention of journalists. One diplomat in Kigali, who did not want to be named, said, "Without our pressure on the government, those boys [journalists at *Umuseso*] would be in prison, and their newspapers would now be history." Some diplomats have played a key role in helping journalists to survive, tell their story, or secure safety in exile.

Although there is strong consensus that Rwanda's embattled journalists urgently need political support, such support is sometimes criticized for tending to be arbitrarily connected to certain individuals, inconsistent, and appearing to convey a political alliance between foreign governments and opposition political forces. Some journalists who receive international sympathy incorrectly see themselves as opposition figures or activists rather than reporters.

Establishment of Regulatory Media Framework

International expertise and assistance played an important role in the adoption of more enlightened media legislation in the form of a press law and new constitution. One official from a major donor country said, for example, that the contribution of his government to the establishment of the press law was decisive, especially with regard to deleting an article in the law that included the death penalty.[22]

Research indicates that these laws have already started to produce an important impact, allowing independent and private broadcasting for the first time. Radio 10 started in early February 2004, while Radio Kibungo (also known as Radio Izuba) started in late 2004. Other radio stations that have so far started include Flash FM, Radio Contact, City Radio, and Radio Maria—the latter owned by the Catholic Church. Campus Radio, at the National University of Rwanda, started in November 2005, after some delays in procurement of machinery. In the long term, international efforts to help reform media law may prove to be the single most important donor contribution toward expanding the free flow of information and enabling a robust media sector to flourish. The effect of the media law reform will depend on the Rwandan judiciary's willingness to uphold the spirit and letter of the law as well as the readiness of journalists and other activists to lobby for their rights.

Limitations of Media Assistance

Donor-Driven Approach

We encountered widespread concern that international media assistance has tended to overlook the advice or perspective of Rwandan journalists and partner organizations. This "donor-driven," inflexible approach has meant that generic projects have been launched in Rwanda that failed to take into account the particular conditions and attitudes prevailing in Rwandan society. Potentially promising local initiatives were often ignored. Instead of treating Rwandans as partners, the donor agencies pursued a "patron-client" relationship. In addition, donors often communicated only with certain individuals rather than the governing bodies of Rwandan partner organizations, which may have contributed to disputes over finances plaguing certain projects. According to a range of sources in the media sector interviewed for this assessment, the donor-driven approach represents the biggest failing of media development assistance.

However, Rwandan organizations bear a share of the blame for this situation, due to their reluctance to question or disagree with donor representatives. Rwandan partners may have to learn to be more assertive about their needs, while donors may have to learn to present themselves as more open to new ideas.

Incoherent Donor Criteria and Strategies

The absence of clear criteria for donor funding has also limited the efficacy of international media assistance. It remains puzzling why certain organizations have received funding while others have not. The lack of coherent, transparent criteria has fostered distrust of donor intentions at times, and fed unnecessary rivalries among organizations pursuing similar work.

Too often, international aid has been fragmented, ad hoc, and lacking coordination among donor organizations. Editors or journalists who managed to grab the attention of a particular donor were able to secure funds, which sometimes produced short-lived, unsustainable projects and publications.

Donors have lacked clearly defined goals or benchmarks that could shape assistance over time. Short-term training has tended to take a priority over building the elements of a permanent "infrastructure" that could sustain the media sector. The government's attempts to suppress editorial independence and critical reporting have exploited the lack of a united front among donor governments and organizations.

Media Treated as a Low Donor Priority

In the wider international effort to build democracy in Rwanda, media may be the most neglected, underfunded sector. Initially, donor governments were naturally reluctant to venture into the media field given the role of radio broadcasts in the 1994 genocide. Other pressing issues took priority as well, including resettlement of refugees, justice for the victims of genocide, and alleviation of poverty. Still, a robust, independent, inquisitive, and professional media industry that fosters open debate is crucial if Rwandan society is to evolve toward genuine democracy and the rule of law.

■ Remaining Problems Plaguing the Media Sector

Repression and Self-Censorship

In Rwanda today, one cannot talk of outright state censorship. However, in spite of a new press law and the constitution, media freedom continues to be curtailed in practice. Whenever a newspaper is suspected of having written articles critical of the government, state operatives confiscate the particular publication. Government campaigns of intimidation, harassment, unlawful arrests, and detention produce a de facto censorship or "self-censorship." Few journalists are willing to risk prison or to jeopardize their publication and instead choose to avoid sensitive subjects.

As a result, journalists and others familiar with the media sector agree that political support from foreign missions has been instrumental for the accused. In spite of this support, however, some journalists are still fleeing the country amid persistent state intimidation, harassment, and imprisonment.

Some sources interviewed for this assessment argued that irresponsible reporting has contributed to the problem. The informal survey conducted by Internews, mentioned previously, revealed that while 53 percent of forty-nine respondents believed that lack of professional training was responsible for the poor quality of reporting, only 15 percent thought political manipulation was to blame. Journalistic recklessness notwithstanding, press freedom is clearly under threat, considering that most detentions of journalists are arbitrary and conducted without a legal basis.

There are signs that media freedom is on the decline. Since 2001, four independent newspapers have folded and a number of journalists have fled to exile. *Rwanda Newsline* closed down due to financial and managerial problems, and its editor, Eddie Muagbi, sought exile in the Netherlands. State authorities shut down the *Rwanda Herald* and deported its editor, Asuman Bisiika, to Uganda. Deo Mushayidi, editor of *Imboni* (The Retina) and *Le Messager,* was forced to abandon his papers and seek exile in Belgium.

Some publications, such as *Umuseso,* have defied the persecution. This is not because *Umuseso* is the best or the most independent newspaper, but because it has courageously defended its editorial line and defied pressure and harassment. Rwandan authorities frequently sought to punish the journalists and particularly the editors at *Umuseso.* The former managing editor, now in exile, was a regular visitor to the Kigali prosecution office and was imprisoned for six months in 1999. His successor, Ismail Mbonigaba, also faced similar problems and was jailed, allegedly for embezzling funds. After Mbonigaba was punished, the authorities jailed the new managing editor, Robert Sebufirira, and his deputy, McDowell Kalisa, for three weeks, allegedly on trumped up charges. Robert Sebufirira now lives in exile in Canada.

In total, ten court cases were brought against *Umuseso* between 2001 and 2004, most of them filed by government officials. The paper has yet to be convicted in a court ruling. Some journalists contend that *Umuseso* itself is at fault, as it sometimes attacked individuals without sufficient evidence of wrongdoing. In addition, the fact that its two former managing editors openly identified themselves with opposition political parties can also be seen as a move that could undermine the paper's editorial independence and journalistic credibility.

Limitations of Print Media

The reach and circulation of the press is mainly limited to Kigali. The only exceptions are *Imvaho Nshya* and *La Nouvelle Relève,* which are distributed through ORINFOR offices in all the provinces, and *Kinyamateka,* which is distributed through parishes across the country. Other regular papers are concentrated in Kigali and bought primarily by an affluent elite who can afford them. Most ordinary people who read newspapers do so at kiosks throughout the city. In addition, few newspapers are sold because of the high level of illiteracy among Rwandans.

Weak Advertisement Market, High Costs, and Fragmentation

The Rwandan economy sustains a lackluster advertising market. Most major companies are monopolies without serious competition and have no interest in antagonizing the authorities by advertising in nonstate media. Moreover, the print media have a small readership limited to the capital Kigali, which makes advertising in newspapers less attractive. As a result, many newspapers struggle to secure sufficient revenue to continue operating.

In addition, the per-copy cost of printing is so high that it exceeds the price of a newspaper sold at the kiosk, as publisher and editor Burasa Jean Gilbert of *Inganzo* (The Winner) told us in an interview.[23] Casmiry Kayumba, editor in chief of *Ukuri* and a member of the High Council of the Press, cites this as the main reason why most independent Rwandan newspapers and periodicals are printed in Uganda, where costs are somewhat lower.[24] Gaspard Safari, chief editor of the *New Times,* said in an interview that if the government was really interested in developing a strong independent media, it should waive taxes on printing materials.[25]

Finally, most newspapers and periodicals are individually owned and operated. Owners may not have either the financial resources or the professional capacity to run a newspaper as a business. Therefore, most rely either on government handouts (mainly in the form of advertisements by state agencies or enterprises) or on small grants from donors. This has led to the proliferation of numerous unsustainable publications that appear irregularly, dispersing scarce resources and talent.

Lack of Solidarity Among Journalists

The Association of Rwandan Journalists was created to protect the interests of journalists. However, since its formation in 1995, it has been dogged by controversies that have diminished journalists' faith in the organization. Some have called it a public relations organization stocked with "government spokespersons." Others say that since the end of the genocide, journalists who lead the ARJ and the Press House end up representing state interests instead of reporters' concerns. Instead of displays of professional solidarity, this discord among working journalists has prevented journalists from speaking with a united voice when media freedom is jeopardized.

Restrictions on Registration

The media sector is also hampered by arbitrary state power over the registration of publications. Newspapers, periodicals, and journals are required to register with the Ministry of Information, which is attached to the Office of the Prime Minister. After consultation, the High Council of the Press, a purportedly independent media regulatory body provided for by the constitution, grants or denies permission for any newspaper to register or operate. The High Council of the Press also retains, together with cabinet, the right to allow or refuse the opening of a radio or television outlet. Due to the involvement of many governmental and nongovernmental institutions, the process of launching radio and television stations has become unnecessarily bureaucratic and serves to discourage the opening of new media outlets.

◾ Lessons and Recommendations

Sustainable, Coordinated Strategies Based on Local Needs

Most of those interviewed for this assessment complained about inflexible donor terms and a lack of regard for local initiatives and priorities. In too many cases, donors came with their own agendas that tended to undermine local initiatives and encourage dependency. Donor-driven approaches, along with the lack of clear funding criteria and the ad hoc nature of some assistance, negatively affected the results of many projects as well as relationships between donors and indigenous organizations. Moreover, fragmented and uncoordinated donor aid led individual journalists to launch newspapers with the sole aim of gaining international funds. This approach wasted limited resources, dispersed talent, and gave birth to numerous unsustainable publications of dubious consequence.

To ensure the efficacy of international media assistance, donors should agree on a common strategy with clear goals and benchmarks based on respectful consultations with local partners. Projects should aim to bolster the entire media sector and plant the seeds for further development, instead of expiring as soon as international funding evaporates. Rwandan journalists should also learn to be more assertive about their needs when communicating with donor governments and organizations. In addition, assistance should be designed for and delivered to an institution or organization instead of relying exclusively on a particular individual. For example, instead of merely donating funds to individual outlets it would be more effective to help finance the establishment of a printing house that could serve as a pillar of an independent media sector. This idea was proposed by a number of editors and publishers whom we interviewed.

Journalism Training Focused on the Long Term

Donor assistance has enabled numerous reporters and aspiring reporters to receive valuable training in journalism skills. The state radio has particularly benefited from this training and advice, with radio programming improving as a result. Training should remain a high priority for donors, but it should be treated as a long-term, systematic endeavor. Ad hoc courses or projects are of little use. Bolstering longer-term training strategies should be the goal, including extended internships or other forms of on-the-job training at particular news organizations or institutions. In addition, there should be continued support for young professionals to earn a bachelor degree in journalism at the School of Journalism and Communication at the National University of Rwanda, as well as training for practicing journalists in basic journalism, ethics, and media law. In addition, donors should consider initiatives aimed at educating a broad section of Rwandan society—including government officials—about the concept of media freedom. This remains a new and largely misunderstood idea, and a public discussion of the principle of freedom of expression could prove constructive.

Diplomatic and Political Support

Political support from foreign embassies and organizations for media freedom and embattled journalists represents perhaps the most crucial element of international assistance. International protests expressed publicly and privately have helped discourage some excesses by the government and served to protect journalistic inquiry. As *Umuseso*'s former managing editor, Ismail Mbonigaba said, "such support is a prerequisite to building a robust media sector." In order to work, he said, "we need to feel safe and protected first."[26]

Political support and legal expertise has also been crucial for the adoption of more liberal media legislation. Donors should continue to extend assistance for the reform of media law and seek to raise awareness of legal issues among journalists.

Political support for media freedom needs to be consistent, because at times it has appeared somewhat arbitrary. Donors should extend such support to all legitimate journalists and should ensure that material assistance is not exploited in a way that makes the international community complicit in any kind of repression.

Renewed Commitment to Media Assistance

A number of donors have overcome initial reluctance and embraced media assistance as an important ingredient in the promotion of democracy in Rwanda. Such a vital element of democratization deserves more generous funding and a long-term commitment. Given the international community's failure to intervene decisively during the tragic events of 1994, donors have an obligation and duty to help build a robust "Fourth Estate" that holds power accountable and ensures open debate.

Notes

1. Prunier, *The Rwanda Crisis,* p. 133.
2. Human Rights Watch, *Leave None to Tell the Story,* p. 67.
3. Prunier, *Rwanda Crisis,* p. 133.
4. Chrétien, *Rwanda,* pp. 383–386.
5. *Akazu* is the Kinyarwanda word for a small hut. In local political jargon, it is understood as a powerful symbol representing the very few individuals who held

real power during the Habyarimana regime. They mainly included the president's wife, his brothers, his cousins, and some senior military officers from the president's birthplace, Gisenyi prefecture. Des Forges, "Face au Génocide," p. 67.

6. Prunier, *Rwanda Crisis,* p. 134.

7. Human Rights Watch, *Leave None to Tell the Story,* p. 68.

8. This information was provided by Charles Nahayo, a longtime technician at Radio Rwanda. Author interview, Kigali, July 1, 2003.

9. A reference to the 1961 referendum banning the Tutsi monarchy identified as a regime used to control the majority Hutu masses.

10. Prunier, *Rwanda Crisis,* p. 223; cited in Chalk, "Hate Radio in Rwanda," p. 98.

11. Prunier, *Rwanda Crisis,* pp. 222–223.

12. Ibid., p. 224; Chalk, "Hate Radio in Rwanda," p. 98.

13. Chalk, "Hate Radio in Rwanda," p. 99.

14. *Agatashya: The History of a Radio Station in 10 Dates,* http://www.hirondelle .org/hirondelle.nsf.

15. Fondation Hirondelle argued that Bukavu was a secure location. Ironically, the defeated génocidares were also heading in this direction. Some RPF sources say that this made the organization suspect and led to it being denied permission to open offices and a station in Kigali.

16. According to various sources, the cold relationship between the RPF-led government and the French government may explain why the project was never realized.

17. Federal Republic of Germany and Republic of Rwanda, *Réunions de Travail Concernant la Coopération Economique et au Développement.*

18. The *Rwanda Herald* is now out of circulation, due to the deportation of its chief editor and proprietor on grounds of operating without a work permit.

19. Author interview with Charles Nahayo, June 30, 2003.

20. Internews survey, October 22–23, 2003, Kigali. Of the sixty-one delegates of a seminar titled "Discussions on Free Media: Journalists, Civil Society, and the Private Sector, Working for Democracy in Rwanda," forty-nine returned questionnaires. This was "not a formal or statistically relevant survey," as Internews recognizes, but it helps to gauge some general views about the media in the country, considering that the delegates included journalists, editors, media managers, legislators, government officials, academics, and civil society representatives.

21. Author interview with Faustin Karangira, July 1, 2003.

22. This law was passed by parliament but the president, allegedly because of pressure from donor governments, refused to sign it and referred it back to parliament. In the end, the article was deleted and the amended version was adopted. It is the same law that provides for the establishment of independent radio and television stations.

23. Author interview with Burasa Jean Gilbert, August 25, 2003.

24. Author interview with Casmiry Kayumba, July 10, 2003.

25. Author interview with Gaspard Safari, June 26, 2003.

26. Author interview with Ismail Mbonigaba, August 4, 2003.

10

Promoting Independent Media in El Salvador

Anne Germain Lefèvre

After decades of deep social inequality and authoritarian rule in which political dissent was brutally crushed, civil war erupted in El Salvador in 1981. The conflict pitted the Salvadoran government and army against the insurgent Farabundo Martí National Liberation Front (FMLN).

The government enjoyed generous backing from the United States, which saw the conflict as part of the Cold War and donated an estimated US$3 billion in military aid. Although the FMLN could not match the strength of the government's well-equipped military, it had significant popular support and was able to assert control over substantial territory and to recruit an estimated 7,000 soldiers. An offensive on the capital by the FMLN in November 1989 demonstrated the government's failure to defeat the insurgency despite years of bloodshed, and made clear that neither side could secure a military victory. During the offensive, the assassination of six prominent Jesuit priests by the army drew international outrage and added pressure on both the government and its US patrons to negotiate an end to the conflict.

As part of the peace talks, the two sides signed agreements in 1990 on human rights and constitutional reforms that included limits on military authority, rules for free elections, a stronger legislative branch, and a more independent judiciary. The peace accords were signed on January 16, 1992, ending a war that claimed more than 40,000 lives.

The peace settlement marked a break with the country's authoritarian legacy, creating conditions for democratic reform and media freedom. The more open political climate gave birth to a more pluralistic media, allowing a wider range of opinions in the public arena, a degree of critical reporting, and a reform of broadcast licensing regulation.

El Salvador received substantial aid from the international community in the postwar period, with most of the assistance targeting reconstruction, poverty relief, sanitation, health, and education. While a smaller portion of aid was focused on the democratization process, donors attached a relatively low priority to the media sector. Few studies have examined the relationship between international assistance, democratization, and the development of the media in Central America or in El Salvador in particular.

This chapter seeks to determine the effect of international assistance on the media sector, looking at the role of the media in El Salvador's democratic evolution. Following an overview of the media at the time of the peace accords, it summarizes international media assistance initiatives, ranging from journalism training to donations of radio transmission equipment, analyzes the impact of international assistance on the media, and sets out several lessons and recommendations for donors based on the El Salvadoran experience.

Media at the End of Civil War

Before the civil war, a tabloid style of journalism tended to prevail, with an emphasis on entertainment, sports, and the social life of the rich elite. Political news was often ignored or given a low priority. Out of three private television stations, only one offered a news program, which focused mainly on society news. Those publications that attempted to report on social unrest and delve into political news in a serious manner were subject to repression by state authorities or quasi-governmental elements. These outlets were sometimes shut down or bombed, and journalists were persecuted or even murdered.

During the civil war, martial law was imposed and freedom of expression was systematically constricted in clear violation of the country's constitution.[1] According to the truth commission that was established to investigate the most serious acts of violence that occurred during the war, all political opposition was treated as subversive. Newspapers or broadcasters who refused to bow to the repression were forced to go underground. Two radio stations allied with the FMLN broadcast throughout the conflict, though the programming tended to display a similar propagandistic approach.

International pressure and US demands that the Salvadoran regime present a more democratic image allowed a limited degree of media freedom to take root. A few critical, balanced news shows appeared, including *Entrevista al Día* and other programming on Channel 12, which took on subjects that other media were unwilling to address.[2]

At the time of the signing of the peace accords in 1992, there were 103 media outlets in El Salvador, including 81 radio stations. With a few exceptions, these publications and broadcasters were all privately owned and highly commercial in outlook. The large number of print and electronic media did not translate into genuine pluralism or robust journalistic inquiry.

The legacy of the civil war and the threat of repression, either direct or indirect, mostly discouraged critical reporting. The media also shied away from airing robust public debates on pressing issues. Journalistic skills and training were seriously lacking, as was a sense of professional solidarity. Business interests were accustomed to bribing reporters to receive favorable coverage. With a smaller number of investors owning a greater number of outlets, a trend toward concentration of ownership had begun to develop.

The most important daily newspapers in 1992 were *La Prensa Gráfica* and *El Diario de Hoy,* the first with an average circulation of 128,000 and the second with 95,000. This dominant market position continues to this day. Both eighty-page papers had nationwide distribution and were sold abroad as well. Other daily newspapers had a much smaller readership and fewer pages, including *La Noticia* (circulation 26,000, twenty-eight pages) and the afternoon papers *Diario Latino* and *El Mundo* (both with a circulation of 15,500 and a length of approximately thirty pages). There were also smaller weekly and biweekly publications, some of which focused on particular cities or regions.[3] Most of the newspapers (88 percent) began as private businesses. Both *La Prensa Gráfica* and *El Diario de Hoy* have been, and continue to be, family owned.

There were eighty-one radio stations in 1992, most of which were private (sixty-eight stations), with ten associated with religious or university institutions. Radio Farabundo Martí and Radio Venceremos were unique in that they began as underground stations politically allied with the FMLN during the war. The AM station La Versátil (Radio YSLV), was also unusual, as it carried a participatory format with programs aimed primarily at women's organizations. La Versátil became Radio Cabal in 1994. Ten stations belonged to religious or university institutions.

The television stations that existed at the time of the peace accords were privately owned, with the exception of Channel 10, and mostly relied on outdated technology and techniques. The country's oldest television stations—Channels 2, 4, and 6—all belonged to the same owner, Boris Eserski. The other stations—Channels 12, 19, and 25—began in the 1980s during the civil war as family-run commercial stations. Channel 12, owned by the Zedán family, presented itself as an editorially independent channel and fought for openness and freedom of expression in the media, giving voice to nongovernmental organizations (NGOs).

The civil war exposed Salvadoran journalists to a more independent, inquisitive approach to reporting due to the presence of numerous foreign correspondents covering the conflict. These foreign journalists, many of them Americans, "brought with them an entire school for the Salvadoran press,"[4] setting a higher standard for the reporting craft. Foreign correspondents hired local assistants to whom they taught the tricks of the trade, who then began to report in a more hard-hitting, timely manner.

The presence and professionalism of foreign reporters highlighted the need to improve training for local journalists. In the latter years of the war, several local universities started journalism degree programs and hired veteran reporters to help design the programs and teach. During the 1990s, several attempts were made to put the investigative approach displayed by foreign correspondents into practice, including the launch of the weekly *Primera Plana* and projects initiated by *El Diario de Hoy* and *La Prensa Gráfica.*

The peace accords brought an end to arbitrary regulation by the national communications secretariat of the presidency, which had blocked certain journalists or organizations from obtaining permission to publish or broadcast. The FMLN, as part of its political participation, was granted the right to obtain media operating licenses and to publish paid advertisements.

Under the new political environment created by the peace settlement, older media outlets adopted a more open format and new outlets offering a wider range of information and opinions appeared.

■ International Media Assistance

International assistance to El Salvador's media sector, albeit modest, could not have arrived at a better moment. The end of a long civil war and constitutional reforms set out in the peace settlement created an opening for a new era for the media.

Donor governments and organizations varied in their approach and goals. Some supported the production of specific television programs, while others funded the creation and development of new media outlets. Some chose to strengthen several NGOs that worked closely with Salvadoran journalists. Several donors focused on improving journalistic skills, and others preferred to support legal reform.

Assistance for New Media Outlets

Newspapers and periodicals. Several new periodicals started with support from international assistance agencies, including the weekly newspaper *Primera Plana* and the monthly magazine *Tendencias*. The editorial approach of both publications was a radical departure from customary journalistic practices in a society permeated by authoritarianism and conservatism for decades.

Primera Plana was launched in September 1994 with financial aid from the German Buntstift Foundation (now known as the Heinrich Böll Foundation) and other organizations. The Buntstift Foundation hoped the new publication would bolster public debate by offering critical, investigative coverage of current events. At the time, the prevailing opinion among donors was that the existing media could not be democratized and that new organizations would need to be established.[5] The Buntstift Foundation was the primary source of aid, providing a grant of US$262,857, while funds from other donors totaled US$28,000. These funds were invested in the project's initial design, feasibility studies, infrastructure, training, salaries, rent, the newspaper's layout, travel expenses, and the three-month marketing campaign to launch the weekly. It should be noted that only US$57,142 was invested in infrastructure, the rest being spent on nonrecoverable operating expenses. For 1995 and 1996, the Böll Foundation committed US$457,142 in aid, to be disbursed in quarterly payments. The paper offered a fresh, investigative style that was new to the Salvadoran market and covered subjects previously overlooked. Nevertheless, after publishing for ten months and despite significant donations, *Primera Plana* collapsed in July 1995.

The Danish International Development Agency (DANIDA), part of Denmark's Central American Human Rights Program (PRODECA), and the Humanist Institute for Cooperation with Developing Countries (HIVOS), of the Netherlands, funded a monthly magazine titled *Tendencias*. HIVOS donated about US$60,000 annually for seven years. The magazine, published without a break between 1990 and 1997, sought to offer readers an alternative source of news and opinions.[6]

Tendencias addressed topics related to politics and culture, and the 3,000 copies produced each month were aimed at opinion leaders. The founders (including Executive Director Roberto Turcios), were supporters of democratic reform in El Salvador. This view was reflected in the magazine's pluralistic editorial line, which offered a range of perspectives. *Tendencias* broke new ground in El Salvador by allowing writers from different political currents to express opinions on the same subject. However, as the magazine proved unable to become self-supporting, it shut down in 1997.

In the late 1990s, PRODECA also funded newspaper supplements that were distributed with the larger daily papers but prepared by journalists from *Tendencias*. Most of these supplements were inserted in *La Prensa Gráfica* and some in *El Diario de Hoy*, since these dailies have the widest circulation in El Salvador. The first supplements covered issues related to development efforts, a subject generally overlooked by the main media outlets. Other supplements had a more cultural bent. *El Búho*, published monthly for one year with an average run of 100,000 copies, provided a critical perspective on cultural issues, with the idea of offering cultural diversity to a newspaper readership accustomed to conservative cultural and literary productions. The PRODECA aid came as a result of suggestions by *Tendencias* editors to produce a product that would reach a wider audience and disseminate alternative information in the largest circulation newspapers.[7]

Radio. Financial and technical assistance from the Netherlands and Denmark, mostly solicited by the Association of Participatory Radio Stations and Programs of El Salvador (ARPAS), helped launch or sustain numerous local radio stations. The stations, which received radio equipment and training, provided groundbreaking participatory programming, reporting on local news, and discussions about current events. The Communication Assistance Foundation (CAF/SCO), of the Netherlands, supported stations such as Radio Izcanal and Radio San Pedro. For Radio Cabal (now Radio La Klave), the Dutch NGO HIVOS provided annual support of $32,000 for several years. The Danish Association for International Cooperation MS provided the primary funding and assistance for Radio Cabal, covering a period from 1993 to 1999. Initially, Denmark's priority was to ensure the station could fulfill its programming goal as a forum for open discussion. By 1998, more emphasis was placed on sound management and finances.

The aid to community radio was modest but useful, and most community radio stations managed to cover their costs through advertising, local donations, and volunteers. Some stations that received aid have since become self-sufficient. Some other radio stations receive regular funding from religious institutions, though station managers maintain that the financial support does not restrict a station's autonomy.

Donors belatedly supported Internet-based projects. Oxfam America, CAF/SCO of the Netherlands, and the Swedish International Development Agency (SIDA) helped launch three electronic publications. These sites are supposed to target opinion shapers, decisionmakers, and international assistance agencies. *El Mirador de Gobernabilidad* follows governance issues, a daily electronic bulletin provides an analysis of current events in El Salvador, and a biweekly online newsletter explores specific issues in-depth.

Television. During the postwar period, donors have supported the production of several television shows that sought to delve into current events and social issues with in-depth, balanced reporting and open discussion. With one exception, these programs have been broadcast by the innovative Channel 12 (which became TV 12 in 1996).

The weekly show *A Fondo* was produced in 1992–1993 with financial and technical aid from the Spanish government, the mayor's office of a Basque city, and the French organization Comité Inter-Mouvements Auprès des Evacués (CIMADE).[8] Combining feature stories with interviews, the program's main objective was to contribute to shaping opinion on diverse topics such as the peace accords, the democratization of Salvadoran society, and the causes of the civil war. The Canadian International Development Agency (CIDA), in 1995–1996, also funded the weekly program *En la Mira*, which addressed the country's economic and social problems. The program *Realidades: Periodismo de Fondo* was launched with financial aid from SIDA in 2001 and continues to air, covering topics of national interest. Since its launch during the civil war, the daily interview show *Entrevista al Día* has become a well-known program with a significant audience. Airing on TV 12 (previously Channel 12), the investigative and research work that provided the foundation for this program was supported by the same donors that funded production of other programs. *Entrevista al Día* was one of the first opinion shows where representatives from different political and social camps appeared, stimulating open, democratic debate. As evidence of its desire to foster political pluralism, *Entrevista al Día* was the only show that dared to allow FMLN leaders to appear on air during the civil war.[9]

These four programs, *Entrevista al Día, A Fondo, En la Mira,* and *Realidades: Periodismo de Fondo,* won large audiences and shared a common mission. The programs sought to open up and raise the quality of public debate by introducing fresh perspectives and well-informed reporting. These programs likely would not have been broadcast if it was not for the attitude of TV 12's daring owner, who employed his channel to give voice to groups long ignored and to promote a more tolerant, informed tone to political discussion. Two of the shows, *Entrevista al Día* and *Realidades: Periodismo de Fondo,* received an average rating of about 60 percent of the television audience as well as a flood of telephone calls and e-mails from viewers. The shows helped set a higher editorial standard for the industry and have become models of broadcasting excellence.

A station operated by the Technological University, Channel 33, broadcasts the weekly program *Emisión Especial* with assistance from Denmark's PRODECA. Financing for one year began in January 2003. The aid covered a six-person team (two camera persons, three journalists, and one producer) that produced investigative feature stories about different political, economic, and social topics, complementing the work of the Channel 33 news department. As an investigative reporting program, *Emisión Especial* fulfilled the strategic vision of PRODECA by helping to educate the public about important issues in a balanced, engaging manner.

In addition, donors have delivered substantial assistance to the public television station (Channel 10), though without sponsoring specific programs. Channel 10, which airs mainly cultural and educational programming, is run by the National Council on Culture and the Arts (CONCULTURA), a state agency within the Ministry of Education. Most international assistance has come from similar cultural agencies in France, Germany, Mexico, Colombia, and Japan. The aid has included broadcasting equipment, training, technical assistance, and educational and cultural books and materials.

Support for Media NGOs

To promote professional solidarity among journalists, bolster community radio stations, and promote ethical standards and freedom of expression, donors have also supported nongovernmental organizations. The main recipients of such aid have been the Association of Journalists of El Salvador (APES), the Association of Participatory Radio Stations and Programs of El Salvador, and PROBIDAD (meaning "Probity"), the last of which is a nonpartisan, nonprofit civic organization that works to defend freedom of expression and promote investigative journalism. These organizations have yet to secure financial sustainability without relying on outside funding.

PROBIDAD has become recognized as an authority on freedom of expression issues and questions of corruption. The international assistance provided tends to be short-term, covering a period of one year. According to PROBIDAD chairman Jaime López, the organization has maintained its autonomy in its decisionmaking while pursuing its primary objective: to stimulate investigative reporting and improve the legal conditions for practicing journalism in El Salvador.

The Association of Participatory Radio Stations and Programs of El Salvador has received international assistance since its founding in 1994. This association works to bolster community radio, lobbying on pertinent legal and regulatory issues and helping the stations share resources and produce joint programming. During its initial five years, ARPAS received financial aid from the Communication Assistance Foundation (Netherlands), DanChurchAid (Denmark), the Canadian Executive Services Organization (CESO), the Programa de Reconstrucción Social El Salvador (Canada), Misereor (Germany), and Diakonia (Sweden). In addition, certain agencies, such as HIVOS (Netherlands) and the World Association for Christian Communication, have provided targeted grants. Since 2000, ARPAS has received financial contributions from Diakonia and the CAF/SCO. ARPAS has also received technical advice from several donors: CAF/SCO, World Communications (United States), the Centro de Desarrollo Internacional (Spain), and Diakonia.

According to information provided by ARPAS's executive director, donors provided a total of US$500,000 from 1994 to 2003, most of which covered a medium-term period of about three years. A significant portion of this aid was invested in radio equipment. A small percentage (5–10 percent per project) supported institutional development.

In 1999 the Association of Journalists of El Salvador was the beneficiary of financial and logistical aid from Radda Barnen (a Swedish NGO dedicated to the protection of children) for the drafting of a code of press ethics. The joint efforts of journalists, scholars, journalism students, and representatives from diverse sectors of civil society produced the code, which was an attempt to raise professional standards for the press. One part of the code refers to the appropriate, responsible handling of information regarding children.

Some journalists and members of existing NGOs have suggested the creation of a monitoring organization that would serve as an independent watchdog of the country's news media, but it has yet to be established.

Journalism Training

Several multilateral organizations and foundations have funded journalism training programs in El Salvador during the postwar period. One of the most important was the Central American Journalism Project (PROCEPER), sponsored by Florida International University with US$13.8 million in funding from the US Agency for International Development (USAID) between 1988 and 1997. The initiative focused on "improving the professional abilities, journalistic ethics, and managerial capabilities of journalists and editors."

PROCEPER provided training through brief or extended seminars that focused on editing techniques, news reporting, investigative journalism, election coverage, and other skills. More than 2,000 journalists from Guatemala, El Salvador, and Honduras participated in the project's training seminars. PROCEPER began work in El Salvador during the civil war, with thirty-five to fifty journalists attending every year.

To reinforce the training process, PROCEPER sponsored various publications. One of these initiatives led to the creation of *Pulso del Periodismo,* a journal devoted to training and education in journalism, which became a forum for discussing and devising journalistic standards and techniques. This journal continues as a website, funded by the Robert R. McCormick Tribune Foundation, and is used by Salvadoran journalists and professors. Another project compiled a Latin America media directory in 1993, providing information on institutions linked to the media and journalists. The directory is now available online.

The UN Educational, Scientific, and Cultural Organization (UNESCO) also has sponsored journalism training programs, including two media seminars as well as more extensive courses in cooperation with universities. As part of its Media and Freedom of Expression in the Americas Program, the US-based International Center for Journalists organized several lectures in 2002 designed to stimulate discussion among journalists about the role of the media and freedom of expression.

The Konrad Adenauer Stiftung of Germany, a foundation that seeks to strengthen democratic structures, funded a research project in 1995 on the Salvadoran media and its effect on democratic development. Organized in cooperation with the Department of Literature, Communication, and Journalism of the José Simeón Cañas University of Central America, the study sought "to deepen knowledge of the issue and its effect on society . . . to contribute to democratic development, the consolidation of peace, and the store of scientific quality texts."

The Friedrich Ebert Stiftung (FES), another German foundation that supports democratization efforts in El Salvador, has offered full scholarships to journalists to attend intensive journalism courses in the United States and Germany. The two-week courses seek to encourage ethical practices and improve journalism skills. Prominent Salvadoran journalists have participated, including Mauricio Funes (of TV 12), Narciso Castillo (of Channel 33), and Carlos Dada (of *La Prensa Gráfica*). FES has also been promoting investigative journalism through research on specific topics. The studies are then used as reference material by journalists and commentators in different media outlets preparing a particular story. For example, a study done by FES on the middle class in El Salvador provided background information for a report appearing in *La Prensa Gráfica,* published in the investigative supplement "Enfoques" in August 2003.

Donors have delivered assistance to several communications and journalism schools, including the communications and journalism unit in the Department of Literature, Communication, and Journalism at the José Simeón Cañas University. Since this unit opened in 1990, it has received support from a Spanish Jesuit organization, Noticias de España, for the purchase of technical equipment.

International agencies have funded training courses for media executives, though I could not confirm the degree of participation by the executives. One of these courses is a joint seminar by Northwestern University and the Press Institute of the Inter-American Press Association (IAPA), funded by the John S. and James L. Knight Foundation and the Robert R. McCormick Tribune Foundation. The two-week course began in 2001 and is designed for media executives working in editorial, production, or administrative positions. The seminar's core objective, according to the organizers, is "to provide the executive with a comprehensive corporate vision and forge new leaders for the journalistic endeavour."[10] The seminar's content revolves around four themes: strategy, marketing, journalism, and leadership.

Assistance for Legal and Regulatory Reforms

In the 1990s the telecommunications sector was privatized with technical assistance from the Inter-American Development Bank (IADB). A new telecommunications law, which dismantled the state monopoly, was adopted in 1996 that created a new regulatory body to oversee the allocation of spectrum and broadcast licenses. A previous state commission that had used arbitrary power to block some organizations or journalists from working was disbanded.

The new regulatory agency, the General Electricity and Telecommunication Superintendence (SIGET), has come under criticism from some quarters, because its authority is tied exclusively to a presidential appointee and because of rules requiring auctions to govern the allocation of frequencies. According to one published analysis, the new law's reliance on auctions fails to take into account public interests, leading to "the radio spectrum, which is a public good, being subject to the private interests at play in the free market."[11] The original version of the telecommunications law also failed to acknowledge the existence of community radio stations. After lobbying by ARPAS, an amendment was adopted in 1998 that secured recognition for community radio stations.

Salvadoran law includes various provisions that run counter to freedom of expression, placing constraints on the practice of journalism. Under the country's libel law, journalists run the risk of losing their press credentials or even a prison sentence if they are found guilty of a libel offense. Access to trials and information held by governmental authorities is severely restricted as well. Yet international donors have only recently taken up legal issues.

In early 2003 the government requested technical assistance from UNESCO to help review national laws related to free speech to ensure compliance with international conventions signed by El Salvador. Ensuring public access to information held by governmental authorities has emerged as an issue of concern. Discussions under way could lead to the creation of a task force made up of representatives from across the political spectrum, professional journalists, and scholars. The commission's mandate would be to create a democratic legal framework that would foster a more robust media sector in El Salvador.

◼ Effect of Media Assistance

The 1992 peace settlement brought dramatic political change to El Salvador, including changes that have transformed the media sphere. Any assessment of the effect of media assistance must take these political events into account and acknowledge that domestic factors—not outside aid—were the main influences shaping the media. Moreover, aid to media projects was relatively modest compared to the international assistance devoted to reconstruction, poverty relief, democratization initiatives, and other areas. Still, donor assistance has played a role in shaping the evolution of Salvadoran media toward a more democratic model.

By sponsoring the production of innovative broadcast programming and publications, and funding training and the expansion of community radio, donor assistance has helped improve the quality of journalism in El Salvador. Media organizations funded by donors have bolstered professional solidarity among journalists, supported lobbying efforts, and promoted investigative reporting. By helping media outlets offer a wider range of opinions and perspectives, international assistance has reinforced a trend toward pluralism and democratic debate. Finally, international expertise has helped plant the seeds of a reformed legal framework for the media sector.

Improving Editorial Quality, Pluralism

In contrast to the civil war era, the news media now report in a critical manner and give voice to a broader range of voices and opinions. News outlets report on dubious bids for public works, corrupt officials, police officers involved in crimes, and the fraudulent or irresponsible handling of public resources. In some cases, news coverage has forced institutions to launch investigations into wrongdoing. International assistance, in the form of support for programming and publications as well as training initiatives, has contributed to this improvement in the quality and breadth of reporting.

Donor assistance combined with visionary entrepreneurs at two television stations paved the way for the production of innovative current affairs programming that attracted large audiences. This fresh approach employed investigative reporting, a more balanced, thorough presentation, and greater participation of ordinary citizens. While many of the programs, such as *A Fondo, En la Mira, Realidades: Periodismo de Fondo, Entrevista al Día,* and *Emisión Especial,* could not be maintained in the long term, the editorial quality set a new standard for journalistic excellence.

One program, *Entrevista al Día,* on TV 12, which was on air until 2005, influenced other broadcasters to embrace live debates and discussions, especially during election campaigns, as a standard feature. This approach, which has been undertaken at some newspapers as well, has clearly bolstered pluralistic debate in El Salvador.

In the print media, donor-funded publications also helped serve as a model for a more inquisitive, informed style of journalism and a greater degree of pluralism. The weekly newspaper *Primera Plana* folded after only ten months, but its investigative reporting inspired other journalists. The monthly magazine *Tendencias,* which was launched with support primarily from the Danish agency PRODECA and published for seven years, has been recognized as a groundbreaking endeavor for its presentation of a broad range of comments and political ideas. Quality investigative supplements prepared by journalists from *Tendencias* and *Primera Plana* also appeared in the country's large daily newspapers. Investigative reporting has contributed to a degree of healthy competition among journalists seeking to hold the government accountable and to provide their readers with the most up-to-date, complete account of current events.

Unlike the repressive atmosphere of the 1970s and 1980s, the news media now serves as a platform for "debate, criticism, and dissent," according to analysts of the Salvadoran media.[12] Factions or opinions that were once totally excluded from the public arena are now openly quoted and interviewed. The more tolerant tone was on display at the municipal and legislative elections of March 2003, when "different political parties were pressured to leave aside classic propaganda aimed at destroying the opponent, and instead to stress educating the electorate and discussing concrete political platforms."[13] Some analysts have cited "considerable progress" by leading media in distancing themselves from government authorities and adopting a more critical stance.[14]

Strengthening Community Radio

International assistance has helped community radio by providing direct aid to six stations as well as helping an association working to promote the interests of the industry. Community radio has stressed participatory, grassroots programs that involve the local population and social issues often ignored by the national media. Donors helped the six stations develop programming and improve sound quality and technical capacity. With help from SIDA, ARPAS has helped build up a network of stations and secured the legalization of community radio stations, contributing to the movement's longer-term sustainability. In 2005, there were twenty-two community radio stations, up from fifteen in 1996. Research shows that between 200,000 to 300,000 persons regularly tune in to the community radio stations. This corresponds to roughly 10 percent of the estimated rural total audience, constituting 2 million potential listeners.[15]

Raising Professional Standards

Over the past decade a new generation of more professional, more responsible journalists has emerged. Editors and producers are more willing to pursue sensitive stories and to raise tough questions for the government. News outlets now often serve as watchdogs, pointing out abuses of authority or social problems. A more open political climate and an end to military rule, in El Salvador and elsewhere in the region, helped create conditions that gave rise to this new generation of reporters. Extensive training and education initiatives sponsored by donors also played an important role, ensuring that the shift in the political atmosphere was fully exploited.

As mentioned previously, the US-funded training program PROCEPER, organized by Florida International University, was among the most influential training initiatives, with more than 2,000 journalists from El Salvador, Guatemala, and Honduras learning about editing techniques, news reporting, investigative journalism, and election coverage over a nine-year period.

Other projects organized with international assistance helped universities launch and expand journalism education and raised awareness of legal issues surrounding media freedom.

The code of press ethics, drafted with assistance from a Swedish NGO, has helped stimulate discussion within the journalistic community about what constitutes responsible, independent reporting. A commission set up by the media industry has sought to encourage voluntary compliance with the code.

Strengthening Professional Solidarity and an Independent Media Industry

International assistance has helped establish media organizations that have promoted journalistic solidarity, media freedom, and investigative reporting. PROBIDAD and ARPAS, which were both created with donor assistance, have emerged as influential NGOs. PROBIDAD has helped shape public debate on media-related issues and fostered quality investigative reporting. It has educated the public about corruption and supported greater access to information held by government authorities. ARPAS has helped improve the technical operation of radio stations, organized training courses, encouraged joint programming projects, produced programming that invites citizen participation, and lobbied to improve the legal status of community radio.

Improving Technical Presentation

Donor aid has contributed to a marked improvement in the operation and technical production of media outlets. Compared to the early 1990s, news organizations are better organized, employing more efficient technologies and modern management techniques. Major newspapers have automated printing and graphic design systems, and television has moved into the digital age, with live broadcasts, better graphics, and upgraded signals. Radio stations are converting to digital technology and are forming broadcast networks and business consortiums. In certain cases, international assistance made this technical progress possible, with editors or managers learning about new techniques and technologies through training seminars. For example, the daily newspaper *El Diario de Hoy* was redesigned under the tutelage of Lafitte Fernández, a Costa Rican editor and instructor for the PROCEPER training program at Florida International University.

Reforming Media Law

International assistance helped clear the way for a sweeping reform of the communications sector, introducing a more transparent regulatory framework for the airwaves. Financial aid and technical advice from the Inter-American Development Bank was a crucial factor in the privatization of the communications industry, resulting in the adoption of a new law and the creation of a regulatory body overseeing the issuing of broadcast frequencies through public auction. Although not free from flaws, the new framework is an improvement over the closed, repressive system that prevailed previously.

■ Challenges Facing the Media Sector

While newspapers and broadcasters now operate in a more open atmosphere compared to the repressive era of military rule, the media sector still faces challenges and obstacles that hold back the free flow of information and journalistic inquiry.

Concentration of Ownership

Perhaps the greatest threat to media freedom in El Salvador is an insidious trend toward monopoly ownership. Telecorporación Salvadoreña (TCS) owns the three television channels with the largest audience and controls 85 percent of the advertising market. This concentration of commercial power discourages competition in programming and news gathering while also obstructing the emergence of innovative new media outlets. The lack of journalistic competition is especially worrying, given that 58 percent of the population relies on television for its news, according to a recent survey.[16] State agencies charged with regulating the airwaves and commerce so far have taken no effective action to limit such concentration of ownership.

Apart from this virtual television monopoly, the print media are dominated by two large daily newspapers. These large media firms have developed close ties to major economic interests and their monopolistic position makes them reluctant to confront these powerful interests. In some cases major corporations own shares in these media firms.

Even though the media have improved their investigative reporting techniques, the main media outlets remain reluctant to touch on the vested economic interests. In some cases, government or business groups have punished certain media for critical coverage by withholding advertising or restricting access to information. According to a report by the UN Development Programme (UNDP), the country's "openness to pluralism shows clear limits, associated with the economic interests of the groups that own the media and to the polarization of Salvadoran society."[17]

Another product of the monopolistic trend is an emphasis on commercial considerations instead of serving the public interest. It is the media business owners, not journalists or editors, who decide "what is disseminated,

how it is disseminated, where it is disseminated, and when it is disseminated."[18] The result is a tendency among media outlets, especially the TCS
television stations, to dwell on scandal, crime, and tales of pathos. Moreover, this sensational approach tends to blur the line between news and
opinion beyond recognition.

The Salvadoran public also lacks a thoughtful weekly or monthly magazine that could allow more in-depth analysis and provide a balance to the
heavily commercial fare offered by the major newspapers and broadcasters.

Legal Obstacles to Media Freedom

Salvadoran law poses certain restrictions on journalistic inquiry and freedom of expression. The penal code carries excessive penalties for libel or
slander offenses, including the possible revocation of press credentials and
imposition of prison sentences. Public access to information held by governmental bodies is also curtailed by existing law and practices, allowing
the state to operate often in virtual secrecy.

Weak Public Broadcasting

The public television station (Channel 10) remains stuck in another era,
despite substantial international assistance. It fails to offer compelling current affairs and news programming that might offer a counterbalance to the
heavily commercial style of private stations. As a result, viewers must rely
on flawed private channels that often offer superficial news coverage that
caters to the agenda of the country's vested business interests. While successive governments have chosen not to use the public television as a political instrument, funding and support have been sorely missing. The political
leadership has failed to put forward a vision of genuine public broadcasting
free of political control.

▣ Lessons and Recommendations

For other countries emerging from war and civil conflict, there may be
valuable lessons to be drawn from El Salvador's experience with international media assistance. By coinciding with dramatic political changes,
aid for the media in El Salvador played a role in shaping a more open, tolerant tone for political debate and a more dynamic news media. Although
the assistance was relatively modest, it came at a pivotal moment after the
signing of the peace accords. To realize the full potential of media assistance
in any society, conducive political conditions are crucial. Donors could have

better exploited the opportunity in El Salvador with a more generous, coordinated, farsighted strategy.

Emphasis on Editorial Quality and Selection of Local Partners

In some cases, donor governments and agencies ensured the success of assistance projects in El Salvador by carefully selecting talented local partners with promising ideas. Government agencies from Sweden, Denmark, the Netherlands, Spain, Canada, and elsewhere sponsored the production of innovative television and radio programming that set a new journalistic standard for the Salvadoran media industry. The visionary managers at Channel 12 television proved to be an excellent investment, with new programs influencing how the news media cover elections, social issues, and state institutions. Moreover, consistent support for training and education initiatives has steadily raised professional standards and practices, shaping a new generation of reporters and editors.

Toward Financial Sustainability

Media donors often struggle to balance the need for short-term impact and longer-term financial viability. Many of the television programs sponsored with donor aid in El Salvador have since gone off the air. Two worthy publications that emphasized investigative reporting and in-depth analysis could not survive once international assistance was withdrawn, though they left a legacy of investigative reporting. Some community radio stations have managed to become self-sustaining and to wean themselves off donor funding. Given that the country's political environment has improved while monopolistic trends have intensified, donors should now examine how to nurture and sustain media outlets that emphasize editorial excellence and independence. Donor aid helped achieve the immediate goal of promoting a more pluralistic environment and setting out a model of journalistic integrity. Financial sustainability now needs to receive a higher priority, including advice and expertise for media business managers.

Donors might consider creating a network of eminent reporters, media owners, and others committed to independent journalism. Such a panel or network could work with donors to forge joint projects using soft loans or other assistance to help new media outlets thrive over the long term.

Media associations and organizations such as PROBIDAD and ARPAS have also played an important role in cultivating an independent news media, but these groups remain heavily dependent on outside assistance. Donors also will need to work with these valuable NGOs to help them find local sources of funding, explore possible alliances with universities, and establish a longer-term financial plan.

Supporting Media Self-Regulation and Higher Ethical Standards

International assistance has bolstered efforts by journalists to improve professional standards through self-regulation. Support for the drafting of a code of press ethics, which required a relatively modest financial commitment, allowed journalists to engage in constructive discussion about how the news media should balance its responsibilities. The code has become a reference for working journalists and a measure for assessing the performance of media organizations. To build on the success of the code, donors should consider promoting the position of ombudsman (or readers' editor) at news publications. Such a position has proved effective elsewhere in Latin America, providing a forum for readers and making news organizations more accountable. Donors also could help the media industry disseminate the code more widely through public discussions.

The Important Role of Media NGOs

Donor aid for media NGOs has helped cultivate solidarity among journalists, promote investigative reporting, and nurture community radio. The experience of El Salvador illustrates how associations and NGOs play an important role in the evolution of a free and independent media.

Although it has been discussed, journalists and donors have yet to organize a media monitoring group that could serve as a watchdog and an auditor for media coverage. Such an organization could reinforce efforts at self-regulation such as the code of press ethics, and stimulate constructive discussion about the quality of news reporting, especially at a time of increasing concentration of media ownership. Perhaps existing media NGOs could create a media monitoring organization in a joint effort.

Recognizing the Importance of Legal Reform

Apart from IADB assistance in the telecommunications sector, donors have been slow to recognize the importance of media law and regulation. Journalists still work under restrictive provisions that impose criminal punishments on libel offenses and allow government officials to withhold information of great public interest. Donor governments and organizations should view legal issues as a top priority to ensure a free flow of information and unfettered journalistic inquiry.

Media NGOs, donors, and journalists are increasingly focused on access to public information, which is not fully guaranteed at present. Donors could provide expertise in this area, possibly assisting domestic experts to adapt Salvadoran laws to ensure compliance with signed international agreements.

According to some experts in El Salvador, a new national law on access to information is not necessarily needed. Public authorities could amend existing laws or could "delineate this regulatory framework and enforce it through a memorandum, a municipal ordinance, a ministerial agreement, or an internal regulation."[19] Additionally, experts have argued for the recognition of "habeas data," which is a means for showing documents in the public interest to the media and for a journalist to investigate information sources that have been closed to him or her.

The media industry's trend toward monopoly poses a potential threat to pluralism and editorial independence in El Salvador. Indeed, concentration of ownership poses a challenge throughout the world. In emerging democracies, donors and journalists need to consider how to safeguard media freedom in the face of commercial pressures. Legal reform, through antitrust or other provisions, should be examined as one way of countering monopolistic trends.

Notes

1. Before the civil war, El Salvador ratified three international conventions establishing the right to free speech: the Universal Declaration of Human Rights, the International Covenant on Civil and Political Rights, and the American Convention on Human Rights. The Salvadoran constitution does not explicitly establish freedom of the press, but it contains elements that provide grounds for such a right.
2. Herrera, "Influencia de la Guerra Civil en El Salvador (1980–1992) en el Desarrollo de la Prensa Nacional."
3. Figures and facts about the media during this period are drawn from Ramos et al., "Los Medios de Difusión Colectiva en El Salvador."
4. Ibid.; Herrera, "Influencia de la Guerra Civil," p. 2.
5. Author interview with Lina Pohl, director of the Central America Office of the Heinrich Böll Foundation, January 27, 2004.
6. Author interview with Beatriz Barraza, consultant for HIVOS, San Salvador, January 26, 2004. HIVOS does not have its own staff representative in El Salvador.
7. Author interview with Roberto Turcios, San Salvador, September 19, 2003; Rasmussen, "Danida Supports Freedom of Speech and Investigative Journalism in Central America."
8. CIMADE is an ecumenical mutual aid service, with its international activities focused on promoting solidarity, peacebuilding, and strengthening civil society in countries of the South. See http://www.cimade.org/qui/region-idf.html.
9. Author interview with Franzi Hasbun, San Salvador, September 25, 2003; Funes, "Medios de Comunicación en El Salvador," p. 98.
10. See http://www.sipiapa.com/espanol/seminario/capacitacion.htm.
11. Perez and Ramirez, "La Radio Comunitaria en El Salvador," pp. 75–76.
12. Chamorro and Arene, *El Turno de los Medios,* p. 4.
13. Chacón, "Los Medios de Prensa en El Salvador," p. 2.

14. Chamorro and Arene, *El Turno de los Medios,* pp. 4–5.

15. Information provided by Héctor J. Vides, executive director of ARPAS.

16. Carlos S. Melgar, chief of social investment of the Statistics and Census Department, personal communication, November 28, 2003. See also http://www .latinobarometro.org/ano2003.

17. UNDP, *Segundo Informe Sobre Desarrollo Humano,* p. 275.

18. Cantarero, "Periodismo en El Salvador," p. 5.

19. López, "El Derecho a la Información Pública y su Importancia en el Combate de la Corrupción," p. 4.

11

Building a Community Radio Network in Afghanistan

Krishna Kumar

*Radio Karabagh may be a microscopic study in how to build a wide pro-
prietary interest in one of the essential pillars of democracy, a vigorous
media and a free press. As Afghanistan has prepared for its first national
elections . . . small stations such as Radio Karabagh have borne much of
the burden of educating the populace about the candidates, the process
and importance of voting. But they are also part of a deeper construction
of local identity.*[1]

When the Taliban regime fell in 2001, Afghanistan was in a state of ruin.
More than two decades of warfare had left a landscape of devastation,
poverty, disease, and social anarchy. The fanatical rule of the Taliban,
beginning in 1996, had introduced yet more deprivation and repression.

A constitutional monarchy had begun to make strides in development
and education until a coup in 1973. A communist dictatorship seized power
in 1978, and when its leader, Noor Mohammad Tarraki, was assassinated in
1979, the Soviet Union invaded to sustain its control. The Soviet occupa-
tion met with stiff resistance from Islamic factions who fought an effective
guerrilla campaign. To undermine the Soviet military, the United States and
Pakistan provided substantial aid and arms to the Islamic insurgents. Following Soviet withdrawal, civil war raged among rival warlords and ethnic
groups. By 1996 the Taliban had seized control over most of the country
and introduced a degree of order along with an extreme interpretation of
Islam that banned women from schools and the workplace.

Under the Taliban, freedom of expression was crushed. Taliban leaders instituted a highly repressive political system, banning television foot-
age as blasphemous. The state radio network was renamed Radio Sharia

and employed for religious and political indoctrination. The radio relayed sermons, religious debates among preachers, and political tirades against the opposition. A handful of newspapers were published under strict censorship. No opposition newspapers were allowed, although some newspapers published in Pakistan found their way into the country. The Taliban virtually cut off the country from the outside world, only permitting correspondents from a few friendly countries such as Pakistan and Saudi Arabia. Although some Afghans listened to local-language broadcasts by the British Broadcasting Corporation, Voice of America, Radio Pakistan, and All India Radio, they faced severe punishment if caught. As a commentator aptly put it, Afghanistan under the Taliban was a country without news and pictures—literally. In the regions controlled by the Northern Alliance, the media situation was only marginally better. Local media dutifully repeated the official line and glorified ruling warlords.

The Taliban had allowed the Al-Qaida terrorist network to operate training camps on Afghan territory. Following the attacks on the United States on September 11, 2001, the United States led a coalition that quickly ousted the Taliban regime.

The media sector in Afghanistan had been practically wiped out, according to Ahmed Rashid, a journalist and often-quoted expert on Afghanistan. "The state of media in Afghanistan today is not zero, it is minus zero," Rashid said.[2]

Conditions began to change quickly with the establishment of a new interim government in December 2001. Censorship was abolished. The victorious Northern Alliance swiftly took over the state-owned radio stations. With the end of the Taliban's draconian rules, radio stations started playing popular music for the first time in six years. Independent newspapers sprouted up in major cities. Foreign correspondents from around the world descended on the country, covering local and national news. Major Western powers, particularly the United States, the United Kingdom, and Germany, bolstered information services to counteract the legacy of Taliban propaganda.

Since the collapse of the Taliban regime in 2001, the international community has funded a substantial media assistance effort in Afghanistan. The assistance has been designed to promote political stability and a pluralistic, democratic society. Donor governments and organizations have sponsored numerous projects to improve programming at the state-owned Afghanistan Radio and Television, help newspapers and periodicals, and build an institutional infrastructure for the media sector. Donors also have sponsored programs to help local entrepreneurs, nongovernmental organizations (NGOs), and community organizations launch new radio and some television stations. This chapter focuses on one project that established a network of community radio stations broadcasting local and national current affairs programming. The nature of international assistance, the challenges faced by the newly launched radio stations, and the impact of the project are examined. The chapter also considers prospects for the stations' survival after international assistance expires.

The radio project in Afghanistan carries special importance, because it represents the first attempt by donor governments and organizations to establish a network of community stations in a war-torn society. Prior to Afghanistan, most international aid in war-torn societies had gone to television and print media while ignoring radio stations at the grassroots level. Moreover, Afghanistan is an extremely poor, agrarian society with low literacy and per capita income. The social and economic infrastructure of Afghanistan is extremely fragile. The media development experience in Afghanistan can provide insights about the suitability of community radio stations in other developing countries traumatized by armed conflict.

The concept of community radio and how it is pursued in Afghanistan requires clarification. Although in theory a community radio station is owned by the community and is responsive to its needs and interests, such stations tend to vary in their ownership the world over. In Afghanistan, these stations fall into two categories. Most of the stations are owned and managed by individuals but are supported by the community. Such support usually comes in the form of a gift of land, a building, or even volunteer work by community members. In addition, there are stations that are owned and managed by nongovernmental organizations. These stations were originally started by NGOs but later incorporated in a community network. For example, the Canadian NGO Institute for Media Policy and Civil Society (IMPACS) started three women-oriented stations: Radio Rabia-e-Balkhi in Mazar-e-Sharif, Radio Zorah in Kunduz, and Radio Sahar in Heart.

■ International Media Assistance

In a country where the flow of information had been stifled since the 1970s and the fundamental conditions for a free media were lacking, international donors and aspiring Afghan journalists faced a daunting task in building up a "Fourth Estate." Shortly after the fall of the Taliban, the international community started promoting indigenous media through a variety of projects. Donors provided transmitters, computers, and other equipment to the state broadcaster, Afghanistan Radio and Television, and trained its journalists and management staff. The broadcaster's operating expenses were also covered in some cases. Such assistance helped Radio Afghanistan to expand its reach and improve its operations, though its efficiency and balance remained in question. In addition, donor governments and organizations helped revive state-owned television, which had been shut down by the Taliban. Several international organizations also gave financial and technical assistance to emerging print media. Because of widespread illiteracy and the high cost of newsprint, the newly established publications were unable to cover their expenses through sales and advertising. Timely international assistance enabled the initial survival of these fledgling newspapers and magazines.

The donor community has also launched initiatives meant to safeguard and nurture a free media sector. Donors established local NGOs committed to democracy and press freedom and provided grants to local educational institutions to develop journalism courses. Some donors also provided technical assistance to the government to reform the legal and regulatory environment. Finally, the international community assisted local entrepreneurs, NGOs, and community organizations in launching independent radio and television stations, which are run as commercial or nonprofit enterprises. The objective of such aid was to lay the foundation of an independent broadcasting sector exhibiting editorial excellence and commercial viability.

Since the establishment of the provisional government, the US Agency for International Development (USAID) has funded numerous media projects. It particularly focused on radio, which is the most popular and easily accessible medium in Afghanistan. Like other international donors, USAID provided material and technical assistance to Afghanistan Radio and Television. It funded Radio Arman, which has the distinction of being the country's first independent commercial station. Radio Arman, which went on-air in March 2003, has been an instant commercial success, playing Pashto, Hindi, Persian, and Western pop music, lonely heart shows, and sports features. The agency also has supported a network of community stations to disseminate local and national news and information, a project that bears further examination.

■ Building Community Radio

In February 2003, USAID signed a cooperative agreement with the US-based media NGO Internews, which was already managing many of USAID's media initiatives. The agreement called for the establishment of fourteen radio stations across Afghanistan. Internews was to select locations and owners for the stations, loan necessary equipment, train radio staff and journalists, and take other steps necessary to ensure the stations' long-term survival and growth. Once the project ended in June 2004, it provided additional resources to establish twenty more radio stations by March 2005.

Internews explored two models for the project. One was to develop a national network carried by repeat FM stations. The second option was to initiate a network of community stations, which would enjoy autonomy over their own programming but also broadcast centrally produced content.

After discussions with USAID, Internews settled on the second option, for a number of reasons. First, instead of a national project imported and imposed from a faraway city, the project encouraged local participation and ownership. Local leaders, entrepreneurs, and communities would have a stake in the management and successful operation of the radio stations. Second, community radio stations would provide an unprecedented voice and a forum for isolated villages and towns by covering local news, personal and community announcements, and other topics. They could cultivate dialogue and discussion on important local issues. Third, the overall costs and operating expenses of community radio stations would be much less compared to repeat FM stations.[3]

To select locations for radio stations, Internews developed three main criteria. The stations chosen should be dispersed throughout the country, and not concentrated in a single or few regions; the community to be served should be large enough to support an independent station, as very small communities cannot generate enough advertising or revenue from public announcements; there should be demonstrable local support for the venture, with the local community either donating land or housing the station and pledging to pay a part of building and maintenance costs. For prospective entrepreneurs, they should have at least US$1,000 to invest in the station. Internews also has screened potential managers and owners to assess their interest and business capabilities.

Each new station receives a "radio station in a box," which includes cased racks of recorders, players and amplifiers, a small mixing desk, a computer loaded with the recording software Cool Edit Pro, microphones, and portable tape recorders for reporting. In addition, the new station receives a 150-watt FM transmitter at minimum and, if necessary, a thirty-meter tower. Because of the chronic shortage of power, Internews also provides a generator to run the station and transmitter. All equipment remains the property of Internews, which has the right to reclaim it. The total cost of the package varies depending on the needs of the station, ranging from US$12,000 to US$100,000. It includes US$3,000 for six months of salaries for a station's director, general producer, and technical director (US$150, US$100, and US$100 per month, respectively), and supplemental fuel and transport expenses.[4]

Once a community is selected, Internews invites senior staff of the planned station to Kabul for three weeks of journalism and technical training, including practical instruction on a dummy radio station. Internews also sends an expert to the station before it becomes operational. The expert helps managers and reporters to install the necessary machinery and equipment, institute an organizational structure, and solve teething problems. When necessary, Internews also helps in building makeshift "studios" with locally available material, ranging from cardboard to canvas.

Once the station is launched, Internews provides regular technical advice and assistance. It has two full-time business development specialists to help stations raise revenues, including preparing fees for advertisements, paid requests, and community announcements. Since September 2004, Internews has started funding the position of an advertising/business director for each station. Selected candidates receive sales and advertising training in Kabul. Internews and other organizations also provide special grants. For example, USAID gave the Killid station a powerful transmitter to boost its signal over Kabul and US$170,000 for training its management and business staff.

All community stations receive radio programming produced by Internews and other organizations, which is distributed by Tanin (Echo) distribution network. Funded jointly by USAID and the European Commission, Tanin delivers as many as thirty-four separate programs, which "vary from Internews' *Shahrak Atfal* (Children's City) to AINA's *Dar Velayat, Tchi Migzarad* (What's Happening In The Provinces?) to the farmer's program, *Kesht-e Khob, Haasil e Khob* (Good Planting, Good Production)."[5] Making up for a lack of newspaper distribution, Tanin also delivers the most popular newspapers and magazines, from which broadcasters often read to their listeners. Tanin's packets are delivered daily via a network of taxi drivers to community radio and state-owned stations.

Since June 2004, community and a handful of state radio stations have started receiving *Salaam Watandar* (Hello Nation), a ninety-minute morning and evening broadcast of news and entertainment programming produced by Internews. Radio stations receive the program via standard digital television satellite decoders, and rebroadcast the show over their local transmitters. *Salaam Watandar* employs a network of local journalists around the country to report on events in their areas. Internews plans to expand the *Salaam Watandar* feed to five, and even eight, hours of daily programming. It is exploring various options so that the program can be self-sustaining.

Salaam Watandar and Tanin programming provide community stations with an essential base to build an audience. The material helps fill airtime with useful, professionally produced news and current affairs features. Moreover, *Salaam Watandar* has become a steady source of income to the stations, as they receive a share of revenues from commercial and public service announcements on the program.

■ Progress and Performance

By the end of November 2004, twenty-five community stations had become operational. Most stations operate for a limited time, ranging from eight to twelve hours. Practically all are located in modest premises, even with

makeshift arrangements. Because of an unreliable power supply, most stations also use electric generators, which unfortunately increases operating
costs. A few stations have now started employing solar panels to cut their
fuel bills.

In addition to programs provided by Internews and other organizations,
all stations play music from tapes and compact discs. Hindi, Pashto, Dari,
and Persian music are all popular in Afghanistan. Radio stations entertain
requests from listeners for songs, poetry, and other entertainment items, and
usually charge a fee for such requests. Most stations have put small boxes
in selected shops, where potential listeners drop their requests in an envelope, which is purchased from the shop for about US10¢. Such requests are
a source of income to radio stations and of increased customer traffic to
participating shops. The *Washington Post*'s description of the letters received by Radio Karabagh conveys the effect of these community stations
on an audience hungry for communication:

> The letters that arrive at the three-room studio of Radio Karabagh are
> small works of folk art. They come on elaborate stationery, covered with
> glitter applied by hand, pictures cut from newspapers and small bits of
> metal foil applied like gold leaf in patterns. . . . More important for Radio
> Karabagh . . . are the envelopes the letters arrive in. Sold by the local mer-
> chants for the price of four Afghanis—about 10 cents—the envelopes
> raise revenue for the station. They contain requests for music, praise for
> the station and sometimes facts offered in the interest of greater general
> knowledge.[6]

Still more important are community and personal announcements. Stations announce upcoming community events, meetings, and other information either free or for a nominal fee. Personal announcements about wed-
dings and funerals are most popular. Such announcements save a family
considerable time and effort, as otherwise they would need to roam the
countryside on foot or donkey to inform their relatives and friends. The fee
for such announcements ranges from US$2 to US$4 (100 to 200 afghanis).

Most radio stations also produce local news, interview community
leaders, and read interesting stories and poems from newspapers and magazines. A few stations hold discussions on important topics affecting the
community. Some stations also air religious programs. Stations owned or
run by women-focused NGOs discuss health, sanitation, child rearing, cooking, literacy, and other more sensitive issues such as forced marriages and
domestic violence.

In Kandahar, Azad Afghan Radio acts as a watchdog and advocate on
local issues such as the power supply, availability of drinking water, and
performance of the municipal administration.[7] A few other stations have
started relaying "people's voices" programs in which ordinary people are

interviewed at random about their views on various topics. Such interviews often highlight specific problems and occasionally force local leaders to find solutions. In Logar province, Radio Milli Paygham conducted interviews with local farmers and traders, revealing that a lack of reliable public transportation to Kabul was a major problem. The farmers had difficulties ferrying local produce to Kabul and bringing back consumer goods. "The station's reporters embarked on an on-air odyssey from local to provincial governments to find out who was responsible for the transport situation. When they finally found the provincial minister responsible, they elicited a promise to arrange more buses for commuters to Kabul."[8] While the outcome of the complaints is still unknown, the incident illustrates the potential role that community radio stations can play in articulating public concerns and bringing them to the notice of local authorities.

The community stations also relay news features and public service announcements on important national issues. Such programs carry substantial educational value in a country where only 30 percent of the populace is able to read and write. Community stations played a useful role educating voters before the presidential elections held in October 2004. They provided information about candidates, locations of polling booths, time and dates of elections, procedures for voting, and voters' rights and obligations. In many remote areas, community radio stations were the only source of such information. Sometimes the election campaign coverage produced instant results. For example, a promotion on Mazar-e-Sharif's Radio Rabia-e-Balkhi calling for increased registration of women resulted in 500 women turning up in front of the station before going to register en masse.

The quality of programming and local reporting at the stations remains poor, which is hardly surprising given the country's recent history and the existing physical and institutional constraints. Most journalists lack both training and journalism experience. Their general educational background tends to be lacking as well. These journalists and producers are learning on-the-job and they have no one to guide them. It naturally will take time before community radio stations conform to the standards of professional journalism in developing societies, much less to those of more mature democracies.

Anecdotal evidence indicates that community stations have become popular and have succeeded in gaining a substantial audience. With the exception of Killid, all community stations visited by a USAID assessment team reported an audience share in their local communities of between 70 and 100 percent. This confirms anecdotal evidence that Afghans tend to prefer FM stations over shortwave and AM stations. Moreover, in small communities such as Ghoriyan, Bamiyan, and Karabagh, the stations face no competition except from shortwave and state-owned regional programs. Therefore an FM channel carrying local and national news and Hindi, Pashto, and popular music can attract a large audience. In relatively larger media markets such as Mazar-e-Sharif and Kabul, community stations face more intense competition.

One measure of audience involvement is the amount of listener mail flowing to the stations. Every week the stations receive 100 to 400 letters, containing community and personal announcements, requests for songs and poems, and complaints about local officials or government. In Bamiyan, the station manager reported that the station also receives five or six "walk-in" visitors a day, who come to read poems or make announcements.[9]

Community radio served a crucial public service when a dam collapsed on March 29, 2005, near the city of Ghazni, south of Kabul.[10] Shortly before the dam broke, journalists from the *Salaam Watandar* program interviewed the governor of the province. Speaking live on-air, the governor urged residents of Ghazni and surrounding villages to evacuate immediately. The warning, which was carried on the local community station Radio Ghaznawiyaan, saved lives in one village, Zamin Kola, which was severely damaged by the floodwaters of the Ghazni River, according to Internews. With the city of Ghazni cut in half by the flooding river, the radio station later provided a vital communications link between the two sides of the city.

The community radio project has already had a significant impact on Afghan society and planted the seeds for a free media, an achievement that seems especially impressive given the difficult conditions prevailing. A quality radio news and current affairs program, editorially independent and balanced, is now heard across the country via the Tanin distribution network. This programming provided crucial information prior to Afghanistan's first post-Taliban election, in 2004, helping to educate voters about the electoral process. The project also has provided local news in many communities for the first time, with radio stations serving as a platform for public discussion and as a training ground for aspiring reporters. By airing family announcements and events as well as poetry readings and music, the stations act as a kind of social network and cultural center for poor, rural communities. While the editorial quality of many community stations remains amateur and there are clear constraints on journalistic inquiry, the stations have introduced a grassroots democratic impulse into Afghan society. In some cases, the stations have sought to hold local authorities accountable or have shed light on human rights, social, and women's issues previously ignored. The project has strengthened the flow of information, empowered local communities, and created conditions for a more open, more professional media sector.

▪ Journalistic Independence and Self-Censorship

Although Afghanistan's radio stations are not subject to official censorship, most seem to exercise extensive self-censorship. Staff at the stations are keenly aware that there are cultural, social, and political boundaries that cannot be crossed. Women's issues constitute an example of how the stations tread cautiously. Even the stations owned by women-focused NGOs are careful not to give the impression that they question the traditional status and roles of women in Afghan society. As the director of Radio Rabia-e-Balkhi reported to a USAID assessment team: "If we acted freely for one day, our office would be closed down. We're trying to help women deal with their difficult family problems, their kids that are out of control. If we just tell her 'you know, a woman can be president,' we will be criticized, and get in trouble. And what good will that do these women?"[11]

Rabia-e-Balkhi, which is named after a famed Afghan woman poet, has still managed to broach delicate women's issues while retaining a large audience. Devoting about 70 percent of its programming to shows catering to women's concerns, the station discusses child rearing, cooking, and hygiene, as well as formerly taboo subjects such as forced marriages, domestic violence, divorce, and female suicide. When certain subjects are too volatile, the station sometimes raises issues indirectly through dramatic productions.

Almost all stations are reluctant to cover sensitive political topics and prominent personalities. They tend to ignore subjects such as political corruption, intimidation by warlords, the role of local elites in poppy cultivation, or the unethical practices of powerful businessmen. In interviews with a USAID assessment team, the radio stations were candid about their cautious approach. The country still suffers from the legacy of prolonged civil war and the political and economic uncertainty associated with it. Community stations have little or no protection against powerful vested interests, especially in small communities and remote areas. The consequences of exposing the privileged and the powerful could be disastrous for the survival of a station and its staff members. However, there are cases in which a community station has succeeded in taking a bold stand and remained on air. Radio Karabagh reported from listeners' letters that Kabul's mayor exploited a teacher's-day ceremony to make a political speech praising the mujahidin. The mayor denied it and demanded that he review all critical letters about him before they were read on the air. When the station refused, the mayor took the case to the local council, or Shura. The council backed the station.

Some stations play it safe by avoiding local news and events. Radio Tiraj-e-Mir in Pul-e-Khumri has not expanded its programming beyond *Salaam Watandar* and popular music. As one local observer described it, "Tiraj e Mir is treated by the local commanders like their personal jukebox. They send their men around to make requests for their favourite songs for their boys to dance to."[12] The same is true with Radio Sharq in Jalalabad. Given the deep and violent divisions between rival warlords and militia commanders and the absence of the rule of law, the station has yet to air any local news program and has primarily focused on a diverse mix of music.

Some community stations are also facing a potential problem due to their relationship with donor governments. Provincial reconstruction teams (PRTs) are under the jurisdiction of the US Department of Defense and include military civil affairs units and USAID advisers. Many PRTs view the community radio stations as useful partners for their public affairs and psychological operations messages. PRT representatives believe that because the community radio stations are funded by the US government, the stations should fully cooperate with them, particularly on poppy eradication and counterterrorism campaigns. Many PRTs are even willing to heavily subsidize the stations. However, a close identification of community stations with PRTs could compromise the independent status of the stations. There is the risk that Afghans may start seeing the stations as instruments of foreign authority rather than independent media outlets. In war-torn societies such as Afghanistan, the dividing line between propaganda and news is thin indeed, and economically struggling stations may be tempted to cross it. Both USAID and Internews are aware of the potential pitfalls and challenges posed by the presence of the PRTs.

■ Commercial Viability

A major unanswered question concerns the sustainability of Afghanistan's community radio stations. Can they survive without international assistance in one form or the other? It is too early to say, because community stations are an entirely new phenomenon in the country and there is little empirical evidence to make future predictions. Even so, a few general observations can be made to illuminate the issue.

Since the beginning of the program, Internews has been concerned about the financial viability of community radio stations and has taken steps to cultivate it. Internews gives preference to those proposals in which managers and local leaders demonstrate the motivation and skill to run stations as sound business enterprises. Internews emphasizes business skills in its training activities and provides technical assistance to secure advertising and sponsors. It has recently recruited experts to provide advice to interested community stations in seeking greater revenue. Internews also is exploring other possible revenue streams, such as supplying stations with systems that can provide a feed to fee-charging Internet cafés.

All community stations raise revenues from different sources—national advertising, local advertising, announcements, and listeners' requests. National advertising revenues come through the program *Salaam Watandar*. Internews negotiates advertising contracts with commercial firms, intergovernmental organizations, and NGOs that want to get their message out on radios. It then shares advertising revenue among the participating stations on the basis of each outlet's market size. While large stations in major cities currently earn between US$1,000 and US$1,500 per month, small stations average around US$400. At present, *Salaam Watandar* is the largest source of income to community radio stations.

Other revenue sources, particularly for the smaller stations, are paid requests for songs and personal announcements. Stations charge a few afghanis for an envelope to be deposited in special request boxes around town. In some cases the boxes attract so much traffic that merchants are willing to pay stations to put them in their stores. No precise data are available, but for many stations such requests are the second most important source of income. Some stations have been able to earn US$100 to US$200 per month from announcements and requests. Finally, stations, particularly in major cities, solicit advertising from local traders and businessmen.

Internews remains optimistic that most stations will be able to raise enough revenues to meet operating expenditures. Moreover, many more will manage with modest assistance from the international community. While this may be true, one should not ignore the structural barriers to long-term sustainability in such a difficult setting as Afghanistan, barriers that are beyond the control of the stations or international NGOs.

The limited local market for commercial advertising represents one obvious obstacle to sustainability. Afghanistan is extremely poor, and most people depend upon subsistence agriculture that generates little surplus. Although manufacturing and trading sectors are growing, most of the firms operate at such a small scale that they have little use for advertising. Consequently, many community stations find it difficult to generate significant advertising revenues. For example, Radio Nadaye Sulhe in Ghoriyan, which enjoys 100 percent of the local audience share and strong public support, has been unable to earn more than US$100 a month from local advertising. Another station, Milli-e-Paygham in Logar province earns only US$250 a month by selling advertisements to local merchants. Only the stations located in large urban areas can realistically expect significant advertising revenues from local enterprises.

Some experts believe that there is still considerable untapped potential for advertising revenues in local markets. They argue that many small firms can be persuaded to advertise on radio stations, provided the rates are reasonable and benefits of advertisements visible. Exponents of this view argue that Afghani businessmen, who returned from foreign countries after the fall of the Taliban, are aware of modern sales and advertising practices. They are also very entrepreneurial and enterprising. So the task of obtaining advertising is not as difficult as it seems, according to this view. There are already cases of enterprising radio managers who have been able to tap the local market. The advertising manager of Radio Naw-e-Bahar in Balkh City was able to solicit commercials worth US$1,500 during his first week. The manager approached small traders and farmers and succeeded. Although other stations might not be able to replicate his achievement, it does point to the potential for advertising in provincial towns.

Another potential obstacle to sustainability is that public service announcements, which are the major source of revenues to community radio stations, are likely to decline in the future. At present, most advertising revenues, which stations receive from the program *Salaam Watandar,* come from the advertising funded by international intergovernmental organizations, European and US NGOs, and major development agencies. However, the experience of recent postconflict societies indicates that as countries achieve political and economic stability, the volume of public service announcements declines. Gradually, the international community no longer sees the need to run media campaigns and withdraws funding for public service spots.

It also seems doubtful that *Salaam Watandar* or similar programs would be able to attract substantial commercial advertising to meet the losses incurred by declining public service announcements. Afghanistan does not have many multinational or national firms that advertise nationally. It will take at least ten to fifteen years before large firms, which allocate significant budgets to sales and advertising, emerge on the national scene. And even if they emerge, large firms are more likely to advertise in greater urban markets than in small towns and villages, where people have little disposable income to spend on consumer goods.

The last obstacle is competition from commercial radio. As the independent media sector grows, many commercial radio stations will compete with community stations for advertising and public service spots. Indeed, USAID has already given grants to a Kabul-based commercial station, Arman FM, to establish repeat stations in Afghan provinces. As a result, community stations in Mazar-e-Sharif, Herat, Ghazni, and Kandahar, would have to compete with well-funded network stations that could drain away audience and advertising.[13]

Under these circumstances, it would be unrealistic to assume that a majority of the stations could secure financial viability. Some stations that are able to meet most of their operating expenses might be in trouble if *Salaam Watandar* fails to obtain the current volume of public service advertising or is no longer subsidized by USAID and other donors. At the time of the USAID assessment in October 2004, Internews reported that six out of fifteen operating community stations had become self-sufficient. A closer examination by the assessment team indicated that only three were actually functioning without any direct support from Internews or other NGOs.

The long-term survival of community stations will depend upon several factors, including continued political stability in the country, economic growth in the areas where the stations operate, the entrepreneurial abilities of station directors, the degree to which operating expenses are kept under control, and priorities of donor governments and organizations. Finally, the legal and regulatory framework for media that evolves in Afghanistan may shape the future health of the stations. If the government provides some protection to community stations against commercial or state-owned media, these stations may have a better chance for survival.

In the meantime, many stations will require financial assistance for years to come, though the amount will be relatively small, ranging from US$500 to US$1,500 per month. As the stations gain experience, they will be able to manage with even less. For example, Radio Rabia-e-Balkhi receives only US$550 a month (US$500 from IMPACS and US$50 from Internews) and has been able to survive. International donors and NGOs may be ready to aid those stations that serve their communities and aggressively seek local revenues. If the international community fails to provide necessary support, many stations would have to fold.

■ Lessons and Recommendations

Internews has succeeded in establishing a network of independent community stations in Afghanistan within a time span of two years, an extraordinary achievement given the daunting conditions. These stations broadcast the national news program *Salaam Watandar,* providing national and international news. They also provide useful information on a range of vital problems facing the country and educate people on public issues. Most stations also have their own local news programs, giving a voice to the local community for the first time. The stations also provide useful social services, such as airing community and personal announcements. Although the quality of local programming is sometimes flawed and amateur, it is improving. While long-term economic viability remains a question mark, most stations can survive for another five to seven years with modest donor assistance.

The experience of establishing community stations in Afghanistan provides four distinct but interrelated lessons. First, many media experts initially doubted the wisdom of establishing community stations in Afghanistan, favoring instead a national, centralized network. They were concerned that the local communities might fail to provide necessary support for such a project. They also were apprehensive about the provision of training and technical assistance because of poor transportation links. Some even doubted the ability of these stations to produce local programming in the absence of experienced journalists. These concerns have proved to be unjustified. Most stations are running reasonably well and are charting new territory in towns that never enjoyed the benefits of any local broadcast media.

The project has demonstrated that international organizations can promote community stations in impoverished, war-torn societies that have had no experience of independent or commercial media.

Second, community radio can provide not only news but also a stimulus for grassroots democracy and social networks. Such an empowering effect is less likely through a centralized network. In settings similar to Afghanistan, a local radio station can serve as a kind of town hall, providing a platform for discussion, a center for cultural enlightenment, and a source of information on public health and schools.

Third, the Afghanistan example also suggests that community radio stations can raise modest resources locally. As mentioned earlier, community radio stations have succeeded in earning revenues from diverse sources— local advertising, requests for songs and poems, community and personal announcements, and national programming. Although the revenues are insufficient to meet operating costs, they are significant nonetheless. The project also suggests that the staff of the newly established stations can be trained to tap these revenue sources even more efficiently.

Fourth, in a politically and economically fragile environment, most community stations may require long-term financial support, though the level of aid would decline over time. It is unrealistic to assume that community stations could become economically viable within a year or two in such difficult conditions. Although some may succeed, most are unlikely to achieve such a feat. Therefore it is important that donors prepare a long-term strategy for supporting Afghanistan's radio stations. While every effort should be made to promote economic sustainability from the outset, international donors should be prepared to offer a helping hand to the needy stations. Otherwise, the whole investment might be wasted.

Notes

A revised version of this chapter has been published in Kumar, *Promoting Independent Media*. In addition, the chapter draws heavily from an assessment of the US Agency for International Development's media assistance program in Afghanistan, conducted by Colin Soloway and Abubaker Saddique; see Soloway and Saddique, *An Assessment of USAID Assistance to the Radio Sector in Afghanistan*. I am grateful for the comments and suggestions by Colin Soloway in preparing this chapter.

1. Kennicott, "Radio Karabagh," p. 7.
2. Quoted on the Internews website, http://www.internews.org/regions/centralasia/afghanistan.htm.
3. Soloway and Saddique, *Assessment of USAID Assistance*.
4. Ibid.
5. Ibid., p. 11.
6. Kennicott, "Radio Karabagh," p. 7.
7. Soloway and Saddique, *Assessment of USAID Assistance*.

8. Ibid., p. 13.

9. Ibid.

10. See http://www.internews.org/news/2005/20050407_afghan.html, April 7, 2005, "Radio Helps Save Lives in Afghanistan Dam Collapse."

11. Soloway and Saddique, *Assessment of USAID Assistance,* p. 14.

12. Ibid.

13. Ibid.

PART 4

Conclusion

12

Findings and Recommendations

Jeroen de Zeeuw and Luc van de Goor

The case studies in this volume have analyzed international assistance for electoral, human rights, and media initiatives in postconflict settings, and examined the strengths and limitations of such assistance. The varying conditions in each country shaped how the assistance was delivered and received. This chapter highlights some of the key overall findings for each area of assistance, showing that some of the major achievements of assistance were offset by important limitations of assistance programs. In addition, we argue that, while a number of lessons have been learned, some key problems of democracy assistance have not been resolved. Finally, we suggest a set of policy recommendations to improve democracy assistance to postconflict societies.

■ The Mixed Record of More Than Fifteen Years of Democracy Assistance

The preceding chapters show that democracy assistance has made a positive difference in postconflict countries, but that the impact it has had on democratic development in these countries since the early 1990s has been rather limited. When we look at the overall picture of strengths and weaknesses of the three areas of assistance analyzed in this volume, the outcome is mixed.[1]

Strengths and Weaknesses of Electoral Assistance

Based on the findings in Part 1 of the volume, on Uganda, Ethiopia, and Mozambique, three major achievements of electoral assistance can be highlighted. First, international support for the election administration was instrumental for the organization of the first and subsequent postconflict elections. In Ethiopia, for instance, donors helped establish the National Election Board of Ethiopia, which was responsible for the country's first postwar elections, in 1992. Additional technical and financial support assisted the board in preparing and carrying out subsequent elections in 1994, 2000, and 2005.

Second, financial assistance from the international community helped domestic civil society organizations in Ethiopia and Uganda to monitor the elections and develop voter and civic education programs to raise popular awareness about the elections.

Third, international political foundations played a useful role by training political party activists on how to formulate party programs and develop messages to communicate with their constituencies, especially in the run-up to elections. In the case of Mozambique, this type of electoral support was said to have had a positive effect on the internal organization of some political parties.

The weakness, however, with all these forms of electoral assistance, is that they have focused mostly on improving technical aspects. As a result, none of them has had a very significant impact on the political aspects of the electoral process in these countries. The logistic and financial support to the national election commissions in Ethiopia and Uganda did not address the problematic political issue of impartiality and independence. In Uganda, for example, the members of the election commission continue to be appointed by the president and approved by a parliament that is dominated by supporters of the incumbent National Resistance Movement. By focusing merely on the technical aspects of the election commission's work and effectively ignoring its perceived political bias, electoral assistance has done little service to the development of an impartial and independent institution that is key to Uganda's future democratic development. A comparable argument can be made in the case of Ethiopia.

Similarly, international support for election monitoring and civic education by domestic civil society organizations seems of limited relevance in situations where the key to further democratization is not public awareness-raising or election observation, but lies in the openness of political debate, access to both print and broadcast media for all candidates, and electoral competition between multiple political parties. The ongoing crises between incumbent parties and political opposition groups both in Ethiopia and in Uganda, which occasionally turn violent, indicate that some of the basic obstacles to sustained democratic reform have not been addressed.

Finally, the various training initiatives for political party activists that have been supported by the international community in Mozambique have not brought about the expected political changes. In Chapter 4, on political party aid, Marc de Tollenaere argues that international assistance was crucial for leveling the playing field for the country's main political contestants (the Mozambican Liberation Front and the Mozambican National Resistance) during the first postconflict elections, in 1994, and indirectly helped the emergence of new parties in subsequent elections. However, despite several internationally supported initiatives to create more political pluralism and the formation of multiparty coalitions in the country's legislature, Mozambique's political scene remains characterized by a multitude of small and weak opposition parties that enjoy limited grassroots support and are unable to compete with the increasingly powerful Mozambican Liberation Front.

Strengths and Weaknesses of Human Rights Assistance

The chapters in Part 2 of the volume, on Guatemala, Cambodia, and Sierra Leone, regarding the impact of international human rights assistance, show a slightly more positive picture. First, the deployment of international human rights monitoring missions helped protect civilians in these three countries from continuing human rights violations and was said to be crucial for the promotion of basic human rights norms in their societies. As Dinorah Azpuru indicates in Chapter 5, "it was not until the first MINUGUA mission arrived in 1994 that the [human rights] situation started to improve significantly." The chapters on Cambodia and Sierra Leone show that UNTAC and UNAMSIL respectively have had a similar positive impact on the most flagrant human rights violations and the institutionalization (or even codification as in the case of Cambodia) of respect for basic human rights.

Second, without the generous technical and financial assistance as well as necessary political pressure from the international community key human rights institutions, like the Commission for Historical Clarification and the Office of the Human Rights Ombudsman in Guatemala, the new police force, Special Court, and the Truth and Reconciliation Commission in Sierra Leone, as well as the Khmer Rouge Tribunal in Cambodia would not have existed.

Finally, these three country chapters prove that international financial support was essential for supporting the activities of existing civil society organizations and enabling the emergence of many new human rights nongovernmental organizations (NGOs). Before the war in Sierra Leone, for example, human rights work was conducted in a piecemeal fashion by a few volunteer lawyers and journalists. Now there are several dozen NGOs working on human rights issues. In Cambodia, the total number of human rights NGOs rose by a factor of ten, from only four organizations in 1992 to more than forty in 2000. Moreover, in a few postconflict countries, training and financial assistance also helped some of the more specialized human rights NGOs to become more professional. This is illustrated by two examples from the case study on Guatemala, where various human rights NGOs are said to have moved from merely denouncing violations to making constructive proposals for change in the form of drafting alternative legislation and providing suggestions for candidates of important national human rights institutions (see Chapter 5).

At the same time, international human rights assistance has suffered from several problems that have limited its overall impact. First, although the international human rights monitoring missions to Guatemala, Cambodia, and Sierra Leone helped guarantee a basic respect for human rights, their mandates required them to focus mostly on civil and political rights. Their monitoring activities gave little attention to socioeconomic rights and other issues like ordinary criminal violence, corruption, and abuse of power by police officers, judges, and other state officials. In Guatemala, for example, this focus did not correspond with what ordinary citizens thought to be most important: the increase of common and violent crime. A similar point is raised by Mohamed Gibril Sesay and Charlie Hughes in Chapter 7, on Sierra Leone, where international human rights programs have only given limited attention to (petty) corruption that continues to fester in Sierra Leonean society. Due partly to their preoccupation with more "abstract" civil and political rights, international human rights initiatives have been less effective in addressing more ordinary human rights problems, making them "not directly relevant" in the eyes of the local population.

Second, the internationally supported human rights missions and mechanisms generally gave little consideration to the objective of leaving behind strong and sustainable domestic human rights institutions. In Chapter 5, on Guatemala, Azpuru stresses that MINUGUA only belatedly started discussions with the human rights ombudsman to ensure a proper transfer of responsibilities and skills needed to strengthen the country's domestic human rights monitoring capacities. In Chapter 7, on Sierra Leone, a similar point is made with reference to the Special Court: "the Special Court, a one-time institution that will try about two dozen people, will consume US$58 million while the Office of the Ombudsman, a permanent state-level institution that many more citizens relate with regularly for human rights protection, has not received a thousand dollars from the international community." Both examples indicate that long-term institution building is not always considered a first priority in international assistance programs. This will not only have a negative effect on the legacy of certain temporary or transitional international mechanisms, but more importantly will also hinder the development of capable and sustainable domestic human rights institutions.

Finally, all four chapters in Part 2 of the volume indicate that the unconditional support by many international agencies to NGOs—especially during the 1990s, regarded by some as the "high time" for civil society support[2]—created a number of problems. The explosive growth of local civil society organizations in Cambodia and Sierra Leone is not a bad thing in and of itself. As indicated previously, most of these organizations performed useful tasks especially in the field of human rights monitoring and awareness-raising. However, the boom of human rights NGOs caused by substantial international financial support also included organizations that had little to do with protection and promotion of human rights. As Sesay and Hughes indicate in Chapter 7, in Sierra Leone, "many organizations remain one-person setups or have unclear objectives and are willing to do anything for which funding is available." In addition, as the case studies on Cambodia and Guatemala illustrate, decisions to provide financial assistance are not always based on a critical assessment of organizational potential. Moreover, once assistance has been given, it is fairly common not to inquire what has happened with the money or evaluate the impact of a particular assistance program. Of course, donor agencies cannot be held directly responsible for the emergence of certain "bad apples," but their unwavering financial support and lack of critical assessment definitely contributed to the conditions in which such organizations could thrive.

Strengths and Weaknesses of Media Assistance

The impact of media support is perhaps a bit more difficult to assess compared to electoral and human right assistance. Due to relatively low levels of international funding for media assistance programs, it is less easy to identify the contribution that the international community has made in this area of democracy assistance. Nevertheless, the case studies in Part 3 of the volume, on Rwanda, El Salvador, and Afghanistan, show a predominantly positive impact of postconflict media support.

First, international actors contributed to the establishment of a more open legal framework regulating the media sector. In Chapter 9, Christopher Kayumba and Jean-Paul Kimonyo argue that international expertise and assistance played an important role in the adoption of a more democratic press law in Rwanda. Similarly, in Chapter 10, Anne Germain Lefèvre describes how, in El Salvador, international technical assistance helped design a new telecommunications law, effectively dismantling a state monopoly over the country's media outlets and installing a new regulatory body overseeing the licensing process for broadcasting media.

Second, material and financial support was vital for the reconstruction of damaged infrastructure and the establishment of completely new media outlets. In Rwanda, international assistance helped rebuild and reequip the studios of the country's national radio station. Moreover, international donors contributed significantly to the development of a journalism and communications school at the National University of Rwanda. In war-ravaged Afghanistan, the international media NGO Internews set up an unprecedented network of community radio stations that provides news and information throughout the country and educates citizens on public issues.

Finally, international media support generally had a positive effect on the quality of journalism in the selected postconflict countries. International training programs in Rwanda have improved the professional skills of most journalists, although sloppy reporting remains a problem. In the case of El Salvador, the quality of journalism has been raised through international support for the production of innovative broadcasting programs, financial assistance for the expansion of the community radio network, and training on investigative reporting skills. In Afghanistan, quality of programming and reporting is slowly improving, but still remains poor, as most journalists lack both training and journalistic experience.

Despite these substantial achievements, the long-term effect of international media assistance is negatively influenced by two main problems. First, the experiences in Rwanda indicate that the journalism training courses organized by international assistance agencies are rather ad hoc and usually too short to have a lasting impact. Instead, longer-term training programs, including on-the-job training for journalists, are essential to fundamentally improve the limited experience and professional knowledge of young journalists in postconflict societies.

Second, the sustainability of most media interventions remains problematic. In postconflict countries, where economic conditions are usually poor and markets for advertisements are tiny or nonexistent, new media outlets struggle to generate income and can often only survive with the help of international assistance, as the chapter on Afghanistan illustrates with regard to community radio stations. However, with the gradual phasing out of international assistance in most postconflict countries, it is likely that most of these media outlets will eventually disappear.

Conclusion: A Mixed Picture

The preceding assessment of strengths and weaknesses shows clearly that democracy assistance has made a difference in postconflict countries, with positive effects discernible on a small scale and in the broader, national arena. At the micro level, international assistance contributed to the growth of new organizations in the public and private sectors and helped improve the capacities and capabilities of already existing organizations that are essential for democratic development. At a higher level, the impact of international assistance is visible in the conduct of competitive elections, and the fact that in all of the postconflict countries studied, successive elections have been held without a return to war. Moreover, in most cases international support also had a positive effect on domestic efforts to protect human rights. And finally, the media space has become more open in practically all postconflict societies.

At the same time, democracy assistance has suffered from a number of shortcomings. The above discussion on electoral assistance shows that the international community has typically favored technical solutions to what are essentially political problems. This approach has had a detrimental effect on the development of key electoral institutions and, according to some, has effectively legitimated undemocratic practices. In the area of human rights, international agencies have neglected the issue of organizational strengthening, skills transfer, and long-term institutionalization of domestic human rights organizations. Moreover, in many postconflict countries, careless international financial support sparked the emergence of an unsustainable sector of human rights NGOs, sometimes at the expense of a handful of organizations that are committed, professional, and effective enough to have a real influence. Finally, the international preference for short-term journalism training and insufficient attention for long-term sustainability has led to suboptimal results in the area of media assistance.

■ The Link Between Democracy Assistance and Democratic Development

The main conclusion that follows from the preceding analysis is that, despite some serious flaws, international democracy assistance was instrumental for postconflict peacebuilding and had a mixed but predominantly positive effect on democratization. Most of the regimes established in the aftermath of conflict have survived; in all of the nine countries analyzed here, there has been no relapse into conflict. They have endured many political and economic crises, often with the generous support of the international community, which moreover has provided some of the building blocks for democratic development.

Yet the political process of democratization in these countries remains fragile at best and highly problematic at worst. Only El Salvador and Guatemala have continued to consolidate their fragile democratic structures. In Mozambique, despite substantial international democracy assistance, limited progress has been made in terms of the institutionalization of democratic procedures and political pluralism. In the failed states of Afghanistan and Sierra Leone, it is still too early to talk about democratic progress, but it is likely that these countries' political future will be marked by regular setbacks. Most worrying, however, is the situation in Ethiopia, Rwanda, Uganda, and Cambodia, where the process of democratic development shows clear signs of backsliding.

This raises an important question: Is there a link between the earlier-mentioned shortcomings of international assistance and the limited democratic progress in some postconflict countries? Moreover, can this limited progress even be attributed to the failing of international democracy assistance? On the basis of the material presented in this volume, our answer to the first question would be: yes, but only indirectly. The answer to the second question: no, not really.

As has been argued in this volume, many institutions conducive to democracy, like elections, civil society organizations, print and broadcast media, as well as human rights NGOs, would probably not have existed or survived in many postconflict countries without international technical, financial assistance and diplomatic pressure. Although some (serious) errors have been made with this support, we believe there is sufficient evidence that the net effect has been positive. Setbacks in the process of democratization in some countries and clear resistance to political reform in others are therefore not so much caused by bad or inadequate assistance programs but by a combination of poor socioeconomic, regional, and political factors, and foremost by unwilling domestic political leaders. Although external actors can perhaps do more to avoid legitimating political window-dressing and thwart the incentives for corrupt activities, in the end it is up to domestic political leaders to stop these practices.

This indicates one of the most important limitations of international democracy assistance: although external assistance can provide some of the seeds for democratic development, in the end it requires strong domestic political will and commitment to political reform in order to strengthen democratic institutions and consolidate the process of democratization.

Recommendations

In recent years, several studies have underscored the need to learn from previous mistakes to improve the efficacy of democracy programs and other forms of assistance to postconflict countries. Suggestions put forward include: applying more realistic mandates and better planning of major assistance programs, making clear trade-offs and mastering techniques,[3] delaying democratic (and market-oriented) reforms until the appropriate institutions are in place,[4] adopting a different approach to obstructionist or "semi-authoritarian" regimes,[5] and fundamentally rethinking some of the conventional assumptions behind democracy programming.[6]

In addition to these suggestions, the authors in this volume have presented a number of concrete recommendations to improve future support to elections, human rights, and media in the particular postconflict countries studied. Finally, we would like to make a few suggestions for future postconflict democracy programming.

Building Democratic State Institutions

Most countries studied here, particularly in Africa and Asia, inherited a devastated state with diminished capacities and legitimacy. Public bureaucracies were in disarray and were often demoralized. Many civil servants were killed or had migrated; still others had quit the civil service. Many governments had no resources to attract and train new staff to run and manage state agencies. Moreover, the government was unable to provide essential public services because of the lack of economic and human resources. Corruption was widespread, further undermining the legitimacy of the government.

During the early stage of transition from war to peace, governments, particularly in Africa, lacked the resources to even build rudimentary state organizations. Yet international donors have been reluctant to focus on state institutions, sometimes out of concern that aid could merely expand the authority of a state apparatus that helped trigger war in the first place. Others took the view that the state should perform minimal functions and that the private sector and NGOs could deliver services more effectively than the government. Still others have been concerned that the resources donated to the state would be wasted. Attitudes have shifted in recent years amid growing concern about failed states and the anarchy that accompanies them. Some donor agencies have begun to invest in the state sector and in efforts to improve governance.

Our country studies strongly suggest the need for focusing on building and reforming the state. An effective and legitimate state is essential not only to promote economic development but also for democratic governance.[7] The reality is that many democracy promotion programs cannot be launched in the absence of a functioning state bureaucracy. For example, all postconflict societies require a well-trained and well-managed electoral administration to hold free and fair elections, professionally trained law enforcement agencies, and regulatory agencies to ensure fair access to electronic media.

However, donor agencies have to be extremely careful not to re-create the dysfunctional institutions that contributed to the original conflict. To avoid this, international assistance should not only focus on increasing state efficiency, but also foster legitimacy and popular support.[8] This not only depends on creating the "hardware" through institutions such as the police, judiciary, army, civil service, and parliament, but also requires cultivating the "software" that ensures these institutions can operate in a transparent, accountable, independent, and participatory fashion. Technical reconstruction, training, and legal reform programs are necessary, but not sufficient in this respect. More attention needs to be devoted to initiatives that change the internal incentives for avoiding or diminishing corruption, that promote a free and independent media serving as a public watchdog, and that exert strong political pressure on governments resistant to democratic reform.

Fostering Security Sector Reform as an Integral Element of Democracy Promotion

The current situation in the Democratic Republic of Congo, Burundi, Iraq, and Afghanistan illustrates how difficult it is to achieve sustainable peace, let alone build a democratic political system, without adequately equipped and professionally trained security organizations. Armed militias and marginalized groups with access to weapons, as well as corrupt and ineffective security forces, pose a constant threat to democratic transition. Unless security forces are accountable to democratically elected civil authorities and oversight bodies under the rule of law, the sustainability of democratic transition of postconflict societies will remain fragile. Unfortunately, the importance of security sector reform is insufficiently recognized by international actors engaged in democracy assistance.

In our view, security sector reform should be viewed as an integral part of the international agenda for democracy promotion in postconflict societies. The international community should aim for comprehensive reforms in the security sector and make these changes an integral part of a broader democratization agenda. Such reforms will require both adequate service delivery in terms of improved security at all levels from individuals and communities to the country as a whole, as well as adequate democratic oversight and control by elected civilian authorities. Mandates should be clearly demarcated in the constitution, and security forces should adhere to internationally accepted codes of conduct and international law. There should also be transparency on the expenditures of the security sector and access to all relevant information by formal civilian oversight bodies in order to be able to execute their role adequately.

As such reforms often encounter stern opposition from vested interests, it is important that the international community build a consensus and seek the cooperation of civil society, political parties, and the judiciary. This may require capacity building of these institutions as regards expertise, knowledge, and insight on the security sector. Training of civil society organizations and parliamentarians is in this regard essential, as is the training of security actors in terms of knowledge of the requirements of democratic societies. It is therefore important that these reforms are integrated into broader democracy assistance programs.

Making Grassroots Civil Society Organizations a Priority

The international community has provided significant assistance to civil society in the majority of the postconflict countries investigated here. However, the organizations that benefited most from civil society assistance were indigenous NGOs. While many of these organizations successfully provided basic services, lobbied governments for more equal rights, and informed public opinion, several problem areas have surfaced. Most of the recipient NGOs have been located in capital cities and have virtually no presence outside major urban areas. They tend to be controlled by a few individuals and are not membership-based. Most of them are not run as democratic organizations. In addition, many NGOs do not disclose the financial details of their activities, adding to the popular perception that some of them are merely set up for personal benefit or profit-making. Furthermore, most of the NGOs suffer from the problem of long-term sustainability, because of weak organizational skills and dependence on international aid. Most important, these NGOs have failed to mobilize large numbers of citizens behind causes or civic efforts. Combined with a lack of access to policy circles, such NGOs tend to have limited political influence.

While providing assistance, the international community should not ignore these problems. It should be more discriminating in its support to democracy NGOs. Instead of relying on the good intentions of NGOs, donors should critically analyze what they do in practice and focus only on those organizations that are democratically run, that are transparent in their operations, and that have the potential to make a meaningful contribution to the democratization process. Moreover, they should focus more on capacity building of membership-based civil society organizations, not only in the national and provincial capitals but especially in the rural areas.

More important, the international community should not equate NGOs with civil society. Civil society comprises a broad range of actors, operating outside the state and the market. Thus it includes, in addition to NGOs, interest groups like labor unions, women's groups, professional associations, religious and cultural organizations, and other grassroots community groups. In fact, only membership-based civil society organizations nurture norms of trust, reciprocity, compromise, and cooperation, which are essential for democratic ethos. Therefore it is important that the international community should try to reach a wider spectrum of civil society organizations.

Assisting Political Parties

International donor agencies have been extremely reluctant to assist political parties in postconflict societies. Assistance to political parties is highly sensitive, posing potential risks to relations between a donor and the host government. In a few countries, such as Ethiopia and Afghanistan, external support to political parties is legally prohibited. Moreover, international actors consider some political parties to be the driving forces behind political tensions and violent conflict. International actors often lack expertise on how to best engage with political parties.[9] These considerations have contributed to the benign neglect of political parties by international donors.

Yet the overriding importance of a political party system in a democracy is beyond dispute. Political parties perform many critical functions that cannot be taken on by other actors, articulating societal aspirations and forging alliances among different interests. Parties also help reconcile diverse needs and demands of various communities and groups, translating grievances into manageable programs. Political parties select and groom candidates for government and legislatures, ensure electoral competition, and help to educate and socialize citizens on political processes.[10] The problem is that in most postconflict countries, the institutional and political infrastructure for party development is lacking. Often, parties are organized around a charismatic personality and lack the capacity to create large constituencies to foster national unity. In a few cases the organizations are led by hard-liners representing sectarian interests. Although civil society organizations can perform some social, civic functions, these organizations cannot serve as a substitute for political parties.

The international community therefore must provide assistance to political parties in postconflict societies. For bilateral and multilateral donor agencies, such assistance should be provided on a nonpartisan basis. All political parties that subscribe to democratic norms and meet well-formulated criteria should be eligible. More than direct and indirect assistance to political parties, institutional reforms that nurture a multiparty system should be promoted. Such reforms involve providing a constitutional basis for the existence of political parties, transparent and fair procedures for registration, codes of conduct for parties, and regulations governing donations. Political foundations such as the National Democratic Institute, the International Republican Institute, the Netherlands Institute for Multiparty Democracy, or German foundations like the Friedrich Ebert Stiftung and the Konrad Adenauer Stiftung have a bit more room for maneuver in this respect, and can be used by bilateral donor agencies to provide support on a fraternal or multiparty basis.[11]

Supporting Independent Media

Our studies show that the media have received relatively little attention in democracy programming, especially when compared to projects related to elections and human rights. Most donor agencies developed only modest efforts, focusing on supporting urban-based newspapers and journalism training courses. Yet the importance of an independent and diverse media cannot be overemphasized for promoting democracy in postconflict societies. A genuinely pluralist political system cannot exist without a free flow of information and a "marketplace of ideas." Media also help to create a responsive political culture and accountable public institutions. By spreading information and ideas, they also promote a better understanding among competing interests and groups. There also is a consensus now among development theorists that economic growth and media freedom are intertwined.[12]

It is vital that the international community allocates more resources for developing media outlets that are free from state control. Several steps can be taken by donors, in addition to providing journalism training. The international community can offer technical assistance to government to support a legal environment conducive to a free and independent media. Apart from constitutional guarantees of media freedom, independent regulatory agencies should be established to prevent political interference in broadcast licensing. It is also important that international donors assist media outlets to operate as profitable commercial enterprises.

We also suggest that donors focus particularly on radio, as it is the most popular and cost-effective means for the dissemination of news and information in developing countries. In most war-torn societies, particularly in Africa, newspapers and other print media fail to reach a majority of the population, because literacy rates are low, transportation services are poor, and the printing and distribution costs of publications are relatively high. Moreover, public access to television is limited to urban areas. Where possible, the international community should support the establishment of community radio stations and networks. The Afghanistan example proves that this is possible even in the most difficult circumstances.

Exerting Political Pressure, Especially in Semiauthoritarian Contexts

Semiauthoritarian governments have come to power through elections in many postconflict societies.[13] Such governments play the game of democracy through undemocratic means, manipulating elections, public bodies, media, law enforcement agencies, and public bureaucracies in order to cling to power. The Cambodian People's Party represents a good example of a regime that has succeeded in attracting international support for holding multiparty elections, ratifying international human rights treaties, and allowing growth of media. Yet the Cambodian government's semiauthoritarian rule has effectively neutralized the main opposition forces since 1991. Not only does the Cambodian People's Party retain a strong influence on the judiciary and security forces, but senior government and party officials also control the most profitable land and businesses. Incumbent regimes in Ethiopia, Uganda, and Rwanda also display many attributes of a semiauthoritarian government.

Out of fear of jeopardizing the fragile peace in these countries, however, most donor agencies have neglected the undemocratic behavior of these governments. Although understandable in the politically volatile contexts of Uganda after 1986, Ethiopia after 1991, and Rwanda after the 1994 genocide, the accommodating stance of the international community seems to have legitimized the regressive national policies and governance styles of the incumbent rulers.

Sustained political pressure is sometimes necessary to keep the new government from deviating from the path of democracy. In countries where incumbent governments engage in gross violation of democratic precepts, the international community should step up efforts for a more critical political dialogue. It should also not shy away from taking more forceful measures, including targeted sanctions and strict conditionalities. After all, providing democracy assistance itself is a political endeavor, and an underlying strategy must take into account the full range of political options.

Improving Donor Coherence and Coordination

Several authors, particularly from Guatemala, Sierra Leone, and Rwanda, have voiced their concern about the lack of donor coordination. Indeed, the need for better coherence and coordination is probably one of the most-cited recommendations in the Clingendael project. Many researchers have wondered why there is so little coordination in practice despite declarations to the contrary, numerous meetings, and basket funding arrangements.

Several steps can be taken to improve coordination among donors. First, in those countries where in-country coordination structures between international donor agencies do not yet exist (such as in Guatemala and El Salvador), it is crucial to set up an appropriate forum where donor agencies can regularly meet and exchange views on important developments. In other countries where such donor forums do exist (Uganda, Ethiopia, and Mozambique), it is important to fully exploit the opportunity. Second, there is a need to devote more attention to strategic planning. In practice, it implies that donors together with national actors should reach a general agreement on the direction of reform in a particular country and identify some of the main long-term benchmarks of democratization as a basis for measurable programming. Positive experiences with the "governance matrix" in Uganda indicate that such an approach can help to provide more direction to the overall donor effort, while still allowing sufficient freedom to individual agencies to design programs according to national priorities. This also allows an appropriate division of labor among different donors that can each focus on a particular sector or actor.

Making Use of Regional Experience and Expertise in Democracy Assistance

Many developing countries, such as India, Botswana, South Africa, Brazil, and Mexico, have now established democratic institutions. In numerous other countries, several rounds of free and fair elections have been held, power has been transferred peacefully, and democratic parliaments and other institutions are able to operate in a relatively independent and effective manner. More important, these countries have a new generation of political leaders, parliamentarians, civil society activists, and journalists who exemplify the democratic political culture in their respective countries. Although not all of these societies have experienced major violent conflict, the way in which these and other states, such as Indonesia, El Salvador, and Nicaragua, managed their democratic transition provides useful lessons for postconflict countries. Unfortunately, their experiences and expertise are rarely taken into account in the planning and design of new democracy assistance programs.

We suggest that the international community should make sincere efforts to use best practices from the region, hire regional and local democracy experts, and work more through regional organizations such as the African Union and the Organization of American States. Such efforts will confer many advantages. The population of postconflict societies in Africa and Asia can better relate to democratic experiences of a neighboring country than those from Western societies. By using regional experiences and examples, donor agencies can help to avoid the paternalistic or even imperialist connotations that the intelligentsia in the developing world often attach to Western support in the field of democracy and governance. The donor agencies may want to support the execution of certain regionally developed initiatives, such as the African Peer Review Mechanism or the New Partnership for African Development, wherein African Union countries have committed themselves to monitor and stimulate democratic governance on the African continent. The involvement of regional and local experts is also likely to promote local ownership of assistance programs. Finally, the heavy reliance on local and regional experts will reduce program expenses due to lower salaries of consultants and savings in transportation costs.

* * *

International democracy assistance to postconflict societies is a difficult though not impossible enterprise. This book has shown that international actors can have a significant impact in some of the key areas and institutions needed to support democratic change. However, the unique conditions of societies shattered by violent conflict pose a major challenge to conventional donor thinking and programming. In the preceding chapters, researchers from postconflict countries have tried to come up with concrete suggestions for improving the strategy, design, and implementation of future democracy programs. It is now up to the policy community to engage in discussions with local actors and apply these lessons in practice.

▨ Notes

1. A similar argument has been put forward in de Zeeuw, "Projects Do Not Create Institutions."

2. For a critical analysis of civil society aid, see Ottaway and Carothers, *Funding Virtue.*

3. Newman and Rich, *The UN Role in Promoting Democracy.*

4. Paris, *At War's End.*

5. Ottaway, *Democracy Challenged.*

6. Carothers, *Critical Mission.*

7. This has recently been recognized in policy documents by the DFID, the UK Prime Minister's Strategy Unit, USAID, and the OECD/Development Assistance Committee. See DFID, *Why We Need to Work More Effectively in Fragile States;* UK Prime Minister's Strategy Unit, *Investing in Prevention;* USAID, *Fragile States Strategy;* and OECD, *Chair's Summary.*

8. See also Chesterman, Ignatieff, and Thakur, *Making States Work.*

9. Two notable exceptions to this lack of expertise include Salih, *African Political Parties;* and Burnell and Randall, *Politics in the Developing World.*

10. Kumar, *International Political Party Assistance,* p. 1.

11. For an excellent overview of some of the challenges of political party assistance, see Carothers, "Political Party Aid."

12. World Bank, *The Right to Tell.*

13. Ottaway, *Democracy Challenged.*

Acronyms

AAAS	American Association for the Advancement of Science
AACC	Addis Ababa Chamber of Commerce (Ethiopia)
AAI	African American Institute
ACFODE	Action for Development (Uganda)
ACI	Alliance Against Impunity (Guatemala)
ADB	Asian Development Bank
ADHOC	Cambodian Human Rights and Development Association
AD-NET	Advocacy Network (Ethiopia)
AFRC	Armed Forces Ruling Council (Sierra Leone)
ALF	Afar Liberation Front (Ethiopia)
ALIMO	Independent Alliance of Mozambique
AMODE	Mozambican Association for the Development of Democracy
ANDM	Amhara National Democratic Movement (Ethiopia)
ANDO	Argoba Nationality Democratic Organization (Ethiopia)
ANDP	Afar National Democratic Party (Ethiopia)
APC	All People's Congress (Sierra Leone)
APES	Association of Journalists of El Salvador
ARJ	Association of Rwandan Journalists
ARPAS	Association of Participatory Radio Stations and Programs of El Salvador
ASC	Civil Society Assembly (Guatemala)
ASEAN	Association of Southeast Asian Nations
ASIES	Association of Investigation and Social Studies (Guatemala)
AWEPA	European Parliamentarians for Africa
BBC	British Broadcasting Corporation

BGPDUF	Benishangul-Gumuz People's Democratic Unity Front (Ethiopia)
CAF/SCO	Communication Assistance Foundation (Netherlands)
CALDH	Center for Human Rights Legal Action (Guatemala)
CAVE	Campaign Against Violation Events (Sierra Leone)
CCSL	Council of Churches in Sierra Leone
CCSSP	Commonwealth Community Safety and Security Project
CDF	Civil Defense Forces (Sierra Leone)
CDHG	Commission on Human Rights in Guatemala
CDHR	Center for Democracy and Human Rights (Sierra Leone)
CDIID	Complaints, Discipline, and Internal Investigations Department (Sierra Leone)
CDU	United Congress of Democrats (Mozambique)
CEDE	Center for the Study of Democracy and Development (Mozambique)
CEH	Commission for Historical Clarification (Guatemala)
CEJOCU	Civic Education Joint Coordination Unit (Uganda)
CERJ	Council of Ethnic Communities— "We Are All Equal" (Guatemala)
CESO	Canadian Executive Services Organization
CETU	Confederation of Ethiopian Trade Unions
CG	Consultative Group
CGG	Campaign for Good Governance (Sierra Leone)
CHRRCC	Cambodian Human Rights Action Committee
CICIACS	Commission for the Investigation of Illegal Bodies and Clandestine Security Groups (Guatemala)
CIDA	Canadian International Development Agency
CIEPRODH	Center of Human Rights Investigation, Studies, and Promotion (Guatemala)
CIMADE	Comité Inter-Mouvements Auprès des Evacués
CIVPOL	Civilian Police (United Nations)
CLCBS	Center for Local Capacity Building and Studies (Ethiopia)
COG	Commonwealth Observer Group
COHCHR	Cambodian Office of the High Commissioner for Human Rights
CONADEHGUA	National Coordination for Human Rights in Guatemala
CONAVIGUA	National Coordination of Guatemalan Widows
CONCULTURA	National Council on Culture and the Arts (El Salvador)

MPRU	Media and Public Relations Unit (Sierra Leone)
MRND	National Revolutionary Movement for Development (Rwanda)
MWVA	Ministry of Women's and Veterans' Affairs (Cambodia)
NACSA	National Commission for Social Action (Sierra Leone)
NAWOU	National Association of Women's Organizations of Uganda
NCDHR	National Commission for Democracy and Human Rights (Sierra Leone)
NDF	National Democrats Forum (Uganda)
NDI	National Democratic Institute
NEBE	National Election Board of Ethiopia
NED	National Endowment for Democracy
NEMGROUP-U	National Election Monitoring Group of Uganda
NFHR	National Forum for Human Rights (Sierra Leone)
NGO	nongovernmental organization
NIHR	Norwegian Institute of Human Rights
NIMD	Netherlands Institute for Multiparty Democracy
NMJD	Network Movement for Justice and Development (Sierra Leone)
NOCEM	National Organization for Civic Education and Election Monitoring (Uganda)
NORAD	Norwegian Agency for Development Cooperation
NPRC	National Provisional Ruling Council (Sierra Leone)
NRA	National Resistance Army (Uganda)
NRC	National Reconciliation Commission (Guatemala)
NRM	National Resistance Movement (Uganda)
NRM-O	National Resistance Movement–Organization (Uganda)
NZA	Dutch Foundation for the New South Africa
OAS	Organization of American States
OAU	Organization for African Unity
ODA	Overseas Development Agency (United Kingdom)
ODHA	Human Rights Office of the Archbishop (Guatemala)
OECD	Organization for Economic Cooperation and Development
OFDM	Oromo Federalist Democratic Movement (Ethiopia)
OHCHR	Office of the High Commissioner for Human Rights (United Nations)
OLF	Oromo Liberation Front (Ethiopia)
OPDM	Oromo People's Democratic Movement (Ethiopia)

ORINFOR	Rwandan Information Office
OSIWA	Open Society Initiative for West Africa
OUMWU	Organization of University Muslim Women of Uganda
PAC	African Conservative Party (Mozambique)
PADELIMO	Democratic Liberal Party of Mozambique
PADEMO	Democratic Party of Mozambique
PADRES	Democratic Alliance and Social Renewal Party (Mozambique)
PALMO	Liberal and Democratic Party of Mozambique
PAREDE	Democratic Reconciliation Party (Mozambique)
PARTONAMO	Party of All Mozambican Nationalists
PASOMO	Mozambique Social Broadening Party
PAZS	Party of Freedom and Solidarity (Mozambique)
PCN	National Convention Party (Mozambique)
PDD	Party for Peace, Democracy, and Development (Mozambique)
PDH	Office of the Human Rights Ombudsman (Guatemala)
PEC-MT	Ecological Party–Land Movement (Mozambique)
PEMO	Ecological Party of Mozambique
PIMO	Independent Party of Mozambique
PMAC	Provisional Military Administrative Council (Ethiopia)
PNC	National Civilian Police (Guatemala)
PPD	Popular Democratic Party (Mozambique)
PPPM	Mozambique People's Progress Party
PPU	Presidential Protection Unit (Uganda)
PRD	Democratic Renewal Party (Mozambique)
PRIDE	Postconflict Reintegration Initiative for Development and Empowerment (Sierra Leone)
PRK	People's Republic of Kampuchea (Cambodia)
PROBIDAD	Probity (El Salvador)
PROCEPER	Central American Journalism Project
PRODECA	Central American Human Rights Program
PROPAZ	Culture of Dialogue: Development of Resources for Peacebuilding (of the OAS)
PRT	provincial reconstruction team
PSM	Mozambique Socialist Party
PUN	National Unity Party (Mozambique)
PVM	Green Party of Mozambique
RA	Reform Agenda (Uganda)
RENAMO	Mozambican National Resistance
RIMEG	Rwandan Independent Media Group
RPF	Rwandan Patriotic Front

RSF	Reporters Without Borders
RSG	Referendum Support Group (Uganda)
RTLM	Radio Télévision Libre des Mille Collines (Rwanda)
RUF	Revolutionary United Front (Sierra Leone)
SAHRE	Society for the Advancement of Human Rights (Ethiopia)
SARDC	Southern African Research and Documentation Center
SCSL	Special Court for Sierra Leone
SEPDC	South Ethiopia People's Democratic Coalition
SIDA	Swedish International Development Agency
SIGET	General Electricity and Telecommunication Superintendence (El Salvador)
SLP	Sierra Leone Police
SLPP	Sierra Leone People's Party
SMPDUO	Sheko and Mezenger People's Democratic Unity Organization (Ethiopia)
SNC	Supreme National Council (Cambodia)
SOC	State of Cambodia
SPDP	Somali People's Democratic Party (Ethiopia)
SRP	Sam Rainsy Party (Cambodia)
SRSG	Special Representative of the Secretary-General
TAFFORD	Technical Assistance Foundation for Rural Development (Uganda)
TCS	Telecorporación Salvadoreña (El Salvador)
TFM	The Free Movement (Uganda)
TGE	Transitional Government of Ethiopia
TPLF	Tigray People's Liberation Front (Ethiopia)
TRC	Truth and Reconciliation Commission (Sierra Leone)
TVR	Télévision Nationale du Rwanda
UCOBAC	Ugandan Community-Based Association for Child Welfare
UDENAMO	National Democratic Union of Mozambique
UDF	United Democratic Front (Mozambique)
UEDF	United Ethiopian Democratic Forces
UGACEF	Ugandan Civic Education Foundation
UHRA	Ugandan Human Rights Activists
UJA	Ugandan Journalists Association
UJCC	Ugandan Joint Christian Council
UJSC	Ugandan Journalists Safety Committee
ULS	Ugandan Law Society
UM	Union for Change (Mozambique)
UMWA	Ugandan Media Women's Association
UMYA	Ugandan Muslim Youth Assembly

UN	United Nations
UNAMI	National African Union of Independent Mozambique
UNAMIR	UN Assistance Mission to Rwanda
UNAMO	Mozambican National Union
UNAMSIL	UN Mission in Sierra Leone
UNDP	UN Development Programme
UNEPA	Ugandan Newspaper Editors and Proprietors Association
UNESCO	UN Educational, Scientific, and Cultural Organization
UNHCHR	UN High Commissioner for Human Rights
UNHCR	UN High Commissioner for Refugees
UNICEF	UN Children's Fund
UNOMSIL	UN Observer Mission in Sierra Leone
UNOPS	UN Office for Project Services
UNTAC	UN Transitional Authority in Cambodia
UPC	Ugandan People's Congress
UPDF	Ugandan People's Defense Forces
UPIMAC	Ugandan Project Implementation and Management Center
URNG	Guatemalan National Revolutionary Unity
USAID	US Agency for International Development
USAMO	Union for the Salvation of Mozambique
UWONET	Ugandan Women's Network
VOA	Voice of America
WFP	World Food Programme
WTO	World Trade Organization

Bibliography

Aalen, Lovise. 2002. *Ethnic Federalism in a Dominant Party State: The Ethiopian Experience, 1991–2000.* CMI Report no. 2/2002 (Bergen: Chr. Michelsen Institute).

Abbink, Jon. 2000. "The Organization and Observation of Elections in Federal Ethiopia: Retrospect and Prospect." In Jon Abbink and Gerti Hesseling (eds.), *Election Observation and Democratization in Africa* (New York: St. Martin's Press).

Abbink, Jon, and Gerti Hesseling (eds.). 2000. *Election Observation and Democratization in Africa* (New York: St. Martin's Press).

ADHOC. 2003. *Human Rights Situation Report 2002* (Phnom Penh).

———. 2005. *Human Rights Situation Report 2004* (Phnom Penh).

AFROBAROMETER. 2003. *Eight Years of Multiparty Democracy in Mozambique: The Public's View.* Working Paper no. 30. August. http://www.afrobarometer .org.

Amnesty International. 1991. "Cambodia."

———. 1992. "Cambodia."

———. 1994. "Cambodia."

———. 1997. "Cambodia."

———. 1999. "Sierra Leone." http://www.amnesty.org/ailib/aireport/ar99/afr51.htm.

———. 2000. "Cambodia."

———. 2000. "Sierra Leone: Childhood—A Casualty of Conflict." August. http:// web.amnesty.org/library/index/engafr510692000?opendocument&of=themes% 5cchildren+juveniles.

Anderson, Mary. 2001. *Do No Harm: How Aid Can Support Peace—Or War* (Boulder: Lynne Rienner).

Arnson, Cynthia. 1999. *The Popular Referendum and the Future of the Peace Accords in Guatemala.* Working Paper no. 243 (Washington, D.C.: Woodrow Wilson Center for International Scholars).

Asian Watch. 1992. *Political Control, Human Rights, and the UN Mission in Cambodia* 8 no. 55.

Asnake Kefale. 2001. "Regime Transition and Problems of Democratization in Post-Insurgent African States: The Case of Ethiopia." Paper prepared for the thirteenth biennial conference of the African Association of Political Science, Yaoundé (Cameroon).

Austin, Reginald, and Maja Ternström (eds.). 2004. *Handbook of Political Party Funding* (Stockholm: International IDEA).

AWEPA. 1993. *Mozambique Peace Process Bulletin.* "Unarmed Opposition" supplement (Maputo).

———. 1994. *Mozambique Peace Process Bulletin.* "Political Party" supplement (Maputo).

Azpuru, Dinorah. 1999. "Peace and Democratization in Guatemala: Two Parallel Processes." In Cynthia Arnson (ed.), *Comparative Peace Processes in Latin America* (Stanford: Stanford University Press).

———. 2001. *La Cultura Democrática de los Guatemaltecos en el Nuevo Siglo* (Guatemala: ASIES).

Azpuru, Dinorah, Carlos Mendoza, Evelyn Blanck, and Ligia Blanco. 2004. *Democracy Assistance to Post-Conflict Guatemala: Finding a Balance Between Details and Determinants.* Conflict Research Unit Working Paper no. 30 (The Hague: Clingendael Institute).

Baregu, Mwesiga. 2004. "From Liberation Movements to Ruling Parties in Southern Africa." In CPS/IDASA/NIMD, *Southern Africa Post-Apartheid? The Search for Democratic Governance* (Pretoria).

Barya, John-Jean. 1993. *Popular Democracy and the Legitimacy of the Constitution: Some Reflections on Uganda's Constitution-Making Process.* Center for Basic Research Working Paper no. 38 (Kampala).

———. 2000. "Political Parties, the Movement, and the Referendum on Political Systems in Uganda: One Step Forward, Two Steps Back?" In J. Mugaju and J. Oloka-Onyango (eds.), *No-Party Democracy in Uganda: Myths and Realities* (Kampala).

Barya, John-Jean, Samson Opolot, and Peter Otim. 2004. *The Limits of "No-Party" Politics: The Role of International Assistance in Uganda's Democratisation Process.* Conflict Research Unit Working Paper no. 28 (The Hague: Clingendael Institute).

Bennett, Richard. 2001. "The Evolution of the Sierra Leone Truth and Reconciliation Commission." In *Truth and Reconciliation in Sierra Leone.* October. http://www.sierra-leone.org/trcbook-richardbennett.html.

Berhanu Nega and Meleskachew Ameha. 2001. *Report on the Media in the 2000 Elections in Ethiopia* (Addis Ababa: Forum for Social Studies).

Bratton, Michael, and Nicolas van de Walle. 1997. *Democratic Experiments in Africa. Regime Transitions in Comparative Perspective* (Cambridge: Cambridge University Press).

Brown, Michael E., Sean M. Lynn-Jones, and Steven E. Miller. 1996. *Debating the Democratic Peace* (Cambridge: MIT Press).

Burnell, Peter (ed.). 2000. *Democracy Assistance: International Co-operation for Democratization* (London: Frank Cass).

Burnell, Peter, and Vicky Randall. 2004. *Politics in the Developing World* (Oxford: Oxford University Press).

Bwengye, A. W. F. 1985. *The Agony of Uganda: From Idi Amin to Obote* (Uganda: Regency Press).

Cantarero, Mario Alfredo. 2003. "Periodismo en El Salvador: En Casa de Herrero Cuchillo de Palo, una Fiscalización Pendiente." *Razón y Palabra.* http://www.cem.items.mx.

Carbone, Giovanni. 2003. *Emerging Pluralist Politics in Mozambique: The FRELIMO-RENAMO Party System.* Crisis States Programme Working Papers Series no. 1 (London: London School of Economics and Political Science).

Carothers, Thomas. 1999. *Aiding Democracy Abroad: The Learning Curve* (Washington D.C.: Carnegie Endowment for International Peace).
——. 2004. *Critical Mission. Essays on Democracy Promotion* (Washington, D.C.: Carnegie Endowment for International Peace).
——. 2004. "Political Party Aid: Issues for Reflection and Discussion." Unpublished paper prepared for SIDA.
Carter Center. 2005. *Ethiopia Elections: Postelection Statement, May 16, 2005* (Addis Ababa).
CEH. 1999. *Guatemala: Memoria de Silencio (Memory of Silence)* (Guatemala).
Center for Advanced Study. 2001. *Democracy in Cambodia* (Phnom Penh: Asia Foundation).
Center for Democracy and Governance. 1999. *USAID Political Party Development Assistance.* USAID Technical Publication Series (Washington D.C.: USAID).
Chacón, Ricardo. 2003. "Los Medios de Prensa en El Salvador: De la Trinchera al Debate Público." *Pulso del Periodismo.* http://www. pulso.org.
Chalk, Frank. 1999. "Hate Radio in Rwanda." In Howard Adelman and Astri Suhrke (eds.), *The Path to a Genocide: The Rwanda Crisis from Uganda to Zaire* (New Brunswick, N.J.: Transactions).
Chamorro, Carlos F., and Alberto Arene. 2001. *El Turno de los Medios: El Periodismo Centroamericano Frente a la Agenda de la Democratización* (Washington, D.C.: PRODECA).
Chan, Stephen, and Venancio Moises. 1998. *War and Peace in Mozambique* (London: Macmillan).
Chesterman, Simon, Michael Ignatieff, and Ramesh Thakur (eds.). 2005. *Making States Work: State Failure and the Crisis of Governance* (Tokyo: UN University Press).
Chrétien, Jean-Pierre (ed.). 1995. *Rwanda: Les Média du Génocide* (Paris: Karthala).
Ciorciari, John D. "Great-Power Posturing and the Khmer Rouge Tribunal." Unpublished paper.
CLCBS. 2003. "Civic Education in Ethiopia: The Experience of Voter Education Activities Prior to the May 2000 National Elections in Ethiopia, and Planning for the 2005 National Elections." Workshop proceedings, May 6–9, Addis Ababa.
Colm, Sara. 1997. *Cambodia: Emerging Civil Society Faces an Uncertain Future* (Phnom Penh).
Commonwealth Secretariat. 1980. *Uganda Elections, December 1980.* Interim report of the Commonwealth Observer Group (London).
Council for the Development of Cambodia. 2002. *Development Cooperation Report 2001* (Phnom Penh).
de Tollenaere, Marc. 2000. "Democratisering in Mozambique: Optimale Imperfectie en Virtualiteit." In Rudi Doom. *De Structuur van de Waanzin: Conflicten in de Periferie* (Gent: Vrije Universiteit Brussel).
——. 2000. "Sustainable Electoral Democracy in Mozambique: International Support and Self-Reliance." In International IDEA, *Promoting Sustainable Democratic Institutions in Southern Africa,* conference proceedings (Gaborone).
——. 2002. *Support to the 1999 General Elections in Mozambique.* Final report, unpublished (Maputo).
——. 2004. "Democracy and Elections in Mozambique: Theory and Practice." In Brazão Mazula (ed.), *Mozambique. Ten Years of Peace* (Maputo: CEDE).
de Zeeuw, Jeroen. 2005. "Projects Do Not Create Institutions: The Record of Democracy Assistance in Post-Conflict Societies." *Democratization* 12, no. 4 (August): 481–504.

des Forges, Alison. 1995. "Face au Génocide: Une Réponse Désastreuse des Etats-Unis et des Nations Unies." In A. Guichaoua (ed.), *Les Crises Politiques au Burundi et au Rwanda (1993–1994)* (Paris: Karthala).

Dessalegn Rahmato. 2003. "Poverty and Agricultural Involution." In Dessalegn Rahmato (ed.), *Some Aspects of Poverty in Ethiopia: Three Selected Papers,* FSS Studies on Poverty no. 1 (Addis Ababa: Forum for Social Studies).

Dessalegn Rahmato and Meheret Ayenew. 2004. *Democracy Assistance to Post-Conflict Ethiopia: Building Local Institutions?* Conflict Research Unit Working Paper no. 27 (The Hague: Clingendael Institute).

DFID. 2004. *Drivers of Change: Public Information Note* (London).

———. 2005. *Why We Need to Work More Effectively in Fragile States* (London).

Diamond, Larry. 1991. *Developing Democracy: Towards Consolidation* (Baltimore: Johns Hopkins University Press).

Dougherty, Beth K. 2004. "Right-Sizing International Criminal Justice: The Hybrid Experiment at the Special Court for Sierra Leone." *International Affairs* 80, no. 2: 318–319.

Drachman, S. S. 1992. "The War in Cambodia and the Case for Judicial Enforcement of Human Rights Conditions on Foreign Aid." *Columbia Journal of Transnational Law* 30: 661–695.

Duffy, Terence. 1994. "Toward a Culture of Human Rights in Cambodia." *Human Rights Quarterly* 16, no. 1: 82–104.

Dunn, J. 1978. *West African States: Failure and Promise—A Study in Comparative Politics* (Cambridge: Cambridge University Press).

EISA. 2004. *Election Update 2004: Mozambique,* no. 1 (Johannesburg). November 10. http://www.eisa.org.za.

European Union Election Observation Mission to Ethiopia. 2005. *Assessment of Vote Counting and Release of Electoral Results: Mission Statement* (Addis Ababa).

Fambon, Samuel. 2003. "The Funding of Elections and Political Parties in African States." Paper prepared for the Africa Conference on Elections, Democracy and Governance, April 7–10, 2003 (Pretoria).

Federal Republic of Germany and Republic of Rwanda. 2000. *Réunions de Travail Concernant la Coopération Economique et au Développement* (Bonn).

Findlay, Trevor. 1995. *Cambodia: The Legacy and Lessons of UNTAC* (New York: Oxford University Press).

Finkel, Steven E., Aníbal Pérez-Liñán, and Mitchell A. Seligson, with Dinorah Azpuru. 2005. *Effects of U.S. Foreign Assistance on Democracy Building: Results of a Cross-National Quantitative Study* (Vanderbilt University, University of Pittsburgh, and USAID).

Freedom House. 2003. *Freedom in the World 2003: Country and Related Territory Reports.* http://www.freedomhouse.org/research/freeworld/2003/countries.htm.

Funes, M. 1996. "Medios de Comunicación en El Salvador: Modernización Tecnológica sin Modernización Política." In R. Bracamonte and S. Roggenbuck (eds.), *Medios de Comunicación y Democracia en El Salvador* (San Salvador).

Geffray, Christian (ed.). 1990. *La Cause des Armes au Mozambique: Anthropologie d'une Guerre Civil* (Paris: Karthala).

Halperin, Morton H., Michael M. Weinstein, and Joe Siegle. 2004. *The Democracy Advantage: How Democracies Promote Peace and Prosperity* (New York: Council of Foreign Relations and Routledge).

Harbeson, John W. 1998. "Elections and Democratization in Post-Mengistu Ethiopia." In Krishna Kumar (ed.), *Postconflict Elections, Democratization, and International Assistance* (Boulder: Lynne Rienner).

Hauck, Volker. 2000. *Building of Political Parties in Southern Africa: Reviewing the Strategy of the Netherlands.* European Center for Development Policy Management Discussion Paper no. 15 (Maastricht).

Hayner, Priscilla B. 2001. *Unspeakable Truths: Confronting State Terror and Atrocity* (New York: Routledge).

———. 2004. *The Sierra Leone Truth and Reconciliation Commission: Reviewing the First Year.* International Center for Transitional Justice Case Study Series (New York).

Hearn, Julie. 1999. *Foreign Political Aid, Democratization, and Civil Society in Uganda in the 1990s.* Center for Basic Research Working Paper no. 53 (Kampala).

Heder, Stephen. 2002. "Dealing with Crimes Against Humanity: Progress or Illusion?" In *Southeast Asian Affairs 2001* (Singapore: Institute of Southeast Asian Studies).

Herrera, Antonio. 1998. "Influencia de la Guerra Civil en El Salvador (1980–1992) en el Desarrollo de la Prensa Nacional." http://www.ull.es.

Howard, Ross. 2003. *International Media Assistance: A Review of Donor Activities and Lessons Learned.* Conflict Research Unit Working Paper no. 19 (The Hague: Clingendael Institute).

Human Rights Watch. 1991. *Human Rights Watch World Report 1990* (New York).

———. 1993. *An Exchange on Human Rights and Peace-Keeping in Cambodia* (New York).

———. 1993. *Human Rights Before and After the Elections* (New York).

———. 1995. *Cambodia At War* (New York).

———. 1996. *Deterioration of Human Rights in Cambodia* (New York).

———. 1996. *World Report 1996* (New York).

———. 1998. *Sierra Leone: Sowing Terror* 10, no. 3(A) (New York).

———. 1998. *World Report 1998: Events of 1997* (New York).

———. 1999. *Hostile to Democracy: The Movement System and Political Repression in Uganda* (New York).

———. 1999. *Leave None to Tell the Story: Genocide in Rwanda* (New York).

———. 1999. *World Report 1999: Events of December 1997–November 1998* (New York).

———. 2000. *World Report 2000: Events of 1999* (New York).

———. 2002. "Cambodia." In *Human Rights Watch World Report 2002* (New York).

———. 2002. *World Report 2002: Events of 2001* (New York).

———. 2003. *Human Rights Watch World Report 2003: Sierra Leone* (New York).

———. 2005. *Human Rights World Report 2005* [Events of 2004] (unpublished text).

IADB. 2003. *Guatemala: Cooperation of the International Community—Consultative Group Meeting* (Washington, D.C.).

ICG. 2002. *Sierra Leone's Truth and Reconciliation Commission: A Fresh Start?* December 20 (Freetown).

———. 2003. "The Special Court for Sierra Leone: Promises and Pitfalls of a New 'Model.'" *Africa Briefing* (Freetown), August. http://www.crisisweb.org/home/index.cfm?id=1803&l=1.

———. 2004. *Liberia and Sierra Leone: Rebuilding Failed States* (Brussels).

ICTJ. 2002. *Exploring the Relationship Between the Special Court and the Truth and Reconciliation Commission for Sierra Leone.* http://www.ictj.org.

Jay, Alice, et al. 2002. *Sierra Leone: A Framework for DFID Support to Civil Society.* Draft version.

Kandeh, Jimmy. 1999. "Ransoming the State: Elite Origins of Subaltern Terror in Sierra Leone." *Review of African Political Economy* 26, no. 28: 349–366.

Kanyeihamba, G. W. 2002. *Constitutional and Political History of Uganda: From 1894 to the Present* (Kampala: Century).

Karistedt, Cecilia. 2001. *Cambodian Human Rights and Democracy Organizations: Relations Between Partners.* Experts for Community Research Report no. 39 (Phnom Penh).

Kasfir, Nelson. 1998. "No-Party Democracy in Uganda." *Journal of Democracy* 9, no. 2: 49–63.

Kennicott, Philippe. 2004. "Radio Karabagh: The Station with Local Identification." *Washington Post,* October 8.

Kiiza Besigye vs. Y. K. Museveni & Anor. 1997. "Petition 1/2001: Makara, Sabiti—Linking Good Governance, Decentralization Policy, and Civil Society in Uganda." http://www.afrst.uiuc.edu/makerere.

Kimonyo, Jean-Paul, Noël Twagiramungu, and Christopher Kayumba. 2004. *Supporting the Post-Genocide Transition in Rwanda: The Role of the International Community.* Conflict Research Unit Working Paper no. 32 (The Hague: Clingendael Institute).

Kohl, Richard, and Steven Schoofs. 2005. "Measuring the Impact of Democracy and Governance Assistance." Summary report of a USAID–Clingendael Institute workshop, March 11 (Washington, D.C.: USAID).

Koroma, Abdul K. 1996. *Agony of a Nation* (London: Andromeda).

Kulldorff, Martin. *Organizations in Guatemala.* http://www.peacebrigades.org/guate.html.

Kumar, Krishna (ed.). 1997. *Rebuilding Societies After Civil War: Critical Roles for International Assistance* (Boulder: Lynne Rienner).

——— (ed.). 1998. *Postconflict Elections, Democratization, and International Assistance* (Boulder: Lynne Rienner).

———. 2005. *International Political Party Assistance: An Overview and Analysis.* Conflict Research Unit Working Paper no. 33 (The Hague: Clingendael Institute).

———. 2006. *Promoting Independent Media: Strategies for Democracy Assistance* (Boulder: Lynne Rienner).

Lalá, Anícia, and Andrea Ostheimer. 2003. *How to Remove the Stains on Mozambique's Democratic Track Record: Challenges for the Democratization Process Between 1990 and 2003* (Mozambique: Konrad Adenauer Stiftung).

LAWCLA. 2003. *Twenty-one Month Report: March 2001–December 2002* (Freetown).

LICADHO. 2002. *Situation of Human Rights Defenders in Cambodia* (Phnom Penh).

———. 2004. *Cambodia Human Rights Report 2004: A Brief on Current Human Rights Issues* (Phnom Penh).

López, Jaime. 2001. "El Derecho a la Información Pública y su Importancia en el Combate de la Corrupción." http://www.probidad-sv.org.

López-Pintor, Rafael. 2004. "Postconflict Elections and Democratization: An Experience Review." Unpublished manuscript (Washington, D.C.: USAID).

Lundin, Iraê. 1996. "Political Parties: A Reading of the Ethnic and Regional Factor in the Democratization Process." In Brazão Mazula (ed.), *Mozambique: Elections, Democracy, and Development* (Maputo: CEDE).

Machochoko, Phakiso, and Giorgia Tortora. 2004. "The Management Committee for the Special Court for Sierra Leone." In Cesare P. R. Romano, Andre Nollkaemper, and Jann K. Kleffner (eds.), *Internationalized Criminal Courts: Sierra Leone, East Timor, Kosovo, and Cambodia* (Oxford: Oxford University Press).

Macuane, José Jaime. 2000. "Instituiçoes e Democratizaçao no Contexto Africano: Multipartidarismo e Organizaçao Legislative em Mozambique (1994–1999)." Unpublished PhD thesis (Rio de Janeiro: Instituto Universitario de Pesquisas).

Mahony, Chris. 2002. *Access to Justice for the Ordinary Citizen in Sierra Leone* (Freetown: CGG).

Makara, Sabiti, Geoffrey B. Tukahebwa, and Foster E. Byarugaba. 2003. *Voting for Democracy in Uganda: Issues in Recent Elections* (Kampala: LDC).

Mamdani, M. 1993. *Pluralism and the Right of Association.* Center for Basic Research Working Paper no. 29 (Kampala).

Manning, Carrie. 1998. "Constructing Opposition in Mozambique: RENAMO as Political Party." *Journal of Southern African Studies* 24, no. 1: 161–190.

———. 2002. *The Politics of Peace in Mozambique: Post-Conflict Democratization, 1992–2000* (Westport: Praeger).

Mansfield, Edward D., and Jack Snyder. 2005. *Electing to Fight: Why Emerging Democracies Go to War.* BCSIA Studies in International Security (Cambridge: MIT Press).

Marks, Stephen P. 1999. "Elusive Justice for the Victims of the Khmer Rouge." *Journal of International Affairs* 52, no. 2: 691–718.

Marshall, Monty G., and Ted Robert Gurr. 2005. *Peace and Conflict 2005: A Global Survey of Armed Conflicts, Self-Determination Movements, and Democracy* (College Park, Md.: Center for International Development and Conflict Management).

Marston, John. 1996. "Cambodia News Media in the UNTAC Period and After." In Steve Heder and July Ledgerwood (eds.), *Propaganda, Politics, and Violence in Cambodia: Democratic Transition Under United Nations Peace-Keeping* (Armonk, N.Y.: M. E. Sharpe).

Mayombo, N. 1997. "Constitution-Making and the Struggle for Democracy in Uganda, 1998–1995." LLM diss. (Kampala: Makerere University).

MINUGUA. 1995. *First Report of the Director of the United Nations Mission for the Verification of Human Rights and of Compliance with the Commitments of the Comprehensive Agreement on Human Rights in Guatemala* (New York).

———. 2000. *Compendio General Sobre el Proceso de Paz de Guatemala—Tomo II: Informes del Secretario General de las Naciones Unidas, del 4 de Junio de 1997 al 31 de Octubre de 1999* (Guatemala).

———. 2001. *Twelfth Report on Human Rights of the United Nations Verification Mission on Guatemala* (Guatemala).

———. 2002. *Décimotercer Informe Sobre Derechos Humanos de la Misión de Verificación de las Naciones Unidas en Guatemala (1 de Julio 2001–30 de Junio 2002)* (Guatemala).

MINUGUA and PROPAZ. 2005. *Paz y Democracia en Guatemala: Desafíos Pendientes.* Memoria del Congreso Internacional de MINUGUA, "Construyendo la Paz: Guatemala Desde un Enfoque Comparado," October 27, 28, and 29, 2004 (Guatemala City).

Mugaju, J., and J. Oloka-Onyango. 2000. *No-Party Democracy in Uganda: Myths and Realities* (Kampala: Fountain).

NDI and AAI. 1992. *An Evaluation of the June 21, 1992, Elections in Ethiopia* (Washington, D.C.).

NEBE. 1997. *Report to the House of Representatives* (Addis Ababa).

———. 2001. *Overall Narrative and Financial Report of the Utilization of the Provisional Fund for Assistance to Political Parties for the 2000 National Elections of Ethiopia* (Addis Ababa).

———. 2005. *Data on 2005 National Assembly Elections* (Addis Ababa).

Neou, Kassie. 2000. *Human Rights in Action: Developing Partnerships Between Government and Civil Society—Our Unique Non-Confrontational Approach in Cambodia.* Human Development Report Office, Occasional Paper no. 35 (Phnom Penh: UNDP).

Newman, Edward, and Roland Rich (eds.). 2004. *The UN Role in Promoting Democracy. Between Ideals and Reality* (Tokyo: UN University Press).

NIHR. 2001. *Uganda Presidential Elections 2001.* Working Paper no. 8/2001, May (Oslo).

NIMD. 2003. *Draft Report on the Evaluation of the NZA/IMD Program in Mozambique, 2000–2003* (Maputo).

————. 2004. *A Framework for Democratic Party-Building* (The Hague).

OECD. 2005. *Chair's Summary: Senior Level Forum on Development Effectiveness in Fragile States.* London, Office of the Development Assistance Committee Chair, January 13–14 (Paris).

Olaleye, Wole. 2003. *Political Parties and Multi-Party Elections in Southern Africa.* EISA, SADC INSIGHT IV. http://www.eisa.org.za.

Ondoga ori Amaza. 1998. *Museveni's Long March: From Guerrilla to Statesman* (Kampala: Fountain).

O'Neill, William. 2003. *International Human Rights Assistance. A Review of Donor Activities and Lessons Learned.* Conflict Research Unit Working Paper no. 18 (The Hague: Clingendael Institute).

Ottaway, Marina. 2003. *Democracy Challenged: The Rise of Semi-Authoritarianism* (Washington, D.C.: Carnegie Endowment for International Peace).

Ottaway, Marina, and Thomas Carothers. 2000. *Funding Virtue: Civil Society Aid and Democracy Promotion* (Washington, D.C.: Carnegie Endowment for International Peace).

Oyugi, Walter O. 2003. "The Link Between Resources and the Conduct of Elections in Africa." Paper prepared for the Africa Conference on Elections, Democracy, and Governance, April 7–10 (Pretoria).

Paris, Roland. 2004. *At War's End. Building Peace After Civil Conflict* (Cambridge: Cambridge University Press).

Pásara, Luis. 2003. *Ilusión y Cambio en Guatemala: El Proceso de Paz, sus Actores, Logros y Límites* (Guatemala: Universidad Rafael Landívar, Instituto de Investigaciónes Jurídicas).

Pausewang, Siegfried, and Kjetil Tronvoll (eds.). 2000. *The Ethiopian 2000 Elections: Democracy Advanced or Restricted?* (Oslo: University of Oslo).

Pausewang, Siegfried, Kjetil Tronvoll, and Lovise Aalen (eds.). 2002. *Ethiopia Since the Derg: A Decade of Democratic Pretension and Performance* (London: Zed).

Peou, Sorpong. 2000. *Intervention and Change in Cambodia: Toward Democracy?* (New York: St. Martin's Press).

Peou, Sorpong, with Ham Samnang, Sisowath Chanto, Bophany Un, Kum Kim, and Sovirak Seng. 2004. *International Assistance for Institution-Building in Post-Conflict Cambodia.* Conflict Research Unit Working Paper no. 26 (The Hague: Clingendael Institute).

Peou, Sorpong, with K. Yamada. 2001. "Cambodia." In Shepard Forman and Stewart Patrick (eds.), *Good Intentions: Pledges of Aid for Postconflict Recovery* (Boulder: Lynne Rienner).

Perez, O., and C. Ayala Ramirez. 1997. "La Radio Comunitaria en El Salvador." In C. Ayala Ramirez (ed.), *Comunicacion Alternativa y Sociedad Civil* (San Salvador: Konrad Adenauer Foundation).

Pettersson, Bjorn. 2004. *Postconflict Reconciliation in Sierra Leone: Lessons Learned.* Biannual IDEA-OHCHR consultations (Geneva).

Physicians for Human Rights. 2002. *War-Related Sexual Violence in Sierra Leone: A Population-Based Assessment.* http://www.phrusa.org/research/sierra_leone/report.html.

Polhemus, James. 2002. *An Action Plan for Useful Donor Involvement in Ethiopia's 2005 National Elections.* Submitted to the Royal Netherlands embassy (Addis Ababa).

PRIDE and ICTJ. 2002. *Views of Ex-Combatants on the Truth and Reconciliation Commission and the Special Court* (Freetown).

Prunier, Gérard. 1997. *The Rwanda Crisis: History of a Genocide* (New York: Columbia University Press).

Rahman, Abdul Lamin. 2003. "Building Peace Through Accountability in Sierra Leone: The Truth and Reconciliation Commission and the Special Court." *Journal of Asian and African Studies* 32, nos. 2–3: 295–320.

Ramos, Alfaro, Julia Ester Bracamonte Gómez, Lucio Ricardo Flores Gutiérrez, José Víctor López Trejo, Silvia Lorena Mira Palomo, and Martín Alonso. 1993. "Los Medios de Difusión Colectiva en El Salvador." Unpublished BA thesis (San Salvador: Universidad Centroamericana José Simeón Cañas).

Randall, Vicky, and Lars Svåsand. 2001. "Party Institutionalization in New Democracies." *Party Politics* 8, no. 1: 5–29.

———. 2002. "Introduction: The Contribution of Parties to Democracy and Democratic Consolidation." *Democratization* 9, no. 3: 1–10.

———. 2002. "Political Parties and Democratic Consolidation in Africa." *Democratization* 9, no. 3: 30–53.

Rasmussen, Finn. 2000. "Danida Supports Freedom of Speech and Investigative Journalism in Central America." http://www.comminit.com/danida.

Reilly, Benjamin. 2003. *International Electoral Assistance: A Review of Donor Activities and Lessons Learned.* Conflict Research Unit Working Paper no. 17 (The Hague: Clingendael Institute).

Richards, Paul. 1996. *Fighting for the Rain Forest: War, Youth, and Resources in Sierra Leone* (Portsmouth, N.H.: Heinemann).

Rubio-Fabián, Roberto, José Antonio Morales Tomás, Florentín Meléndez, and Anne Germain Lefèvre. 2004. *Democratic Transition in Post-Conflict El Salvador: The Role of the International Community.* Conflict Research Unit Working Paper no. 29 (The Hague: Clingendael Institute).

Salih, Mohamed (ed.). 2001. *African Political Parties: Evolution, Institutionalisation, and Governance* (London: Pluto).

SARDC. 1997. *Peace and Reconstruction: Interview with President Joaquim Alberto Chissano of Mozambique* (Harare).

Sen, Amartya. 1999. "Human Rights and Economic Achievements." In Joanne R. Bauer and Daniel A. Bell (eds.), *The East Asian Challenge for Human Rights* (New York: Cambridge University Press).

Sesay, Amadu. 1999. "Paradise Lost and Regained? The Travails of Democracy in Sierra Leone." In Dele Olowu, Adebayo Williams, and Kayode Soremekun (eds.), *Governance and Democratization in West Africa* (Dakar: Codesria).

Sesay, Mohamed Gibril, and Charlie Hughes. 2005. *Go Beyond First Aid: Democracy Assistance and the Challenges of Institution Building in Post-Conflict Sierra Leone.* Conflict Research Unit Working Paper no. 34 (The Hague: Clingendael Institute).

Shaw, Rosalind. 2005. *Rethinking Truth and Reconciliation Commissions: Lessons from Sierra Leone.* US Institute of Peace Special Report no. 130 (Washington, D.C.).

Shugarman, D. 1997. "Combating Corruption: Regulating the Funding of Political Parties." Presentation at the eighth International Anti-Corruption Conference (Lima).

Soloway, Colin, and Abubaker Saddique. 2005. *An Assessment of USAID Assistance to the Radio Sector in Afghanistan* (Washington, D.C.: USAID).

Stanley, William, and David Holiday. 2002. "Broad Participation, Diffuse Responsibility: Peace Implementation in Guatemala." In Stephen John Stedman, Donald Rothchild, and Elizabeth M. Cousens (eds.), *Ending Civil Wars: The Implementation of Peace Agreements* (Boulder: Lynne Rienner).

Stedman, Stephen John, Donald Rothchild, and Elizabeth M. Cousens (eds.). 2002. *Ending Civil Wars: The Implementation of Peace Agreements* (Boulder: Lynne Rienner).

Tejan-Cole, Abdul. 2001. "The Special Court for Sierra Leone: Conceptual Concerns and Alternatives." *African Human Rights Law Journal* 1, no. 1: 107–126.

TGE 1991. *The Transitional Charter of Ethiopia* (Addis Ababa).

Tronvoll, Kjetil. 2000. *Ethiopia: A New Start?* Minority Rights Group report (London).

Tronvoll, Kjetil, and Q. Aadland. 1995. *The Process of Democratization in Ethiopia: An Expression of Popular Participation or Political Resistance?* Human Rights Report no. 5 (Oslo: NIHR).

Turner, Michael J., Sue Nelson, and Kimberly Mahling-Clark. 1998. "Mozambique's Vote for Democratic Governance." In Krishna Kumar (ed.), *Postconflict Elections, Democratization, and International Assistance* (Boulder: Lynne Rienner).

Ugandan Commission for the Constituent Assembly. 1995. *Report of the Constituent Assembly Elections 1993* (Kampala).

Ugandan Electoral Commission. 1999. *1997/98 Local Government's Councils Elections Report* (Kampala).

———. 2000. *Report on the Referendum 2000 on Political Systems in Uganda* (Kampala).

———. 2001. *Parliamentary Election Report, June 2001* (Kampala).

———. 2001. *Report on the Presidential Election, March 2001* (Kampala).

Ugandan Interim Electoral Commission. 1997. *The Uganda Presidential and Parliamentary Elections 1996* (Kampala).

UK Prime Minister's Strategy Unit. 2005. *Investing in Prevention: An International Strategy to Manage Risks of Instability and Improve Crisis Response* (London).

UN. 1990. *Report of the United Nations Fact-Finding Mission on Present Structures and Practices of Administration in Cambodia: 24 April–9 May 1990* (New York).

———. 1995. *The UN and Mozambique, 1992–1995* (New York).

———. 1996. *Elections in the Peace Process in Mozambique: Record of an Experience* (New York).

———. 1998. *The Guatemala Peace Agreements* (New York).

———. 2003. Press Release GA/SHC/3762, November 10 (New York).

———. 2003. UN Doc. A/58/317, August 22 (New York).

UN Economic and Social Council. 2001. *Situation of Human Rights in Cambodia*. UN Doc. E/CN.4/2002/118 (New York).

UN General Assembly. 2001. *Situation of Human Rights in Cambodia*. UN Doc. A/56/209 (New York).

UNDP. 1995. "Consolidation of the Democratic Process in Mozambique: Some Priority Areas for Assistance." Unpublished report (Maputo).

———. 2000. *Democratic Governance in Mozambique: Priorities for the Second Generation, 2002–2006* (Maputo).

———. 2002. *Human Development Report 2002* (New York).

———. 2003. *Segundo Informe Sobre Desarrollo Humano en Centroamérica y Panamá 2003* (San José).

———. 2004. *Institutional Flexibility in Crises and Post-Conflict Situations: Best Practices from the Field* (New York).

UNDP and Chr. Michelsen Institute. 2004. *Governance in Post-Conflict Situations.* UNDP background paper for working group discussions, Bergen Seminar, May 5–7 (Oslo).

UNDP and Ugandan Commission for the Constituent Assembly. 1994. *Placing the People First: Elections to the Constituent Assembly.* Republic of Uganda, March 28. Report of the UN project: Support to the Electoral Process in Uganda (Kampala).

US State Department. 2001. *Country Reports on Human Rights Practices.* Bureau of Democracy, Human Rights, and Labor (Washington, D.C.).

———. 1995. *Uganda Human Rights Practices* (Washington, D.C.).

USAID. 2000. *Conducting a DG Assessment: A Framework for Strategy Development* (Washington, D.C.).

———. 2002. *The State of Democracy and Governance in Mozambique* (Washington, D.C.: Management Systems International).

———. 2005. *Fragile States Strategy* (Washington, D.C.).

Vestal, T. 2000. *Ethiopia: A Post–Cold War African State* (Westport, Conn.: Praeger).

Vijghen, John L. 2002. "Guilty by Association: The Inaction of Donors and NGOs." *Phnom Penh Post,* June 7–20.

Vines Alex. 1996. *RENAMO: From Terrorism to Democracy in Mozambique?* Rev. ed. (York: Center for Southern African Studies).

World Bank. 2002. *The Right to Tell: The Role of Mass Media in Economic Development* (Washington, D.C.).

The Contributors

Dinorah Azpuru is assistant professor in the Department of Political Science at Wichita State University in the United States. She is a member of the Guatemalan research center Asociación de Investigación y Estudios Sociales. In addition to her academic activities, she has worked at the Supreme Electoral Tribunal and at the Ministry of Foreign Affairs in Guatemala. She has published extensively on the peace process in Guatemala.

John-Jean Barya is associate professor and former head of the Department of Public and Comparative Law at Makerere University, as well as senior research fellow at the Center for Basic Research in Kampala, Uganda.

Marc de Tollenaere is head of governance at the Swiss Agency for Development and Cooperation in Maputo, Mozambique. He has worked as senior program officer at the European Center for Development Policy Management in the Netherlands, and spent more than nine years in Mozambique in various positions related to support for democratization and public sector reform.

Jeroen de Zeeuw is research fellow at the Conflict Research Unit of the Netherlands Institute of International Relations 'Clingendael', The Hague. From April 2002 to August 2005, he was project coordinator of the Democratic Transition Project, an international comparative research project that formed the basis of this volume.

Dessalegn Rahmato has been a senior research fellow at the Institute of Development Research at Addis Ababa University, and was the executive director of the Forum for Social Studies in Addis Ababa, Ethiopia. He has

311

published numerous works on land and agrarian issues, food security, poverty, environmental policy, civil society, and democratization.

Charlie Hughes is director of the Forum for Democratic Initiatives in Sierra Leone. In 2002 he was a Reagan-Fascell democracy fellow at the International Forum for Democratic Studies in Washington, D.C. He has served as a member of the board of directors of the National Forum for Human Rights in Sierra Leone.

Christopher Kayumba is a lecturer at the National University of Rwanda. His research interests include media, peace research, democratization, civil society, and gender in transition societies.

Jean-Paul Kimonyo was the founder and director of the Center for Conflict Management at the National University of Rwanda. He is now an independent researcher and consultant, based in Kigali, Rwanda.

Krishna Kumar is a senior social scientist with the Center for Development Information and Evaluation of the US Agency for International Development. He is editor of *Rebuilding Societies After Civil War: Critical Roles for International Assistance; Postconflict Elections, Democratization, and International Assistance;* and *Women and Civil War: Impact, Organizations, and Action.*

Anne Germain Lefèvre has been a consultant on various topics with Oxfam America, El Salvador's Ministry for Environment and Natural Resources, the US Agency for International Development, the UN Development Programme, Inter-American Foundation, and the José Simeón Cañas University of Central America. She is currently a project coordinator and researcher at the Fundación Nacional para el Desarrollo, El Salvador.

Meheret Ayenew is assistant professor in the Department of Management and Public Administration within the faculty of Business and Economics at Addis Ababa University, as well as a member of the Forum for Social Studies in Addis Ababa, Ethiopia.

Sorpong Peou has held positions at the Institute of Southeast Asian Studies in Singapore and at the Center for International and Security Studies at York University in Canada. He is now an associate professor in the faculty of Comparative Culture at Sophia University in Tokyo, Japan. He is author of *Conflict Neutralization in the Cambodia War: From Battlefield to Ballot-Box* and *Foreign Intervention and Regime Change in Cambodia.*

Mohamed Gibril Sesay is cofounder of the Forum for Democratic Initiatives. He has held various positions as sociology lecturer, governance consultant, and journalist for various newspapers in Sierra Leone. During the 2002 national elections, he was the director of the Resource Center for Political Parties. He is now a lecturer with the faculty of Social Sciences and Law, Fourah Bay College, Sierra Leone.

Luc van de Goor is head of the Conflict Research Unit at the Netherlands Institute of International Relations 'Clingendael', The Hague. He is coeditor of *Between Development and Destruction: An Enquiry into the Causes of Conflict in Post-Colonial States.*

Marieke Wierda is a senior associate with the International Center for Transitional Justice in New York. Her work includes Liberia, Uganda, Afghanistan, and Sierra Leone, the latter of which has involved advising both the Truth and Reconciliation Commission and the Special Court. She is trained as a lawyer and previously spent three years at the International Criminal Tribunal for the Former Yugoslavia.

Index

About the Book

Few would dispute the importance of donating funds and expertise to conflict-ridden societies—but such aid, however well meant, often fails to have the intended effect. This study critically evaluates international democracy assistance in postconflict societies to discern what has worked, what has not, and how aid programs can be designed to have a more positive impact.

The authors offer a unique recipient perspective as they explore three dimensions of democracy promotion: elections, free media, and human rights. Drawing on the experiences of Afghanistan, Cambodia, El Salvador, Ethiopia, Guatemala, Mozambique, Rwanda, Sierra Leone, and Uganda, they suggest concrete ways in which the international community can better foster democratization in the wake of conflict.

Jeroen de Zeeuw is research fellow in the Conflict Research Unit at Clingendael, the Netherlands Institute of International Relations. **Krishna Kumar** is senior social scientist with the US Agency for International Development. His recent books include *Rebuilding Societies After Civil War: Critical Roles for International Assistance* and *Postconflict Elections, Democratization, and International Assistance.*